Meet Tom Cruise…

"I get it. He has that deliciously indescribable magic that cannot be analyzed or replicated. He is in every sense a movie star."
—Steven Spielberg

"He was pushing limits all the time…. I never thought of him ever becoming an actor. He was more of an Al Capone character, a maverick, the kind of kid who wouldn't back down."
—A childhood neighbor

"Don't let that smile and those teeth fool you. He could have a really nasty streak."
—A high-school girlfriend

"His acting was so good it was almost bizarre. You'd look into his eyes and he'd really be there, he'd really be in love with you. You could see his heart and soul. And then the director would shout 'Cut,' Tom would leave the set, and you'd have to go into therapy for six months."
—Renée Zellweger

"I'll bet all the money I've ever made, plus his, that he doesn't have a mistress, that he doesn't have a gay lover, that he doesn't have a gay life."
—Nicole Kidman

"You can't drive past an accident, because as a Scientologist you are the only one who can help."
—Tom Cruise

Also by Andrew Morton

Madonna

Monica's Story

Diana: Her True Story in Her Own Words

TOM CRUISE
AN UNAUTHORIZED BIOGRAPHY

Andrew Morton

St. Martin's Paperbacks

TOM CRUISE: AN UNAUTHORIZED BIOGRAPHY

Copyright © 2008 by Andrew Morton.

Cover photo © Rene Johnston/*Toronto Star*/Zuma Press.

For information address St. Martin's Press, 175 Fifth Avenue, New York, NY 10010.

ISBN: 0-312-94337-7
EAN: 978-0-312-94337-0

Printed in the United States of America

St. Martin's Press hardcover edition/January 2008
St. Martin's Paperbacks edition / February 2009

St. Martin's Paperbacks are published by St. Martin's Press, 175 Fifth Avenue, New York, NY 10010.

10 9 8 7 6 5 4 3 2 1

For Max and new beginnings

CHAPTER 1

If truth be told, Tom Cruise Mapother IV has always been something of a ladies' man. Sweethearts, girlfriends, lovers, and wives; it has been a rare day in his life when he has not been wooing, wowing, or wedded to a young woman. In fact, he first walked down the aisle when he was just eleven in an impromptu ceremony under the spreading oak tree in his school playground. There is no record of who officiated or whether there were bridesmaids or even a best man, but the bride, a pretty, open-faced girl with a halo of blond ringlets, felt sufficiently confident of their plighted troth to sign herself Rowan Mapother Hopkins when she autographed her school friends' yearbooks.

Maybe it was a dash of Irish blarney in his soul, as much as his winning smile, that made him so popular with the ladies. There is Celtic ancestry—albeit of confused genealogy and origin—on both sides of his family. Some historians assert that the first member of the Mapother clan to set foot in the New World was an Irish engineer named Dillon Henry Mapother. He was the younger of two sons, age just eighteen, who left his home in southeast Ireland in 1849 to escape famine and poverty. This is endorsed by the passenger list on the ship *Wisconsin,* which docked in New York on June 2, 1849. A certain Dillon Mapother, who listed his occupation as engineer, was one of the many seeking a new life in the New World. Other genealogists, notably used by the TV show

Inside the Actors Studio, tell a different story. They claim that the same Dillon Henry Mapother was a Welshman, from Flint in north Wales, who had arrived in America several decades earlier, in 1816. All are agreed that he settled in Louisville, Kentucky, and married a woman named Mary Cruise, who bore him six children. Tragically, Dillon Mapother, by now a surveyor, died of a severe case of food poisoning in 1874, leaving Mary, then only thirty-one, to bring up her large brood alone.

She was not on her own for long, meeting Thomas O'Mara, who made a decent living in the town as a wholesaler of chemist supplies. While he was born around 1835 in Kentucky, as his name suggested, the O'Mara family hailed from Ireland. The couple married in February 1876 and promptly started a family. Their first son, Thomas O'Mara, was born just over nine months later, on December 29. In the 1880 census, the toddler was still called Thomas O'Mara and was listed as living with his parents and two half brothers, Wible and deHenry, who were both still at school, and a half sister, Dellia, then eighteen, who worked as a store clerk. Mysteriously, at some point during his childhood, Thomas O'Mara's name was changed to Thomas Cruise Mapother. Perhaps it was to give him the same surname as his half brothers and sisters, or his parents later divorced and his mother altered Thomas's name, but as genealogist William Addams Reitwiesner noted, "The reasons for him changing his name are not entirely clear." Indeed, this confusing family tree could serve as a metaphor for the actor's own contradictory and elusive history.

So while the family name of Mapother seems to be Irish rather than Welsh in origin, the actor's paternal bloodline can be traced back to the O'Mara clan from Ireland. Yet Mapother the surname stayed, and for the next four generations the actor's father, grandfather, and great-grandfather were all named Thomas Cruise Mapother.

Not only did they keep the same name, they lived in the same place, putting down deep roots in the rich Kentucky soil. Over the years the Mapothers, from both the O'Mara and

Mapother bloodlines, produced an array of well-to-do professional men: mainly lawyers, but also engineers, scientists—and even a railway president.

The first Thomas Cruise Mapother (born Thomas O'Mara) went on to become one of the youngest attorneys in Louisville. He married Anna Stewart Bateman, who bore him two sons, Paul and Thomas Cruise Mapother II. "They were a good, solid family, pillars of Louisville society and very loyal and dependable," recalled Caroline Mapother, a family cousin.

His younger son, Thomas Cruise Mapother II, born in 1908, followed in his father's footsteps, becoming a lawyer and later a circuit court judge and a well-known Republican Party activist. After his marriage to Catherine Reibert, the couple went on to have two boys. His younger son, William—father of the actor William Mapother—became an attorney, bankruptcy consultant, and judge like his father, while his elder son, Thomas, born in 1934, inherited the family's inquisitive scientific bent. His cousin Dillon Mapother, formerly associate vice chancellor for research at the University of Illinois, is probably the best-known scientist in the family, his work on superconductivity and solid-state physics earning him a considerable reputation. The professor's academic papers alone take up 8.3 cubic feet in the college library.

As a teenager, Thomas Mapother III continued that tradition. After graduating in the early 1950s from St. Xavier's, a private Catholic school in Louisville that has been the alma mater to generations of Mapother boys, he went on to study electrical engineering at the University of Kentucky. At the time it was viewed as one of the better colleges in the country, but was mainly for white kids—the university was not desegregated until 1954. After graduating in the mid-1950s, he started seriously courting an attractive brunette, Mary Lee Pfeiffer, who was two years younger and had a family history equally established in Jefferson County, Kentucky. Like her future husband, she could trace her lineage back to Ireland and her roots in Louisville to the early nineteenth century. Her father, Charles, had died in March 1953, so only her mother, Comala, who lived to the ripe old age of ninety-two, and her brother Jack were present to watch the twenty-one-year-old walk down the aisle at a Catholic church in Jefferson County just a few days after Christmas Day, on December 28, 1957.

For a young electrical engineer like Thomas Mapother, it was an exciting time. Recruited by the giant General Electric Corporation, he apparently took a keen interest in the development of laser technology, which had just been introduced in a paper by scientists Charles Townes and Arthur Schawlow in 1958, their pioneering work ultimately revolutionizing the world of medicine and communications. "Thomas was fascinated by technological developments of the day," Professor Dillon Mapother later observed. "He spent every waking moment on new projects." While he was establishing himself in his new corporation, it was not long before the newlyweds began a family: four children born in just four years. Their first child, Lee Anne, was born in 1959 in Louisville, their second, Marian, two years later, after the family had moved to Syracuse, New York. Thomas Cruise Mapother IV was born on July 3, 1962—the day before Independence Day. His younger sister, Catherine—known as Cass—who was named after her paternal grandmother, arrived a year later.

It did not escape notice that with his dark hair, strong jaw, straight nose, blue eyes, pouchy dimpled cheeks, and slim, well-proportioned features, together with a winning smile, little Tom was very much his mother's son. The two developed an intensely close bond of mutual love and admiration, an adoration he has never been shy of expressing. "My mother is a very warm, charismatic woman, very kind, very generous," he later told TV interviewer James Lipton. As the only boy in the family, he found himself doted on by his sisters as well as his mother.

A young child with a vivid imagination—often caught daydreaming instead of helping his mom—he was constantly creating his own real-life adventures, eagerly exploring the domain beyond his backyard on his tricycle. At times his daring spirit caused a degree of consternation in the Mapother household, the youngster regularly having to be gently coaxed down by his mother from the trees he had climbed. It did not help his mother's equanimity that he dreamed of emulating his hero, G.I. Joe, a plastic action man who came complete with a parachute. Then only three or four years old, he achieved his ambition with potentially tragic results. He remembers pulling the sheets from his bed, using monkey bars to climb onto the garage roof, and then jumping off. "I knocked myself out. I was laying there looking at stars," he later recalled.

Even as early as the tender age of four, he daydreamed of becoming an actor. "It just evolved," he once recalled, and it was no surprise that from a young age he was fascinated by the drama, action, and adventure of the movies. A family treat was to go to a drive-in, buy popcorn, and let young Tom lie on top of the station wagon to watch the film. He was mesmerized by the wartime yarn *Lawrence of Arabia*, even though nothing in his young life enabled him to grasp the notion of an endless rolling desert. Around the dinner table he enjoyed performing, making his family laugh with impersonations of cartoon characters like Woody Woodpecker and Donald Duck. Later he graduated to the voices of Elvis Presley, Humphrey Bogart, and James Cagney. His mother, who had a love of theater, encouraged Tom and his sisters to perform skits she had written.

In some ways his early experience of school was a more painful adventure than jumping off the roof. When he was still a toddler, the family moved frequently, living for a time in New Jersey, then moving to St. Louis, Missouri, and returning to New Jersey when he was six. In 1969 he was at the Packanack Elementary School in Wayne Township. It soon became apparent to his teachers that young Tom was struggling to learn the rudiments of reading. He felt humiliated and frustrated, embarrassed every time he was called upon to read aloud in class. It was not long before he was diagnosed as suffering from dyslexia, a learning disability that apparently affected his mother and, to a greater or lesser degree, his three sisters. Dyslexics find it difficult to distinguish letters, form words, spell, or read with any degree of comprehension. Even though sufferers are of average or above-average intelligence, this invisible handicap, if unrecognized, can produce deep psychological trauma, notably a sense of isolation, inadequacy, and low self-esteem.

Tom has since spoken of the shame he felt as he grappled with the disorder: "I would go blank, feel anxious, nervous, bored, frustrated, dumb. I would get angry. My legs would actually hurt when I was studying. My head ached. All through school and well into my career I felt like I had a secret." Like other sufferers, he developed coping strategies, rarely volunteering to answer teachers' questions, or behaving like the class clown to deflect attention from his academic failings. His Woody Woodpecker impersonations now amused his classmates as well as his family.

Tom's own frustrations were seemingly mirrored by his teachers' impatience with him. He would later claim that when he was seven—the time he attended Packanack Elementary School—one teacher hurled him over a chair in class, the implication being that the teacher was angered by his inability to grasp the subject. Other teachers, he later recalled, were similarly irritated. The current principal of the five-hundred-pupil school, Dr. Kevin McGrath, who has been teaching for more than thirty years, finds the actor's claims difficult to accept. "That kind of behavior by a teacher toward a pupil would not have been tolerated then or now," he says. "It is tantamount to locking a child in a closet or taking a switch to them."

In the winter of 1971, when he was halfway through third grade, his family packed up again and headed north for Ottawa, the Canadian capital, where his father had apparently gotten a job working for the Canadian military. They moved into a tidy clapboard house at 2116 Monson Crescent in Beacon Hill North, a leafy middle-class suburb that attracts government workers, diplomats, and other itinerant professionals. "Hello, my name is Thomas Mapother the Second," announced Tom proudly if incorrectly when he knocked on the door of his new neighbors, the Lawrie family, and introduced himself. "I liked him," recalls Irene Lawrie, whose sons Alan and Scott became regular playmates. "He was always very active, always on the go, but a bit of a loner."

Beneath the surface bravado there was, as he admitted later, an American youngster understandably worrying about whether he would fit in at a new school with new friends in a foreign country. "You know, I didn't have the right shoes; I didn't have the right clothes; I even had the wrong accent," he recalled. Small for his age, "Little Tommy Mapother," as he was known by teachers and pupils alike, soon found himself picked on by playground bullies. He had to learn to stand tall. "So many times the big bully comes up, pushes me, and your heart is pounding, you sweat, and you feel you are going to vomit," he said later. "I'm not the biggest guy in the world, I never liked hitting someone, but I know if I don't hit that guy, he's going to pick on me all year."

Tough lessons from his father, which he painfully learned at home, as well as his own obdurate nature gave him the inner resilience to face down those who opposed him. When his own father was at school, he, too, had been bullied, an experience that emotionally scarred him for life. Determined that young Tom not go through the same trauma, he always pushed him to stand up for himself. If Tom was in a fight and lost, his father insisted that the youngster go out and take on his opponent again. Physically, Tom Senior was "very, very tough" toward his only son, seemingly crossing the boundary between stern parenting and abuse. "As a kid I had a lot of hidden anger about that. I'd get hit and I didn't understand it," the actor later told celebrity writer Kevin Sessums.

Young Tom's bloody-minded obstinacy and refusal to back down soon earned him respect among local youngsters. "Tom was the school tough guy," recalls Scott Lawrie, now a police officer. "He wasn't a pushover and could handle himself." As his brother Alan observes, "If there was trouble with the local kids, he would be the first to say, 'Let's get involved.'" In the cruel world of playground politics, Tom needed a thick skin. He stood out not only because he was

American but also because of his learning difficulties. "I remember some kids making mockery of him because he couldn't read," recalls Alan Lawrie.

Ironically, in spite of the inevitable taunts from thoughtless classmates, Tom was enrolled in the perfect elementary school for a child with his learning needs. So new that pupils had to take their shoes off before walking on the purple carpet, Robert Hopkins Public School was years ahead of its time: progressive, enlightened, and nurturing, with ample funding. When Tom and his sisters were enrolled, his parents alerted the school principal, Jim Brown, to their children's various learning difficulties. The principal explained that before the Mapother children could be placed into special-needs classes, they had to be given a routine assessment by an educational psychologist.

When he was at the school, which was open plan, Tom and other youngsters with similar problems—normally there would be eight or so in a class—would go into a smaller room away from the hubbub for more intensive tuition in reading, writing, spelling, and math under the watchful eye of the school's special-needs teacher, Asta Arnot. Even by today's standards, this was high-quality care. His mother supplemented the work of the school at home: Tom would dictate the answers to his assignments to her, then she would hand the work back to him so he could painstakingly copy it out.

While there is no recognized cure for dyslexia, teaching programs help sufferers to make sense of everyday life—from distinguishing the numbers on currency to reading a menu. The fact that he was diagnosed early worked heavily in his favor. At that age—he was at Robert Hopkins between eight and eleven—the brain is at its most adaptable, able to interpret and consolidate the basic building blocks of reading, writing, and arithmetic even in the face of a condition like dyslexia.

While the school was professionally equipped to help children with learning difficulties, the actor later complained about his treatment in the educational system: "I had always felt I had barriers to overcome. . . . I was forced to write with my right hand when I wanted to use my left. I began to reverse letters, and reading became difficult," he said later. Unsurprisingly, his former teachers meet the actor's grievances with disbelief. Both Pennyann Styles, who taught him at Robert Hopkins, and special-needs teacher Asta Arnot emphatically reject these claims. Styles, who is left-handed herself, was a self-confessed "zealot" about helping lefties to write as they wished—even bringing left-handed scissors to school.

In spite of his learning difficulties, the teaching staff at Robert Hopkins remembered Tom as a creative pupil who simply needed more time and attention. Another former teacher, Shirley Gaudreau, observes: "He was a right-brain kid—very creative but not in academics. It takes a lot more work with them." Like other pupils with similar problems, he was encouraged to excel at a nonacademic subject like sports, drama, or art in order to bolster his confidence. He joined the school's drama club and soon became a regular fixture in plays and other theatrical events. This was not entirely surprising, as there was acting blood on both sides of his family. Among the Mapother clan, his cousins William, Katherine, and Amy were enthusiastic childhood performers, William and Amy later becoming professional actors, while Katherine now works with the Blue Apple Players in Louisville. During their time in Ottawa, Tom's mother and father were so keen on drama that the American newcomers helped found the Gloucester Players amateur theater group, appearing together in the group's first-ever performance.

A fellow founder was school drama teacher George Steinburg, who, together with Tom's mother, was instrumental in kindling the boy's enjoyment of theater. "He had good raw energy that had to be channeled," Steinburg recalled. "You could tell there was some talent." In June 1972, at the end of his first school year in Ottawa, Tom and six other boys represented Robert Hopkins in the Carlton Elementary School drama festival. The group, dressed in tunics and tights, performed an improvised play to dance and music called *IT*. Their aim was to interpret the full title of the piece, which was "Man seeks out and discovers some unknown power or thing. He is affected by it."

In the audience was drama organizer Val Wright. Even though she has since watched and judged hundreds of youngsters, she has never forgotten that "superb" production. "The movement and improvisation were excellent. It was a classic ensemble piece."

Other performances were equally memorable. In her mind's eye, teacher Wendy Santo can still remember the youngster in a fifth-grade performance where he played the sun, frozen in a sideways pose. "Even thirty years later it still gives me goose bumps. He was just another kid, but you would have been impressed," she says.

When he took on roles that demanded reading and learning lines, teachers were on hand to help him out. Teacher Marilyn Richardson remembers how she was asked to read his lines out loud to help him memorize them. "He could read, but it took him a long time," she recalls. "He had a very good memory and it didn't take him long to learn his lines." Certainly his performances always left an impression—although sometimes for the wrong reasons. Fellow pupil Louise Giannoccaro (née Funke) recalls the day when the "really cool" Tom Mapother appeared in a school play about Indians and cheekily played to the gallery to get a laugh. "He was supposed to pick an apple and say, 'An apple, what's an apple?' but he was eating the apple and couldn't say the line." As his teacher Marilyn Richardson recalls, "He was a joker who liked to kid around. Everything was a bit of a laugh."

While his acting garnered attention, his sporting prowess was more notable for tough, unbridled aggression than for any natural ability. He scraped into the school's second team for hockey and earned a reputation for spunk and determination, flinging himself into "impossible situations" where the sticks were flying. "He was rough in floor hockey," recalled his school friend Glen Gobel. "He was hardheaded but not talented." For his pains, he ended up chipping a front tooth in one game. His belligerent streak got him into more trouble during a robust game of British Bulldogs—a rough version of "Piggy in the Middle"—in the school playground that left him writhing on the floor in agony. He was taken to the hospital in an ambulance with a busted knee, prompting headmaster Jim Brown to ban the game.

Doubtless it was an incident that made his father proud. Tom Senior's robust approach to teaching his son sports emphasized taking the knocks without complaint. When they played catch with a baseball glove in their backyard, Tom's father would throw the hardball violently and fast at the head and body of his nine-year-old son. "Sometimes if it hit my head, my nose would bleed and some tears would come up," he later recalled. "He wasn't very comforting." Noticeably, it was Tom's mother rather than his father who took him to his first ball game. This tough training did help Tom win a place on the North Gloucester baseball team, and as he adapted to local sports, he became much more proficient. When neighbor Scott Lawrie played against him in an ice hockey match, he couldn't believe how good Tom was. "I just couldn't get the puck by him," he recalls. "He became a good hockey player, always ready to try new things."

It should not have come as too much of a surprise. Tom and his gang, which included Scott and Alan Lawrie, Lionel Aucoin, Scott Miller, Glen Gobel, and Tom Gray, spent endless hours playing street hockey or baseball in the summer and ice hockey in the winter. For a change they played pool on a miniature table given to Tom by his sister Lee Anne's boyfriend, rode their bikes to nearby Ottawa River, or went fishing in Green's Creek.

The same reckless daring he showed on the sports field was evident when his gang was out having fun. Tom was the acknowledged tough guy, a thrill seeker who pushed the edge of the envelope when his friends cried chicken. "He was cocky, confident, and cool," recalls Alan Lawrie. "When the kids got together, he set the agenda." At Tom's prompting, the boys became blood brothers, pricking their fingers with a pin and then mixing their blood together. When they went bike riding, he was the one who constructed rickety ramps to perform Evel Knievel–style stunts, the one who used a hockey net hung on a frame or a tree to perform Tarzan tricks, and the one who performed a daring back flip from the roof of his house but missed the soft landing of a snowbank and broke his foot when he landed on the sidewalk. This experience failed to curb his daredevil antics. At a nearby building site, he climbed on the roof or started the builder's tractor while the rest of his friends ran off. "He was pushing limits all the time," recalls Alan Lawrie. "I never thought of him ever becoming an actor. He was more of an Al Capone character, a maverick, the kind of kid who wouldn't back down."

Tom had a belligerent side, a cussed indomitability that seemed to stop him from knowing when to retreat and move on. One episode demonstrates the stubborn streak of the alpha male in Tom Mapother. He and his friend Glen Gobel were walking home when two older and bigger boys made disparaging remarks about Tom's new haircut. He fiercely denied having his hair cut, and it was only the intervention of his school friend that stopped a fight—and Tom taking a beating. Afterward, when Glen asked why he had been so insistent, Tom replied, "It's not a haircut, it's a hairstyle." As Glen recalls, "Even though he was a pretty popular kid, this 'my way or the highway' attitude did lose him friends."

Of course, there was another reason Tom was so concerned about his hairstyle and why he took the trouble to go home at lunch every day to change—girls. "Little Tommy Mapother" punched way above his weight in the romantic arena. His teacher Pennyann Styles remembers him well. "He had charisma. He was a standout because he was so good-looking. Even then he had that smile that he has today. Little Tom was attractive, outgoing, and slightly mischievous, but not bad. The kind of kid you recognize and remember." He had long eyelashes that the girls adored and, for some inexplicable reason, they swooned over the fact that he had a sty under one eye. "The way his hair fell was so dreamy," recalls Carol Trumpler, a fellow pupil at Robert Hopkins. "He had a cute way about him, certainly the gift of gab." More than that, he had a swagger, a confidence that made him seem to stand much taller than he was. "We all had a crush on him; even then he was very cute," recalls former pupil Nancy Maxwell.

He was the precocious kid, the one who organized parties

for girls and boys at his house just as the sexes were becoming interested in each other. "He was sort of a bad boy, on the outside of the rules," recalls Heather McKenzie, who enjoyed her first smooch with the future star. Even the boys in his gang now have to admit he had something that they lacked. "All the girls liked him and he thought he was pretty hot, too," recalls his friend Lionel Aucoin pointedly. Tom had a distinct advantage over his friends, as living with three sisters had given him an insight into the fairer sex. "Women to me are not a mystery. I get along easily with them," he observed later. That his sister Lee Anne, nearly three years his elder, would let her friends use him for kissing practice gave him a practical edge in the endless battle of the sexes. "It was great; there were no complaints," he recalls.

One of his first girlfriends was fellow pupil Carol Trumpler. He was her first sweetheart, and even now, two marriages and four children later, she comes across all misty-eyed when talking about her first-ever kiss. "When you talk about first loves, I will always remember mine . . . Tom Cruise," she says. "He was a very good kisser, very much at ease with it all. But what do you know at eleven?"

Carol got in trouble when she and Tom were caught smooching behind the picket fence by the playground perimeter. The young lovebirds were hauled up before school principal Jim Brown. As a result Carol was grounded by her parents and ordered to stay in her room. Undeterred, young Tom knocked on her door a few days later, a gray pup tent slung over his shoulder, to ask if she wanted to go camping in the woods. "It was probably so he could spend the day kissing me," she recalls. "He was quite precocious and promiscuous, as far as you are at that age. He was trying to kiss me all the time." Even though her father, Rene, sent Tom packing, the youngster was reluctant to take no for an answer, prepared to stand his ground before the older man.

After Carol—"I was trying to be a good girl, and when I didn't give in to his ways he moved on"—there was Heather, Louise, Linda, Sheila, and, of course, his "bride," Rowan Hopkins. Athletic, adventurous—she loved camping and hiking—and with a lively imagination, Rowan was one of the darlings of her year. As Lionel Aucoin recalls, "When you look back, it was just one of those funny things, Tom Cruise marrying his sweetheart in the school playground."

In his official class photograph, taken in 1974 when he and his classmates had moved from Robert Hopkins to Henry Munro Middle School, it is easy to imagine why the eleven-year-old American was known as the coolest kid in school. With his head half cocked at the camera with a look of inquisitive insolence, his long hair in a fashionable, almost pageboy cut, and his checked shirt daringly unbuttoned, as was the style in the early 1970s, he looks more confident and at ease than other youngsters standing beside him. "As a kid he was famous even before he became properly famous, if that makes sense," recalls Scott Lawrie. "He was one of those kids that you wanted to be around. I thought it was cool that Tom Mapother lived next door to me." (Tom did, however, have competition to be king of the heap. On the next street lived Bruce Adams, now better known as rock star Bryan Adams, who also attended Henry Munro Middle School at the time.)

Cool, confident, charismatic, energetic; an occasionally cussed but popular boy: This is the presenting portrait of Tom Cruise Mapother IV as he approached his teenage years.

While academically he was seen as a middle-of-the-road student, it seems that he was coping well enough with his dyslexia not to need any extra help or coaching at Henry Munro. His homeroom teacher, Byron Boucher, who later specialized in special-needs children, taught him in a variety of subjects, including English and math, and as far as he is concerned, twelve-year-old Tom Mapother had no unusual learning difficulties. If he had struggled with reading and writing, the school principal would have been automatically informed and necessary remedial action taken.

At his new school he continued to excel at acting, taking part in Friday-afternoon drama sessions where, if they had worked hard, pupils were allowed to perform in front of the class. "He liked that very much and was very convincing," recalls Boucher.

Less convincing was his behavior. During the transition from Robert Hopkins to Henry Munro, Tom's image as a boy who got up to mischief but not into trouble began to change—for the worse. It wasn't just the parents of his sweetheart Carol Trumpler who now viewed him with suspicion. He gained a reputation as a bit of a troublemaker, a youngster whose friendship should not be encouraged. "Parents would say, 'Watch that kid,' " Alan Lawrie recalls.

He had started to get into more serious scrapes toward the end of his time in elementary school. His teacher Sharon Waters was hauled up by the school principal and threatened with dismissal when Tom and another student played hooky from Robert Hopkins. The local police escorted the pair, then eleven, back to class, and Sharon was severely reprimanded for failing to take attendance. On another occasion, Tom and Lionel Aucoin found a cache of firecrackers, which they threw into backyards in the neighborhood before running off. One irate householder gave chase, caught them, and threatened to turn them over to the police. Another time, Alan Lawrie's father, Murray, cuffed him around the ear when he spotted him using three pine trees he had just planted in his garden for high-jump practice. (Tom didn't do permanent damage to the trees, which are now over thirty feet tall.) As Tom later admitted, "I was a wild kid. I'd cut school. Everything had to do with my wanting always to push the envelope to see: Where do I stand with myself? How far can I go?"

In truth, his truculent behavior coincided with the collapse of his parents' marriage, his wilder excesses a manifestation of his confusion and unhappiness. In an attempt to sort out his personal problems, his father sought professional counseling. "After the breakdown you could see big changes," recalls George Steinburg. "Tommy was a problem. His dad was coming home from therapy and teaching him about opening up. Tommy really got into it and got into some trouble at school. You know, cussing and swearing."

During the three years they lived in Ottawa, stresses and strains were developing that neighbors and friends could only imagine. It had all started so well. When they first arrived in Ottawa, the family made an effort to fit into their new community.

Tom's mother earned the nickname "Merry Mary Lee" for her sunny personality. For a time she worked at the local hospital and helped out at the children's school, taking part in school trips and other activities. "The first year and a half they lived here I think was a very happy time for the whole family," recalled George Steinburg. "They were all popular." The children pitched in, too, Tom remembering how he and one of his sisters took part in a forty-mile walk (the distance has probably been exaggerated) to raise money for local charities. Tom remembers that grueling walk mostly for the fact that a woman gave him a quarter for a soda to quench his thirst just as he was silently praying for a cool drink.

Around the neighborhood, he and his gang were seen as helpful kids who made two dollars a job for mowing lawns. Tom himself earned a little extra by cleaning out people's yards. But after the first flush of neighborliness, the general judgment on the block was that Tom's father was distant and uncommunicative—a shadowy, elusive figure. "He was not sociable at all," recalls his neighbor Irene Lawrie. "He could barely bring himself to give you the time of day." There was talk that he had quit his job to write a book—certainly the family never had any money—rumor that he was a heavy drinker, gossip, too, that social services had been called in to help the family.

After the early efforts to socialize during their first years in Canada, it became clear to friends, teachers, and neighbors that the Mapother marriage was unraveling. "It was not a happy time for the family," recalls Tom's former teacher Shirley Gaudreau. The polarized local opinion about the Mapothers matched the schisms inside the family. While Tom has never uttered a critical word about his "beautiful, caring, loving" mother, who doted on her only son, he has rarely had a kind comment about his father. The relationship

seemed one of mutual, confusing antagonism, his father singling his son out for his own interpretation of tough, almost
brutal, love. While Tom and his sisters could not do enough
for their strong, jovial mother, they tiptoed warily around
their unpredictable father.

On one occasion the Mapother children asked Irene
Lawrie for help in secretly baking a cake as a surprise for
their mother's birthday. Their oven wasn't working and they
didn't have any baking equipment, so they threw themselves
on her mercy. Irene ended up baking the cake, but the affection the Mapother children felt for their mother was clear
from their excitement. By contrast, when Tom's father took
him for a two-hour drive to go skiing in the hills outside Ottawa, he refused to stop to let his hungry son buy a snack.
Perversely, he told Tom to eat imaginary food, the duo
spending a long time making and then eating a make-believe
sandwich, complete with soda and chips. "And we had nothing," Tom later recalled of his father's bizarre behavior.

He would eventually describe his father as a "merchant of
chaos" and life as "a roller-coaster ride" where he could never
trust or feel safe with his father. For a boy who once said that
all he really wanted was "to be accepted" and be given "love
and attention," life with a father who was a "bully and a cow-
ard" was almost unbearable. One of his more poignant memories concerns seeing the movie *The Sting,* starring Robert
Redford and Paul Newman, which spoke to him not only because of the catchy theme song and audacious story line about
con men, but because it was one of the few pleasurable experiences he remembered sharing with his father. His verdict on
his father is damning: "He was the kind of person where, if
something goes wrong, they kick you. He was an antisocial
personality, inconsistent, unpredictable."

The fear Tom felt in his father's presence may help explain
his natural affinity for acting, as the great skill of a child in
an abusive, difficult home is the ability to split off, to hide in
the imagination, to simply no longer be present when things
get bad. In short, to fake it. This ability gets in the way later in
life, when victims cannot connect to really important emotions

like love and happiness because they are inextricably linked to fear. As adults, they are able to express emotion but not feel it.

At the same time, perhaps the indulgence of his mother, her obvious devotion to her son, generated a primal jealousy and resentment in his father, a rage that only served to diminish his authority and cement the bonds among mother, son, and daughters. Every inexplicable outburst, every ugly tirade against his son, merely served to create protective sympathy for Tom, while edging his father further to the margins of family life.

As he became more of an outsider within the family, Tom Senior seemed to be increasingly at odds with society at large. He slowly transformed into an angry young man, a renegade who had little time for the system. Brought up a Catholic, he denounced organized religion and expressed contempt for doctors and conventional medicine. A restless, seemingly unfulfilled soul, he quit jobs while nursing dreams of making a fortune with various inventions. Doubtless his secret drinking fueled his tirades, the lurching unpredictable moods of brutality and remorse. "He was a very complex individual and created a lot of chaos for the family," Tom later remarked. Finally, it all got too much for Mary Lee. It is a vivid testament to how difficult life with Thomas Mapother III had become that it was Mary Lee, a stalwart, strong-minded, churchgoing Catholic, who made the decision to leave her husband. "It was a time of growing, a time of conflict" is her only comment on this distressing event.

For a woman with a sense of the theatrical, the family departure was indeed dramatic. Mary Lee painstakingly planned the great escape with the precision of a military operation. She told Tom and her daughters to pack their suitcases and keep them by their beds in readiness for flight. At four-thirty one spring morning in 1974, when for some reason her husband was out of the house, Mary Lee roused her children, packed them into their station wagon, and headed for the border. "We felt like fugitives," recalls Tom, the secrecy surrounding their flight predicated on the false assumption that, under Canadian law, Mary Lee's husband could prevent them from leaving the country.

They drove the eight hundred miles from Ottawa to Louisville, where Mary Lee knew that her mother, Comala, and brother, Jack, were waiting for her. The route was not unfamiliar to the Mapother children, the family often driving to Kentucky during the summer break to spend time with relations from both sides of the family. As they sang along to the radio to keep their spirits up, it is doubtful that any of the children realized that they would only see their father three more times. They hadn't said any sort of good-bye to him, nor had they a chance to say their farewells to their school friends. Later, Tom's younger sister, Cass, did take the trouble to send her teacher a "sweet" note thanking her for all her help.

After the initial excitement and sense of adventure wore off, the enormity of what they had done began to sink in. They had left a safe, well-to-do neighborhood, excellent schools, and a familiar circle of friends for an uncertain future. In addition, the full extent of their financial calamity became clear once they realized that Tom's father was either unable or unwilling to pay child support. At first Mary Lee's mother, brother, and other family members rallied round to help, paying for a rented house on Taylorsville Road in the eastern suburbs. It also seems that they and the Mapother family helped pay the fees to send Tom to the local Catholic school, St. Raphael, which takes children up to eighth grade.

The move south had at least one advantage for Tom: When he joined the school hockey team, he was a star player thanks to his Canadian experience. During one match in Indiana, the opposing player was so frustrated by Tom's quicksilver ability that he unceremoniously grabbed him by the collar and threw him off the ice.

There was, however, no disguising the difficulties the family now faced. They could not rely on the kindness of relatives forever. Everyone had to chip in. The two eldest girls, Lee Anne and Marian, got part-time jobs as waitresses, and

Tom got back into the old routine—taking on a paper route, mowing lawns, and cleaning neighbors' yards. This time the money he earned was not to spend on movies or indulging his sweet tooth, but in putting food on the table. "No job was too dirty or difficult for Tommy, as long as it paid money to help his mom out," recalled neighbor Bill Lewis, a former Marine who befriended the youngster. Not that Tom was as saintly as he is portrayed. He later boasted that he saw *Star Wars* some fourteen times, paid for from his part-time jobs, while he once skimped on tidying a neighbor's yard so that he could catch an early showing of his favorite war movie, *Midway,* a dramatized account of the World War II sea and aerial battle in the Pacific Ocean.

His mother was the main breadwinner, taking on three part-time sales jobs to pay the bills. "My mom could have sat there every morning and cried and cried," Tom later recalled. "She didn't. My mom was very proud. She had dignity. She's going to work hard." Even though the family received federal food stamps, they were ineligible for full welfare benefits because she had too many jobs. Juggling those three jobs took its toll. Mary Lee slipped a disk in her back when her boss in the electrical store where she worked part-time ordered her to move a washing machine on her own. She was in traction for eight months, so incapacitated that a family friend had to move in to help out. The store never apologized or offered compensation.

The new young man about the house was incensed, consumed with an impotent fury at his mother's treatment. Even today the incident rouses him to rage. "He [the store manager] didn't give a shit about his employee. My mother's not a bitter person, but I remember just being very, very angry about that." Solicitous of his mother, protective of his sisters, Tom took his new role very seriously. At an age when most teenage boys have little time or patience for their mother, Tom became even closer to her. He admired Mary Lee for her unconditional love, steadfastness, and optimism. She was the kind of person who always sees a glass as half full, sings in the morning, and offers hospitality to strangers. When Mary Lee eventually returned to work, she enjoyed a treat from Tom, at least during Lent. Every day for six weeks, he washed and massaged her feet for thirty minutes when she came home.

Tom was sternly possessive toward his older sisters, giving their boyfriends his stamp of approval and on several occasions threatening them if they crossed the line of propriety. Once he threatened "to kill" his sister Marian's boyfriend if he touched her because he knew that the boy was dating another girl. Another time, a fellow pupil at St. Raphael who criticized one of his sisters found himself doing battle in the school bathrooms with an outraged Thomas Mapother. "I didn't care, I'm fiercely loyal," he says. His eldest sister, Lee Anne, observes that he has always acted more like a big brother than a little brother. "He was very caring and protective of us," she recalls. "Whenever any of us girls started dating anybody we were serious about, having them meet Tom was a big deal. His opinion has always weighed very heavily with all of us."

While he always felt comfortable surrounded by women, once observing that he trusted women more than men, they did get to be too much at times—so he called on his cousin William Mapother for company. "He only has sisters and I only have sisters, so we turned to each other for protection," recalls William. "We have a lot of strong verbal women in both our lives."

A hero to his uncritical mother, adored by his sisters, and with a father now held in contempt, it all rather went to his head. "It gave him a real sense of entitlement," recalls a family friend, speaking on the condition of anonymity. "He was the king of all he surveyed." Tom's authority quickly extended beyond his immediate family, the youngster displaying the daredevil leadership that had made him so popular among his Ottawa friends. His tall tales of his life outside the provincial confines of Kentucky, combined with his edge of dangerous audacity, gave him a patina of glamour and excitement. "To the neighborhood kids he became leader of the pack," recalled his onetime pal Tommy Puckett. "He would reward our loyalty by either buying or stealing cigarettes from the corner store for all of us to smoke." The youngsters would go off into fields with Puckett's BB gun and take potshots at the local wildlife. Tom was apparently a good shot.

Still, he wasn't quite the master of all he surveyed. On one occasion he came close to severely injuring himself when he rode a motorbike into the side of a house. He had boasted to older teenage friends that he was experienced with motorbikes, when in fact he had never ridden one. Mistaking the accelerator for the brake, he roared through a clump of bushes and into a brick wall. "I nearly killed myself trying to be one of the guys," he later admitted.

Closer to home, the new monarch had an unexpected and uneasy encounter with the deposed king, his father, on the streets of Louisville. Tom's father had eventually followed his family back to Kentucky, where he reportedly tried unsuccessfully to reconcile with his estranged wife. Tom Senior had abandoned all pretense of a professional life, living hand-to-mouth and taking on casual, unskilled work. At one point it was said that he was working on the crew of a highway construction gang. During his awkward encounter with them after months of separation, Tom Senior asked Tom and his sister if they wanted to go to a drive-in movie with him— a once-happy family event. While Tom has never spoken of this confrontation, his father later said to a local reporter that his son had told him to "stay the hell out of everything."

In fact, he came back into his son's life in a way that many in Louisville found incomprehensible. On August 1, 1975, just three weeks after Tom's thirteenth birthday, Mary Lee and Thomas Mapother were officially divorced and Mary Lee reverted to her maiden name of Pfeiffer. Just six weeks later, after a whirlwind courtship lasting all of two weeks, Tom's father remarried. In August 1975, the month he officially divorced, he met Joan Lebendiger, the widow of a well-respected local doctor who had died the previous November at the age of just forty-six. The attraction was instant and mutual, and within a matter of days they decided to wed.

Certainly Joan Lebendiger was measuring up to the translation of her German surname: "full of life." If the Mapother clan was surprised, the four Lebendiger children were utterly stunned. "My mother told us on a Tuesday over dinner that she was getting married, and they married on the Saturday," recalls Jonathan Lebendiger, who at thirteen was the same age as his future stepbrother. Tom and his sisters attended the civil ceremony, which took place in their home at 2811 Newburg Road, a leafy suburb of Louisville. Apart from making desultory conversation with the four Lebendiger children at the wedding, Tom has never contacted his "second family" again.

If the wedding was rushed, no sooner had Jonathan Lebendiger, his brother, Gary, and his sisters, Jamie and Leslie, absorbed the news that their mother was marrying for the second time than they literally found themselves abandoned, their mother and her new husband setting off for a new life in Florida. In this family crisis the Lebendiger children were taken in by relatives or family friends, with only the money left by their dead father to support them. Neither their mother nor her new husband contributed in any way to clothe, feed, or educate the children, just as Tom Mapother Senior did nothing to help his blood family.

Understandably, this incident has left the Lebendiger children with a legacy of anger and bitterness toward the man who turned their lives upside down. "He was the black sheep of the Mapother family," says Jonathan Lebendiger, now a real-estate agent in Philadelphia. "I don't know what his relationship was like with his son, but I know that he was a bad apple. His family were all lawyers and he opposed everything they stood for. I was angry about it at the time but I am not anymore." This union—a grand passion or passing desperation—lasted for just a year before Jonathan's mother and Tom's father went their separate ways. Joan Lebendiger, a bridge fanatic, eventually retired to Los Angeles. She and her children were reconciled before she died in 2005. "She said that she did the best she could but admitted that she didn't have the normal parenting skills like other people," recalls Jonathan. "Let's leave it at that."

If the Lebendiger circle was aggrieved, the Mapother clan was "appalled" by Tom Senior's behavior. "I don't think anyone normal would go off and abandon a wife and four children like he did," Caroline Mapother told writer Wesley Clarkson. The family did not hear from Thomas Mapother III for years—not a note or a letter or even a Christmas card. Tellingly, Tom recalls the first Christmas after the 1975 divorce as the best ever. As they only had enough money to put food on the table, his mother suggested that they each pick a name out of a hat in advance, then perform secret acts of kindness for the recipient and reveal their identity on Christmas Day. On that day they all read poems and put on skits for one another. "We didn't have any money and it was actually great," he has since said of this life of hand-me-downs, early-morning paper rounds, and making do.

Curiously, at that time, they lived in a handsome four-bedroom house on Cardwell Way, a neighborhood where backyard swimming pools are not uncommon. For their part, the greater Mapother family bridles at suggestions that they abandoned Mary Lee and her children to a life of struggle and poverty. As Caroline Mapother observed, "These claims make me angry because his grandmother did everything in the world to try and help support those children, especially after Tom III went off."

Tom became particularly close to his grandfather Tom Mapother II, a retired lawyer with a wealth of tales about the colorful characters he'd encountered in his practice, as well as stories about Tom's now-absent father when he was young. One summer he took Tom and his cousin William on a visit to Washington to see the sights; and after Tom left St. Raphael in 1976, he offered to pay the fees at St. Xavier's, a prestigious all-boys Catholic high school that William was destined to attend.

Tom spurned his grandfather's generous offer, arguing that unless he could pay for his sisters to attend private schools, too, he was reluctant to be singled out simply because he was a boy. This seems an odd argument, given the fact that St. Xavier's was all boys and his older sisters, Lee Anne and Marian, were already settled in their high schools and only a couple of years from graduating. Tom later told TV interviewer

James Lipton that this was the compelling reason he traveled one hundred miles north to enroll in a Catholic seminary in Cincinnati. His yearlong sojourn at the St. Francis boarding school run by Franciscan priests has been widely interpreted as indicating his desire to train for life as a priest. As he later explained, the reason was much less romantic: "We didn't have the money back then, and I went for the education for a year, and it was free." Still, he insists that he did indeed toy with the idea of joining the brotherhood. "I looked at the priesthood and said, 'Listen, this is what I'm going to do,' " he told Dotson Rader.

Perhaps his family felt that this truculent teenager, who was forever getting into scrapes and fights, might benefit from a stiffer regime than the "monstrous regiment of women" who enveloped him. This was now the fifth school he had attended since he was seven—not the fifteen institutions he claimed to attend before he was fourteen years old to emphasize his rootless childhood. He spent a school year at the remote seminary, from September 1976 to the following summer, and he described this period with one hundred other pupils, many the children of divorced parents, as the best year of his academic career.

Tom may have appreciated the discipline and regimentation of a religious boarding school—Mass was said every day—as well as the jostling, boisterous camaraderie of twenty boys sharing a dormitory. A sense of belonging, a need to be part of an identifiable group, is a recurrent theme in Tom's emotional lexicon. While his family fulfilled that need, the cloistered world at St. Francis seemed to become his emotional home away from home. "He always had a smile," recalled Father John Boehman, rector and guardian of the now closed seminary. "But he stood out because he was the smallest in his class and he couldn't get away with anything."

He joined the glee club, played basketball—even though he was the shortest player in his freshman year—and played on the Saints soccer team. There were hobby shops and remote-control boats and planes available, which, for a boy who had a passion for flight, was thrilling. Even more thrilling, for the first time in his academic career he made the honor roll.

Given his fond memories, it is surprising that he stayed at the seminary only until the summer of 1977, deciding to return to Louisville to continue his education—especially since he had to go and live with his aunt and uncle, the Barratts, because Mary Lee and his sisters could no longer afford the rent on their house and had squeezed in with her mother. He enrolled at St. Xavier's Catholic school and says that he paid the tuition by taking on a paper route and, for a time, working in an ice cream parlor in downtown Louisville. It seems a perplexing choice. He knew that his grandfather had previously offered to pay his fees, and now that Lee Anne had graduated and his other sisters were established in their own schools, there was no obstacle to accepting his generosity.

Teenage pride and a realization that model planes were no substitute for hanging out with the fair sex probably helped explain his return to Louisville. When he was at the seminary, he and other boys had visited the homes of local girls, to chat and play spin the bottle. "I started to realize that I love women too much to give all that up," he later recalled. He and his friends cruised the streets of Louisville looking for action or hung around in the local mall playing pinball. His easy way with women, evident from his numerous conquests in Ottawa, was equally apparent in his new hometown. For years Laurie Hobbs, who met Tom when she was a student at the Sacred Heart School in Louisville, boasted that she was the first to teach one of the world's sexiest men how to kiss. He was probably too much of a gentleman to discuss his numerous previous experiences, although she should have realized as much from her own comments. "I remember thinking how surprised I was that he could kiss like that. We just floated along clinging to each other. I even had to tell him to keep his hands to himself."

The frenetic fumblings and mumblings were part of a typical teenage rite of passage. When he and his friends were not looking for girls, they were just barely keeping themselves out of trouble. Even though, at fifteen, he was too young to have a driver's license, he cruised around town in borrowed cars. On one occasion he was stopped by police when he tried to drive the wrong way down a one-way street. The police officers watched him impassively as he struggled to turn the car around.

Never one to refuse a dare, he once stripped naked and streaked down the street as his friends watched. He literally ran into trouble when a passing police patrol car caught him in its headlights. According to a former school friend, he had the wit to tell the skeptical officers that he had locked himself out of his home after taking a bath. For his pains he was given a ride home wrapped in the officer's coat. Tommy Puckett recalls one Halloween when Tom and others dressed as flapper girls for a laugh.

Tom was not smiling, however, when he discovered that his mother was dating plastics salesman Jack South, whom she had met at an electronics convention. For a young man used to being the head of the household, cosseting his mother and vetting his sisters' boyfriends, the interloper was an affront to his authority. Gruff, tough, and straight-talking, Jack South was more than a match for the young whippersnapper. There was an inevitable clashing of heads, and for a long time their relationship was uneasy. Their common interest in sports, movies, and "guy stuff," notably gambling, eventually helped bring about a thaw. The fact that Tom made the right choices during their betting duels seemed to forge a degree of friendship between them. After all, Jack South was now permanently in his life. He and Mary Lee were married in 1978, and shortly afterward he took a job in New Jersey. As a result the family was on the move again. But this time all the family traveled together.

CHAPTER 2

She was the heartthrob of her high school. As the beautiful head cheerleader, it was only to be expected that, in the student hierarchy, she would be dating the hunkiest football player. Her fame, though, went beyond the well-heeled but insular borders of her high school. Lorraine Gauli was the star of a teenage TV show, *The New Voice*—a precursor to *Dawson's Creek*—that regularly took her to Boston for filming. To her fellow students the beautiful blond actress was the girl most likely to hit the big time. Success was hers for the taking. Or so it seemed.

If only her love life had run quite so smoothly. While she and football player Frank Gerard were seen as the school's glamour couple, they fought like cat and dog. He was possessive and very jealous, a strapping six-footer with a temper. On the night of a party at fellow pupil Kevin Forster's house, the golden couple was fighting. It was nothing unusual; everyone knew that they would make up later. She was crying and went outside to get some air. The new kid at school was in the yard, too. Short, skinny, one hundred pounds soaking wet, and with prominent teeth, sixteen-year-old Tom Mapother—or Maypo, as he was known—was hardly the catch of the county. But the newly arrived sophomore was a nice enough kid. Lorraine was his partner in chemistry class. He was chatty, easy to talk to, and funny.

Tom asked if Lorraine was okay and tried to comfort her.

Then he made his first big mistake. He put his arm around her, just as her boyfriend and his fellow jocks came outside looking for his girl. It was all the encouragement burly Frank needed. There was a flurry of fists and a torrent of venom. "Since you've come to this town you've been nothing but trouble" was one of the cleaner insults yelled by the jocks as Frank pummeled the slightly built weakling. Lorraine ran into the house, screaming hysterically, and little Maypo was left lying, barely conscious, in the bushes. Eventually he picked himself up, confirmed he had no broken bones, and made his way home. Welcome to Glen Ridge.

The town of Glen Ridge is the Beverly Hills of New Jersey, a compact, white, upper-middle-class suburb of Montclair, where a Porsche, BMW, or Mercedes is the traditional transport of choice. With streets lined with mature trees and quaint gaslights, and most of the substantial family homes dating back to Victorian days, Glen Ridge is as elegant as it is affluent. While surgeons, accountants, lawyers, and media folk are attracted to the area because of the short commute to Manhattan, many of the 7,500 residents move here for the quality of the schools, particularly Glen Ridge High School, widely acknowledged to be the finest in the state.

The sprawling Victorian house on Washington Street in the desirable South Ender district, which Tom's stepfather, Jack South, rented for the Mapother brood in 1978, was larger than they were used to, but the well-to-do environment was not unfamiliar. They had seen it all before in Ottawa and Louisville. Although they lived in pleasant surroundings, the family was not well off and often the pantry was literally bare. Tom's stepfather worked as a plastics salesman and his mother sold real estate, while his sisters worked as part-time waitresses in Glen Ridge and the nearby suburb of Bloomfield. Tom took a part-time job as a waiter at the upmarket Glen Ridge Country Club, where Ridgers, the nickname for Glen Ridge locals, gathered on weekends. Here he served the parents of fellow pupils, and the pupils themselves.

If the family's means were modest, at least the street where they lived was rich in history. George Washington stayed at one home after the Battle of Monmouth, and another substantial house was the residence of composer William Bradbury, who wrote the music for such famed hymns as "Jesus Loves Me," "Savior, Like a Shepherd Lead Us," and "Just As I Am."

There was, however, a less-than-angelic side to Glen Ridge that Tom experienced early on: the culture of athleticism. Here the jock was king of a miniature domain where he played hard but partied harder. A decade later, the darker side of young men being lionized by their schools and community for their exploits on the field was graphically exposed when a group of popular athletes from Glen Ridge High School were accused of raping a mentally disabled seventeen-year-old girl. It was an incident that split the community, the social fallout documented in a book (later a TV movie) in which author Bernard Lefkowitz explored the sinister secret life of a seemingly perfect suburb.

For Tom and his sisters, being uprooted at a critical time during their teenage lives meant making friends again. Proving themselves. Fitting in. And Glen Ridge was a tough ticket. Most of the students at the six-hundred-pupil Glen Ridge High School had been together since kindergarten. Everyone knew everyone else. A new kid, especially a short, skinny sixteen-year-old who didn't have a hope of making a place in the Holy Trinity of sports—football, baseball, and basketball—had to work hard simply to overcome knee-jerk hostility. Tom was damned if he did, damned if he didn't, as fellow pupils prodded and poked this latest specimen on the social petri dish. "He was in a class of mine in the first couple of days he arrived here," recalls former Glen Ridge student Philip Travisano. "He called the teacher 'ma'am,' so I thought he was kissing ass. Later I realized he was just naturally polite."

It must have been all the more galling for a teenager who was used to being the leader of the pack to be considered a small fish in a hostile pond. Having learned the art of disguise from his relationship with his father, Tom played out a role, displaying a mask of affability in order to survive the blackboard jungle. Fellow pupil Nancy Armel was asked by her uncle and vice principal Jack Price to show Tom around his new school. When they first met, she sensed his uncertainties and insecurities. "He was eager to make an impression," she recalls.

Make an impression he did. As she lived around the corner, he came over, ostensibly to do homework together, but really to hang out. In short order she went from school guide to classmate to girlfriend. They became so close that they were separated in English class for chatting too much. The young couple went horseback riding together and, because they were too young to drive, one of their parents would take them to the movies. Mostly, though, their dates consisted of fooling around at each other's homes. She liked him because he was fun and personable. Certainly not for his looks. "He was not the Don Juan of the year," she recalls dismissively of her boyfriend. She did, however, stick around long enough to date him for three years and become his first lover. They even talked of marriage.

At that stage in his life, young Maypo had to get by on sheer personality. "He was fresh meat but kind of goofy-looking," recalls fellow pupil Diane Van Zoeren. It was at his first school dance that fellow students began to sense that there was more to the kid from Kentucky than they originally thought. Everyone formed circles, and one by one, teenagers went into the middle to show off their moves. When it was Tom's turn, he stunned the watching crowd with a series of lunges, leaps, and spins that had them mesmerized. "We all realized then that there was something different about this guy," recalls Travisano. "He was a kid with charisma. After that display he started making friends, and it was totally obvious that he was a cool guy." Before he arrived at the dance hall, Tom had spent hours rehearsing so that his performance would look relaxed and natural. It was a trick he was to pull off throughout his future career. He watched shows like *Soul Train* and copied the dance moves of teenagers in the audience. "I taught myself how to do the robot spinning and stuff like that," he once said. But however hard he tried, he was never cool enough to be in with the hot crowd.

Cheerleaders and jocks, the Lorraines and Franks of this little world, ruled the corridors and bowers of Glen Ridge. Tom was on the fringes, mixing with the jocks, but never making the sporting grade. He joined the soccer team, then in its infancy. The fledgling sport, in Glen Ridge, New Jersey, at least, had been left in the tender care of the school's history teacher, Dr. Don Voskian, known imaginatively as "Doc Voc." Young Tom achieved about the same standard as the rest of the squad, which was, as one spectator observed, "pretty hopeless." He fared much better in the winter, when he took up wrestling, practicing every day after school under the watchful eye of Coach Angelo Corbo. Not only was it a way for the small boy—in tenth grade he was only around five feet, six inches tall—to compete with others his same weight, but it was a chance to make new friends. "I think he was quite lonely and found it tough to fit in," recalls Corbo.

Even so, he was unfailingly polite, dedicated, and determined. The sport had such an influence that his mother once told Corbo that the psychology of wrestling, matching up to another, one on one, had been a great help in his later acting career. Of course, in later life his sparring partners were Dustin Hoffman, Paul Newman, and Jack Nicholson rather than students from rival schools in Jefferson Township and Hillside. What he lacked in technique, he made up for in enthusiasm, and he was thrilled when his picture appeared in the local Glen Ridge paper in January 1979, showing him defeating a rival wrestler. Inevitably his mother, Mary Lee, came along to show her support. His younger sister, Cass, eventually became manager of the team.

If victory was sweet, defeat was hard to bear. "He was a very intense person," recalls his girlfriend Nancy Armel. "He took things very seriously. If he lost a wrestling match, you couldn't talk to him for hours. You knew to stay away."

While he took his wrestling seriously, he could never lay genuine claim to academic ability. He was, as in his previous schools, a middle-of-the-road student, never really excelling at any subject. Still, in the three years that Tom and Nancy studied English together—and did homework at each other's houses—she never noticed any signs of a learning disorder. A straight-talking New Jerseyan, Nancy gives little credence to his later claims that he was a "functional illiterate": "I dated him through high school and it was never an issue. It cracks me up. Maybe he wanted to boost his career by saying that he was dyslexic. He seemed fine to me. I don't remember him ever going to special classes and I would have known. He was an average student like me, a B/C student. He didn't stand out academically." Fellow students also point out that in a small school like Glen Ridge, every little imperfection is noticed and pounced upon. As a contemporary, Pamela Senif, observes, "He wasn't in those classes for kids pegged as slow. Quite frankly, other kids would have teased him about it. If he was dyslexic, no one knew about it."

While it may stretch credibility to think that he could disguise his reading disability from his girlfriend for three years, his academic shortcomings were well noted. In a couple of acerbic postings on a Glen Ridge school Internet site, former students were dismissive of the school's most famous old boy. One student who took history with Tom remembered him as a "phony" who used to charm the teacher, Dr. Voskian, to cover up for his lack of preparation. A great smile but a "confused and empty mind" was his verdict. Others were more forgiving, a former classmate noting that while he wasn't reading "Tolstoy or Trollope, he could read and write and add and subtract." That said, European classics are hardly the literary diet of most American teenagers.

Tom may have been only an Average Joe academically, but he was a boy with ambition. When he and Nancy sat around the kitchen table discussing their futures, Tom expressed one burning desire: to be an airline pilot. It was an ambition he had harbored since childhood. As a kid he was plane crazy, collecting every model plane he could lay his hands on. Every time he left for a new home, he brought models of two of the most famous Second World War fighter planes, the Spitfire and the P-51 Mustang. His toy box, stenciled with the lettering

"Tom's model airplanes," still remains in the attic of his Glen Ridge home in Washington Street and is enduring testimony to his fascination.

There were other ambitions stirring between Tom and Nancy. By senior year he told her that he loved her, wrote her poetry and love letters. One Easter, because he couldn't afford to buy her flowers, he stole daffodils from a neighbor's front yard. It was a typical high-school romance: intense, fanciful, and passionate. By now they were both able to drive, and Tom would borrow his parents' car for evenings out. As she says, with the rather coy remembrance of times long past, "Yes, he was my lover. Absolutely. I was his first. At least I think I was. I hope I was a good tutor. We definitely fooled around in the parked car like all teenage kids. I was black and blue from the gearshift, I can tell you that."

When they weren't making out, they were talking about their future together. He wanted to go to the famous Embry-Riddle flying school in Florida to learn to be a pilot. Nancy was going to be a flight attendant—which she eventually became—and they planned to work side by side. "We were going to spend the rest of our lives together, children, a white picket fence, the whole nine yards," recalls Nancy, who now has two boys from two marriages. "Back then I would have married him; we were high-school kids in love."

But even in the midst of their dreams, Nancy was beginning to sense the changes in her boyfriend. She didn't entirely like what she saw. By the fall of 1979, his senior year, he was hanging with the jock crowd, now accepted as one of the guys. His crowd included Michael LaForte, who later became a Marine, Randy MacIntosh, Mark Worthington, Joe Carty, Mario Ponce, now a top attorney in Manhattan, Steve Pansulla, John Jordan, now a model, and the Travisano brothers, Vinnie and Phil. Several of them would remain Tom's lifelong friends. They went to the Meadowlands to watch the Giants football team, drank in the Star Tavern—in those days the legal drinking age was eighteen—went to the Regency cinema in nearby Bloomfield, or just hung out in the school parking lot. They got into the usual scrapes, rumbles, and fights that come with teenage territory. As Sam LaForte, Michael's older brother, recalls, "They knew how to enjoy themselves, they were a tight-knit group, just like the Rat Pack. They always got attention when they went out, and if they were in trouble, they would come running to me, the big brother."

Typically, it was Tom Mapother who was caught drinking beer before a school football game—in his senior year he made the third team—and was unceremoniously kicked off the squad. He was not the only one drinking; he was just the only one who got caught. Banished from the football team and with no chance of earning academic honors, he seemed to be drifting. Nancy Armel noted with some concern that while other students were applying to colleges, Maypo had not stirred himself even to send off for a brochure from the flight school in Florida.

Even his wrestling career seemed to be taking a tumble. Ironically, over the past year the skinny little kid had filled out, putting on so much weight that he was now over the limit for his class. If he wanted to wrestle in the individual, rather than team, events at the end of that winter's wrestling season, his coach told him that he would have to scale down a tad. Even though he would not have gotten very far in the competition, where he would have been up against much more accomplished athletes, he was determined to take part. In an effort to lose weight, he ran up and down the stairs of his Washington Street home. As he was coming down the stairs, he tripped on a pile of school papers left by his sister Cass and tore a ligament in his ankle. Crestfallen, the teenager told his wrestling coach that he would have to pull out of the tournament. "He felt pretty bad about it because he wanted to go out and wrestle," recalls Coach Corbo. It seemed that the final months of his school career were simply petering out.

He was still in the school choir—he has a good voice—and joined his friend Steve Pansulla and other singers like Cathy Carella and Kathy Gauli, Lorraine's sister, for that season's Christmas concert. Steve, who had taken him under his wing in his first few months in a new school and encouraged him to join the choir and the wrestling squad, now suggested that he try out for a part in the school's production of *Guys and Dolls.* Cathy Carella and Kathy Gauli made up the chorus of encouragement as they tried to wheedle the reluctant teenager into giving it a shot. "Just do it, it will be fun," Steve Pansulla told him.

After all, now that he could no longer enter the wrestling tournament, what else did he have going on? For a long time, Tom would not entertain the idea. He told his friends that he couldn't sing or act and that he had never appeared in a drama, let alone a musical. The hesitant thespian was being far too modest—as his family's theatrical tradition and his enjoyment of the limelight on the various stages of his previous schools demonstrated.

It is testimony to the actor's ability to disguise his real self, to play a role, that even now, the same school friends who encouraged him to audition for *Guys and Dolls* at Glen Ridge High are stunned by the knowledge that he had been performing for much of his life. "I didn't have a clue that he had acted before," says former school friend Pamela Senif, her shock matched by other thespian school friends. "Wow, I didn't know that. As far as we were concerned, it was the first time he was in a play," his friends chorused.

Eventually he was persuaded to go for an audition. Under the critical gaze of the show's musical director, Nancy Tiritilli, and director, Bill D'Andrea, he sang a couple of songs and read from the script. His friend Cathy Carella was watching the audition and knew immediately that he was going to get the lead of Nathan Detroit. "People were blown away by how good he was. He was a natural. I knew he was going to be famous." As far as she is concerned, he read from the script without any trouble, echoing the view of his contemporaries that if he had any reading difficulties, he disguised them extremely well.

Before he formally accepted the part of Nathan, he asked permission from his wrestling coach to make sure that he was not needed for the team. Then he began a transformation that would change his school status—and his life—forever. In the beginning, seasoned performers Steve Pansulla, who had the role of Nicely-Nicely Johnson, and Kathy Gauli, who played Agatha, gave him tips on how to handle himself on-stage. "Just be yourself, act natural," Steve told him. "Forget about the audience and don't be nervous." Steve, his self-appointed mentor, encouraged him even as Tom was saying that he just couldn't handle the part.

His diffidence soon evaporated. The cast had not been re-hearsing long before they began to realize that they were watching a star being born. "As everyone says, he was a natural from the beginning," recalls Kathy Gauli. "He could sing and act, it was almost effortless for him. It was amazing. It was really something to watch this creative seed being planted and a natural talent emerging."

It was not long either before those qualities that have become his trademark—an ability to focus, a fiery intensity, and a relentless professionalism—began to surface. Just as he demonstrated an easy command of the stage, he visibly grew in self-assurance among his peers. The cocky leader of the pack from Ottawa and Louisville now came swaggering back. Even his erstwhile guide Steve Pansulla felt the lash of his tongue. During one rehearsal Tom and his fellow actors were told to use the school cafeteria. At the moment when Steve, as Nicely-Nicely Johnson, was due on the improvised stage, he missed his cue. Without missing a beat, Tom, as Nathan Detroit, said, "Nicely, get your fat ass out here." Fellow actors didn't know if it was a performance or if Tom was genuinely annoyed at his buddy. They found Steve in the kitchen raiding the ice cream freezer. "He just didn't goof around like the others," recalls Phil Travisano. "He was deadly serious."

When *Guys and Dolls* was performed in April 1980, the school's theater was packed with family, friends, and well-wishers. Phil Travisano's father, Ronald, a commercial film director, came along to support his son. The movie professional was so "blown away" by Tom Mapother's performance that he went backstage and told him that he should take up acting seriously. "He was awesome. Most high-school students are self-conscious and just plain bad. He was fluid, outside of himself, and not hung up on who he was."

Opinions vary about how Tom Mapother got his first foot on the theatrical ladder. One version has it that school starlet Lorraine Gauli brought her agent, Tobe Gibson, to watch her sister, Kathy, in the hopes that she would sign her. "Ironically, he would not have been discovered that night if my sister's agent had not come to see me," Kathy recalls, ruefully admitting that she was never signed herself. Lorraine, who was then riding high on TV, was in the audience with her agent, and realized from the moment she saw Tom's command of the stage that he had what it took to be a star. So did her agent. "She went gaga about him," she recalls. "He was so charismatic."

While Tobe herself has no memory of that evening, she vividly recalls her first encounter with the teenager in her Manhattan office. She had previously asked Lorraine if she knew of any good-looking, talented teenage boys, and she recommended, among several others, Tom Mapother. Tom even took his photographs to the Gauli sisters' house so that Tobe could look at him before they met. As soon as he walked into her Fifty-seventh Street office, she knew that she had found the gold dust all agents dream of . . . a charismatic youngster with raw talent. As she says, "I am very psychic, and when he came to see me and shook my hand, I said to him, 'Listen to me. You are going to be a great star.' "

His audition, such as it was, was perfunctory. Tobe just knew. As her daughter Amy, who has starred in several TV soaps, says, "Her instincts were uncanny. She has done it several times with clients. It has made me believe in intuition." Tobe entered Tom's name and address into her Rolodex and he signed a standard contract, giving her 15 percent of his future earnings. They spent much of the audition discussing his stage name. Various surnames were considered before Tobe, who was going on a vacation to the Caribbean, spotted a holiday brochure in the corner of her office and suggested the name "Cruise." As corny as it sounds, this was how he came to be known as Tom Cruise. At the time, Tobe didn't even know it was his middle name—once she found out, it merely confirmed her initial impulse. Indeed, his later assertion that he dropped his family name after his father left when he was twelve seems odd, as he was known at Glen Ridge High School as Maypo, an abbreviated version of Mapother and a reference to a breakfast cereal popular at that time.

Over the next few months Tobe became like a second mother to him, lining up auditions and giving him advice and encouragement. As with much of his own version of the events of his life, she disputes his story that he found an agent only after he and his ever-loyal mother schlepped around Manhattan for days. "That's not true," she says. "Lorraine was a client of mine and she recommended him to me. She was the instrument of his success." Tobe's former client Lorraine Gauli is much more forgiving of the way she has been forgotten in the later story of Tom's rise to stardom. Now a flourishing criminal defense lawyer, she believes that he would have been discovered no matter what. "He was a talented, good-looking guy, and that is quite unusual in the business."

It was perhaps inevitable that the brash, controlling side of his personality began to surface, young Maypo now believing he could be the king of the world. His girlfriend at the time, Nancy Armel, watched the transition and decided there were better fish in the sea. She went to Florida for spring break and started dating an older guy behind his back. When she finally confessed her infidelity, he was furious. "Don't let that smile and those teeth fool you," she recalls. "He could have a really nasty streak and was very mean to people. Toward the end of his senior year he felt he could control people and he was starting to show his darker side. He felt that he could do no wrong."

While he had every right to feel angry at her behavior, he didn't let the grass grow under his feet for long. During a "wild" cast party, he danced the night away with any number of new admirers. Around this time, the school campus was swept with rumors that vitamin E was good for sexual performance. So there were raised eyebrows among the guys standing in the kitchen when Tom walked in and asked party host Andrew Falk if he had any tablets. After grabbing a handful, he quickly left, leaving the guys rolling their eyes and smiling. "I never saw any evidence other than he was a red-blooded high-school student," recalls Phil Travisano. "He was a regular masculine guy."

At times there was just too much testosterone flying around. At the end of yet another cast party, this time at the home of Kim Thorne, he was sitting in the basement shooting the breeze with a handful of stragglers when he tried to pin down two of the girls, including Cathy Tevlin, by their ankles. While he and the other guys laughed uproariously, Cathy and her friend failed to see the funny side, squirming away from his grasp before making their excuses and leaving. "It was kind of gauche and sexual at the same time. These days I don't think women put up with that goofy kind of behavior," observes one of those present at that late-night impromptu wrestling match.

Certainly not everyone was impressed by his newfound fame. Ditched by Nancy Armel, he struggled to find a date for the senior prom. Ellen Hurley, for one, turned him down. "I have to tell you he wasn't a chick magnet. Girls just weren't that into him," says her friend Pamela Senif. He managed to convince Ann Stoughton to be his partner for the evening— but only "as a friend." In the end, it was one of those flouncing, tear-filled, whispering, intense, in-the-moment evenings that teenagers live for. He spent two angst-filled hours talking on the lawn to his old girlfriend Nancy Armel—before going off into the night in his battered green car looking for Diane Van Zoeren. Even though she was a year behind him in school, he had had a crush on her since he first arrived in New Jersey. That night, driving up and down empty streets in Glen Ridge, the lovelorn youngster tried but failed to find out where she lived. Soon after, however, he tracked her down, and for the next year or so he convinced her to be his girlfriend as he made the improbable transition from school to the silver screen.

After his triumph in *Guys and Dolls,* he was seriously bitten by the acting bug. With Hollywood in his sights, he missed much of the last few weeks of his final semester at Glen Ridge because he was traveling to Manhattan for auditions. His next role, though, was not so much "off Broadway" as "off Broad Street," a local joke about a tiny theater that staged amateur productions in Bloomfield, New Jersey, near Glen Ridge. A few weeks after playing Nathan Detroit, he was rehearsing the part of Herb in the musical *Godspell,* based on the Gospel According to St. Matthew. Big time it wasn't. But even though it was an amateur production, recruiting aspiring actors from Bloomfield Community College, for Tom it was another step forward into a world that he had edged around since he was a boy.

His enthusiasm and dedication to his chosen career were such that he decided to miss his high-school graduation ceremony in June 1980 rather than drop out of a *Godspell* performance. Later he attributed his absence from the ceremony to embarrassment about his dyslexia: "I graduated in 1980 but didn't even go to my graduation," he said. "I was a functional illiterate. I loved learning, I wanted to learn, but I knew I had failed in the system."

As is often the case, the memories of his contemporaries vary from his own recollections. When he was appearing in *Godspell,* he told numerous friends that he was prepared to skip the ceremony to appear in the show. His friend Lorraine Gauli told him that he was mad to miss this undoubted highlight of the school calendar. He shrugged and smiled, but later she realized that he possessed a quality that she lacked—a burning ambition to succeed and a willingness to sacrifice short-term enjoyment to achieve that goal. As Phil Travisano, who went to see him in the show, recalls, "He was dedicated and so excited about acting that he was prepared to miss the fun of graduation." So as the names of the graduating students were read out on the lawns of Glen Ridge High, he was pursuing his dream in a different kind of ceremony: singing, dancing, and rousing the audience with songs and stories that popularized the Christian gospels. "Did you like it? Was I good?" he eagerly asked his new girlfriend, Diane Van Zoeren, when she and her mother came to the show. He visibly preened as he accepted her complimentary verdict.

As the senior class celebrated the end of school, there were endless graduation parties thrown by the parents of departing classmates. That summer, Tom, beer in hand, dressed in T-shirt and shorts, was a familiar fixture at numerous gatherings. At one party Sam LaForte asked Tom about his future plans. His reply was as forthright as it was revealing: "Sam, I am going to New York and I am going to be a star."

CHAPTER 3

It was the perfect night for romance. Hand in hand, Tom Cruise and Diane Van Zoeren walked along the beach, watching the waves shimmer in the moonlight as they rolled along the New Jersey shoreline. When they paused by a lifeguard stand, it was clear that Tom was not in the mood to whisper sweet nothings. He was more concerned that he *had* nothing— no money, no job, and no contacts. That night in the summer of 1980, just a few weeks after leaving Glen Ridge High School, eighteen-year-old Tom felt vulnerable and frustrated, barely able to hold back his tears as he poured out his fears to his sweetheart.

Rich in ambition—he told Diane he would give himself ten years to succeed as an actor; otherwise he would train as an airline pilot—he was dirt poor financially. Money—or rather the lack of it—had always been a nagging issue in his life. Now it was more pressing than ever. He often talked about being a self-made millionaire by the time he was thirty, and had a standing bet with his great friend Michael LaForte that the first one to earn a million dollars would buy the other a Mercedes. It was a bet he never honored, a failing that still rankles with some members of the Glen Ridge Brat Pack.

On the beach at Lavallette, a popular New Jersey resort, that night, it was not the idea of future millions that consumed his thoughts, but scraping together enough cash to rent an apartment in New York. With his agent, Tobe Gibson, based in Manhattan, he reasoned that he needed to be in the city so that he would be easily available for auditions and acting classes. But more than just money was worrying him. Even though he had an agent, Tom was concerned that he didn't have the experience or wider contacts in the film industry to make it big as quickly as he would like. The confidence he had shown after his school success in *Guys and Dolls* seemed to be evaporating.

When the couple returned from Lavallette, Tom made do with the resources at hand. For part of the summer of 1980, he commuted into Manhattan from the family home in Glen Ridge. He was a familiar figure in his dirty green Ford Pinto, rarely parted from a ratty T-shirt that read: EYEING ICE COLD GIRL. If his own car was out of commission, he borrowed his mother's or asked Diane Van Zoeren or his actress friend Lorraine Gauli, who lived around the corner, to give him a ride. If he had an early audition, he spent the night on the couch in the living room of Tobe Gibson's Sixty-second Street apartment. Tobe's daughters, Amy and Babydol, were amazed at her enthusiasm for a young man they thought was "nothing special." At least not in the looks department. They concentrated on the superficial—his rather lumpy, stocky physique and inoffensively polite demeanor—and missed their mother's instinctive feel for his nascent star quality.

After a day in the city, he would regularly take the commuter bus to Glen Ridge, sometimes bumping into neighbors and old school friends at the Port Authority bus station. Curiously, Tom's version of events is much more exotic. He later claimed that he had so little money that he would often walk to the Holland Tunnel, which takes traffic under the Hudson River from Manhattan to New Jersey. In those days, whores offered sex to commuters on their way home. "There were prostitutes, who used to be around the tunnel, who knew me," he told writer Dotson Rader. "They'd see me and they'd go, 'Look, I'll pick up a john, and you jump in.' So I'd ride through the tunnel to New Jersey. The driver's a little like, 'What's this guy doing in the backseat?' but he saw I'm just this eighteen-year-old kid. I didn't look dangerous. And they didn't do anything sexual in front of me. I'd get out in New Jersey and say, 'Thank you very much.' Then I'd hitch-hike home."

This extraordinary story seems as implausible as it is impractical. Why would a hooker risk a trick so that a teenage boy could hitch a free ride through the Holland Tunnel? And why would a nervous driver, worried about being stiffed or mugged, allow him to get in his car in the first place? Unsurprisingly, Diane Van Zoeren has no memory of this unusual method of transportation. "Tom borrowed his mother's car, but I don't recall him hitchhiking or catching rides with hookers," she said.

At some point during the summer, Tom very reluctantly swallowed his pride and asked his stepfather, Jack South, for a loan to help pay his rent and expenses in Manhattan while he got a professional toehold in the city. "How much is this going to cost me?" his stepfather asked warily when Tom outlined his vision of his future. He borrowed around $850, which he agreed to pay off on an informal installment plan. While the incident has now become a standing family joke, at the time Diane Van Zoeren recalls that Tom was loath to ask his "intimidating" stepfather for anything. He wanted to make it on his own and did not wish to be beholden to the rather grudging largesse of a man he frequently clashed with.

With money in his pocket, he found a small apartment on the Upper West Side, which he shared with a fellow struggling actor. To supplement the loan from his stepfather, he worked as a porter and cleaner in his new apartment building, got a part-time job busing tables at the now-defunct Mortimer's restaurant, and spent the summer unloading trucks. It was a time of transformation. "He lost that dorky look," recalls Diane. "He was running and working out. Quite frankly, he was adorable." One of her favorite memories of that time is a fun shot of Tom taken during one of the weekends they spent in Lavallette. Bare-chested to show his "cut" physique, a beer in hand, he and a friend covered their faces in shaving cream before the picture was taken.

At that time, though, he saw himself and his life in much

darker shades. During his days in Manhattan that summer, he recalled how he fed hungrily off cheap hot dogs and rice, living, as he later recalled, "like an animal in the jungle." Albeit a jungle animal who went home on weekends for his mother's roast chicken dinners. Indeed, as jungle lairs go, his apartment on the Upper West Side was rather "neat and tidy," the romantic youngster making sure there were flowers in the room and strawberries and cream waiting in the refrigerator when Diane visited.

All his animal instincts were focused on capturing a career in the movies. When he could afford it, he attended half a dozen or so evening classes run by veteran actor Phil Gushee at the Neighborhood Playhouse School of the Theatre on Fifty-fourth Street. Not that his agent thought it was money well spent. In Tobe Gibson's eyes, Tom was a natural talent who could be spoiled by the shaping and molding of an acting studio. It was a view shared by his friend Lorraine Gauli, who recognized, albeit reluctantly, that his raw ability and passion far outstripped her own theatrical talent. When he came to her house one day to practice a scene from David Mamet's play *American Buffalo,* she was struck by how natural and instinctive was his acting. "This kid was innately good. He didn't need any method or training," she recalls. In fact, he was highly critical of her own decision to take the conventional route and sign up for a three-year course at a New York acting school. He felt she should follow his lead and audition for stage and screen roles immediately. The single-minded young man believed he could pick up acting experience on the hoof.

Even those friends who did not have a background in drama could see the talent bursting forth. One weekend back in Glen Ridge, he stood with his friend Vinnie Travisano in the hallway of his family home, trading lines from the 1980 hit movie *Raging Bull.* "He got so emotional and into the moment, you could see that this was his calling," recalled Vinnie. "It was amazing."

Having given himself ten years to become king of the acting jungle, he was already making a noise in that wild world within ten weeks. "From the minute he started to audition he was a hit," Tobe Gibson recalls. He snagged a part in a commercial for Hershey's chocolate and received callbacks for several other TV commercials. Intense and dedicated, he explored every avenue to gain an advantage over all the other hopefuls in search of stardom. For a time he took guitar lessons from Laura Davies, a Glen Ridge High School musician, to give him a better chance of snagging a part in a TV version of the hit movie *Fame*. The show's producers were holding auditions in Hollywood, and Tobe managed to get Tom's name added to a very long list of hopefuls. Somehow he scraped the money together for the flight from New York to Los Angeles, packed a bag, and embarked on a journey that gave him the opportunity to experience firsthand the indifferent, offhanded reality of the industry he was determined to conquer.

The experience left the East Coast boy somewhat perplexed. He arrived at the director's office and proceeded to give, as he later recalled, a "terrible" reading. When the director asked him how long he intended to stay in town, the young actor, thinking he might get called back to read again, said that he was there for a couple of days. "Good, get a tan while you're here," came the reply, and he was promptly shown the door. As he later recalled: "I walked out and thought it was the funniest thing. Tears were coming out of my eyes. I was laughing so hard, I thought, 'This is Hollywood. Welcome, Cruise.'" Given his raw ambition and intense, rather humorless character, it is hard to reconcile his later glib recollection with the likely reality: all those days of hopeful guitar practice and rehearsals dashed in an unforgiving minute.

Certainly one person who wasn't laughing was his girlfriend, Diane Van Zoeren, who phoned him for two days straight without any response. She only later discovered that he had teamed up with a couple of other acting hopefuls and spent forty-eight hours trying his luck at the gaming tables of Las Vegas.

While he hadn't made the grade for the *Fame* TV show, Tobe secured him an audition for a walk-on role in *Endless*

Love, a story of teenage passion and obsession starring Brooke
Shields. Tobe had to use all her negotiating skills to get him
in to see the director, Franco Zeffirelli. The film's casting
agent, Sally Dennison, wanted a taller, slimmer character for
the part of a high-school football player, but Tobe convinced
her at least to look at her protégé, who she admitted had the
look of a stocky wrestler.

Before he left for the audition, Tobe reminded him of the
golden rules for a young actor. At the first meeting, always
say thank you, keep eye contact, and arrive fresh and full of
enthusiasm. If you get a part, watch the director's every move
on set and never party before the filming is finished. Her
words fell on deaf ears. Tom later admitted that he had committed the cardinal sin of drinking heavily the night before
his audition and arrived with a hangover. Eventually he was
asked to deliver lines from *Romeo and Juliet* and walk up and
down the room, presumably to give the director a sense of his
screen presence. For someone so passionate and committed
to his craft, his confession that he drank too much before his
first big opportunity seems strange. Was it nerves, bravado, or
the exaggeration of hindsight?

Hangover or no, Tom won for himself the tiny part of Billy,
while another of Tobe's clients, Sean Gauli, the kid brother of
Tom's actress friend Lorraine, also snagged a "blink and you'd
miss it" role. Filming was in Chicago in the fall of 1980, and
before he boarded the plane, his mother made sure her young
lion was properly attired—taking him shopping for T-shirts,
shorts, and fresh underwear. It was a necessary precaution, as
his first screen character is notable more for the tiny Daisy
Duke shorts he wore during the filming of a soccer kickabout
than for any lines he delivered. His role, such as it was, called
for him to take off his undershirt before chatting to the lead
character, David. During their brief conversation he whimsically suggests that David should set fire to his girlfriend's family home, a suggestion that has tragic consequences for the
star-crossed lovers.

While Tom was a lifelong film fan, he was a novice when

it came to the mechanics of making a movie. Once he got on the set, he started to realize what a technical process it was. As he later recalled, he spent as much time worrying about camera angles and hitting his marks as about the handful of lines he had to deliver. Even though the film earned lukewarm or downright hostile reviews, Tom was thrilled with the whole experience. While on the set in Chicago, he made a fleeting background appearance in a *60 Minutes* TV documentary about the film's director, Franco Zeffirelli. When it aired, he was literally jumping up and down on the sofa with excitement as he, his girlfriend, and family watched his first appearance on the small screen. It was a precursor of a rather more public performance some twenty-five years later.

When *Endless Love* opened, Tom was one of the first in line to see it, going to the Regency cinema in Bloomfield, New Jersey, with a bunch of friends. Literally as he was coming out of the door after seeing the matinee performance, fellow actor Sean Gauli was lining up to see the evening show. In some ways it served as a metaphor for their respective careers. By then doors were opening for Tom while they were banging shut for Sean, who is now a motor home salesman in Florida. It annoys him that his old school buddy exaggerates his struggle to make it in the industry, as it diminishes those who helped him get his start and, ironically, demeans Tom's own talent, which includes an uncanny ability to make everything look easy.

Although Tom later told writer Jennet Conant, "I was a starving actor for a few months," it is an assertion Sean finds difficult to accept. "What he says and what the reality was are two different things," he recalls, dismissing as myths the stories of Tom hitchhiking around the country seeking fame and fortune. "The plain facts are that he was a natural and didn't struggle at all. I know because I went to hundreds of auditions and he didn't do any of that shit. It would be good for the truth to come out instead of this fictitious crap. We were all struggling actors, and when he made it he never made any attempt to help us out." There remains residual resentment that the actor has never acknowledged the help of people like his Glen Ridge school friends Steve Pansulla and Lorraine Gauli or his first agent, Tobe Gibson, in promoting his career.

This comes as no surprise to Tom's onetime friend Vinnie Travisano, now a successful art director. "He is a very talented guy, and very talented people give themselves all the credit for their success and move on." It is the way of the world. Stars tend to limit their thank-yous to Oscar acceptance speeches.

In fall of 1980, after he returned from filming *Endless Love,* any kind of success still hovered in the distance. While those few days in Chicago had served to confirm his ambitions, back in New York he was still an out-of-work teenage actor busing tables and scraping by. Nevertheless, his experience on the film seemed to have reinforced his confidence and willingness to assert himself. He was furious with his agent for sending out promotional pictures to the most popular teen magazines, *Tiger Beat* and *Teen Beat.* Even though later in his career he was featured on the cover of *Tiger Beat,* he made it clear that he did not want to be pigeonholed as some cheesy pinup. It was a point he made time and again in later interviews. "I'm not locking myself into a teen idol stereotype," he said.

Far more bothering was a set of black-and-white studio photographs of Tom wearing a gym top and short shorts that reportedly found their way into *Parlée,* a gay magazine that circulated in New York and Long Island. Diane Van Zoeren remembered that it was a big enough issue for him that Tom drove to his agent's office for a face-to-face confrontation. "He was very serious with her," she recalled, the incident revealing a young actor who, even this early in the game, wanted to control his image.

Diane also realized that he wanted to control much more than his image; he wanted to be in charge of everything and everyone. She found his behavior oppressive and even relayed her concerns to his younger sister, Cass. "We had a volatile relationship," recalls Diane, who was then in her senior year at Glen Ridge High School. "I didn't get how intense and dramatic he could be. He was so controlling and I wasn't used to that."

Still, he was romantic and considerate—when he could afford it. So while she became used to cheap Chinese meals and fooling around in the back of her father's Oldsmobile— "Typical high-school stuff, doing what you are not supposed to," recalls Diane—when he returned from filming *Endless Love* he bought her a pretty necklace adorned with a locket and a key which, as he told her romantically, was "a key to her heart." Their romantic interludes were punctuated by arguments and recriminations. At the Candy Kane Ball in December 1980, they had a huge falling-out because she danced with another boy. The next day he sent her twelve yellow roses to apologize. Single-minded and go-getting, Tom was not in a placatory mood for long. A few weeks later he was furious because she was too busy to read through the script for *Taps,* a rite-of-passage movie about a violent rebellion among military cadets facing the closure of their academy.

Early in 1981, veteran casting agent Shirley Rich was looking for young talent for the film, which already included the legendary George C. Scott and recent Oscar winner Timothy Hutton in the lineup. She was looking for a black actor and a "WASP-type" kid to fill a couple of small parts. So far no one fit the bill. "I told her that I've got what you're looking for," Tobe Gibson recalls, and promptly sent Tom along for an audition one Friday afternoon.

This time he was clearheaded as he read out lines before director Harold Becker, who asked Tom to put up his hair so that he would get an idea of what he would look like as a shaved army cadet. It was a brief audition, leaving the teenager uncertain about whether he had made the cut. By the time he arrived back in Glen Ridge, the beaming grin on his mother's face gave the game away. She told him, "You got *Taps*!" It was a moment he will never forget, a moment that changed his life forever. Not only did his reputed $50,000 fee enable him to pay off the $850 loan from his stepfather, it was his first step on the ladder to stardom. The part he had landed was that of a friend to one of the main characters, David Shawn, an uptight cadet at the military academy who goes violently off the rails during the student rebellion. "He was acutely aware that this role could make or break his attempt at a career in Hollywood, and so took it very seriously," recalls Diane Van Zoeren.

In many respects Harold Becker was the ideal director for a raw, inexperienced actor like Tom Cruise. He insisted on a long rehearsal period, putting the kids through forty-five days of basic training at a real boot camp—Valley Forge Military Academy in Wayne, Pennsylvania—to get a true flavor of the brutal gung ho camaraderie of cadet life. They spent half the day rehearsing their roles, the rest undergoing military training and learning to march and handle weapons, as well as studying the relentless intricacies of military protocol. By the end, Becker reasoned, they would feel like the characters they were playing and give the film an air of authenticity. Later, when filming began in earnest, he let Tom view the day's rushes, talking him through the technical process.

All the young actor cadets thrived in the military atmosphere except for one—a talented youngster from a Shakespeare youth theater in Tennessee. He was earmarked to play the part of David Shawn, the gung ho war lover who acts as a macho foil for the more conciliatory voices in a cadet rebellion. "But he couldn't cut it, which was heartbreaking," recalled Becker. With the youngster from Tennessee now out of the picture, Becker looked closely at the other actors to see who had the power, as he recalled, to "walk the walls." A young man with the build of a wrestler who was already outmarching the other kids on the parade ground came to mind. It was Tom Cruise. "There was something in Tom that attracted me," recalls Becker. "He's one hundred percent. He was able to strut down that field and he had a crispness that a kid at a military academy might work three or four years for. I can't say I thought, 'This kid is going someplace.' But I put him in."

To his credit, Tom was more concerned about the fate of the young man originally chosen to play David Shawn than taking his own opportunity. Becker explained that, even though Tom and the other actor had become friends, he had to replace him, and if he didn't want the part, Becker would look elsewhere. So Tom took it.

Watching from the wings with wry amusement as this off-screen drama unfolded was a young Sean Penn, who was inked in to play Alex, a thoughtful soldier who becomes the dramatic linchpin between the warring cadet factions. The son of director Leo Penn and actress Eileen Ryan, the California-born actor, two years older than Cruise, was already a theater and film veteran. He had directed his first movie, *Echoes of an Era,* about a Vietnam veteran's experiences, while he was a student at Santa Monica High School. It helped that the screenplay was by his school friend Emilio Estevez, whose father, Martin Sheen, was the star of the seminal war movie *Apocalypse Now.*

After Sean left high school, where, perversely, he studied auto mechanics and speech, he obtained small parts in several TV series, including *Barnaby Jones* and *The Killing of Randy Webster,* before buying himself a one-way ticket to New York to try his hand at off-Broadway theater. Knowing and cynical about the workings of Hollywood—his father had been blacklisted for refusing to testify during the notorious McCarthy Communist witch hunts during the 1950s—he was a passionate, intense, and talented actor, with the curmudgeonly self-confidence to challenge directors and fellow actors, but above all himself. At his audition for *Taps,* for example, Sean jumped on the desk to illustrate how he would address a crowd of fellow recruits. When he watched Tom Cruise in action, he sensed a kindred spirit, another furiously driven young man. "Cruise was like he was training for the fuckin' Olympics," he later recalled. "I think he was the first person I ever said 'Calm down' to. A fun guy, too."

Tom, Sean, and Timothy Hutton soon became fast friends, the youngster from Glen Ridge deferring to the experience and success of the two older men. The high-testosterone trio lived and partied hard, and their rooms on the same hotel floor in Valley Lodge soon became known as Fraternity Row. "Yeah, there was a lot of rock and roll going on on that floor," recalled Sean Penn. On set, though, friendship was set aside.

The characters that Penn and Cruise played were opposites, always at each other's throats. They matched each other for intensity, Penn insisting that he be addressed by his character's name of Alex even when the cameras had stopped rolling. During one scene, where Tom's character shoots off a rifle, director Harold Becker thought Sean and Tom were going to kill each other after Sean said something to Tom, who suddenly started chasing him angrily around the set. It was only when Becker and members of the cast intervened that the fracas ended. "Sean likes to push buttons, and he said something to Tom," recalled Harold Becker. "So Sean found a way to have Tom not like him for a moment."

Tom, too, submerged himself in the character he had taken over, eagerly exploring the cruelly manic qualities of the psychotic cadet. "I remember being nervous, really nervous, because at that point, when you're young, you just don't want to get fired," he later told director Cameron Crowe. It was a nervousness born of ambition and an almost visceral drive to succeed. The experience was so intense that it took him months to come down from the role. "I had no sense of humor whatsoever," he confessed later to one profiler, who observed drily, "This isn't hard to believe."

During that period of collegiate self-absorption on the movie set, both his screen character and the real Tom were undergoing a rite of passage. Personally and professionally, Tom's life was changing. Secretly, a new representative, Gerry Silver, the nephew of his existing agent Tobe Gibson, was courting Tom. With the promise of bigger and better roles whispered in his ear, Tom decided to ax the woman who had given him his first break. Midway through the filming of *Taps,* she received a curt telegram from her client telling her bluntly that her services were no longer required. Tobe, who considered herself a second mother to him, was devastated, all the more so because it was her nephew who stole him. She didn't speak to her nephew for four years as a result of this perceived treachery, and even today finds it difficult to talk about that experience. "He met Tom behind my back, wined and dined him, promised him this and that," she says. "I treated Tom like a son."

Tom later told Lorraine Gauli that he had fired Tobe because she could not take him where he wanted to go. "She was heartbroken about that," recalls Lorraine. "She knew he was going to be a star and felt that this would catapult her agency as well." It is the price that talent agents who spot young actors and actresses often have to pay, as Tobe's daughter Babydol, who hit the headlines herself years later when she was exposed as a Hollywood madam, fully understands. "It is a cross my mother has to bear," she says. "She finds people, gets them started, and then they leave her. She did, though, play an integral part in developing his career."

At the same time that he was severing links with his "surrogate mother," he was saying good-bye to his longtime girlfriend, Diane Van Zoeren. While he was away, Diane, who always felt that they would eventually go their separate ways, had secretly started dating an old boyfriend. When Tom's friend Michael LaForte confronted her and asked if she was cheating on his buddy, Diane denied it. In a frantic last-ditch attempt to save her eighteen-month romance, she hailed a taxi, headed for the Newark railroad station, and caught a train to Valley Forge, where she knew Tom was rehearsing. She was in such a hurry to make up with her boyfriend that she didn't have enough cash to pay the taxi when she arrived at his hotel. They spent two days together, but both knew it was their last hurrah. With his shaved head, muscular body, serious demeanor, and easygoing friendship with Tim Hutton and Sean Penn, Tom had changed almost overnight. He looked good and knew it. More than that, he truly realized that he had found his true calling. Diane was no longer part of the package.

In truth she was rather starstruck, silenced by the presence of Tim Hutton, who was then a teen pinup. Her parting with Tom was friendly, but final. She recalls: "He said, 'I love you but I'm not in love with you anymore.' I was cheating with someone else, and we were growing apart. He could be very cold—when he was done with you, he was done with you." In some ways her behavior had done them both a favor. They were both moving on, Diane to college and Tom to Hollywood.

He wasted little time finding a replacement. Shortly afterward, he took time away from filming *Taps* to escort Melissa Gilbert, a former girlfriend of Timothy Hutton best known as the freckled-faced moppet from *Little House on the Prairie,* to a performance of *Sophisticated Ladies* on Broadway. Dressed in a preppy sport coat and tie, the unknown Tom Cruise looked awkward and rather gauche as photographers snapped the young couple in the theater foyer. By contrast, Melissa, at the time a well-known child star, seemed relaxed and at ease with the publicity. "I date different people and I'm not serious about any of them," she later said.

It was perhaps his first taste of the life that lay before him. After a short break at an uncle's holiday home in Kentucky at the end of filming, he flew to Hollywood, where he joined up with Sean and Tim, who had arrived at the airport with his Oscar for *Ordinary People* casually tossed into a duffel bag. To save money, he divided his time between staying with Sean at Zumirez, his Malibu home, and in West Hollywood with composer and longtime friend of the Penn family, Joseph Vitarelli.

According to those who saw him at the time, it was a Spartan existence. He lived in a bare room, a mattress on the floor and a telephone by the pillow. The only decoration was a pile of film scripts, empty beer bottles, and pizza takeout boxes. While the home comforts were rudimentary, as far as Tom was concerned he was living at the best address in the world . . . Hollywood.

For the boy from Glen Ridge it was an intoxicating brew. Not only was there the excitement of being at the heart of the movie industry, but Sean Penn quickly introduced him to the in-crowd of young guns eager to make a name for themselves. They hung out at the then trendy Hard Rock Cafe or On the Rox, a private club on Sunset, spending time with Sean's brother Chris, whom Tom taught how to wrestle, as well as other longtime friends like Emilio Estevez and Rob and Chad Lowe. Of course, he already knew Tim Hutton. As Sean Penn's former fiancée Elizabeth McGovern says, "I do

think that Sean is an absolute Hollywood animal." They would
later become known as the Brat Pack, a dismissive term based
on the 1950s Rat Pack of Frank Sinatra, Dean Martin, and
Sammy Davis Jr. It was a term that rankled with these young
men, not only because they didn't think their party behavior
was so outrageous, but also each considered himself a star in
his own right, not part of a group. As Emilio Estevez, who was
deemed to be dean of the fraternity, later remarked, "We were
just guys being guys. We'd meet to let off steam, that was all."
And part of that behavior was having the good looks and nerve
to pick up a *Playboy* centerfold model, as Emilio did one evening at the Hard Rock Cafe.

Certainly Tom was not slow in following his friend's lead.
When he first arrived in Los Angeles, the nineteen-year-old
started dating Melissa Gilbert again. According to Melissa,
who was later engaged to another member of the Brat Pack,
"I can honestly say that he's a very sexual person. He gave
me butterflies in my tummy and there was a lot of making out
on the couch in my mom's living room." Their brief dalliance
ended when he was introduced to Heather Locklear, a beautiful blond model and actress who had already snagged several
small parts in TV series, including an episode of *CHiPs*. One
day Tom was taking a shower in his Hollywood condo when
Heather called him. At the time his best friend from Glen
Ridge, Michael LaForte, was staying with him. Michael answered the phone and introduced himself as Tom's better-
looking "cousin"—their joke reference to each other—and
started hitting on her. It was, he told Tom afterward, just harm-
less fun . . . but he repeated the story for years, especially after
Heather shot to stardom in the fall of 1981 when producer
Aaron Spelling cast her as Sammy Jo Dean in the TV soap
Dynasty.

Certainly the Brat Pack of arrogant, talented young actors
seemed destined to be Hollywood's future dynasty. Sean's father, film director Leo Penn, sensed their potential, singling
out his son and Tom Cruise for special mention. He told
Joseph Vitarelli that if this duo got a couple of breaks in Hollywood, "you could all be in for a hell of a roll."

Not everyone was so impressed by the cocktail of conceit and ability. Tom's pal Vinnie Travisano, who came to visit Cruise for a few days during the summer of 1981, noticed the changes in him when he took his girlfriend along to the set of *Diff'rent Strokes* and watched the action in the company of his old school buddy and Sean Penn. Neither he nor his date were impressed by these leading lights of the Brat Pack fraternity. "I got a feel for what an asshole Sean Penn was at that time," recalls Vinnie. His school friend did not fare much better. He and his girlfriend found the new Tom Cruise to be "insufferably arrogant, utterly self-absorbed and unapproachable." When Tom suggested that he and Heather go on a double date with Vinnie and his girlfriend, the girl refused point-blank. As Vinnie recalls, "She hated him, she just saw this cocky kid who only cared about himself." While Vinnie, having known Tom for years, was much more forgiving— "He was a young man feeling his oats," he says—he was still surprised by the transformation.

Vinnie and his girlfriend were not the only ones. Even Tom's loyal family was concerned. His mother and his sisters—then working in local restaurants—felt that everything was happening too fast for him. Calls to his mother and the rest of his family had become more and more infrequent. He had "gotten cocky" and, as his sister Cass confided to friends, he was "hard to be around," which, given his busy schedule, was not often. Tom had sufficient self-awareness to realize that, as he later admitted, he was "the most unpleasant person to be around," blaming his aggression in part on his intense role in *Taps*.

His friend Sean Penn was worried about him, too—not because of his behavior, but because of his next career choice. Tom had followed Sean's lead and signed up with the influential Creative Artists Agency in Beverly Hills. While Sean had gone with Todd Smith, Tom had chosen Paula Wagner, a former Broadway actress and sometime playwright. Their introduction, in July 1981, was tentative—but it was to last much longer than most Hollywood marriages. "How do you do, Miss Wagner," said the polite young man in the same brown corduroy jacket he had worn when he took Melissa Gilbert on a date on Broadway. "Nobody had a clue who he was," Wagner told writer Fred Schruers. "But from the day I met him, there was something about his eyes and his presence. He was all there."

While his choice of agent met with Sean Penn's approval, his next film pick did not. Tom signed on for that season's Hollywood fashion—the teenage coming-of-age film. The movie *Losin' It* was in the same genre of the successful *Porky's* series, where horny adolescents spend ninety minutes trying to raise a laugh and lose their virginity on the way. "That is when his tension started to go," recalled Sean rather censoriously. "I said to him, 'What are you doing? You're gonna destroy your career.'"

Tom didn't see it that way. He was rather flattered that word was out about him even before *Taps* was released. Producer Garth Drabinsky was looking for a "handsome, fresh-faced kid" for *Losin' It* and had heard about young Cruise. He made inquiries and approached *Taps* director Harold Becker as he was in the editing room cutting his film. After watching a mere eight seconds of Tom, the Canadian producer decided to sign him. Even though he was only offered $35,000 for a three-picture deal, Tom quickly agreed, eager to see his name in lights. He began to have doubts when he looked at the script more closely. Tom later recalled, rather shamefacedly, "When I first read it, it was worse than the released film. I worked hard, but it was a terrible time in my life."

However bad the movie, it was his first starring role. Tom played one of a group of California school friends who go to a brothel in Mexico to lose their virginity. When confronted with a group of prostitutes, his sexual desire, like the film, flops badly. In his best dramatic moment, he stands in front of the whores, hands in pockets, confidence and desire draining from his face. Finally he finds romance in the arms of a young divorcée played by Shelly Long.

Whatever Tom's misgivings—and those of his friend Sean Penn—the movie helped launch the careers of Shelly Long, who starred in the TV comedy *Cheers,* and director Curtis Hanson, who went on to make the film noir *L.A. Confidential.*

Certainly Drabinsky was more enthusiastic about the movie and Tom's input than the actor himself. "He was terrific," he says. "Respectful, hardworking, and humble, with a very professional approach on set."

As in his school days, however, trouble had a way of finding Tom. When a late-night fight broke out near his trailer on the set of *Losin' It,* rather than call for assistance, he tried to break up the brawl himself. He later claimed that he "nearly got killed." As the actor held down one guy, he kept dodging his pumping fist, and it was only after members of the crew heard the shouting and came to help that they discovered that the thug was trying to hit Tom with an ice pick.

Even after film production moved from the border town of Calexico back to Los Angeles, Tom got himself into more scrapes. He was apparently threatened with a gun when he and several members of the film's production team visited the infamous Lingerie Club on Hollywood's Sunset Strip. The young actor was dancing with an attractive Asian girl while some crew members were drinking at the bar. The next thing they knew, she had pulled a gun on her dance partner. "We grabbed Tommy and got the hell outta that club as fast as possible," an anonymous cast member told writer Wesley Clarkson.

Later that year, when Tom headed back east to meet up with his Glen Ridge buddies, his roving eye nearly cost him his career. Tom and his friends Michael LaForte and Vinnie Travisano were out barhopping in Manhattan and ended up at the Ritz nightclub, which then hosted hip-hop bands like Rock Steady Crew and Bow Wow Wow. As was his wont, Tom started trying to pick up every girl in the joint. He was hitting on two girls at the bar, oblivious to the fact that they were with a couple of unamused muscle men. Vinnie saw one guy reach into his pocket and slip brass knuckles on his hand, ready to punch the budding movie star. Michael and Vinnie intervened and hustled their friend out of harm's way. "We always used to say that we had saved his career because we saved his beautiful teeth," recalls Vinnie.

Indeed, Tom's career was nearly over before it had begun.

When Drabinsky tried to sell his movie, he found the studios cool to hostile. Fox Studios had first option on the film, but when Fox's vice chairman Norman Levy sat through a screening, his verdict was damning. He hated the film. Nor did he have kind words for Tom Cruise. He told Drabinsky bluntly: "The film will never sell and Tom Cruise will not be an important actor." Understandably, Drabinsky has never forgotten that meeting—or the verdict on Tom Cruise. At the time the idea of a sequel was out of the question.

What saved his career was the release of *Taps* just before Christmas 1981, several months before the disastrous *Losin' It* came out. While the movie opened to cool critical notices, it made money, attracting the notoriously fickle youth market and earning plaudits for the central performances of Tim Hutton and Sean Penn. Although Tom passed unnoticed when he attended his first black-tie gala premiere, joining Hollywood notables like Michael Douglas and Ali MacGraw as well as fellow cast members at the AVCO movie theater in Westwood, Los Angeles, his portrayal of the psychotic David Shawn did create something of a stir among Hollywood insiders.

The director and writer Cameron Crowe identified the buzz around the young actor at a party for the film version of his book *Fast Times at Ridgemont High,* which propelled Sean Penn to stardom. "The legend of *Taps* was in the air," he recalled. "Sean and Tom had acquired these reputations. Sean was sort of Sean De Niro, this character actor extreme. Tom had both moves, character, and leading man. He was The Guy."

At that time The Guy was still licking his professional wounds after the creative train wreck that was *Losin' It.* The experience taught the nineteen-year-old a degree of humility. Even though the film put his name up in lights, he realized how inexperienced he was. "I had been offered some lead roles, but I didn't feel that I could carry a film," he said of this period in his career. "I hadn't learned enough and I felt that I would be eaten alive to try and carry a movie by himself." Not for the first time, however, fortune smiled on the young man.

When he heard that Francis Ford Coppola, the genius behind *The Godfather,* was casting for a screen version of S. E. Hinton's best-selling book about teenage life, *The Outsiders,* Tom was determined to hustle for a role. At the auditions he literally pulled Coppola aside and told him, "I'll do anything it takes; I'll play any role in this." His tactics paid off: Tom was offered the small part of Steve Randle, a street-smart youngster who works in a gas station. He was a member of the Greasers gang, kids from the wrong side of the tracks, whose sworn enemies were the Socs, kids who get the breaks in life.

Tom was in good company. The cast list reads like a Who's Who of future Hollywood stars, with Matt Dillon, Patrick Swayze, Ralph Macchio, Diane Lane, and C. Thomas Howell taking major roles. It was a plus that his friends Emilio Estevez and Rob Lowe were also chosen for parts. For the greenhorn actor, the real bonus was that, like *Taps* director Harold Becker, Coppola encouraged his actors to spend weeks together shaping and defining their characters. The fact that Coppola had yet to secure financing for the movie meant that rehearsals were extended while the deal was being thrashed out.

In early March 1982, they gathered in the gym of a local school in Tulsa, Oklahoma, where filming was scheduled to take place. For a month the actors were at liberty to explore their roles in convivial but intense daily workshops. It was just what Tom needed. "I remember feeling very good, building up my own instincts on acting," he later recalled. "And understanding more of each level, learning more about film acting and what I wanted to do." As he explored his strengths and weaknesses as an actor, he realized he had a flair for ad-libbing and comic timing.

Coppola, whom Matt Dillon dubbed "Father Film," pushed and stretched his young team in most idiosyncratic and unexpected ways. He encouraged Matt Dillon to go shoplifting and the have-not Greaser characters to mix with real-life greasers for a few days so that they would understand their characters more fully. To make himself fit the part, Tom worked out three times a day, removed the crown from a front tooth he had chipped during a schoolboy hockey game, piled powder into his slicked-back hair, and had a tattoo painted on his arm so that he looked more rugged and unkempt.

But Coppola went even further. Away from the set, members of the upscale Socs were given better hotel rooms and larger daily allowances, while the have-not Greasers were assigned the shabbiest rooms and given measly expense accounts. Even their social lives differed, so that the Socs sipped cocktails at Tulsa's glitzier clubs while the Greasers gulped down beer as they watched mud-wrestling matches. The differing treatment gave rise to tensions between the two groups, ill-feeling that spilled over during an overenthusiastic rehearsal for a rumble in the rain. Emilio Estevez got a cut lip, Tom Howell a shiner, and Tom Cruise a broken thumb. The rivalry continued away from the set. Tom joined in a series of pranks on fellow cast members to celebrate April Fools' Day.

He is widely credited as being the one who smeared honey on Diane Lane's toilet seat and scrawled "Helter Skelter"—a reference to the Charles Manson cult killers—on her bathroom mirror. As she later recalled: "They ransacked a couple of hotel rooms on April Fools' Day. They got the keys from the maid because they were so cute." Not everyone was amused by the actors' antics, guests at the Excelsior Hotel, where the crew stayed, frequently complaining about the noise. On one memorable occasion Tom came up to the front desk, theatrically took out one of his false teeth, and dropped it on the desk in front of the assistant night manager—who calmly told him that they only accepted cash or credit cards.

At the end of filming, Coppola was impressed enough to offer Tom a small part in his next movie, *Rumble Fish,* the third of S. E. Hinton's books to get the big-screen treatment. To Coppola's surprise, the teenager turned down the opportunity to rub shoulders with actors of the caliber of Dennis Hopper and Mickey Rourke, as well as some of his colleagues from the cast of *The Outsiders.* Twenty years later, Cruise still remembers the look of incredulity on Coppola's face as he found himself explaining that he was declining the chance to work with the director of *Apocalypse Now* to make a film about a suburban teenager who runs a brothel out of his home while his parents are out of town for the weekend. "Here I am turning him down to do this movie about hookers," he recalled, trading a bit part in an ensemble movie for a chance at solo glory.

Even so, it was a gamble. The movie, entitled *Risky Business,* was director Paul Brickman's first film, and the budget was so low that the lead actors wore their own clothes onscreen, paid their own air fares, and stayed in cheap hotels. More than that, Brickman, who also wrote the script, was firmly against Tom's participation. He had tentatively cast the male and female leads for his brainchild, and his provisional choices, Kevin Anderson and Megan Mullally, had already read with other potential cast members. Brickman felt that Tom, from what he had seen in *Taps,* was much too muscled and tough to play the soft-bodied, rather weak boy who finds himself in a sexual predicament rife with comic possibility.

Tom's agent, Paula Wagner, heard differently. The Hollywood tom-toms were pounding out the news that whatever the views of novice director Paul Brickman, coproducers Steve Tisch and Jon Avnet were still having trouble casting the male lead. She took Tisch and Avnet for a steak lunch and organized a meeting between the young actor and the moneymen. "Tom stuck his head in the casting office, gave us the twenty-five-million-dollar smile, and that was pretty much it," recalled Tisch.

When he took time from filming *The Outsiders* for a screen test, Tom was still tattooed and pumped up from his role. Even his famous smile was not quite at full wattage after removing the crown from his front tooth to make him look a more credible greaser. As he told writer Tom Shales, "I was like filthy, dirty, stunk, and my hair's all greasy . . . and here I am explaining to Paul Brickman which way I'm going to go with the character in terms of losing the weight and what I would wear. So it's pretty amazing that they cast me in the role."

He was being much too modest. The way he took over the script reading, making slight changes to the dialogue, finding the moment in a scene, left the watching director and producers deeply impressed. He had won over a tough audience. As he had to leave the following morning, he was asked to take a screen test with Rebecca De Mornay, a young actress they had considered and rejected because they were unsure she was up to playing a leading role. Before she snagged the role of the tart with the heart of gold, her screen-acting experience had been limited to one line—"Excuse me, those are my waffles"—in the box office bomb *One from the Heart,* directed by Francis Ford Coppola.

As there was no money in the wafer-thin budget for further screen tests, Tom and Rebecca drove to Tisch's home and, with Avnet holding his own video camera, played six short scenes. Before shooting began, Tom washed the grease out of his hair, cleaned himself up, and put on a preppy, button-down shirt. At five in the morning when filming finished, the director and his coproducers knew they had their leading man and lady. Producer David Geffen was equally thrilled. In fact, he was so pleased with the handsome youngster that he had a copy of the videocassette made for himself, which he displayed in his office with the name "Tom Cruz" scrawled on the side. The producers had solved their casting problem—although Paula Wagner made them pay the full $75,000 asking fee for Tom's services. It meant that Brickman's contender for the lead role, Kevin Anderson, would have to make do with a secondary part.

Tom returned to Oklahoma penciled in for the role of Joel Goodsen, a conventional young man eager to explore his sexuality who finds himself running a brothel from his parents' home. After he finished filming *The Outsiders,* he flew home to Glen Ridge for a couple of weeks before heading off to Florida, where he had asked his friend Michael LaForte, now in the Marine Corps, to help organize a training schedule so that he could sweat off the twelve pounds of muscle he had agreed he needed to lose to give his new persona the soft, preppy look of a middle-class teenager from the Chicago suburbs.

One day, while he was out jogging around Glen Ridge, he

bumped into his old flame Nancy Armel, who had by then realized her own dream and was working as a flight attendant for People Express. They started dating again, and one night he called her to say that he had tickets for a new musical on Broadway, *La Cage aux Folles*. Tom was unaware of the story line—about two gay men living together in St. Tropez, where one of them runs a nightclub featuring drag artists—until they had taken their seats in the theater. As Nancy recalled: "Men dressed as women, he couldn't handle it. We had to leave before the intermission. It really bothered him. He was definitely homophobic."

He was much more comfortable with the joshing male camaraderie that he found when he flew to Sarasota, Florida, with Michael LaForte to begin serious training for his second lead role. As fit as he was ferociously competitive, Michael was a down-to-earth man's man with a robust sense of fun and an eye for pranks and mischief. He lived by the catchphrase "Life is a cabaret." "When they were together after a long absence, they picked up like it was yesterday," recalled Michael's older brother Sam. "That's the kind of relationship they had. Nobody put a spike in their friendship."

Michael had the grace to make himself scarce in their Sarasota condo when Tom invited Nancy Armel to join him for a long weekend. While Tom worked out, she went to the beach or joined her friends at the bar. After a couple of years' absence, she found him a changed person, more confident, rather smug but still pleasant to be around. Before he flew to Chicago to begin filming, his former school friends got the chance to catch up with Tom when he arrived for a beach party at Lavallette resort on the New Jersey coast. Wearing a beret at a rakish angle and what was described as a "Hollywood getup," he left no one in any doubt that he felt he was doing them all a favor just by turning up.

But if the cool dude from the West Coast had meant to impress them, he signally failed. "He just looked silly," recalled his old girlfriend Diane Van Zoeren. The dubious beret aside, he was confident, in control, and "on fire" with drive and ambition, no longer the dorky high-school kid of two years before. He took himself very seriously indeed. At one point during the evening, he took his former girlfriend to one side and announced gravely, "I have taken Hollywood by the balls."

For the self-confessed geek in school, the sudden transformation to cool dude seemed uncomfortable and confusing, his surface brashness possibly a way of coping with the spotlight. One evening he and Nancy left a restaurant prematurely because a fellow diner recognized him from his appearance in *Taps*. "Initially he found the attention somewhat overwhelming," she recalls.

Ironically, it was his portrayal of another geek, Joel Goodsen, the suburban Nice Guy with an ambitiously anarchic streak, that was to propel Tom further into the limelight. When he first arrived on the set of *Risky Business* in Highland Park, Chicago, there was no indication that this movie was going to skyrocket his career. In fact, there was concern on the set that, even though he had lost the requisite twelve pounds in Florida, he was still too chubby to be a believable teen idol. Tom had such a sweet tooth that he had always worried about his weight. Such was his self-absorption that he often wondered out loud if other major actors ate as much candy as he did. "I bet Al Pacino [his all-time screen hero] doesn't have a sweet tooth," he told colleagues.

"He was on the phone endlessly discussing his diet with his agent," recalls his screen mother, actress Janet Carroll. While she found him "attentive, gracious, and serious," a young man who was prepared to listen and take direction, she had no inkling that she was watching the making of a megastar. "Absolutely not," she recalls. "The movie launched many careers. He was in good company." It was a cast that included not only Rebecca De Mornay, but also Bronson Pinchot and Curtis Armstrong.

Tom did apparently try to throw his weight around on set. In the early days of the shoot, the actor complained that he and Rebecca De Mornay were just not jelling on camera. When he told coproducer Steve Tisch that he felt she was miscast, Tisch gave Tom short shrift, explaining that they thought she was doing a terrific job and had no intention of replacing her.

This episode did not particularly endear him to other cast members who, even twenty years later, have little praiseworthy to say. It seemed, at least to those who worked with him, that behind the polite "yes sir, no ma'am" veneer was a young man out to take social and professional advantage of every possible situation. A frequent comment was that he liked to expose the vulnerability in others and then crush them—perhaps reenacting his own father's behavior toward the young Tom Cruise. "It was just put-down after put-down of everyone and everything," observed a former colleague who described him as "bland as tofu but without the flavor."

Yet that blandly disingenuous screen persona and his vulnerable sexuality struck a chord with the teenage audience, who flocked to see the witty, low-budget sleeper film that grossed more than $70 million. As thrilling for Tom was that his childhood idol, Steven Spielberg, took the trouble to send a letter congratulating him on his performance. "He's the all-American everyboy," observed director Paul Brickman. "He has an archetypal quality that makes audiences connect."

The iconic moment in the film, much parodied, was when the actor, dressed in white socks and underpants, danced around his parents' living room to Bob Seger's song "Old Time Rock and Roll." It was an ad-libbed scene that resonated both with the actor and his audience. "I loved it, because of course I'd done it myself. It was a moment I understood," he told Cameron Crowe. Certainly his Glen Ridge friends remember him miming to music and running around their backyards in his underwear—in short, acting just like Joel Goodsen.

Unlike the real lives of teenagers, in the movie world the sexually frustrated boy does get the girl. In a dreamily erotic sequence, Joel has sex with Lana, his hooker girlfriend, on board a Chicago commuter train. While Tom and Rebecca were nervous before playing the scene, those who snuck onto the closed set are convinced that the answer to the question of "did they, didn't they" really get it on on camera is a firm yes.

As Paul Brickman commented afterward, "It was hard to get them started, but it was harder to get them to stop." By then the couple had chemistry both on and off the screen, spending all their time with each other and eventually living together. He made her Toll House cookies while she introduced him to Nicolas Roeg's scary thriller *Don't Look Now.* "He seemed to be looking for somebody to love and somebody to love him back," Rebecca later recalled.

In a moment of social triumph, he returned for the last time to Glen Ridge High School in June 1983 to watch the outdoor graduation ceremony of his sister Cass. With *Risky Business* playing in the local movie theaters and Rebecca De Mornay on his arm, it was easy to flash his increasingly famous grin as his former classmates jokingly pestered "Mr. Cruise" for his autograph.

Tom was now a fully accredited teen heartthrob, his disarming smile and boy-next-door good looks appealing to mothers and daughters alike. As critic Gary Arnold of *The Washington Post* noted, "In Tom Cruise the movies have a new star to conjure with." Nor did it hurt his burgeoning status that he was dating the delectable Ms. De Mornay—even though some thought it was a publicity stunt to promote the film. No matter, in New York they were followed by the paparazzi, asked to pose for the cover of *People* magazine, and gossiped about in the Hollywood trade papers.

So when the actor arrived at his alma mater, it was not so much as the hometown boy made good as it was the outsider, the guy who didn't make the football team or get a date for the school prom, finally showing his former classmates that there was life beyond Glen Ridge. It was a valedictory moment, a knowing acknowledgment of his achievements.

In some ways it was his lesser-known film *All the Right Moves,* released in the same year as *Risky Business,* that more clearly reflected his real life. That movie, coproduced by Lucille Ball, portrayed a high-school football star, Stefen Djordjevic, struggling for a college scholarship to avoid following his father and brother into the steel mills. While the gritty, rather downbeat blue-collar movie did poorly at the box office, it spoke to Cruise's own desire to move on from an unhappy youth and childhood. "I remember getting through high school and thinking, 'Boy, I'm glad I got that behind me,'" he has often said when discussing his formative years. It is a feeling he expressed during conversations with *All the Right Moves* director Michael Chapman, whom he admired for his work as cinematographer on his favorite movie, *Raging Bull.* "I know that as a teenager and a child he had felt a kind of fear of not escaping whatever it is children want to escape from." Cruise's Stefen Djordjevic is the roughly drawn blueprint for the generic character to come, an egotistical, self-absorbed but ultimately successful hero. His character's relentless ambition eventually translates into glorious triumph, an arc of achievement that seemed to mirror the actor's own life.

If *Risky Business* cemented his popular appeal, *All the Right Moves* showed that he had acting range. This young man, still only twenty-one, had started as a junior member of the Brat Pack, but was now showing his rivals a clean pair of heels, consolidating his position as one of the leading stars of his generation.

CHAPTER 4

There is no noise in Hollywood quite like the sweet sound of success. While failure is a silent, rueful companion, the friendly ringing of the telephone, the satisfying thump of the latest delivery of film scripts, and the swish of backs being slapped makes for the most pleasing music. It was a sound Tom Cruise was beginning to enjoy, his future golden with possibilities. But in the fall of 1983, with *Risky Business* the talk of the movie world, it was his past that returned to haunt him.

A phone call from his paternal grandmother, Catherine Mapother, was as unwelcome as it was disturbing. His estranged father, the man he hadn't seen for ten years, had terminal cancer. His grandmother asked if Tom would agree to his father's request and visit him in the Louisville hospital where he was being treated. There were conditions, too. His father did not want any recriminations, any talk of the past. For a young man becoming used to making his own rules, this must have been an irritating imposition, especially coming from a man he at once despised, feared, and still loved.

He agreed, probably reluctantly, to his father's conditions, the last request of a dying man. Financially secure after his $75,000 payday from *Risky Business,* he paid for his three sisters to fly from New York to join him at his father's bedside. It was a trying, emotionally charged, and yet, in time, cathartic encounter. When he had last seen his father, Tom was a twelve-year-old boy watching him marry a woman he had never met. Now he was a young man who had made his own way in the world without any help or guidance from the man lying before him on his hospital bed. The gift he brought to the hospital was a poignant reminder of the happier times they had once shared. It was a musical statue of a ragged Tom Sawyer–like figure that played tunes from his father's favorite film, *The Sting,* one of the few occasions father and son had enjoyed a harmonious public outing.

Since the abrupt splitting of the Mapother family in Ottawa, Tom's father had largely dropped out of sight. After his marriage to Joan Lebendiger, he went to Florida for a time and then headed out west. When that union foundered after just a year, he returned to Louisville, where he apparently lived in poverty and obscurity. "He was a drifter. He obviously regretted what he had done. I felt sorry for him," recalled his cousin Caroline Mapother. For a time he took up with Jill Ellison, the estranged wife of a local journalist, who seemingly helped nurse him during his cancer treatment.

While he was aware that his son had made a name for himself in the movies, Thomas Senior hadn't made the time, or perhaps more accurately the effort, to see any of his work. His seeming indifference served as an epitaph to their uneasy relationship. Ever since their parting a decade before, it seems that his father had adhered resolutely to his son's angry demand to "stay the hell out of everything."

The bullying young man of Tom's childhood was now reduced to a pathetic figure in a hospital bed. His son's "powerful" reaction to the enforced reunion has swung between sympathy and fury, pity at his father's plight and anger at a life of missed opportunities and shared family experience. Tom later told TV host James Lipton that his family was very special and his father had deliberately rejected "a huge life force." Over the years he has become more philosophical about his father's behavior, believing that he created his own suffering and isolation. "He had made some mistakes and he knew it. I wasn't angry at him, I wasn't, I was just looking at a man who was my father who I loved no matter what happened."

They held hands and, in a vainglorious gesture, his father promised that he would soon be well enough to take his son for a steak and a beer. They never had that steak, his father dying of metastatic rectal cancer on January 9, 1984, at the age of just forty-nine. The funeral was a quiet family affair, laying Thomas Mapother III to rest at the Calvary Catholic cemetery in Louisville.

Within weeks of his father's death, Tom found himself with a new name, living in a new country, and consorting with unicorns, goblins, and fairies in an enchanted forest. It was a curious kind of catharsis. Now known as Jack O' The Green, he was the hero in the battle between light and dark, good and evil, in a film that was the brainchild of British director Ridley Scott. Tom had long admired the hand behind the sci-fi movies *Blade Runner* and *Alien,* and was beguiled by the 411 elaborate storyboards that Ridley Scott brought along to convince Tom to star in his latest film fantasy, *Legend.*

Suitably intrigued, Tom signed up, brushing off the advice of his agent Paula Wagner that, because of his father's death, he could pass on the movie if he wished. Leaving behind his family, friends, and girlfriend, Rebecca De Mornay, he made his first overseas flight to London, where filming was scheduled for spring 1984.

He had little time to dwell on the past. When he first arrived at Pinewood Studios in Buckinghamshire, north of London, Ridley Scott ushered him into Theatre 7 on the lot and showed him the 1970 François Truffaut film, *The Wild Child,* the true story of a young boy who emerged from a forest in central France, unable to speak and walking on all fours like an animal. It seemed that the youngster had been raised by wolves. Scott was intrigued by the story and wanted Tom to grow his hair and emulate the jerky gestures and wolverine behavior of the wild child, whom he saw as a heroic force of nature. For once, a childhood spent practicing backflips and Evel Knievel stunts did not go to waste.

Unlike his earlier movies *Taps* and *The Outsiders,* where he had enjoyed the collegiate camaraderie of his fellow actors, this time he was left to his own devices, regularly hanging around the huge stage, normally used for James Bond movies, during the laborious process of setting up the elaborate fantasy world. He helped his costar Mia Sara, a seventeen-year-old who had never acted professionally before, learn her lines, and the Brooklyn-born actress returned the favor by using her circle of London girlfriends to find Tom dates for the evening. More often than not, he went into the office of unit publicist Geoff Freeman to chew the fat, catching up on news and sports back home.

A brief visit to London by his friend Sean Penn did little to change the mood. Sean was wandering aimlessly around Europe with actor Joe Pesci, drinking and partying hard as he tried to come to terms with his split from actress Elizabeth McGovern. Leaving Joe in Rome, Sean flew to visit Tom on the *Legend* set for just one day. It was not a success. Tom was focused and working, Sean brokenhearted and drinking. Sean enigmatically describes their meeting as a "kind of disastrous interaction." He left the following day to go to Belfast in Northern Ireland. "I thought, 'Take me somewhere violent,'" he later recalled, indicating his mind-set at the time.

If being a stranger in a strange land was unsettling enough, the shoot was dogged by accidents. Tom strained his back when a stunt went awry, and was mauled by a live fox he was supposed to cradle during one scene. Four weeks before the end of shooting, Tom and other members of the cast and crew watched helplessly as the giant stage burned down, destroying the carefully constructed polystyrene forest that was the film's setting. While only four days' shooting was lost, the accident served as a metaphor for the film, which was enough of a box-office flop to make director Ridley Scott believe his Hollywood career was over and seek work producing pop videos.

As one film reviewer noted: "Performances tend to get lost in productions like this. I particularly noticed how easily Cruise got buried in the role of Jack. Here is the talented young actor from *Risky Business,* where he came across as a genuine individual, and this time he's so overwhelmed by sets and special effects that his character could be played by anybody." Even Tom admitted that he was "just another color in a Ridley Scott painting" and these days treats the movie as a bit of a joke.

Things were not much better when he returned to New York. His relationship with his girlfriend Rebecca De Mornay soon reached the final reel. They had been apart for the best part of a year, and while he had briefly seen her on the set of her movie *The Slugger's Wife,* and she had flown to London a couple of times, the strain of maintaining a long-distance relationship in the days before cell phones and e-mails had taken its toll. It was a liaison built on mutual ambition, shared careers, and similar backgrounds of broken homes and constant moving.

If anything, Rebecca's early life was much more exotic and sophisticated, as she enjoyed a peripatetic upbringing with a bohemian mother and lived in a number of European countries. "I was desperate to fit in. . . . I've worked hard to be accepted," she once explained. While Tom learned to speak with a Canadian or Kentucky twang, when Rebecca lived in Austria she spoke German with a perfect regional accent. They were two souls striving for acclaim and adulation. "There's definitely something different about kids who come from broken homes," observed Rebecca. "They have this sort of searching quality, because you're searching for love and affection if you've been robbed of a substantial amount of time with your parents. I think that is true of Tom."

Lurking in the background was the old green-eyed monster of jealousy and envy. Both Tom's and Rebecca's careers took off after the success of *Risky Business.* At the time it seemed that Rebecca, who was a much less experienced actor than her boyfriend, had made much smarter choices. During the year or so they were together, she was ostensibly the more successful partner. In 1984, while Tom spent months playing a woodland creature in London, Rebecca notched up three movies that went on to earn critical acclaim.

It is not hard to imagine how Tom, competitive and controlling, would have responded as he watched his girlfriend outstripping him in both the quality and quantity of her film work. Even the $500,000 fee for *Legend* and the magical word "starring" might not have provided enough compensation. For a young man who had grown up bolstered by the uncritical acclaim of an adoring mother and cheerleading sisters, it would probably have been difficult to come to terms with a live-in companion who seemed to be outstripping him in his chosen career, the spotlight shining more brightly on Rebecca, who was then more worldly, polished, and stylish.

In her movie *The Trip to Bountiful,* she was praised for her performance as a young woman who befriends an old lady, played by film veteran Geraldine Page, who won an Oscar. In Rebecca's second film that year, the gritty drama *Runaway Train,* actors Jon Voight and Eric Roberts received Academy Award nominations for their roles as escaped criminals on an out-of-control train. Movie fans regularly vote the film, where Rebecca plays a railway worker on the wrong train at the wrong time, one of the best ever.

On the surface, the third film she made that year, *The Slugger's Wife,* also oozed quality. Not only was she working with a script by Neil Simon, who wrote *The Odd Couple,* but she was directed by the legendary auteur Hal Ashby, who shot *Being There* with Peter Sellers. While Tom was spending his days in makeup, surrounded by fairies and goblins, waiting to utter risible dialogue, his girlfriend was working with the cream of Hollywood. Or so it seemed.

If that wasn't bad enough for Tom's ego, she played a sexy nightclub singer who has a torrid affair with a baseball star played by Michael O'Keefe. For a young man who had been cheated on by his two previous lovers, it was hard to be completely trusting, especially as he knew all about the chemistry that could easily be generated between a leading man and lady. After all, it was how he had met Rebecca. Nor did it help that billboards advertising the film showed Rebecca and her screen lover in an openmouthed kiss. "I go to a movie and see Rebecca doing a love scene with another guy, telling him that she loves him. I'm always facing my fears," he admitted at the time.

Behind the scenes, the movie was suffering from competing egos—Neil Simon refused to countenance changes to his script, and director Hal Ashby was fired for drug abuse. For Rebecca, still learning her craft, her role as singer and actress was too far a stretch. As her costar Michael O'Keefe recalls, "She was in a bit over her head." A long-distance relationship between two ambitious actors on the brink of stardom was also too far a stretch. The parting of the ways was, as an actress friend of Rebecca explained, "a very unpleasant experience for her. She didn't really want to talk about it. It was very abrupt."

When she did speak publicly about the breakup, she admitted that it was a painful experience. "We were both ambitious and hardworking. I'm afraid the ending was not very amicable." Her reasons touched on the clash of egos underlying the amicable public façade. "There's the potential threat of competition, there's a continual threat of long separations, of major love scenes, of adverse publicity, and the transitory nature of the business itself." Tom was much more pragmatic and stern. "When something is not working, you have to face it and move on."

Move on he did, trading the up-and-coming for an established Hollywood star. At thirty-nine, his new girlfriend, Cher, was nearer in age to his mother than to the twenty-three-year-old actor, but she was 24-carat movie royalty, their outings guaranteed to make headlines and keep Tom's name in the news. As a sign of how far and how fast he had traveled, he met Cher at a fund-raising event for dyslexia at the White House in the presence of First Lady Nancy Reagan. Tom, Cher, and Olympic athlete Bruce Jenner, among others, were presented with an award for Outstanding Learning Disabled Achievement. Both Cher and Tom had experienced learning difficulties caused by dyslexia. While Tom was diagnosed early, Cher learned that her problems in reading, telling time, and writing checks were caused by dyslexia only after her daughter, Chastity, had been diagnosed with the condition.

"If I read a script, I read it very slowly and memorized it the first time I read it," she told the White House audience, which included youngsters from the Lab School, which helps students cope with learning difficulties. Tom admitted that he had a dictionary by his side to help him read scripts. "I couldn't read *The New York Times* because I couldn't read the big words," he has said. "It was humiliating for me. When I started working on films, I had to buy a dictionary. I started out with the *Young Reader's Dictionary* and worked my way up to bigger dictionaries. I'd sit on an airplane with a script and a dictionary."

While their perceived mutual disability helped break the social ice, Tom's rising star and Cher's existing place in the Hollywood firmament also drew them together. Cher, who was known for dating younger men before it became fashionable, was instantly attracted to the young actor. His year-long sojourn in London had brought one benefit—he had lost the preppy, pudgy *Risky Business* persona and had honed and toned his body from his role in *Legend*. "I can't take my eyes off the guy," Cher told an associate admiringly. "He's so damn handsome, all I want to do is stare at him." They dated off and on for a few months, becoming regular gossip column fodder. Of course, it didn't hurt that both Tom and Cher had films to promote in 1985. Her second major feature, *The Mask,* a true-life drama about a disfigured teenager growing up in Southern California, cemented the singer's growing reputation as a serious actress.

Even though the age difference meant that neither side really took the relationship that seriously—Cher's daughter, Chastity, was only eight years younger than Tom—they liked hanging out together. "Cher is funny and bright and we're good buddies and that's it," he told *People* magazine. He stayed with her in her Malibu home, and when Cher visited New York she often stayed at his apartment, whether or not he was in residence. In fact, Chastity was staying at Tom's apartment when she made the most painful phone call of her life. A lonely, troubled child, she confessed to her father, Sonny Bono, that not only was she a lesbian, but she had been having an affair with a friend of her mother's who was also gay. Cher was furious and ordered her to leave Tom's apartment and see a therapist. "Mum did not comfort me with kisses and cuddles, because it was not the family way," she later recalled. "Instead, she sent me to a therapist." It took Cher nearly a decade to come to terms with her daughter's sexuality. "It's a difficult thing for a parent," she said later. "It's one thing to be completely liberal when it doesn't affect you. When it does, you really have to search your soul long and hard." It seems that Tom, who had his own issues with homosexuality, played little part in this family drama other than giving Chastity shelter in his New York home. Certainly she always got on well with her mother's younger boyfriends. "It doesn't matter to me if they're closer to my age than hers," she said.

When he was out on a date with Cher in New York one night, there was a poignant reminder of Tom's past. They were dining at a restaurant called Fiorella's on Sixtieth and Third. By chance their waitress was Lorraine Gauli, his friend from Glen Ridge. When he had first arrived at the high school, she was a TV personality and seemingly destined for fame and fortune. After drama school, her acting career had petered out into a sad procession of failed auditions and screen tests. Now the woman who had encouraged him to try his hand at acting faced the indignity of serving as waitress to her protégé. "I was so humiliated," she recalls. "I had told everyone he was a friend of mine, and here I was waiting tables."

In the circumstances it would have been easy for him to ignore his onetime helpmate, but he introduced her to Cher and made pleasant small talk. He had made it, she hadn't: He could afford to be Mr. Nice Guy. It was an episode that symbolized how far and how quickly he had come. Tom had closed the chapter on his past life and opened another book where he was finally in control of his destiny. One that had "success" embossed on the cover.

That may have been how others saw him, but he had a different view. Beneath the cocky, self-assured persona was a young man not entirely comfortable with his newfound fame. In media interviews he was stiff and overly serious, endlessly talking about his "craft." He found the attention of the public, particularly his growing teen fan base, disconcerting. Just as he had walked out of a restaurant in Florida with old flame

Nancy Armel because he was being stared at, so in a New York eatery, Serendipity 3, he generously overtipped a waiter who asked a quartet of teenage girls to stop gawking at him. At his Upper West Side apartment he played detective when he noticed that he was being spied on from an adjoining block by someone using binoculars. After confronting the startled apartment owner, he discovered that the spies were the man's teenage daughters and their friends.

As when looking at a painting close up, he was not yet truly aware of his place in the bigger picture. His only fixed references were his contemporaries. By his standards, the class of '82, the group of young actors who'd appeared with him in his first movie, *Taps,* were all doing just as well—none more so than his wayward friend Sean Penn. While Tom was seemingly making excuses for dating Cher, in January 1985 his buddy met Madonna and fell for the controversial charms of the hottest female in showbiz. With a critically acclaimed movie, *Desperately Seeking Susan,* to her name and a second album, *Like a Virgin,* that outraged the establishment and delighted her teenage audience, she was a startling and unique talent.

Artistically, the career trajectory of his contemporaries should have given him pause for reflection. His friend Tim Hutton, who up to that time was the youngest-ever Oscar winner for his work in *Ordinary People,* had chosen to embrace serious projects, pointedly turning down the lead role in *Risky Business,* the film that jump-started Tom's career, as too lightweight. Although Tom won a coveted Golden Globe nomination for the role of Joel Goodsen, his appearance in *Legend* would have raised eyebrows among his Hollywood peers. While the sets and special effects were extraordinary, the script was laughable—as was Tom mouthing lines like "When I get to heaven I know just how the angels will sound." Meanwhile, Sean Penn and Tim Hutton were working together on *The Falcon and the Snowman,* a stern movie about two young men who are convicted of selling secrets to the Russians. "Two finer performances it would be difficult to find," said *People* magazine when the film was released in January 1985.

After *Legend,* released in the same year, sank without a trace, Tom and agent Paula Wagner were determined to choose his future projects more carefully. His two bombs—*Losin' It* and *Legend*—had struck out because of poorly scripted stories. While there were all kinds of offers on the table, the knack of choosing the right script was ultimately a lottery. As screenwriter William Goldman observed, the first rule of Hollywood is "Nobody knows anything."

This truism perhaps helps explain why the gestation period of the average movie is so long. In May 1983, when Tom was learning his lines for *Risky Business,* producer Jerry Bruckheimer was in his offices at Paramount Studios, absorbed in an article in *California* magazine called "Top Guns," by Ehud Yonay, about the flight school for the U.S. Navy's best pilots in San Diego. "*Star Wars* on earth," he thought to himself as he slid it over the desk to his producing partner, Don Simpson. Simpson was on the phone, and when he glanced at the upside-down story that Bruckheimer put in front of him, he waved it away, thinking it was a "Western." By the time he'd read it, the two hotshots behind the smash hits *Flashdance* and *Beverly Hills Cop* had a new blockbuster in mind: *Top Gun.*

In a way, Simpson's first instincts were exactly right. It *was* a Western; these sexy young pilots were modern-day cowboys with wild names like Viper, Jaws, and Mad Dog, who pushed the edge of life's frontiers with their testosterone-fueled behavior. For all their arrogant swagger, the young men in their flying machines lived by an old-fashioned code of self-sacrifice, comradeship, and patriotism. It seemed like a slam dunk. "It's about Yankee individualism, nobility, excellence of purpose, and commitment to excellence," Simpson explained in his pitch to movie moguls as he tried valiantly to turn the concept into a movie.

The studios and many screenwriters thought otherwise. After some initial interest, Paramount Studios eventually told them, "Who wants to see a movie with too many planes?" Don Simpson was reduced to falling to his knees in a meeting with Paramount boss Michael Eisner and begging him to keep faith with the project. "If they are this desperate, we've got to let them keep developing it," said Eisner. But top screen-writers were not especially interested, and, according to screen-writer Jack Epps, after several drafts of the script, the film "just died."

It was only at the end of 1984—eighteen months after the first discussions—that the new head of Paramount, Ned Tanen, green-lighted the project. They had a budget of $16.5 million to play with. First priority was to bring the navy on board. At a meeting with top brass, including then–Secretary of the Navy John Lehman at the Pentagon in Washington, they gained agreement to film at the navy air base in Mira-mar, outside San Diego, and on board two aircraft carriers. Mindful of the navy's reputation, retired two-star admiral Pete Pettigrew was seconded as technical adviser to ensure authenticity.

Hollywood seemed less enthusiastic. The reluctance of screenwriters was followed by that of directors and actors. Apparently both John Carpenter and David Cronenberg turned down the chance to shoot the film, Simpson and Bruckheimer eventually opting for Tony Scott, brother of *Legend* director Ridley Scott, who was back shooting commercials after his debut feature movie, *The Hunger,* was roasted as "agonizingly bad." His commercial showing a Saab car racing a fighter jet apparently caught the eye of the two producers. Of course, Simpson and Bruckheimer put a brave face on their choice, praising the director for his stylish photography, if not for his storytelling ability. Their pick did not seem to inspire confi-dence among actors or agents.

Breakfast Club star Ally Sheedy turned down the romantic lead of Charlie, the female flying instructor eventually played by Kelly McGillis. "I didn't think anyone would want to see a movie about fighter pilots," she said later. A similar reaction came from actor Val Kilmer, who flatly refused a role and only reluctantly agreed to be involved—he eventually played the part of Iceman—after contractual arm-twisting.

Other stars rejected the lead role of Maverick, the cockily charismatic navy pilot who grows up during the movie—and gets the girl. Chisel-featured Matthew Modine, the star of

Birdy, the story of the damage inflicted on homecoming soldiers by their Vietnam experience, did not like the film's prowar sentiments and passed on the lead role. He had just returned from a visit to East Berlin and discovered that the Russian soldiers were "just people." The heartthrob from *Happy Days,* Scott Baio, said no, as did brooding bad boy Mickey Rourke. Charlie Sheen was considered, but, at only twenty, was thought to be too young, while John Travolta, an authentic pilot, was then seen as a failure at the box office. Finally, they hit on a young man with long hair fresh from the plastic forests of Pinewood, who, at five feet, seven inches, was an inch shorter than the minimum required height for a navy pilot. Rather disingenuously, Bruckheimer would later claim, "There was never anybody in our minds other than Tom Cruise. When the script was first delivered to our doorway, we saw Tom playing the part."

At the time, even Tom Cruise was not wholly convinced. Like other actors, he was not sold on the film's gung ho ethos, worried that it would be "*Flashdance* in the sky." In any case, the actor, who had started his own production company, Kid Cruise, had other projects he was more interested in pursuing. But Simpson and Bruckheimer would not take no for an answer.

It was at this point that the myth of Tom Cruise and *Top Gun* was born. During a two-hour meeting with the two producers, he insisted that he would sign up only if he were involved in the whole production process. He wanted two months to develop the script, which meant that he would effectively be working gratis if there was no deal at the end. Simpson later recalled that Tom would show up at his house and they would grab a beer and spend five or six hours going through the script. "We had a lot of fun," he said. As part of his hard-nosed deal, Tom secured the choice of his costars, oversaw director Tony Scott's work on set, and was consulted during film editing. As Simpson recalled: "I was against it because I like to run things. To me, an actor is generally a hired hand. I like to be the boss. But we talked at great length, and he proved himself to us, and when he walked out of our office, he shook our hands firmly and said, 'Gentlemen, I'm on-board.'" It seemed that the decision to let him become the first actor in their company to be involved in the whole production process was an indication of Tom's ballsy self-confidence and artistic altruism, along with recognition of his as-yet-unseen talents as a cinematic wunderkind.

Others remember the negotiations rather differently. Far from wanting to rework the script without payment for a couple of months, Tom insisted the producers show him the money before he would even contemplate being in the movie. As he played hard to get, Don Simpson relentlessly pursued him, eventually nailing him for a fee of over a million dollars. A final meeting was set for April 1985, but with his agent, Paula Wagner, out of town, Tom was terrified about meeting the two producers on his own in their offices at Paramount Studios. "I can't go over there, they will devour me," he complained. Simpson curtly dismissed Tom's plea to have the meeting in the offices of his representatives, Creative Artists Agency. Instead, CAA head Michael Ovitz accompanied this relatively new young client to Paramount to hammer out the deal.

Still only twenty-two, Cruise had every right to be nervous. In the piranha tank of Hollywood, Bruckheimer and Simpson were authentic sharks. As one industry veteran observed, "Bruckheimer is the one to really watch out for. He'll stab you in the back. Simpson at least will stab you in the chest." Simpson even liked to intimidate visitors to his office by leaving a nine-millimeter handgun on his desk. When director Marty Brest was asked for advice on how to deal with a meeting with Simpson, he said: "Wear a fucking bullet-proof vest."

Simpson liked to pose as a tough guy, once boasting, "I would kill someone with absolutely no compunction." In meetings he was notorious for haranguing scriptwriters, actors, and agents. Only those who did not crumble beneath his bullying earned his respect.

In the weeks when he was wooing Tom Cruise, Simpson's wild excesses were more pronounced than ever, thanks to his wanton drug and drink abuse. He was often so wasted from a combination of hard liquor and lines of cocaine that by four in the afternoon he could barely talk—let alone walk. He became so paranoid that for a time he refused to visit his offices at Paramount because he thought the Mafia had ordered a hit on him. He spent his days barricaded inside his Cherokee Avenue house. The occasional visitor he allowed through the gates noticed numerous surveillance cameras outside the compound. There was copious evidence of drug abuse, as well as an armory of weapons, which he casually brandished.

"He was coked out of his mind," observed screenwriter Chip Proser, who completed the major rewrite of the *Top Gun* screenplay in April 1985, shortly before Cruise came on board. That rewrite, with only a little further tinkering, was essentially the finished script, complete with detailed descriptions of the characters and the story. In fact, at this critical time, Simpson was so delusional that he believed Proser and director Tony Scott were trying to take his movie away from him. It meant that the director and scriptwriter met in cafés in Santa Monica rather than taking the chance of being spotted together in a Hollywood restaurant and incurring Simpson's paranoid rage.

So the idea of Simpson, this wasted genius whacked out on coke, sitting down over a beer with Tom Cruise—who at the time was claiming that he needed a children's dictionary to read a script—to whip the screenplay into shape appears fanciful, especially as the producers were already paying professional scriptwriters $30,000 a week to spin this slim thread of an idea into box-office gold. But that didn't stop the publicity machine for *Top Gun* from repeating the story to anyone who would listen. As Tom Cruise—and the navy—found to their chagrin, truth doesn't always have the same meaning in Hollywood as it does in the rest of the world. This late-night exchange between two movie moguls, reportedly overheard at the Four Seasons hotel in Beverly Hills, sums up this philosophy:

First man: "You're lying! You're lying to me!"

Second man: "Yes, I know. But hear me out."

It was simply part of the negotiation for Bruckheimer and Simpson to promise the Earth to land their quarry, whether it was the cooperation of the navy or the signature of a potential leading man. During filming they simply ignored retired Admiral Pettigrew's concerns regarding accuracy. "I'm just trying to keep them from turning *Top Gun* into a musical," he complained at one point, although he agreed that the changes improved upon reality. So when Tom Cruise, in an initial meeting with the producers and their navy adviser, talked about exploring and developing the film's locker room scenes to make it more like a sports film than a warmongering movie, Simpson and Bruckheimer listened carefully and nodded sagely. When Tom went out of the room and Pettigrew pointed out that navy pilots have private rooms, Simpson was blunt. "Look, we're paying one million bucks to get him. We need to see some flesh," he said cynically.

Once he signed in April, with filming due to start eight weeks later, the reality was that Tom had to concentrate on his own job—doing background research, learning the script, and spending three weeks with a personal trainer working out so that he looked like a trim navy pilot. In fact, his trainer did such a good job in "totally transforming" the actor that producer Jerry Bruckheimer hired him later to get *him* into shape.

Tom, still sporting his long mane after his performance in *Legend,* didn't even have time to get a haircut, let alone rewrite a script, before heading down the freeway to hang out with the "top gun" pilots at Miramar. For all his initial reservations, when Cruise drove past the base's gate, he found himself in boy heaven. Ever since childhood he had dreamed of becoming a pilot, and now he had the chance to mess around with $36 million fighter jets. It was exhilarating for him to fly in F-14 jets and soak up the lifestyle of a group of professional men who had a technical focus, drive, and sense of daring that matched his own. "That was a dream come true," he later recalled. "I dug it, I dug making that movie."

He and his fellow actors soon became familiar figures on the base. Instructor Dave "Bio" Baranek remembers his first encounter over a beer with a "skinny kid with long hair" one Wednesday night in the Miramar club. "Tom asked me, 'What's the most fun part of flying, what's the scariest part?' " recalled Dave. "He was polite and sincere, but like a sponge soaking up the stories we loved to tell. I told him about high-G dogfights, about flying at low altitude and high speed, and the almost unlimited power and maneuverability of the jets."

After that first meeting, a call went around the squadron for a single guy who would like to be a drinking buddy for Tom. Lieutenant Jim Ray answered the call, becoming the squadron's "designated drinker." Instructor Dave Baranek recalls: "He was nothing wild, but they went to lots of parties and had a good time." Mostly Cruise and his fellow actors met at the Rusty Pelican, a seafood restaurant in San Diego, where they would pepper the real-life top guns with questions. Before very long he was walking like a pilot, talking like a pilot, and thinking like a pilot. "The thing that's so impressed me about him is that he's taken so much time to make sure he's doing the job right. He's done his homework," noted Jim Ray approvingly.

Finally, after testing for F-14 certification, which involved learning to withstand high G forces, eject, and escape an ejection seat in water, he was allowed to go for a ride. It was a thrill seeker's dream come true. As Tom recalled, "It's very sexual. Your body contorts, your muscles get sore, and the straining forces blood from your brain. You grab your legs and your ass and grunt as sweat pours over you. I had this grin on my face that wouldn't leave."

The making of the movie reignited what was to become a lifelong need for speed. This time, rather than "drag racing" up and down the streets of Louisville in his mother's car, he was sitting next to studio boss Ned Tanen roaring through the boulevards of Santa Monica at dawn in his vintage Porsche, a car so highly tuned that it burned high-octane aircraft fuel and was housed in an airplane hangar. "He just fell in love with racing," Tanen later recalled. His induction into the world of motorcycles was rather less glamorous, learning to ride in the parking lot next to the House of Motorcyles in El

Cajon, California. However, the vision of him hurtling along a desert road, framed by a blood-red setting sun, became one of the iconic images of the movie and helped establish Cruise as an all-action hero.

Filming, it seems, was just as much fun. Every Friday night was treated like a wrap party, with drinking and carousing by the pool at the officers' club. Director Tony Scott, whose then affair with statuesque actress Brigitte Nielsen ended his marriage, got into the habit, according to navy adviser Pettigrew, of "auditioning" young actresses long after all the roles had been cast. While Scott, a close friend of Timothy Leary, the champion of LSD, kept his activities behind closed trailer doors, the parties really got started when Don Simpson, who jokingly referred to himself as "Beverly Hills Cock," made his raucous arrival on set, often so high on coke that he crashed his black Pontiac Trans Am in the parking lot.

Perhaps the most memorable night was the party held in July at the North Island Officers Club to celebrate Tom's twenty-third birthday. Simpson and his assistants Dave "the Rave" Robertson and Dave Thorne, known as Baby Dave, headed to the beach and invited bikini-clad girls to join the cast and crew for the party. As the drink-fueled evening wore on, one assistant recalls that leading lady Kelly McGillis left the girlfriend with whom she had been dancing, stripped naked, and jumped into the water. Her costars and pilots from the top gun school then grabbed Bruckheimer and Simpson and threw them unceremoniously into the pool. Simpson sank straight to the bottom because he couldn't swim. "It was insane," the assistant told writer Charles Fleming. "Tom had his girls there and Kelly [McGillis] had hers there. She's doing the entire navy plus has her lesbian girlfriend come down on the weekend from Los Angeles. Tony [Scott] has his girls with the huge boobs, plus Brigitte was there."

If life was good during the filming of *Top Gun*, it was about to get a whole lot better. While he was on board the USS *Enterprise*, snatching what rest he could as the jets rumbled overhead, he got a call from the Hollywood director he not just admired, but revered. Martin Scorsese, the man who made *Raging Bull,* wanted him for his latest venture. Just a couple of years before, Tom had been rapping the script with his friend Vinnie Travisano in his home in Glen Ridge. Now he had the great man asking if he wanted to work with him. Oh, and there was the little matter of teaming up with another Hollywood legend—Paul Newman. As Tom later recalled: "I couldn't believe this was happening to me."

The idea was to make a long overdue sequel to the 1961 movie *The Hustler,* where Newman played the pool hall king, Fast Eddie Felson. The new film, entitled *The Color of Money,* would introduce a younger version of Fast Eddie, a talented but arrogant pool player called Vincent who plays the apprentice to the older sorcerer. Scorsese had seen Tom in *All the Right Moves* and thought he would be ideal for the part. Flattered though he was, after a grueling ten-month filming schedule, Tom was looking forward to taking a break. However, the opportunity to work—and learn from—two Hollywood greats was too tempting, and he duly signed up.

This time there was no mythic nonsense about Tom rewriting scripts, editing the film, or choosing camera shots. He was joining committed and talented artists at the height of their powers. Newman, Scorsese, and writer Richard Price had worked on the script and storyboarded the shots for the previous nine months. When filming began in January 1986, Tom simply had to turn up and act. That in itself was an intimidating prospect. Cocky as Tom was, he was duly overawed. Even though they had met before—Tom had read unsuccessfully for Newman when he was casting his 1984 film *Harry & Son*—for the first few days he called the star of the show "Mr. Newman" before the older man told him to call him Paul.

Unusually, Newman insisted on several weeks of rehearsals before filming began, the seasoned actor quietly testing the mettle of his young protégé. Tom practiced pool for hour after relentless hour under the watchful gaze of professional Mike Sigel. It was a dedication that earned the respect of the leading man. "He learned to play pool better in six weeks than I did in five months twenty-five years ago," Newman recalled. During filming, which took place mainly in grimy poolrooms in Chicago, Tom did all his own pool shots, except for a two-ball jump shot executed by Sigel. Even that he could have managed with more practice, but the tight fifty-day shoot schedule would not allow that luxury.

The movie was much more than wielding a pool cue like a samurai warrior's sword, which Tom did during one scene. At its heart it dealt with the complex interplay between the old cynic and the young pretender, the older man teaching his protégé how to hustle and study the psychology of his opponents. Tom had to step up to the plate as an actor, not just a performer. He realized as soon as he first met Newman that he was being quietly and subtly assessed. It was a test he passed. By the end of filming, such was Newman's respect for the younger man that when he was nominated for an Academy Award, he sent Tom a telegram: "If I win, it's ours as much as mine because you did such a good job." Newman did win, and Tom was so proud of the telegram that he framed it and put it on the wall of his New York apartment.

Indeed, Newman later described the filming of *The Color of Money* as the "most creative experience" he had ever had. "During the movie there wasn't any ritual dancing. No egos. Tom Cruise and I were just very, very open with each other." From calling him "Mr. Newman" at the beginning of filming, by the end Tom joined in the "worst joke of the day" competition on set and even gave Newman a bra and garter belt for his sixty-first birthday. There was a real family feeling during the production, Scorsese's wife Barbara De Fina often cooking pasta and other Italian fare for Tom. The convivial, friendly atmosphere spoke to Tom's deep-seated need for family, his yearning for a sense of belonging.

Over the months, his relationship with Paul Newman, rather like the movie they made together, became much more textured and layered, with mutual professional respect giving way to a kind of manly friendship. Newman introduced Tom to his lifelong passion—professional automobile racing. It was a love affair that had led him to enter the Le Mans twenty-four-hour car rally. At the end of shooting he arranged for Tom and Don Simpson to have five days of intensive race training with his driving partner, Jim Fitzgerald. By the end of it, Tom was hooked, and during the summer race season he watched his friend take part in numerous events.

Certainly there was talk that the avuncular Newman had taken on the mantle of surrogate father to the much younger man. Six years previously, his only son, Scott, then twenty-eight, had committed suicide, haunted by his own failures as an actor and his father's divorce from his mother, Jacqueline Witte. Cruise, talented, charismatic, and hardworking, seemed to be occupying the place of the son Newman had lost in such tragic circumstances. As Newman's biographer Daniel O'Brien observed, "Inevitably it was alleged that Newman regarded Cruise as a surrogate son. He enjoyed a close relationship with the young actor, something he'd never had with Scott."

Perhaps even more important, Tom's association with Newman and Scorsese helped prepare him for the road ahead. He had been working with two men, especially Newman, who had been exposed in full measure to the blaze of publicity during their glory years. It had turned Newman from an actor to a star and ultimately a screen icon, defined by his penetrating blue eyes and easy swagger. That he had survived with his sense of self firmly intact was not lost on Tom. "He lives a normal life. He's got several businesses, a wife, a family. That's good for me to see." Now the fickle flame of stardom beckoned a new recruit. This time the focus would be as much on Tom's megawatt if manipulative smile and the way he handled his Ray-Ban sunglasses as on his acting prowess.

The promotional firestorm surrounding *Top Gun* erupted in May 1986, just a few weeks after Tom had finished working with these Hollywood giants. His experience with them helped keep him grounded as he skyrocketed to superstardom. The movie instantly established the Tom Cruise of popular imagination. He nailed his future screen persona from the first frame of the movie, when he flew his plane upside down above a Russian MiG so that he could snap a Polaroid of the Russian pilot for his collection. While his cocky panache was as winning as it was reckless, beneath his easy grin was a young man haunted by the past who found personal redemption through the counsel of a gruff older man. A sex symbol with a soft center: It was a theme he was to explore time and again.

The movie itself was huge, grabbing audiences from the first moment, when a fighter jet roared off the deck of the aircraft carrier, accompanied by a pulsating rock beat, and holding on for 110 stirring minutes. It was so relentlessly gung ho that the U.S. Navy attracted its largest influx of recruits since World War II. So much for Tom's instincts to make a sports movie; *Top Gun* was much more than that. Beyond the fact that it was Paramount's biggest-grossing film that year or that it was nominated for eight Oscars, it became, along with *Wall Street,* one of the iconic films of the 1980s, representing ideals underpinning the American dream.

With its glossy, slick-paced photography, hard-pumping soundtrack, and attractive actors, this was a movie that appealed to almost everyone. As Simpson and Bruckheimer intended, the target audience of "mom and pop in Oklahoma" came in droves. The movie also attracted a huge gay following because of the underlying homoerotic theme of glamorous machismo. A competitive volleyball match involving rivals Cruise and Kilmer, stripped and oiled, was so appealing that it took the breath away of readers of the gay magazine *Suck,* who voted it "favorite scene" in a movie for three years running. Even though Tom had pointedly refused to go bare-chested for publicity pictures, the gay vibe was one that would continue to haunt him.

At the time, he publicly defended this unadulterated beefcake moment as demonstrating how fighter pilots need to keep fit. "They want to beat each other, they want to be the best," he argued in one of an interminable series of promotional interviews. It was not just the grind of a movie tour that he had to contend with, but the realization that he was no longer an up-and-coming actor, but a genuine star. For Tom his life would never be his own again. While the attention made him feel "isolated and lonely"—he was unable to go out with his sisters without being mobbed by fans and paparazzi—he recognized, perhaps instinctively, that the way to control the media was to reveal only what he wanted about himself.

During the filming of *Top Gun* he had seen the destructive power of the mass media, watching helplessly as his friend Sean Penn found himself in their crosshairs as a result of his relationship with Madonna. Not only was the aggressive Penn arrested for throwing rocks at two British journalists, his wedding on the clifftops at Malibu in August 1985 degenerated into a paparazzi feeding frenzy where Tom and the other guests, who included old flame Cher, could barely hear the service above the noise of hovering helicopters.

Tom adopted a different approach, giving away those morsels of his life he was comfortable discussing rather than refusing to feed an ever-hungry media. It impressed the hell out of Sean Penn. As his personal assistant Meegan Ochs recalls, "Sean used to say that Tom Cruise ought to get an award for dealing with the press. His opinion was that Cruise decided early on a few things that he was going to share of himself with the public—his dyslexia, his lack of relationship with his father. Everyone felt they were getting this very sensitive insight, and because of that, he was golden with the press. But basically he just kept repeating these few things ad infinitum and never gave anything else up. Instead of what Sean did, which was just to try and keep things private."

Others, like movie mogul David Geffen, were equally impressed by the way Tom handled himself. Keeping a fatherly eye on the media mayhem was Paul Newman, who had become a star during a gentler, less frenetic time. "It's tough when it happens as fast as it did with Tom," he said. "He's a very savvy kid, a very savvy man. So far he's kept his head on his shoulders, but he's one of the very, very few."

This mutual admiration society was symbolized by the fact that during the publicity for *The Color of Money* in October 1986, Cruise and Newman appeared on the cover of *Life* magazine, lying on top of a pool table. At the charity premiere in New York's Ziegfeld Theater, Cruise, Newman, Joanne Woodward, and Tom's on-screen love interest in the film, Mary

Elizabeth Mastrantonio, turned up *en famille* to face the flash-bulbs. A week later Tom went to Atlanta to watch his friend and mentor in the Valvoline road-racing classic. He presented Newman with a good-luck floral arrangement. "These are for your garden. Go get them," said the note. It was signed Tom and Mimi. It seemed that stardom was not quite so lonely after all.

CHAPTER 5

Even by Hollywood standards she was an exotic creature, her statuesque beauty matched only by her colorful background. Born in 1956 in Coral Gables, Florida, Miriam Spickler's parents soon realized that they had a child prodigy on their hands. Clever, quick, and blessed with a near-photographic memory, young Miriam, or Mimi, as everyone called her, effortlessly rose to the top of her class, especially in science, even though her father Phil's job as a civil engineer meant that they often moved from state to state, school to school. When she was just seven, her parents parted, she and her younger brother Paul opting to stay with their father.

It was a decision that would change her life. Her evident academic ability enabled her to skip several grades so that she graduated from high school by the age of fourteen. Instead of going on to college, she joined her father on his regular forays to the casino resort of Lake Tahoe, Nevada. He had folded his career as a civil engineer and opted to try his hand as a professional gambler. With her good looks and better memory, the voluptuous teenager became an accomplished poker and blackjack player—even though she was under the legal age limit. Years later she competed in professional tournaments.

It wasn't long before her father swapped the vagaries of the gaming table for a surefire bet—selling a man-made religion. He had long since discarded his Jewish faith to become an adherent of Scientology, a cult founded by science fiction writer Lafayette Ron Hubbard in 1954, four years after the publication of Hubbard's best-selling book *Dianetics: The Modern Science of Mental Health*. It was one of the first of the now-familiar genre of self-help books and became a founding text for Scientology. Soon his eager customers were parishioners and his business repackaged as a religion. Hubbard was making good on a boast he had made to a conference of science fiction writers in 1947: "If you really want to make a million, the quickest way is to start your own religion."

Hubbard described Dianetics as a revolutionary and scientifically developed alternative to conventional psychiatry and psychotherapy, arguing that it could alleviate all manner of illnesses, including asthma, arthritis, alcoholism, ulcers, migraines, conjunctivitis, morning sickness, the common cold, and heart disease. In addition, he claimed it could hugely increase intelligence and eliminate burdensome emotions as well as cure conditions like atheism and homosexuality. The basic premise was that the brain remembers everything, and that by recalling and cleansing negative experiences, or "engrams," a person can free himself from repressed feelings and so arrive at a "clear" mental state. Hubbard maintained that the widespread use of Dianetics would lead to a "world without insanity, without criminals and without war." It was an audacious application of the notion of mind over matter.

Hubbard founded his own Church of Scientology not only to exploit the financial success of his book, but also to bypass constant criticism by psychiatrists and other scientists that his theories were little more than untested and unproven pseudoscience, intellectual snake oil for the gullible. Nobel Prize–winning physicist Isidor Isaac Rabi declared in *Scientific American*: "This volume probably contains more promises and less evidence per page than has any publication since the invention of printing."

The scorn of the scientific community did not stop Hubbard from incorporating his first church in California, in 1954. He faced stiff competition in a crowded field. In Los Angeles alone there were one hundred or so cults, one of his fiercest rivals being Krishna Venta, who told his disciples that he had arrived on a spaceship 240,000 years ago. Hubbard's philosophy was much more subtle, promising the spiritual equivalent of the alchemist's dream, turning pewter into gold. In this case it was an impregnable synthesis of faith and reason, science and belief.

While scientists saw man as a body, Hubbard argued that man was an endlessly reincarnated spirit. He did not worship God, but was his own god. By following Hubbard's applied religious philosophy, an individual could fully realize his immortal nature, freeing himself from his body. At its heart, the appeal of Scientology was not to a man's soul, but to his ego. He could become his own god . . . for a price.

On their journey, new members—whom Hubbard called "raw meat"—would undergo auditing. The process bore similarities to the Catholic confessional, except Scientology's parishioners would pay handsomely for the privilege. To give the process an air of scientific inquiry, an auditor would use a device called an electropsychometer, or E meter, akin to a crude lie detector, which measures small changes in the body's electrical current. The theory was that the meter registers thoughts of the reactive mind and can root out unconscious lies. This process of discovery would eventually free the mind.

Gradually—and many thousands of dollars later—Scientologists would go up what Hubbard called "the bridge" to reach a stage of enlightenment. The elite, who had reached upper levels, were seen as superhuman beings who, Hubbard claimed, could communicate telepathically, leave their bodies at will, move inanimate objects with their minds, and be totally free from the physical universe, able to control what Scientologists call MEST: Matter, Energy, Space, and Time. It is possibly the greatest story ever sold: customers spending up to $500,000, or more in today's terms, to progress through Hubbard's labyrinthine courses in the hopes of reaching spiritual fulfillment—and the ability to move ashtrays. From mortal man to immortal superman . . . it was an enticing prospect. All that and saving the planet, too.

Hubbard's particular genius was his ability to create a

parallel universe, a self-contained belief system that promised "total spiritual freedom" while depicting the planet Earth as a dangerous place full of "merchants of chaos." In the Cold War era, amid the threat of an instant nuclear Armageddon, his philosophy struck a populist nerve, particularly with Roman Catholics and later Vietnam war veterans and hippies, who were disillusioned with conventional religious and political structures and inspired by the notion of saving the world from itself. Mimi's father, Phil Spickler, was an early follower. He recalled: "There was a strong feeling that I, we, were making or would be making a difference in this world's future. In the 1950s, after the war, it seemed possible to break the grip that certain institutions held in world affairs, and establish a saner planet."

Altruism aside, it was also a way to make money. Ron's church was essentially a franchising operation, expanding its membership by licensing individuals known as mission holders to set up branches in various parts of the country. Like any pyramid selling scheme, the higher up the chain, the more an individual earned. Typically, a Scientologist who introduced "fresh meat" into the church would earn a lifetime commission of 10 percent, plus more on book sales. Spickler opened his own mission in Palo Alto, California, his daughter, Mimi, rising through the ranks so rapidly that by her late teens she was a Class 8 auditor, able to train the most advanced Scientologists, including celebrities. "It was a religious philosophy that I was shaped and formed by, part of my education. So in that sense it will always be there," she says.

During the 1970s, Mimi was a familiar figure at the Scientology headquarters in Clearwater, Florida, where she took courses. Inside the cult, she was something of a celebrity herself, her high achievement in one so young making her stand out. Even though fellow Scientologists remember her as icy, aloof, and distant, she was beautiful enough to have men falling at her feet. As a teenager she was well aware of her effect on men, dating a string of fellow Scientologists who included fellow auditor James Fiducia, a tall, good-looking New Yorker. When they went their separate ways, she met another high-level Scientology auditor, Jim Rogers, who was in a similar mold to her previous boyfriend, being tall, older, and easygoing. The couple married in 1977, when she was just twenty-one.

After their wedding they opened a small Scientology "field auditing" practice in Sherman Oaks in the San Fernando Valley, which catered to actors, artists, and other celebrities. As many celebrities wanted to keep their association with Scientology private, it was often difficult to encourage them to visit the main Celebrity Centre in Hollywood. The Sherman Oaks venue was a discreet, anonymous setting for a celebrity to explore Hubbard's world vision. As a former Scientologist observed, "Field auditing is about getting people into the cult in a casual, come-round-to-my-house-and-talk-to-me kind of way."

It is also about money, Scientology field auditors earning a decent living from commissions for bringing in raw meat. And celebrities were prime steak. Jim and Mimi had a pleasant three-bedroom home in the valley with a volleyball court and a swimming pool, money earned from the hundred dollars an hour or so they charged for an hour's auditing. She recruited the singer and later politician Sonny Bono into the cult, while her great friend, comedy actress Kirstie Alley, who credited Scientology with getting her off drugs, was a regular visitor.

While Scientology was a vehicle for Mimi to fund her lifestyle, it was also a route to achieve her ultimate ambition: to become a Hollywood star. Beneath her surface charm and good looks was a focused and determined young woman who networked constantly to gain a foot on the ladder of fame. "She knew what she wanted—to be a superstar. If you had nothing to offer her, she wasn't interested," recalls a former girlfriend. Mimi and Kirstie even attempted scriptwriting, one effort featuring a girl who was enjoying a last fling before she reached thirty. Indeed, it took screenwriter and onetime Scientologist Skip Press some time to realize that he was being invited to her home for cookouts because of his contacts and for the chance to have first look at his latest scripts rather than because of his scintillating wit and good looks. "When she and her husband set up an auditing practice, I learned that rather than 'clearing the planet,' she was fiercely focused on Hollywood success. She is one of the most coldly calculating people I ever met and would cast you aside if you could not fuel her ambition."

In 1980, Mimi divorced her first husband, Jim, concentrating full-time on her acting career. The following year she was cast in the hit TV series *Hill Street Blues* and started dating Ed Marinaro, one of the show's stars. Over the next few years she got a number of small roles in TV soaps such as *The Rousters* and *Paper Dolls*. Her ceaseless networking did not impress everyone, a friend of her ex-husband commenting sourly, "Mimi is the only actress I know who could fuck her way to the middle."

While seeking acting work, she continued to recruit new members to the cult. The lifetime commissions she earned helped pay the bills. Dinner parties and other social gatherings were perfect opportunities to quietly introduce Scientology into the conversation, and it was at one such dinner party in 1985 that Mimi first met Tom Cruise. At the time she was dating "an associate" of the young actor, but she later recalled there was a chemistry between them comprised of stolen glances and brief exchanges. "I guess we both thought we were kinda cute," said Mimi later.

For Tom, the fact that she was an actress was a plus. Apart from briefly dating singer Patti Scialfa, whom he met backstage after a concert in New Jersey during Bruce Springsteen's "Born in the USA" tour, he had eyes only for those in his own profession. It meant that when he launched into one of his passionate lectures about his craft, his date would understand what he was talking about. As he later explained, "It's like trying to explain how driving a racecar feels. You can't do it. They've got to get into the car themselves." Certainly Mimi recognized that quality. "He's always been a very intense guy who is openly passionate about some things."

At first sight, Tom was not Mimi's usual type. The men in her life—after her divorce she dated TV detectives Tom Selleck and Ed Marinaro as well as Bobby Shriver, scion of the Kennedy clan—were all older and taller than she was. By contrast, Tom Cruise was two inches shorter and six years younger. Like the others, though, he was well-connected—and busy. "He seemed so young and vulnerable, and she was a very powerful personality who knew how to work her power," recalled a onetime girlfriend who watched her in action. "Quite simply, she rocked his world."

Mimi's romance with Tom followed a similar pattern to her days with Tom Selleck. It was all about mutual ambition and business. Show business. They saw each other in between Tom shooting *The Color of Money* and publicizing *Top Gun*, and Mimi embarking on her first major starring role in the crime thriller *Someone to Watch Over Me*. As Selleck's biographer Jason Bonderoff noted, "Mimi's a go-getter, a real powerhouse, which is one of the things Tom [Selleck] found so attractive about her. The trouble is that they were so busy with their careers they hardly had time to fall in love."

Mimi paid rather more attention to the new Tom in her life, introducing her latest partner to the life and works of L. Ron Hubbard. She was simply performing the Gospel according to Ron. Indeed, when her friend Kirstie Alley married acting heartthrob Parker Stevenson in 1993, he, too, became a Scientologist. Somewhat ahead of his time, Hubbard placed great store on enticing celebrities into his cult, recognizing that their involvement would give the movement credibility and encourage others to join. As early as 1955, he issued a policy known as "Project Celebrity," where he implored his followers to recruit film, theater, and sports stars. He gave celebrities free courses and wooed them further by building or buying buildings he turned into Celebrity Centres, notably a neo-Gothic mansion at the foot of the Hollywood hills in Los Angeles, where artists, actors, and others could take Scientology courses in pleasant, friendly surroundings, away from prying eyes.

His recruitment advice was to go after the "old and faded" or "up and coming," believing that those at the top of their artistic game had no need of Scientology nostrums. For example, John Travolta joined the movement in 1974, when his acting career was in a slump. "Scientology put me into the big time," he later claimed. Others who joined during this period were the musicians Chick Corea and Isaac Hayes, while the influential acting coach Milton Katselas sent and still sends a steady stream of aspiring hopefuls to the Celebrity Centre to try Scientology on for size. Word of mouth and personal endorsements within the Hollywood community were key elements of celebrity recruiting. So when Chick Corea went to a Paul McCartney concert in Hollywood, he had more than music on his mind. Backstage, Corea tried to corral Paul and his wife Linda into the cult. They said no, as did John and Yoko Lennon when the highly regarded session pianist Nicky Hopkins, another cult member, tried to entice them in. Hopkins was more successful with music legend Van Morrison, who joined for a time.

There was little left to chance in the "casual encounters" between a cult follower like Mimi Rogers and a potential celebrity recruit. What the celebrities never realized was that their introduction to Scientology was the result of weeks, sometimes months, of meticulous planning. The first stage was to identify a celebrity target, and then work out a "battle plan" to lure them into the cult. To help them, dedicated Scientologists made clay models of the individual, Michael Jackson for example, outlining incremental scenarios that would help their planning. By turning the idea into clay, the concept was somehow made "real."

On the office wall inside the Celebrity Centre in Hollywood was a three-foot-by-six-foot white magnetic "org board" with the names of targeted celebrities cross-referenced to titles like "Contact," "Handle," "Intro Session," and "Org," which indicated how involved an individual had become. It was a deadly serious business. The staff of the Celebrity Centre was under intense pressure to show results. Former Scientologist Karen Pressley was "commanding officer" of Celebrity Centre International for three years during the mid-1980s and was considered a celebrity herself, as she and her husband, Peter, had written the 1982 smash hit "On the Wings of Love."

She recalls, "I remember David Miscavige [now the Scientology leader] pounding his fists and screaming threats about getting to more celebrities. It was psychotic." With sickening regularity, she and her colleagues were warned that if they didn't get a celebrity into Scientology within forty-eight hours they would face internal discipline, namely a so-called Ethics Commission, or assignment to the Rehabilitation Project Force, the Scientology version of prison, whose punishments included running around a pole for days. This hysterical behavior, though typical, was even more extreme during the mid-1980s. In 1986, when Mimi and Tom started dating seriously, the cult was plunged into crisis following the death of its founder, L. Ron Hubbard.

By then Scientology had become one of the most notorious and feared cults in the world, the movement treated with suspicion in numerous democratic countries, including Britain, Spain, France, Germany, and Australia. On the surface the cult was friendly and inclusive, adherents living by the phrase: "If it ain't fun, it ain't Scientology." The Celebrity Centre in Hollywood, under the warm gaze of Yvonne Jentzsch, was widely regarded as a "friendly and relaxed" venue, a great place to make show business contacts, meet good-looking girls, and, if you were lucky, get laid.

Beneath the seductive smiles, Scientology was a paranoid movement reflecting the schizophrenic personality of the founder, a dogmatic cult dedicated to world domination, dismissive of other religions like Christianity and Buddhism, and accusing psychiatrists and other health workers of being responsible for all the ills on the planet since the dawn of time. As for the gay community, Hubbard wrote in his book *The Science of Survival* that if the Scientology road to salvation was unsuccessful, the solution was to "dispose of them quietly and without sorrow." For a man who wrote policies on everything from cleaning windows with newspapers to how to cheat on taxes and how to use a body vibrator, he was less forthcoming about the methodology to be employed to "dispose of" the world's gay community.

The dark heart of Scientology was a bizarre, closed world, hidden from public view or examination, that reflected the megalomania of the cult's founder. Even Hubbard's second wife, Sara Northrup, described the cult leader as someone who was "hopelessly insane" and should be committed.

During the 1960s and '70s, Hubbard built up the biggest private intelligence agency in the world, hiding behind the shield of the First Amendment to attack, harass, and defame. Church intelligence agents were taught how to make anonymous death threats, smear perceived critics, forge documents, and plan and execute burglaries. They used all means necessary to "shudder into silence"—Hubbard's charmless phrase—any opposition.

As all critics were by definition criminals, their crimes cried out to be publicly exposed. "Start feeding lurid, blood sex crime, actual evidence on the attackers to the press," Hubbard wrote in 1966, this attitude codified in a policy known misleadingly as "Fair Game," where a critic "may be tricked, sued or lied to or destroyed." Not surprisingly, an exhaustive investigation into Scientology by the Australian government in 1965 concluded: "Scientology is evil; its techniques are evil; its practice is a serious threat to the community, medically, morally, and socially; and its adherents are sadly deluded and often mentally ill."

The cult practiced what it preached—to chilling effect. Church members were deliberately infiltrated into government agencies as well as newspapers, anti-cult groups, psychiatric and medical associations, and other organizations deemed antithetical to Scientology. The church's most audacious espionage conspiracy—at least so far publicly known—took place during the 1970s. Code-named "Operation Snow White," it involved the systematic wiretapping, theft, and burglary of eleven government and nongovernment buildings, including the IRS and the Office of the Deputy Attorney General of the United States. Scientology spies had even amassed a dossier on then President Nixon, himself no stranger to dubious behavior. In 1977 these criminal activities led the FBI to launch one of the biggest raids in its history, with dozens of armed police simultaneously breaking into Scientology "centres" in Washington and Los Angeles. As a result, eleven senior Scientologists, including the founder's third wife, Mary Sue Hubbard, went to jail. Hubbard himself and Kendrick Moxon, currently the lead Scientology counsel, were named as unindicted conspirators, along with a further nineteen Scientologists, some of whom remain active in the church today.

While Operation Snow White was breathtaking in its audacity, another conspiracy at this time was bloodcurdling in its calculated cruelty. In 1972 author Paulette Cooper wrote a book called *The Scandal of Scientology,* which by today's standards was a modest and even-handed analysis of the cult. For her pains she was served with a total of nineteen lawsuits by the church. That was only the beginning of her seven-year ordeal. The same attention to planning and detail that was involved in luring celebrities into Scientology was now employed in attempting to destroy those the cult considered enemies.

Unbeknownst to her, high-ranking church officials were discussing whether to employ the Mafia to kill her or frame her for a crime she did not commit. They chose the latter, a conspiracy that involved dozens of church workers in a campaign of harassment designed to send her to jail or a mental institution, or drive her to suicide. For months after the book's publication, Paulette, a pretty, petite blonde, was followed and subjected to obscene phone calls and attempted break-ins to her Manhattan apartment, as well as a vicious letter-writing campaign that accused her of molesting a two-year-old child. (In keeping with Hubbard's teachings, sexually lurid and often ludicrous allegations against opponents are hallmarks of Scientology smear campaigns.)

Paulette's second cousin, who bore a remarkable resemblance to the writer, survived a bungled murder attempt. A few months later, in May 1973, the FBI arrested Paulette for allegedly making two bomb threats against the church of Scientology. It took two years and a "truth test," which Paulette passed, for the FBI to drop its case. In a plan called

"Operation Freakout," Scientologists continued their harassment. At one point a Scientology agent, Jerry Levin, deliberately befriended her, feigning sympathy for her torment while sending details of her every thought and movement to his Scientology bosses. In one of his many reports he noted exultantly: "She can't sleep again, she's talking suicide . . . wouldn't this be great for Scientology?" It was only after the FBI raid on Scientology churches in 1977, which uncovered at least twenty-three thousand documents relating to Operation Freakout, that the full extent of the vicious conspiracy was exposed and Paulette's undoubted innocence proven.

Paulette's explanation about her reasons for investigating the cult is as simple as it is courageous. Born in Auschwitz concentration camp, where her parents were murdered, she says, "My parents were killed by Hitler. Scientology is a Fascist group. If people had spoken out in the 1930s perhaps he wouldn't have come to power. Once I decided the church was evil I had no choice."

After the jailing of high-ranking Scientologists, the cult liked to claim that its nefarious past was over. During the 1980s, two senior judges on different continents begged to disagree. In 1984, in London's High Court, Judge Latey, ruling in a child custody battle, concluded: "Scientology is both immoral and socially obnoxious . . . it is corrupt, sinister and dangerous. It is corrupt because it is based upon lies and deceit and has as its real objective money and power for Mr. Hubbard, his wife and those close to him at the top. It is sinister because it indulges in infamous practices both to its adherents who do not toe the line unquestioningly and to those who criticize or oppose it. It is dangerous because it is out to capture young people, and indoctrinate and brainwash them so that they become the unquestioning captives and tools of the cult, withdrawn from ordinary thought, living and relationships with others."

That same year a judge in California focused on the bizarre mind-set of the cult's founder, L. Ron Hubbard. At the conclusion of a four-week case involving senior church officials and their harassment of former senior Scientologist

Gerry Armstrong, who was at one time Hubbard's personal researcher, Judge Breckenridge launched a forthright condemnation of the cult and its founder: "The organization clearly is schizophrenic and paranoid and this bizarre combination seems to be a reflection of its founder LRH. The evidence portrays a man who has been virtually a pathological liar when it comes to his history, background, and achievements. The writings and documents in evidence additionally reflect his egoism, greed, avarice, lust for power, and vindictiveness and aggressiveness against persons perceived by him to be disloyal or hostile."

By then the cult seemed to be on the point of internal collapse, riven by disputes, splits, and lawsuits. In 1982, Scientology missions were summarily disbanded for seemingly taking too big a slice of the cult's business pie. Many mission holders were harassed, humiliated, and strong-armed into acquiescence. Disgruntled cult members left by the thousands, some even staging a noisy protest outside the cult's British headquarters. Even Scientology celebrities had their doubts about the direction in which the organization was headed. At that time John Travolta was struggling with his commitment. In an August 1983 interview with *Rolling Stone* magazine, he voiced his doubts about the way the cult was being run. "I wish I could defend Scientology better but I don't think it even deserves to be defended in a sense." Alarmed, the cult hierarchy assigned two Scientology auditors, Chris and Stephanie Silcock, a married South African couple, to go everywhere with him, from the movie set to his home, to bolster his allegiance. Other celebrities, like musician Edgar Winter, were given free auditing to keep them happy.

The convulsions gripping the cult proved the last straw for Mimi's father, mission holder Phil Spickler, who watched the movement he had so enthusiastically embraced become perverted from its original purpose. He recalls: "There is a great deal to be found in both Dianetics and Scientology that is truly and absolutely wonderful and that can be used outside the profit motive or the enslavement motive."

As the movement went into meltdown, Hubbard was in

hiding, on the run from the law for fraud and tax evasion. Those who glimpsed this shadowy character, then living under an assumed name in a remote ranch in Crestor, California, recall that he cut an incoherent, unkempt figure reminiscent of the eccentric billionaire Howard Hughes. His teeth were black, his lank, shoulder-length hair dirty and matted, his nails long, gnarled, and curling—hardly an endorsement for the lifestyle he had spent years promoting. The ultimate irony of his bizarre life is that when he died in January 1986, shortly after suffering a stroke, his body was full of Vistaril, a psychiatric drug used to calm frantic or overanxious patients. Yet this was the same man who had devoted his life to fighting psychiatrists, blaming them for all the world's ills.

With his death, the Scientology leadership became embroiled in a vicious power struggle. Youngsters in the fanatical Sea Org—an elite group that signed billion-year pledges to Scientology—staged a coup against Hubbard's inner circle, ousting his anointed successor, Bill Franks, and Hubbard's closest aides. In several countries Sea Org officers, some barely teenagers, snatched control of the entire country's organization. "It's like *The Lord of the Flies*," a former franchise holder told *The New York Times*. "The children have taken over." When the dust settled, a diminutive but ruthlessly ambitious high-school dropout named David Miscavige had taken overall command of the rickety operation. With members leaving in droves, the omens were that Scientology would go the way of so many cults and expire shortly after the death of its founder. Not this time. A Hollywood heartthrob was waiting in the wings to give it the kiss of life. In years to come he would be called the savior of Scientology.

When Tom Cruise was given picture books on Scientology and Dianetics in 1986, he knew little, if anything, about the cult, except that some of those in his circle had joined or, like *Top Gun* producer Don Simpson, were interested. It is doubtful that he would have had a chance to read the article in *Forbes* magazine that year that described the church as "complete with financial dictators, gang bang security checks, lie detectors, committees of evidence and detention camps."

As for Mimi, she was doing what she and her Scientology friends like Kirstie Alley had done for years, enticing friends into her faith. At that time Tom was the most talked-about star in Hollywood, *Top Gun* being that year's blockbuster. To reel in such a big fish would raise her standing inside Scientology and give her film career and earnings a massive boost. Scriptwriter and onetime Scientologist Skip Press, who watched Mimi in action, recalls: "As a former Scientologist who saw all its dark corners, it certainly wouldn't surprise me if she made a play for Tom with the primary intention of bringing him into the cult and leapfrogging over him to an acting career. In the mid-1980s, Scientology was still reeling from the raid by the FBI. They desperately needed new celebrity blood to stay alive."

Ironically, while Tom was becoming quietly intrigued by the philosophy of L. Ron Hubbard, senior Scientologists had other celebrities in their sights. During Tom's romance with Mimi in 1986, prime Scientology targets were his buddy Emilio Estevez, son of actor Martin Sheen, and his fiancée, actress Demi Moore. Indeed, the entire Sheen family was in the crosshairs. With Mimi now on the scene, it was perhaps no coincidence that Scientologists assigned to recruit Demi and Emilio started getting high-grade information about their whereabouts. As Karen Pressley recalls, "A senior Scientology executive would be on the phone telling us that Emilio Estevez was staying in Malibu and that we had forty-eight hours to speak to him and get him in for an auditing session. There was so much heat and pressure on this, it was outrageous." The thinking was that if they could entice Emilio into the fold, Demi would surely follow. Their covert tactics paid off, as both did join for a time, Estevez always refusing to talk about his involvement with the cult for fear that he might "have his phones tapped."

While the Scientology big guns were trained on Estevez and Moore, Tom quietly came in under the radar, joining the cult sometime after the release of *Top Gun* in 1986. As with many celebrities nervous about being publicly associated with such a controversial movement, Scientology auditors visited him privately. It was some time later that he came out, enrolling in the fashionably discreet Scientology Enhancement Centre in Sherman Oaks, which his girlfriend, Mimi, and her former husband, Jim Rogers, had started. Even though they had sold it, Mimi was still friendly with the new owner, Frances Godwin.

While Mimi's blandishments may have encouraged Tom to give the cult a try, he was not, even by Hubbard's standards, typical "raw meat." He was neither up and coming nor old and faded, but at the top of his game, reaching the dizzying peaks of Hollywood stardom without any help from L. Ron Hubbard. Adored by his fans, financially secure, professionally appreciated, in the early throes of a mature relationship with an exciting, sexy woman, he seemed to have it all. So what was missing from his life? What was, as Scientologists call it, his "ruin"?

Invariably people are initially drawn to Scientology because they have deep-seated difficulties in their lives. It may be drugs—as with Don Simpson and Kirstie Alley—or drink, depression, or loneliness. Everyone who joins is searching for some kind of salvation. It is no coincidence that the "Free Stress Test" trumpeted by Scientology centers around the world is the introductory bait used to hook potential clients by indicating what is wrong with their lives. In the question-and-answer induction that follows, one of the primary roles of a Scientology auditor is to find a person's "ruin," the vulnerabilities and sensitivities that can be exploited to sell more Scientology courses.

Peter Alexander, former vice president of Universal Studios, was a member of Scientology for twenty years and spent a million dollars on their services. He observed: "There are only two types of people who join the cult—those with serious personal problems and those who buy into the idea." It is a not uncommon point of view. Now fifty-four, Michael Tilse was a member on and off for twenty-seven years. He says, "People who join are emotionally crippled, trying to find something inside themselves. They long to change something." Others are less critical. "Tom found what we all found—something that worked. Simple as that," observes a recently departed senior Scientology executive. "Hubbard talked about individuals taking responsibility for their own actions and lives. That probably struck a chord with him."

Most past and present Scientologists agree that entry-level courses produce practical benefits—in Alexander's case, Scientology self-help techniques helped him stop smoking. Many years after Tom Cruise joined, he explained that Scientology, in particular Hubbard's "Study Tech," had helped cure his dyslexia. While his claims will be discussed in more detail later in this book, there is evidence to suggest that this claim had more to do with his proselytizing mission on behalf of his faith than with the objective reality of his early life.

Another, perhaps more plausible, explanation for Cruise's belief in Scientology can be found in both his innate character and chosen profession. The Scientology ethos dovetailed nicely into his own personality. Pragmatic, dogmatic, controlling, and guarded are all descriptions that can be applied equally to the cult and to Tom himself. Just as the polite and smiling public face of the actor and cult representative forms a barrier to further inquiry, this smooth façade also masks a fundamental suspicion of the outside world.

In addition, actors respond particularly well to Scientology teachings, the one-on-one auditing technique flattering the actors' skills as the process encourages them to dramatize their lives by turning past events into scenes they can explore. For those working in a profession that is utterly self-involved, the notion of following a faith where the object of devotion and reverence is the self, where a man becomes his own god, is terribly alluring. Scientology strokes the ego as it lightens the wallet.

As much as it is ego-driven, acting, like modeling, nags away at an individual's insecurities. For an artist, no matter how successful, there is always the fear of failure, of falling from the professional tightrope before a gleeful and unforgiving audience. During the early years of his career, Tom expressed this anxiety by throwing himself into work. He told writer Jennet Conant, "In the beginning I was always afraid: 'This is my one shot, I'm going to lose it so I've just gotta work, work, work.' The first ten years, that was it."

Just as successful Hollywood stars surround themselves with a sycophantic coterie to soothe their insecurities and pamper their sense of self, so Scientology "love bombs" the celebrities it has managed to secure, praising, cosseting, and protecting them from the vagaries of the outside world. In particular, it feeds their innate distrust of the mass media.

For Tom Cruise, beleaguered by the post–*Top Gun* hysteria, it was an appealing prospect, especially since the young actor was always looking for a sense of belonging. Dustin Hoffman, who was then trying to recruit Tom for a film he was developing about an autistic man and his evolving relationship with his younger brother, was to observe this trait in his co-star. After making *Rain Man* with Tom, Hoffman recalled: "I think he desperately needed family, whether it was my family or the makeshift family of the crew." Scientology plays on this need. Once inside the cult, celebrities discover the friendly embrace of an instant family, nurtured by a sea of smiley, happy people. From the moment they join, celebrities are always treated like the special people they like to think they are.

Perhaps, though, where Hubbard's philosophy truly resonated with Tom Cruise was that it taught the actor, still only twenty-four, that he could rewrite the script of his life, or perhaps more accurately, the script of his life as he recollected it. As author J. C. Hallman, who investigated America's religious fringe for his book *The Devil Is a Gentleman,* observes, "What Scientologists seem to believe is that events in your life write a script for you and you can break away from that by breaking away from the role that fate has assigned you. You break your own character. You write your own script instead of simply acting out the script that fate has written for you." For a young man who returned time and again to the sour memories of his rootless childhood, alienation from his father, and sense of isolation, the prospect of reinvention and renewal almost certainly struck a deep-seated chord. "I thought, I can't wait to grow up because it's got to be better than this," he once recalled.

Tom began to live his life by Hubbard's famous statement of moral relativism: "If it isn't true for you, it isn't true." By slow, almost imperceptible degrees, he would eventually exchange his family, or his unhappy memories of his past life, for the bright, shiny, new family of Scientology. Eventually all decisions, great and small, would be taken with reference to its teachings. Tom embraced the philosophy so thoroughly that in time he would use one of Hubbard's peculiar phrases to describe his own father. Cruise called him "a merchant of chaos," a phrase Hubbard used to refer to those— mainly journalists, police, politicians, and doctors—who he believed make the outside world dangerous.

One of the ironies of Tom Cruise's journey is that a man who is often described as controlling was ultimately shaped and manipulated by the fiercely doctrinaire religion he embraced in 1986. Like other celebrities who joined the cult, their every move, whether they knew it or not, was discussed, debated, and orchestrated by Scientologists working feverishly behind the scenes to ensure that their prize catch swam in the direction they ordained. "These celebrities never had a clue about the octopus that was taking over their lives," a former Celebrity Centre operative recalled. It would be no exaggeration to say that when they entered Scientology, they were about to take part in a real-world version of *The Truman Show*—Peter Weir's 1998 film starring Jim Carrey as a man who doesn't realize that his life is actually a carefully orchestrated TV reality show.

While Tom's decision to join the Scientology cult would prove to be the most controversial choice of his life, at the time it was all of a piece with his growing intimacy with fellow Scientologist Mimi Rogers. For Tom, the most important decision was asking her to marry him. Not that it was the most romantic declaration of his life. As she later recalled, "He didn't do anything dashing like going down on one knee.

It just, well, it just sort of happened." Perhaps with memories of the circus that surrounded his friend Sean Penn's wedding, Tom and Mimi told no one apart from immediate family. Even his publicist Andrea Jaffe was kept in the dark.

Their wedding was a simple, straightforward, no-nonsense affair. Barefoot and dressed in blue jeans, they were married on May 9, 1987, in a simple Unitarian—rather than Scientology—ceremony, in their rented house in upstate New York. His sisters baked and iced the chocolate wedding cake, his friend Emilio Estevez, who by then had split with Demi Moore, was best man, and his mother, Mary Lee South, shed the customary tears, describing the ceremony as "intimate and beautiful."

Of the fifteen or so guests, the notable absentees were Paul Newman and his wife, Joanne Woodward, who were in Cannes promoting his movie version of Tennessee Williams's *The Glass Menagerie*. Woodward and Newman had heard about the wedding plans a few weeks earlier when the two couples had had dinner at the fashionable Wilkinson's Seafood Café on New York's Upper East Side to celebrate Newman's Academy Award for Best Actor as Fast Eddie Felson in *The Color of Money*. Newman's performance on the racetrack a few days after Tom and Mimi's wedding was not so memorable. As Tom watched from the sidelines, his friend lost control of his Nissan and slammed into the wall at California's Riverside International Speedway. A long, tense moment passed before Newman climbed out the window and walked away from the wreck.

While the incident did not dampen Tom's enthusiasm for his new passion, in the first few months of married life he had little time for racing—or his new bride. Both of the newlyweds went straight back to work. Mimi was putting the finishing touches on *Someone to Watch Over Me*, a sexy crime film costarring Tom Berenger and directed by Ridley Scott, who had made *Legend* with Tom a couple of years earlier. She had high hopes that this would be her breakout role.

While Mimi was still laboring up the slopes of Hollywood

success, Tom was now at the summit. In the months after his marriage, he was about to square the artistic circle, embarking on three movies that would not only expand his bank balance, but earn critical praise. In a journey that took him to the heart of who he was as an actor and a man, he traveled from Jamaica and the Philippines back to New York, Las Vegas, Cincinnati, Oklahoma, and his home state of Kentucky. While it was hardly the best way to nurture a new marriage, he did pick up a brother on the way.

When Tom had first met acting legend Dustin Hoffman in New York a couple of years earlier, it was something of a dream come true. When he was new in Hollywood, Tom and his friend Sean Penn had driven by Hoffman's Beverly Hills home and dared one another to ring the doorbell. Neither had had the nerve to do it. So when Hoffman offered him two tickets to watch his Broadway performance in Arthur Miller's *Death of a Salesman,* Tom needed no second invitation. After the show he went backstage and spent more than three hours chatting to the veteran actor in his dressing room. "There was something between us," recalled Hoffman later. "He was like family. He was treating me like I was his big brother." During their conversation, they recognized striking similarities in their backgrounds. "Neither of us had a nice childhood," recalled Hoffman. "Like we had come out of the same house." Even their career trajectory was remarkably similar: Eighteen years earlier, Hoffman had become an overnight star with *The Graduate*, just as Cruise had with *Top Gun.* After their late-night tête-à-tête, Hoffman went home and told his wife Lisa about the "weird connection" he felt with the younger man.

Filial rapport or no, Tom did not immediately spring to Hoffman's mind when he was discussing actors to play alongside him in his latest movie project. The film, called *Rain Man,* was the story of two brothers; Charlie Babbitt is a normal if avaricious salesman, while his elder brother, Raymond, is an autistic savant who has spent much of his life in an institution.

They meet properly for first time only after the death of their father, who has left his fortune to Raymond. This spurs Charlie into finding his long-lost brother, initially with the aim of fleecing him. During a road trip where, among other adventures, they use Raymond's astonishing memory to win at the gaming tables in Las Vegas, Charlie undergoes an epiphany, learning to love his elder handicapped brother—and himself.

Originally, Hoffman considered Jack Nicholson to play the fast-talking con man brother, and then Bill Murray. It was Michael Ovitz, president of Creative Artists, the biggest agency in Hollywood, who suggested Tom Cruise, not only because he was younger and had terrific box-office appeal, but because both Tom and Dustin were on his books. As in *The Color of Money,* this was a chance for Tom to work with a man he both respected and liked, as well as on a film with artistic integrity that would stretch him as an actor. His challenge was to get the audience to empathize with a character who comes across as a thoroughly unpleasant piece of work.

By September 1987, just four months after his marriage to Mimi, Tom was Dustin Hoffman's neighbor, moving into a beachfront house in Malibu next door to the legendary actor so that they, together with screenwriter Ron Bass and director Steven Spielberg, could work on *Rain Man.*

Both Hoffman and Cruise embraced the research with their customary immersion, Tom taking only a couple of days off in October to accompany his new wife to the premiere of *Someone to Watch Over Me,* which opened to mixed reviews. Then he rejoined Hoffman. In the course of their journey they consulted medical specialists in San Diego and on the East Coast, and hung out with dozens of people with autism, some with extraordinary gifts such as the ability to calculate math problems faster than a computer. The movie stars dined with them, laughed with them, took them bowling, and met their families. Eventually Hoffman was able to perfectly mimic the gestures and movements of a typical sufferer of autism—even down to not making eye contact.

Still, the very nature of the condition proved a considerable artistic stumbling block. The first three directors, used to the convention that called for a character to develop in the course of a movie, found the immutability of autistic people disconcerting. For a central figure to stay the same throughout—and not even make eye contact—was a problem. One director, Martin Brest, had cut and run over endless disagreements with the notoriously perfectionist Hoffman. Brest felt that it was wrong that it took fifteen minutes before Hoffman's character, Raymond Babbitt, first appeared on-screen. "My God, Tom's the biggest star in the world; he can hold a movie for two reels," retorted Hoffman. Next up was Steven Spielberg, who left the project to make a sequel to *Raiders of the Lost Ark,* giving all his notes to the final director, Barry Levinson, who had made *Tin Men* and *Good Morning, Vietnam.* Before he left, Spielberg told Levinson that the movie would make $100 million.

First, however, the movie had to get made. As Tom now realized, there is no such thing in Hollywood as an automatic green light, and for a long time it seemed that the project would get lost in the mire of development. So Tom flew to New York and did a major tour of the bars of Manhattan. He even took up bartending, learning how to mix the perfect martini under the watchful gaze of bartender John "JB" Bandy. In a few weeks he visited around thirty-four bars as he learned his new craft—with the promise of a $3 million payday for a maximum of three months' work at the end. Nice work if you can get it. His new life hanging out with barflies in Manhattan was part of his research for the Disney movie *Cocktail,* which he agreed to make while the production glitches for *Rain Man* were being ironed out.

In *Cocktail,* Tom played a former serviceman who comes to New York to make his fortune and ends up working in a bar with Australian Bryan Brown, where they fall out over a girl, played by Elisabeth Shue. Eventually their pursuit of easy money—and rich women—ends in tragedy, a fitting metaphor for the "greed is good" ethos of the 1980s. During filming on location in Jamaica and elsewhere, Cruise experienced the ugly side of celebrity, whispers circulating in the American tabloids that the recently married star was having an affair with Elisabeth Shue. In fact, the Harvard-educated Shue was wondering why she was involved in a film that was so "empty and superficial." Dismissing the rumored affair as one of the "silliest stories" about her, she later remarked, "If I'd known it was just going to be about these guys throwing drinks around, then I might have had some second thoughts."

While the film was, as Tom's agent Paula Wagner put it, "eviscerated" by the critics as a cocktail of emotional clichés, it demonstrated Tom's star quality nevertheless. Not only did he refuse to knock a penny off his $3 million fee, forcing economies among the production and cast, but, in spite of the critical drubbing, the movie cleaned up at the box office, becoming the seventh most popular film of 1988. "Congratulations, you are now able to open a movie," a delighted Jeffrey Katzenberg, the head of Disney studios, told him. It was the biggest opening in Disney history, taking in $11.8 million, proof that a big name could carry a bad movie. While Tom didn't quite appreciate it at the time, it was a defining moment in his Hollywood career.

In any event, Tom had little time to reflect on his career trajectory. No sooner had he forsaken his cocktail shaker than he was rehearsing for *Rain Man,* which finally started shooting in May 1988. It meant that Tom missed his first wedding anniversary and was on the road for his twenty-sixth birthday and the July opening of *Cocktail,* which, given the reviews, was perhaps just as well. It also meant that he was too focused on filming to get particularly agitated about tabloid stories suggesting that Mimi was finding it difficult to get pregnant. The fact that they were both working hard, often in different parts of the world, was discounted by the gossips. These emotional discomforts were a small price to pay for working alongside Dustin Hoffman. As with his initial collaboration with Paul Newman, he harbored doubts that his own ability would be able to match the older man's screen presence. He saw himself as the student, Hoffman the tutor. "I wasn't sure if I could play in that league. I was excited enough just to be there."

As on the shoot for *The Color of Money,* the chemistry between the two leading men and the coaxing creativity of director Barry Levinson ensured a happy if hardworking set. "I couldn't wait to get up in the morning and I didn't want to finish at the end of the day," recalled Tom, who started the day with a 4:30 A.M. workout. "He was like a machine in that sense," commented Hoffman. "There is a joy in achieving excellence. It's all about the work."

The work paid off handsomely, artistically and financially. *Rain Man* made more than $400 million at the box office and, in another first for Tom, he received a share of the final profits as well as a $5 million fee. It was compensation for the disappointment he felt at failing to receive an Oscar nomination. Members of the Academy of Motion Picture Arts and Sciences were apparently unmoved by his performance as the cocksure hotshot who by the end of the third act is a reformed egomaniac.

However, it pleased the audience and some reviewers, Roger Ebert describing him as a "genuine star and a genuine actor," though not everyone was impressed. Acerbic, influential film critic Pauline Kael described him as "patented": "His knowing that a camera is on him produces nothing but fraudulence." She was no kinder to his screen partner, dismissing Hoffman's efforts as "a one-note performance." Hoffman's note, however, struck a chord with Oscar voters, his quirky performance earning him the award for Best Actor. The film itself went on to win Oscars for Best Director, Best Original Screenplay, and Best Picture.

While hindsight gives the impression that Tom's acting career was a series of carefully considered stepping-stones, in reality much depended on chance and the clout of his agency, Creative Artists. For example, had it not been for the delays and uncertainty surrounding the production of *Rain Man,* he would not have had time to star in *Cocktail,* the movie that sealed his reputation as an actor whose name alone could carry a film. Nor would he have tackled his next film, *Born on the Fourth of July,* especially as this was a movie project that had been hanging around Hollywood for a decade. He might not have even looked at the script if he had not shared the same agent as the film's director, Oliver Stone, or if Tom Pollock, the head of Universal Pictures, had not agreed to provide $14 million in funding because he believed it was one of the "great unmade screenplays of the last decade."

At first sight, this true story of Ron Kovic, an innocent young patriot from Long Island who gets his spine shattered in combat during the Vietnam War and returns home to indifference and life in a wheelchair, was well past its sell-by date. Not only had Hollywood covered the conflict—Oliver Stone's own Vietnam movie *Platoon* had won the Best Picture award in 1987—but the world itself had moved on. With the Cold War thawing fast—the Berlin Wall fell in December 1989—the new generation of moviegoers remembered Vietnam simply as an event, like World War II, in American history.

Tom, however, was intrigued not only by a searing human story that challenged his acting abilities, but also by a curious sense of destiny about the movie. His own birthday was the day before July 4, but more significantly his acting hero Al Pacino had been slated for the starring role a decade earlier, before production was canceled because funding dried up. Even though he was researching his part in *Rain Man,* Tom agreed to meet Oliver Stone in a New York restaurant in January 1988. Not for the first time, Stone's passionate intensity was both mesmerizing and convincing to an actor. By the end of lunch, Tom was as committed to the part of Ron Kovic as Stone was to Tom. "I chose Tom because he was the closest to Ron Kovic in spirit," recalled Stone later. "They certainly had the same drive, the same hunger to achieve, to be the best, to prove something. Like Ron, too, Tom is wound real tight."

As a result, once *Rain Man* was green-lighted, Tom found himself researching and preparing for two demanding roles at the same time, to the point where he would meet Dustin Hoffman and Barry Levinson in the morning, and Stone and Ron Kovic in the afternoon. His schedule was so demanding that Paul Newman sent him a six-pack of beer with a note urging him to sit down, relax, and take a weekend off. No such luck. The pace was remorseless, and understandably, Stone, who had spent ten frustrating years trying to shepherd the story onto the screen, was nervous that it would prove too much for his leading man. He called Tom constantly for fear that he would pull out. "I will give you everything I have, trust me," an exasperated Tom finally told him.

Less sure was Ron Kovic. It may have been a challenging role for Tom and a "sacred mission" for director Oliver Stone, who had fought in Vietnam, but it was Ron Kovic's life. His initial skepticism about the choice of Cruise was blunted when Tom first visited his home in Los Angeles. After he pulled up to the house, Tom slowly eased himself out of his car and into a wheelchair—a clear sign that he was taking the enterprise very seriously. As they sat in his kitchen, Tom convinced Kovic that he was committed to portraying him in an understanding and sympathetic way. Kovic recalls looking at Cruise, who then represented the all-American screen action hero, and thinking: "He's about to go through this hell and he doesn't even know it." Ironically, it was the nature of Tom's public persona that made him so potent in the part—as Oliver Stone and Universal boss Tom Pollock immediately recognized. Pollock recalled: "The film's journey is more powerful when it is made by the maverick from *Top Gun*. It's not only Ron who goes through this wrenching story, it is Tom Cruise—our perception of Tom Cruise."

For the best part of a year, Tom put himself through mental and physical torture as he tried to convey the anger and agonies undergone by Kovic. Routinely described as intense and focused, for once Tom met his match in his director, who was utterly absorbed by the story. Twice Stone sent him to boot camp. "I didn't want his foxhole dug by his cousin," he said afterward. Stone was constantly encouraging his leading man to read more about Vietnam, to meet more veterans and visit more hospitals to truly understand the anguish and helplessness felt by these forgotten heroes.

At one point, in the madness that infects this kind of passionate, close-quarters project, Stone convinced Tom to allow himself to be injected with a chemical that would have rendered him paralyzed for two days so that he could more realistically convey the incontinent, impotent torture of a once-virile young man confined to a wheelchair. As there was a chance that he would have suffered permanent incapacitation, the insurance company wisely vetoed the madcap idea. It was reminiscent of the time Dustin Hoffman went without sleep for two days during the filming of *Marathon Man* so he could better express his exhaustion. His costar, British actor Laurence Olivier, laconically remarked, "Try acting . . . it's easier."

Even without drugs, researching life in a wheelchair showed him how the invisible half lived. It was exhausting, uncomfortable, and frustrating, leaving him weary at the end of the day. Tom went around stores and malls with Ron, watching how he coped with his disability. On one occasion they were asked to leave a store because their wheelchairs were damaging the rubber carpet. "I couldn't believe it," Cruise recalled. "There were nights when I went home and couldn't help but think that this could be me." He stayed in character for meetings with movie executives and journalists, who were nonplussed by the sight of the wild-eyed, wheelchair-bound figure confronting them. Even at home he remained focused on the character he now inhabited, at night his wife watching him slowly struggle into bed from his wheelchair. It probably didn't help his marriage when, in May 1989, the American tabloid the *Globe* insinuated that Tom's low sperm count was the reason why Mimi was not yet pregnant. It was a claim that haunted Tom long after he had left his wheelchair behind, the actor later successfully suing a German magazine for repeating the story.

The three-month shoot, which started in Dallas, with battle scenes filmed in the Philippines, was as raw as the research. Tom shaved his head, lost weight, and became so exhausted by the brutal twelve-hour days that there were times when he would just fall into Stone's arms. "I'm not saying it's the healthiest thing to do, but it was the right thing to do, and the only way to play that character," he later told director Cameron Crowe. It was, as Kovic predicted, a journey to hell and back as Tom tried to convey the horror of accidentally shooting a comrade in Vietnam as well as the rage he felt against his broken body, his unresponsive family, and an uncaring nation. This unrequited fury was finally channeled into Kovic's antiwar activism. Tom admitted that he was just "burnt out" by the intense process. "I have got absolutely nothing left," he recalled after the final battle scenes were shot on location in the Philippines.

It certainly won over Kovic. As filming came to a close in July 1989, he presented Tom with his own Bronze Star as a twenty-seventh birthday present. "He gave it to Tom for bravery," said Oliver Stone, "for having gone through this experience in hell as much as any person can without actually having been there."

It was no coincidence that as Tom was researching his role as Ron Kovic, one of his new, carefully handpicked Scientology companions was Vietnam veteran Pat Gualtieri. A sensitive, intelligent man, he had served with 5th Battalion 2nd Artillery north of Saigon and lived to tell the tale when he and his 180-strong unit were attacked by 10,000 North Vietnamese regulars at the opening of the Tet Offensive. When the Brooklyn-born draftee returned home in 1968, he found a nation ill at ease with itself, and headed to California looking for answers about the mystery of life. He tried numerous "isms" before settling on Scientology. Easygoing and popular, Pat was an ideal guide who, along with his superior, Inspector General Greg Wilhere, explained the language and thinking behind the faith to their star acquisition.

Slowly, carefully, and gently, Tom was eased into the world of Scientology. By the summer of 1989, senior Scientologists felt confident enough to invite Tom to their secret, secluded, and heavily guarded Gold Base, deep in the California desert. When he accepted, new leader David Miscavige gleefully announced to his closest staff, "The most important recruit ever is in the process of being secured. His arrival will change the face of Scientology forever."

CHAPTER 6

As anxious as a teenager on his first date, David Miscavige, the young leader of Scientology, impatiently paced around the immaculately arranged cabana as he waited for his guest on a Saturday night in the late summer of 1989. While no expense or effort had been spared to impress his visitor, by the agreed arrival time of eight o'clock there was still no sign of Tom Cruise. Watches were nervously checked, and as minutes turned into hours, cult minions made frantic phone calls. David Miscavige was not a man who liked to be kept waiting. But wait he did, becoming more and more furious as his carefully laid plans came to naught. By the time Tom, who had recently finished filming *Born on the Fourth of July*, arrived at the Gold Base Scientology fortress, it was long past eleven o'clock, and the actor, tired by the journey from Beverly Hills, went straight to bed.

He had missed a greeting as elaborate as it was incongruous. In the heart of the desert scrub, he was to have been taken to a swimming pool next to a $565,000 life-size replica of a three-masted schooner. In the tropically themed cabana, complete with parrots and other exotic birds, Miscavige and other senior Scientologists would have formed a welcoming committee. Doubtless, as he was being shown the nautical artifacts, he was to have been told about the history of the landlocked ship, the *Star of California*, which had been built on the express instructions of cult founder L. Ron Hubbard.

Even though he served with an utter lack of distinction in the U.S. Navy during World War II, Hubbard liked to think of himself as a military hero, dressing his most fanatical followers, known as the Sea Org, in the regalia and uniforms of a seafaring militia. This fraternal paramilitary organization was zealously dedicated to advancing their faith, signing "billion-year" contracts—pledging themselves to work for Scientology for the next billion years during future reincarnations—as a sign of their utter devotion. In their eyes they were fallen gods, immortal beings or "thetans," who had lived for millions of years and would be reincarnated for billions of years to come.

From their desert lair, a place that had once been so secret that new Sea Org recruits were brought there blindfolded so that they could not divulge the location to outsiders, they pursued their mission of world domination and the defeat of their enemies. As Hubbard once wrote, "All men shall be my slaves. All women shall succumb to my charms. All mankind shall grovel at my feet and not know why." In preparation for the day when they could put the words of the man known as "Source" into practice, they read *The Art of War* by the Chinese military strategist Sun Tzu and *On War* by the Prussian general Karl von Clausewitz. No one and nothing from the inferior "wog world"—the term for nonbelievers—could be allowed to get in their way. Certainly not in this existence. Indeed, the outside world was an unwelcome distraction. Believers were once banned from watching TV, listening to the radio, reading newspapers, making telephone calls, or receiving other communications from outsiders, including their families. Security staff even opened their Christmas presents to make sure they did not contain anything that would deflect them from the cause. (Nowadays newspapers are sold and TV played in the staff dining room.)

In its early years, most public Scientologists had never even heard of Gold Base, let alone visited the onetime holiday resort just outside Hemet, California. The organization deliberately disguised its true purpose, listing the five-hundred-acre compound in the local telephone directory as the "Scottish

Highlands Quietude Club." It was a sign of Tom Cruise's importance that he was invited to stay at this inner sanctum.

Significantly, the invitation was extended only to Tom, even though his wife had been a Scientologist for most of her life. The reason had less to do with the fact that they now seemed to be leading separate lives than with Mimi's own position inside the cult. When her father, Phil, left the faith during the cull of mission holders in the early 1980s, he was deemed an enemy, or, in Scientology-speak, a "suppressive person." Worse, he joined those, dubbed "squirrels" by Hubbard, who offered Scientology-style services at cut prices.

Anyone associated with Mimi's father was supposed to "disconnect"—sever all relations—with him if they wanted to stay inside Scientology. In short, Mimi was expected to choose between her father and the cult, a dilemma that has confronted thousands of Scientologists over the years, leading to hundreds of family breakups. "Tom was a big star, she was a nothing and tainted by association with her father," says a former Scientologist who helped plan that first visit. "David Miscavige wasn't bothered about Mimi. In any case, in his eyes, her father had done all these terrible things to Scientology."

To emphasize how little value the Scientology leadership placed on Mimi, her husband was accompanied by his assistant, Andrea Morse, daughter of actor Robert Morse. Tom paid for her to take numerous Scientology courses, Andrea in turn recruiting her mother, Carole, and sister Hilary to the faith. It was the beginning of a carefully considered strategy that would ultimately see the actor surrounded by Scientologists both at home and in his office, Odin Productions, which in time came to be operated on strict Scientology principles, where crispness, clarity, and military efficiency are the watchwords.

Both sides were keen that Tom's first visit to the base be discreet and secret. Scientology's inspector general, Greg Wilhere—effectively Miscavige's right-hand man—had been assigned to ferry the Hollywood actor from Los Angeles to the secret retreat. Smooth, urbane, and unflappable, Wilhere was Tom's "handler," the senior figure assigned to deflect any outside hostility toward Scientology and ensure that Tom remained enthusiastic about his new faith. He was the perfect choice to groom Cruise: friendly, sincere, and intelligent, even grudgingly admired by those who had become disaffected with Scientology.

Wilhere needed every ounce of his legendary charm to calm his furious leader. Though he was only five feet, five inches tall, Miscavige was known to have a giant temper, lashing out at subordinates whom he deemed to have crossed him. Wilhere managed to soothe him by explaining that Tom had been delayed for several hours because of movie business. Miscavige's frustration was perhaps understandable. At the time his organization was on the ropes, facing a massive IRS investigation into its tax affairs. Not only was the cult spending $1.5 million a month on legal fees, but thousands of ordinary Scientologists were being audited by the tax man. "Things were very grim in 1990, and I don't think a lot of Scientologists knew that," Miscavige later admitted. "We kept it to ourselves. It was terrible."

As far as the beleaguered Scientology leadership was concerned, Cruise was the cavalry riding to their rescue. It had taken years of careful planning to tease Tom through the gates of Gold. During his first years inside the cult, he was termed a "preclear," someone not deemed to be free of his problems and difficulties. (In fact, it was not until 1989 that Tom and his cousin William Mapother were listed in a Scientology magazine as completing "basic training.") While the process of auditing bore some similarities to the Catholic rite of Confession, it was neither free nor anonymous. Tom sat facing his auditor while holding an E meter, the crude lie detector that supposedly detected the truth or otherwise of responses. Under polite but relentless questioning, he was encouraged to reveal his most intimate secrets, every admission jotted down in a supposedly confidential folder stamped with his given name: Thomas Mapother. Following a pattern set by Hubbard himself, auditors would ask Tom, among other things, if he had ever raped someone, practiced homosexuality or cannibalism, been unfaithful, watched pornography, or killed or crippled animals for pleasure.

Although auditing was reportedly designed to clear problems, Hubbard's estranged son, Ronald De Wolf, who audited many early converts, took a more cynical view, seeing the process as a way of controlling and potentially blackmailing Scientologists, especially celebrities. In an interview with *Playboy* magazine, he observed: "Auditing would address a guy's entire sex life. It was an incredible preoccupation. . . . You have complete control of someone if you have every detail of his sex life and fantasy life on record. In Scientology the focus is on sex. Sex, sex, sex. The first thing we wanted to know about someone we were auditing was his sexual deviations. All you've got to do is find a person's kinks, whatever they might be. Their dreams and their fantasies. Then you can fit a ring through their noses and take them anywhere. You promise to fulfill their fantasies or you threaten to expose them . . . very simple." After the interview appeared, the then president of Scientology declined to respond to De Wolf's observations, noting that his credibility was "just out the bottom."

Nonetheless, although the preclear file was supposedly confidential, several auditors could have access to the folders and, it is claimed, senior staff members were known to discuss their contents. Former celebrity Scientologist Karen Pressley, who lived at Gold for years, was present one evening when John Travolta's auditor Chris Silcock openly discussed the actor's sexuality. "It made my head spin," she recalls, "and made me realize that the idea of confidentiality was a chimera." As another Scientology executive admitted bluntly, "These files come in handy if they want to blackmail you."

Ostensibly, Tom had been invited to Gold Base to make sure that his initial auditing, which took place at Sherman Oaks, had been performed correctly. While the questions can be sexually lurid, the auditing process itself is highly technical, Hubbard creating an entire language to describe the procedure. As well as monitoring his auditing progress, Gold

Base asked him to give their propaganda film studio, known as Golden Era Productions, the professional once-over.

Tom's first weekend stay was organized with the precision of a military operation, the planning akin to a visit by royalty. In the weeks before his arrival, the base was a hive of activity as the five hundred or so Sea Org disciples painted, pruned, primped, and cleaned the gardens and buildings so that it was in pristine condition for his arrival. Not that they were ever aware who the visitor was to be. While his assistant was assigned to staff quarters, Tom was housed in a plush guest bungalow with a Scientology chef and butler, Sinar Parman, who had once worked for L. Ron Hubbard, at his disposal around the clock.

To underline the importance of the visit, Sea Org members were ordered to stay indoors or, if that was impossible, to keep away from certain parts of the compound where Tom might be present. If they happened into his line of sight, they were instructed to avert their gaze and under no circumstances speak to him. Those who did come into contact were ordered to address him as "sir" rather than "Mr. Cruise." Disobedience would be punished. "The whole base was on eggshells," recalls one Sea Org member. The scene was set to impress and awe possibly the most important recruit in Scientology history.

During Tom's tour of the compound, it was evident that this was not a place for children. Like nuns and monks, Sea Org fanatics were not allowed to have children; if a woman got pregnant, she faced the heartbreaking choice between her beliefs and her unborn child. For the true believer, abortion was an article of faith. If the woman decided to have the child, she had to leave Sea Org and serve the sect in a lesser capacity. Former Sea Org follower Karen Pressley remembers that she was often approached by fellow Scientologists asking to borrow money to pay for an abortion so that they could stay in Sea Org. "I had a real problem because I don't believe in abortion," she recalls. Scientology officials reject as "simply false" the assertion that Sea Org women are encouraged, as a matter of policy, to have abortions.

As Tom viewed the film production areas, the editing bays, the music studio, and the film studio, known as the Castle, uniformed Sea Org operatives with walkie-talkies relayed his regal progress. In the film studio, handpicked Sea Org operatives rigorously rehearsed the "spontaneous" scenes they were scheduled to shoot. As far as Sea Org film workers were concerned, the tour had an unhappy outcome. Tom commented that when he made a Hollywood movie, he worked flat out until it was finished. At Gold, film technicians were given time off during filming for Scientology study. As a result of his offhand comment, schedules were changed and Sea Org film operatives were forced to work around the clock until films were completed. For the next two years, according to at least one former Sea Org member, the film unit never had a day off.

The difference, of course, was that Tom Cruise was paid millions of dollars, while Sea Org workers earned a mere thirty-five dollars a week. In fact, one Sea Org associate paid an even higher price. When she complained about the new edict, she was sent to Scientology "prison," known as the Rehabilitation Project Force. There, in a former ranch in Happy Valley, eleven miles away in the Soboba Indian reservation, inmates were guarded twenty-four hours a day and forced, among other demeaning punishments, to run around a pole under the blazing sun. While Scientology describes the RPF as a voluntary rehabilitation program offering a second chance for Sea Org members who have strayed from the sect's codes, those who refuse to accept their punishment are "declared," effectively thrown into the outer darkness. For a true believer it means either accepting their punishment—however unjust or arbitrary—or leaving behind friends and family, not to mention relinquishing the dream of eternal life.

People who have been through RPF say it is akin to brainwashing with hard labor. Critics accuse the sect of human rights abuses, comparing the Scientology punishment camps to Stalinist gulags. "One hardly has to point out that the RPF and RPF's RPF [a more extreme punishment regime] are brainwashing programs," notes Professor Stephen Kent of the University of Alberta. "Forced confessions, physical fatigue, and intense indoctrination combined with humiliation and fear are the hallmarks of these camps."

Tom, of course, did not realize that his offhand remarks would have such Draconian repercussions. After showing him around the studio, Miscavige took him on a tour of the estate, Tom riding pillion on his motorbike. Later, they went skeet shooting on a range set up behind Bonnie View, the mansion built by Scientologists for the anticipated return to Earth of the deceased L. Ron Hubbard after his galactic wanderings. Although he had appeared in several military movies, Tom was nervous around guns, and Miscavige, an enthusiastic member of the National Rifle Association, showed him the correct way to handle his weapon. Tom was so impressed that, as a thank-you present, he sent his new friend an automatic clay pigeon launcher to replace the manual pull contraption they used that weekend. Although Tom probably never realized it, his gift meant more work for hapless inmates of the sect's prison. More than two dozen of them worked day and night for three days installing the new launcher and then landscaping the shooting range for Tom's next visit.

As far as Tom was concerned, the visit was an enormous success—and it showed, Tom impressing those Scientologists he met with his energy and enthusiasm. "He was like a walking lightbulb," recalls Jesse Prince, former Scientology deputy inspector general. "He was so bright and enthusiastic, a playful kind of guy. It was like the kid with no friends who had suddenly found a load of people who were now his friends. During this time he was doing lower courses, so it was a honeymoon period. Great fun."

Not only did the visit reinforce Tom's new faith, it introduced him to the man who would have a profound influence on his future life. When David Miscavige finally shook hands with Tom Cruise, he had him at "Hello," the chemistry between the two immediate and apparent. From the start they were like brothers, constantly trying to outdo each other. As controlling, competitive, and macho as he was, Cruise had met his match—and more—in the Scientology leader. Their burgeoning friendship came as no surprise to those who had watched the rapid rise and rise of Miscavige. "It was easy to see why they got along so well," says a former Scientology executive who was present during that first weekend. "They are both driven, demanding, focused perfectionists—let's call it the Short Man Syndrome." Significantly, it was Miscavige, two years older if two inches shorter, who was the dominating force in their friendship, his ferocious will, aggressive ambition, and willingness to live on the edge proving more than a match for Cruise's own alpha male behavior. As Shelly Britt, who worked for the sect leader for fifteen years, recalls, "David would dominate Tom Cruise without him even knowing about it."

Much as Tom talked about his own hardscrabble beginnings, they paled when compared with that of the Scientology leader. Born in a Philadelphia suburb to a Polish father, Ron Miscavige, who earned his living playing trumpet, and an Italian mother, Loretta, he had a twin sister and another brother and sister. Short, slightly built, severely asthmatic, and extremely allergic, he was relentlessly bullied at school for his Polish heritage and his lack of height. Young David was so determined to play sports that on one occasion his father filled his pockets with two-pound metal plates so that he could meet the sixty-pound weight minimum and play as a defensive back for the Pennypacker Patriots football team.

If school was a daily ordeal, his home life wasn't much better; family and friends recalled that his father was an intimidating and ill-tempered man. When Ron discovered Scientology, it stopped his unpleasant behavior to the point where his confused wife felt that he didn't love her anymore because he had become a changed person. Ron's religious conversion was complete when David recovered from a severe asthma attack while undergoing Scientology counseling. "From that moment I knew this is it," David said later. "I have the answer."

By age twelve, David Miscavige was auditing other

Scientologists, becoming the 4,867th Scientologist to reach a state of "clear." He dropped out of high school on the day of his sixteenth birthday, citing the "appalling" drug use of his contemporaries as well as the realization that he wanted to dedicate his life to Scientology. David joined the Sea Org elite in Clearwater, Florida, where he worked as a "commodore's messenger," essentially a gofer for Hubbard. He is remembered from that time as charismatic but ferociously competitive and ambitious—"the jerk who wanted to impress."

Soon the keen and confident teenager was deployed to the secret base at Gold, where he worked alongside Hubbard and others making promotional movies. In 1979, while Tom Cruise was still in school, Miscavige was made "action chief" inside the Commodore's Messenger Organization, sending out teams, or "missions," to improve management at Scientology centers. It was a high-pressure, high-stress job at a time when the top echelon of Scientology, including Hubbard's wife, was in jail, and Hubbard himself was on the run.

As Tom was making his way in movies, Miscavige was asserting his authority inside the rapidly disintegrating sect. In 1981, after two heated confrontations, he forced Hubbard's wife, Mary Sue, to resign. Although he maintains that they are now friends, she has a different view. "He was a tyrant," she told her son-in-law, Guy White. That same year, when he was twenty-one, he married his first and only girlfriend, Shelly Barnett, who had been a commodore's messenger since she was twelve. A year later he oversaw the rout of mission holders, including Mimi's father, Phil Spickler, which led to a bitter schism, akin to the original theological divide between Protestants and Catholics. When his mother-in-law, Flo Barnett, joined a breakaway Scientology group, it caused a vicious family rift that never healed. She committed suicide in 1985, shooting herself three times with a rifle. David Miscavige has always stoutly denied any involvement whatsoever in her death.

During the institutional carnage, Hubbard put the rising young man in charge of his considerable fortune, Miscavige now managing his literary, personal, and business affairs. Most important, he became one of a handful of Scientologists who maintained lines of communication with the fugitive leader, who was hiding at a ranch in California. Fellow Scientologists knew not to ask questions when a black van with darkened windows arrived at the Gold Base in the dead of night and Miscavige, armed with an Uzi submachine gun, loaded paperwork and boxes of cash for the leader. Then he and Scientology executive Pat Broeker, who lived with Hubbard, drove off into the inky blackness, taking circuitous routes in case they were being followed by the FBI or other government agencies. On one occasion they snapped under the strain, heading to Las Vegas and spending a couple of nights gambling. They later explained that they had gone into hiding for fear of being followed. The stress was palpable, Miscavige having a morbid fear of ending up in jail and being sexually abused, possibly raped, by fellow inmates.

Miscavige's dread of jail was matched only by his bewildered attempts to placate the manic demands of Hubbard. Living under this kind of tension brought on terrible asthma attacks. Onetime colleague Jesse Prince, who audited Miscavige, recalls cradling the distraught young man in his arms. "Sometimes he would get so upset that his eyes were bulging and he couldn't breathe," Prince said. "He wouldn't take medication or inhalers, so I would have to calm him down and then he would sleep for days after an attack."

Aides claimed that Miscavige kept an oxygen cylinder under his bed in his quarters at Gold to help him cope in case of emergency. Far from curing him, it seemed that Scientology, or rather L. Ron Hubbard, was exacerbating Miscavige's medical condition. That and smoking three packs of Camel cigarettes a day.

The continual pandering to the insane whims of Hubbard—for example, any whiff of perfume, particularly rose, drove him into a towering rage—profoundly affected Miscavige. There were times when Jesse Prince, who introduced him to the music of Jimi Hendrix, took him to a bar to help drown his sorrows. "Dealing closely with LRH was a traumatic experience," he recalls. "It changed Miscavige from a likable human being, a sports fan, into the monster he has become. We used to clown and trick each other. He loved to make people laugh, but now it is unimaginable that that was his personality." The feelings are now mutual, with Scientology dismissing Prince as a "criminal" after he left the organization.

Once he grabbed power after Hubbard's death in 1986, the twenty-six-year-old Miscavige was in charge of a billion-dollar operation where his word was law and his rule absolute, the young man king of all he surveyed. He lived like one, too, enjoying an "utterly" luxurious lifestyle. While his disciples were paid $35 a week, Miscavige was impeccably dressed in $250 handmade Egyptian cotton shirts with his own emblem, custom-made leather shoes, and the finest Italian wool suits. Neiman Marcus and Hermès in Beverly Hills were regular haunts for him and his wife, Shelly.

On one occasion she bought him a ten-thousand-dollar suit from the South Korean tailor Mr. Lim on Wilshire Boulevard in Beverly Hills—the equivalent to six years' pay for Sea Org disciples. In contrast to his followers' shared, spartan quarters, the sect leader had a number of lavishly decorated apartments around the country that were carefully and expensively refurbished in the style of a gentlemen's club. He enjoyed the services of butlers and maids whose tasks included walking his dogs, Chelsea and Cheslea.

Just as he lived like a king, Miscavige ruled like an absolute monarch. His watchwords were loyalty and control, the new leader followed everywhere by an entourage who slavishly tape-recorded his every utterance, translating his words into a stream of orders, directives, and commands. To ensure that his decrees were carried out to the letter, he created his own Praetorian guard, recruited exclusively from the Religious Technology Center within the Sea Org, whom he dubbed his "SEALs," after the highly trained navy SEALs who have a formidable reputation for performing the impossible. They were given better uniforms, housing, and food— but at a price.

Those "SEALs" were expected to focus night and day on Miscavige's cause—to the exclusion of all else in their lives.

He loved Hollywood movies where the leader, usually an American President, enjoyed the absolute loyalty of his staff, especially when he was surrounded by a phalanx of bodyguards. Miscavige was routinely accompanied by six bodyguards, even when he was on vacation on board private yachts. If he went swimming, three would dive in with him.

Miscavige controlled every aspect of policy: From film sound to building design, nothing escaped his focus on perfection. The diminutive leader was most particular about the surroundings for his speeches, ensuring that the backdrop was blue to match his eyes and the dais was in proportion to his stature. Former Scientologist Karen Pressley worked closely with Miscavige on numerous design projects and watched as he even chose fabrics for new Sea Org uniforms. She recalls: "Men who are obsessed with fabrics tend to be feminine in nature. I can tell you right now there is nothing gay about this guy. He was controlling, dominating, and obsessive. You felt like you were living under a dictatorship."

While he liked to model his behavior on his political hero, Simón Bolívar, the South American independence leader, Miscavige ruled by fear, gaining a reputation for verbally demeaning subordinates and even hitting them, publicly slapping—never punching—those whom he felt had offended him. Some he spat on, a sign of contempt and disdain initially encouraged by Hubbard. In sworn declarations in several lawsuits, he has been accused of striking subordinates. (When asked about such claims, a representative of Scientology denied them.) Guy White, Hubbard's son-in-law, came in for this treatment one evening, when Miscavige and others accused him of committing "crimes." Miscavige ripped the lanyards from his uniform, spat on him, and slapped his face. After what Scientology charmingly calls a "gang bang" audit, where he faced hostile, quick-fire questioning from his accusers, he was consigned to the sect's prison gulag, the Rehabilitation Project Force.

Any hint of criticism of the leader, known as Black PR, was deemed a crime. Miscavige scrutinized even the facial expressions of Sea Org followers, who would be punished for looking hostile or bored. In his book *1984,* about mind control in a future society, George Orwell had a term for that offense—"facecrime." That, however, was a work of fiction.

Understandably, many lived in fear of the man they dubbed Napoleon—even his own family. Karen Pressley, who lived in the same quarters as Miscavige's parents, recalls, "One day his father looked me in the eye and said, 'I'm afraid of my own son.' It freaked me out. He was scared of him because he was so powerful and controlling." Others are more measured, appreciating Miscavige's energy, focus, and charisma while acknowledging his inappropriate aggression. His assistant Shelly Britt saw him as a Jekyll and Hyde character, the nicest or the meanest boss in the world. "If you are on his good side you are on top of the world, on his bad side you couldn't get much lower." Another close aide, Marty Rathbun, averred that in all the years he had known Miscavige he had never been aware that he had hit anyone. "That's not his temperament," he told the *St. Petersburg Times.*

For Tom Cruise, the first meeting with Miscavige in August 1989 was the beginning of an enduring friendship, the Scientology leader becoming a boon companion and adviser, continually challenging, controlling, and competing with the Hollywood star.

If Tom had made a lifelong friend thanks to his faith, his next film was about to change his life. For the previous three years Tom had nursed this movie baby, wanting to make a film about stock-car racing. High on adrenaline and the thrill of speed after doing laps at 190 miles an hour around the famous Daytona International Speedway, he yelled, "I'm going to make a movie about this." Once Paul Newman had introduced him to the sport during the filming of *The Color of Money,* Tom had taken it up with his customary enthusiasm. He raced Nissans for Newman's team, his expertise such that, as far as racing driver Bob Bondurant was concerned, he had the ability to turn pro.

Based on his experience, the actor wrote a crude outline of a story and hired veteran screenwriter Douglas Day Stewart to polish the plot of what became *Days of Thunder.* It centered on a cocky driver, Cole Trickle, played by Tom, who tries to outgun a rival, the two men ending up badly injured in the hospital. Inevitably, Trickle falls for the glamorous brain surgeon who helps heal him, and ultimately learns humility, conquering his demons sufficiently to go on and win the big race.

Known in early discussions as *Top Car,* the hope was to do for NASCAR racing what *Top Gun* had done for the navy flying school in San Diego. Once the project was officially in development, Cruise brought in *Top Gun* scriptwriter Warren Skaaren, who, after writing several drafts, quit in exasperation at Cruise's demands. Undeterred, Tom wooed writer Robert Towne by taking him to the racetrack at Watkins Glen, New York. As they soaked up the atmosphere, Towne told the actor: "I get it, Cruise. This is fantastic." With director Tony Scott and producers Don Simpson and Jerry Bruckheimer on board, the scene was set to make another summer blockbuster.

It wasn't quite so simple. While Paramount gave the green light for filming to start in November 1989, they didn't have a completed script, an agreed title, a leading lady, or even a character that a leading lady could play. In October, when Cruise was invited to a private screening of the Australian thriller *Dead Calm,* which had been making waves for the performances of Billy Zane and Nicole Kidman, he went with a particular sense of urgency. Watching the film with scriptwriter Robert Towne, Tom was as entranced by Nicole's on-screen authority as by her long, elegant legs and translucent skin. He left the screening suitably impressed, instructing minions to bring her to Los Angeles for a screen test.

That she was in Japan promoting *Dead Calm* was no obstacle. Nicole was flown to Hollywood to meet Cruise, the producers, and the director, arriving at the Paramount studios jet-lagged and professionally curious, but not expecting much. "I thought, 'Oh yeah, right,'" she said later. "I'd been to America before. You go in, you audition, you don't get the job." As insurance, she decided to use the trip as an excuse to visit friends and see her sister, Antonia, in England.

When she walked into the conference room to meet Tom and his colleagues, however, the chemistry between them was unmistakable. "The moment I laid eyes on him, I thought he was just the sexiest man I had ever seen in my life," she later told *Rolling Stone*. "He took my breath away. I don't know what it was. Chemical reaction? Hard to define. Hard to resist."

At the time, the girl who was nicknamed "Stalky" by her school friends thought she was unlikely to win a part where, at five feet, eleven inches, she was four inches taller than the leading man. She read a couple of pages of script, though not from the movie in question, and left, ready to enjoy herself in California. So she was surprised when producer Jerry Bruckheimer called the next day to tell her they wanted her to play Tom's love interest. There was a caveat: Her character, like much of the film, had yet to be fully conceived. In the end, the twenty-two-year-old rather improbably played a brilliant brain surgeon, Dr. Claire Lewicki.

What was not in doubt was the attraction the leading man felt toward his new leading lady. "My first reaction to meeting Nic was pure lust," he later recalled. "It was totally physical." At first sight, it was a curious coupling, the tall, ginger-haired, willowy Australian so different from his voluptuous dark-haired wife. While physically different, however, both women had reputations as being aloof, ambitious, and coolly unattainable—perfect foils for a man who liked the challenge of an endless romantic chase.

Tom was soon smitten, the couple sharing a sense of humor as well as the thrill of living on the edge. As with David Miscavige, the Hollywood star seemed to have met his match in the slim shape of a young woman who cited strong, determined actresses like Vanessa Redgrave, Jane Fonda, and Katharine Hepburn as her inspiration. Nicole also sensed his unhappiness, his need for a closer connection than his current relationship. A few weeks later, in late November, scriptwriter Robert Towne had dinner with the couple at Toscana in Brentwood. He immediately recognized their rapport and realized that Tom's two-year marriage to Mimi was surely over.

Certainly Tom was true to form, disposing of his first

marriage with the matter-of-fact alacrity with which he had ended previous love affairs. In the late fall he moved out of their home in Brentwood and went to stay with his friend— and best man—Emilio Estevez for a few days. Then he and Mimi went to the Scientology base in Hemet for what the sect calls "chaplain counseling." Ostensibly, this was to discuss and attempt to resolve their differences by discussing them with a Scientology counselor. Once everything is out in the open, Scientologists argue, there is no reason to split up. In some circumstances this procedure is successful, but in this instance there was a hidden agenda. The Scientology leadership felt such hostility toward Mimi's father that Mimi was stained by association. "They no longer wanted her on the team," says a former Scientologist who was involved in the charade. "The impetus was to help Tom Cruise, and within twenty-four hours they had agreed to split up."

The Hollywood actor was even given the services of a senior Scientology trustee, Lyman Spurlock, director of client affairs, to help sort out the intricate financial fallout. "He was lost, he didn't know what his rights were or understand what Mimi should get," recalls former senior Scientologist Jesse Prince. "They made it as painless as possible for him." Mimi's final settlement was a reported $10 million—with a clause enforcing confidentiality on both sides. Word was that Mimi made it clear that if the Scientology leadership used its black propaganda to try to discredit her, she would open her own Pandora's box of secrets about the cult.

While Tom was dealing with his domestic matters in a typically businesslike manner, Nicole was saying her farewells to her family in Sydney, Australia. She did not, however, say a final good-bye to her longtime boyfriend, fellow actor Marcus Graham, the former star of Australia's top soap *E Street*. Although he was one of the first she told about her new part, she gave no hint of a flirtation with her new leading man. In fact, when she landed in Los Angeles, she called him with the news that legendary New York agent Sam Cohen, whose clients included Woody Allen and Meryl Streep, had flown out west to sign her to a contract. Although he was in something of a career slump, Graham had no reason to believe that their romance—they were living together before she left for America—was over. They planned a holiday in the Pacific, and while she was filming *Days of Thunder,* he racked up over thirteen hundred dollars in phone bills chatting to his erstwhile lover.

It was a forlorn waste. Within days of starting her new life in America, Nicole was spending every moment, both professionally and romantically, with Tom. She was smitten. "I was consumed by it, willingly," she said later. At the end of November the couple was not only filming together in Charlotte, North Carolina, but quietly flying to the Scientology Gold Base, arriving by helicopter in the compound. They had their own VIP bungalow in a remote part of the five-hundred-acre compound, with Sea Org disciples under strict orders to stay away from the area, as well as the services of Sinar Parman as butler and chef. When the couple did emerge, they spent time with David Miscavige, his wife, Shelly, and Tom's handler, Greg Wilhere.

Whatever they did, Wilhere was either with them or watching over them, making sure everything was perfect. "It was clear that they were very much in love, very tactile and all over each other," recalls one former Scientologist who was privy to what was then a closely guarded secret. "Within a matter of days of Tom splitting with Mimi, he and Nicole were coming to Gold. Senior Scientologists helped facilitate this." In fact, Greg Wilhere played such a pivotal role in smoothing the path of romance that Tom named a character in *Days of Thunder* after him. When the name of a "Dr. Wilhere" is mentioned, it was an in-joke between the lovebirds and their Scientology friends.

On December 9, 1989, with filming for *Days of Thunder* in full swing, Tom's lawyers quietly filed a suit for his legal separation from Mimi, the actor citing "irreconcilable differences." Yet Tom continued to play the happily married husband in a series of interviews to promote *Born on the Fourth of July,* released just before Christmas. As high-performance cars burned rubber and fuel around North Carolina's Charlotte

Motor Speedway, Cruise spoke affectionately about his wife to selected journalists. "The most important thing for me is I want Mimi to be happy," writer Richard Corliss quoted him as saying during a flattering *Time* magazine cover profile entitled "Tom Terrific": "I'm just happier now than I've ever been in my life," Tom said, Corliss noting how he and Mimi had visited the Brazilian rain forest as part of their work on the board of Earth Communications Office, an entertainment-industry organization, subsequently infiltrated by Scientologists, that promotes environmental causes.

During another chat with writer Trip Gabriel for *Rolling Stone,* which, because of Tom's friendship with owner Jann Wenner, was effectively his house journal, he stonewalled questions about rumors of marital troubles. As for *Us* magazine, he told them: "I just really enjoy our marriage." It helped cement the fiction of marital bliss when Mimi visited the *Days of Thunder* set during his publicity jag.

Looking back, Richard Corliss sees Cruise's dissembling as part of his character and par for the course in Hollywood. "His marriage to Mimi Rogers was a fiction he wanted to maintain—at least until the magazine profiles attending the release of *Born on the Fourth of July* were published. I wasn't astonished by his insistence that he was sticking with Mimi when he had decided he wasn't. That dodge is a movie star tradition as old as Hollywood."

Tom's faith not only helped ease his separation from Mimi Rogers, it also helped him keep a straight face as he related his story of domestic harmony. The art of controlling the media forms an integral part of Scientology practice, and one of the entry-level courses, on communications, teaches effective techniques for "outflowing false data." Cruise proved himself a nimble and able student, receiving favorable coverage in December for his on- and off-screen personae and winning a Best Actor Oscar nomination for his role in *Born on the Fourth of July.* "Tom Cruise's portrayal of Ron Kovic is proof positive that he is one of the most versatile actors working in Hollywood today," wrote movie critic Edward Gross.

As the flattering profiles of Tom hit the newsstands, his divorce lawyer flew out from Los Angeles to Daytona Beach, Florida, where filming was now taking place, on January 12 so that the actor could sign his divorce papers. A day earlier, Tom had quietly met with Mimi at the Charlotte Hilton University Place Hotel. Some observers believe it was a last-ditch attempt by the actress to save her marriage. More realistically, it was to finalize their official statement and outstanding financial matters. In fact, in keeping with the speed of the split, the divorce papers were filed four days later, the couple releasing a brief statement the next day. "While there have been positive aspects to our marriage, there were some issues which could not be resolved even after working on them for a period of time."

In an interview in *Playboy* three years later, Ms. Rogers mischievously elaborated on those mysterious "issues." Scorned for a younger woman, Mimi got her revenge by kicking her former husband, whom *People* magazine had named the "sexiest man on earth," in the *cojones*. "Tom was seriously thinking of becoming a monk," she told interviewer Michael Angeli. "At least for that period of time, it looked as though marriage wouldn't fit into his overall spiritual need. And he thought he had to be celibate to maintain the purity of his instrument. Therefore it became obvious that we had to split." As for her own instrument: "Oh, my instrument needed tuning," she said. While her comments would help float a flotilla of sexual gossip about her former husband, she admitted afterward that she was just having fun with the clearly besotted interviewer.

Perhaps more accurately, their fiercely demanding work schedules, Tom's stated desire to start a family, the influence of his new faith—and, of course, the sexual chemistry between Tom and a younger woman—all contributed to the breakdown of their brief union. Tom later told *Talk* magazine, "Before Nicole I was dissatisfied, wanting something more. It was just two people who weren't meant to work and it wasn't what I wanted for my life. I think you just go on different paths. But it wasn't Mimi's fault . . . it's just the way it is."

He spent little time reflecting on what had gone wrong with his first marriage, instead, as was his romantic pattern, racing headlong into a new relationship. Ironically, he was behaving in much the same way as his father, who, weeks after his divorce, had married Joan Lebendiger following a whirlwind courtship. Tom, at least, was more discreet. Just five days after formally announcing his divorce, he faced banks of photographers when he accepted a Golden Globe for Best Actor for his performance in *Born on the Fourth of July*. He did have a woman by his side as he walked down the red carpet—but it was his mother, Mary Lee. Otherwise, he was spending all his free time with the new woman in his life, his rented white BMW and Harley-Davidson motorcycle spotted outside the rented Daytona Beach bungalow of his Australian costar when the production moved to Florida. The love match between Nicole and Tom was not the only subject of crew chatter on the set of *Days of Thunder.* Actress Donna Wilson dated producer Don Simpson during the early weeks of filming, then ditched him for director Tony Scott, whom she subsequently married.

Shortly after Tom's divorce was finalized on February 4, 1990, Nicole told her mother, Janelle, who had taken leave from her job as a nursing instructor to visit her daughter and give Tom the once-over, that when work on *Days of Thunder* was completed, she planned to move into Tom's newly purchased $4 million home at Pacific Palisades in California. By all accounts her mother was not surprised, her daughter having pursued previous love affairs with hotheaded abandon.

Like Tom, Nicole had Irish blood coursing through her veins, the Kidman family having immigrated to Australia from Ireland as free settlers in 1839. Born in 1967 in Honolulu, Hawaii, to Australian parents, Nicole was raised a Catholic, attending Mass every week. Yet she was willful and strong-minded, dropping out of school at the age of sixteen to pursue an acting career. "I was a nightmare to my parents," she later told *Movieline* magazine. Rebellious and impetuous, the unconventional seventeen-year-old flew to Amsterdam with her thirty-seven-year-old boyfriend for a vacation. When that relationship foundered, she lived on and off for three years with another older man, fellow actor Tom Burlinson, leaving him after turning down his offer of marriage.

The next man in her life, actor Marcus Graham, never really had a chance once the world's sexiest man arrived on the scene. While Graham pined for her in Sydney, Tom was wooing Nicole, sending her love notes and flowers, usually red roses, almost daily. Marcus realized what was going on only when he watched Nicole walk along the red carpet with Tom—and Nic's mother, Janelle, and Mary Lee—at the Academy Awards in Hollywood in March 1990. It was their first public appearance as a couple, Tom missing out for the Best Actor award to Daniel Day-Lewis for his performance in *My Left Foot*. Tom was gracious in defeat. "It was exciting, just getting nominated. That acknowledgment from my peers."

The evening was glamorous relief from the expensive growing pains associated with his latest movie baby. Bad weather, an unfinished script, technical problems, and a ballooning budget—escalating from $40 to $70 million, including a handsome $7 million fee for Cruise—made *Days of Thunder* a seat-of-the-pants production. Working with an incomplete script meant that Cruise and other actors were being fed new pages of dialogue every day, the leading man reading lines off the dashboard of his 180-mile-per-hour stock car. Disaster was not long in coming: After Tom was involved in a high-speed crash as he squinted at his script, writer Robert Towne dictated dialogue to him through his headset.

Yet the financial tempests threatening to overwhelm *Days of Thunder* did little to dampen the party atmosphere on set. According to Don Simpson's biographer Charles Fleming, there was a steady stream of hookers and drugs to keep everyone happy. Girls who came to parties were regularly rewarded with Donna Karan dresses, which producer Don Simpson kept in his hotel suite. During the day Simpson sent out his two assistants to local beaches, asking girls if they wanted to go to a bash for Tom Cruise. On one occasion a local club, the Palace, was closed for a crew party where rapper Tone

Loc performed. The booze and cocaine, according to Fleming, were in plentiful supply.

If the day-to-day filming wasn't hair-raising enough, during his time in Florida, Tom quietly embarked on a new risky business: skydiving. He made dozens of jumps under the supervision of local expert Bob Hallett, who pronounced him "a natural." Nicole was delighted to accept his invitation to join him, realizing a childhood ambition that had been thwarted by her concerned parents. Here was further confirmation, if any was needed, that Nicole was a partner after Tom's own heart, a woman with a "ferocious" work ethic on set and a fearless daredevil when off duty. After she leapt from the plane, an instructor by her side, her boyfriend swooped in and planted a kiss on her mouth, and then flew away and pulled his ripcord. "Not as good as sex—but almost" was her exhilarated response to the experience. That Easter he performed the same maneuver when he took his mother, Mary Lee, for her first jump.

He was there, too, when his friend David Miscavige, accompanied by an instructor, went skydiving during a visit to the film set. The Scientology leader was so excited by his adventure that, when he returned to Gold Base, he proudly showed a video of himself jumping with Cruise. Not everyone inside Scientology was impressed with their leader's seeming obsession with the Hollywood actor. His father, Ron, was "very upset" when he went skydiving, fearing that he could have an accident. "As head of Scientology he felt that he had a responsibility to his parishioners," recalls Karen Pressley. "But David loves to live on the edge, he enjoys thrills and danger."

Whatever his father's misgivings, the off-screen escapades continued, the two friends racing cars against each other, running red lights, and, according to a former Scientologist, on one occasion narrowly missing a high-speed collision. "They were two guys trying to impress and compete with one another," says an ex-Scientologist who watched them together. But their friendship went beyond macho postures, with Tom endlessly calling his friend for advice and counsel.

During the filming of *Days of Thunder,* for example, he was reading the script for the movie *Edward Scissorhands,* a typically gothic Tim Burton film about a sensitive but misunderstood loner. Unsure about whether to accept the role, he asked Miscavige and others for their opinion. The Scientology leader felt he should reject the part as "too effeminate." Tom did say no, arguing that he wanted a happy ending for the movie rather than the bleak one that Burton intended. Instead, Johnny Depp took the role, going on to carve a niche playing quirky outsiders.

While Miscavige might not have had any training judging scripts, he did have expertise in the technical side of moviemaking, closely monitoring the faith's propaganda films for picture and sound quality. Not only did he have an expensive, state-of-the-art sound system in his apartment to check the sound quality of Golden Era products, Scientology engineers had also developed an in-house system called Clearsound. As a budding film star, Tom had been concerned about his weight. Now that he was an established Hollywood heartthrob, he fretted that his voice was just a tad too high-pitched. He discussed his concerns with his Scientology mentor before filming started on *Days of Thunder*. Miscavige suggested that he listen to the difference a Clearsound system might make.

Although the system was not used for *Days of Thunder,* writer Rod Lurie later claimed that Miscavige lobbied producer Don Simpson about it during his visit to the movie set. Simpson, a onetime Scientologist who accused the organization of being "a con" after spending more than $25,000 on counseling, apparently told Miscavige to "fuck off" when he broached the subject and had him removed from the set. The cult leader subsequently denied any such altercation, although he did confirm that he had earlier discussed sound systems with Tom. The issue of using the Scientology sound system would resurface on future Tom Cruise projects.

With or without Clearsound, *Days of Thunder*—and its leading man—was given a tempestuous reception from the critics when it was released at the end of June 1989. "He is

Cute and he's Great at Something," wrote David Denby in *New York* magazine. "But he's also Cocky and he Shows Off. He is Reckless, Callow, Stupid. He is Out for Himself and he Goes Too Far. He must Mature. . . . There is a Crisis. He is Alone, Confused. Crestfallen. He seeks a Father Figure." What was dubbed a "minor film with major pretensions" by *Boxoffice* struggled to break even. At the final reckoning, Tom's first venture in orchestrating a big-budget film squeaked into the black, making just $89 million in ticket sales against costs of more than $70 million.

After years of back-to-back filming, Tom needed a break, he and Nicole spending a couple of weeks scuba diving in the Bahamas when the movie wrapped. That summer the couple organized their new home in Pacific Palisades while undertaking intensive Scientology courses at their own VIP bungalow on the Gold compound. It was not all study, the couple enjoying the freedom to be themselves away from prying eyes and long lenses. For her birthday in June, for example, a flatbed truck arrived at the base carrying a brand-new Mercedes as a gift from Tom. "They were like teenagers running round the base having fun," recalls one ex-member.

While Tom was now taking advanced Academy-level Scientology courses, Nicole was gently being introduced to Hubbard's writings and basic Scientology tenets. Ironically, she shared one common denominator with Tom's former wife—a troublesome father. Just as Mimi Rogers was seen as a Potential Trouble Source because of the cult's animosity toward Phil Spickler, so technically Nicole had to be treated with grave suspicion. Not only was she a practicing Catholic, but her father, Dr. Antony Kidman, was a clinical psychologist. By definition, he was deemed an enemy of Scientology, a member of a profession responsible for all the ills on Earth, including the Holocaust in Germany and Stalin's purges in Russia.

The destruction of Dr. Kidman's profession was Scientology's stated aim. For Nicole to be truly adopted and accepted by the sect, she should "disconnect" from her father—that is, never communicate with him again. It posed a genuine problem for the Scientology hierarchy. As Jesse Prince recalls, "It definitely counted against Nicole, having a psychologist as a father. She was always considered a Potential Trouble Source inside Scientology. But the leadership figured they could handle it. It was a balancing act. They had Tom in their pocket, so they thought they would worry about Nicole later."

Not for the first time, it seemed that celebrity Scientologists lived by different rules than regular members, following Scientology Lite rather than the hard-core faith. And Tom Cruise was a law unto himself. As far as the Scientology leadership was concerned, nothing was too much trouble to keep him happy. So when the secrecy surrounding Tom's membership in Scientology was exposed that summer in an article written by Janet Charlton in the *Star* tabloid in July 1990, the cult leadership went into overdrive, both to soothe the irritation of their most prized member and to find the source of the story. They used the notorious private investigator Eugene Ingrams, a former Los Angeles cop who was fired for misconduct after allegedly running a brothel, to find the culprit.

During his four-month investigation, journalist Charlton was harassed and people impersonated her, trying to get copies of her phone bill. Eventually, after a series of subterfuges, Nan Herst Bowers—longtime Scientologist, sometime Hollywood publicist, and friend of Janet Charlton—was fingered as the perpetrator. When she faced a Scientology court, she pled not guilty to eight media-related charges, including "engaging in malicious rumor mongering" and "giving anti-Scientology data to the press." She was found guilty and formally listed as a "Suppressive Person Declare," the equivalent to being excommunicated.

The ruling meant that she was not allowed to have any further contact with anyone inside Scientology, including her ex-husband, her three sons, Brad, Todd, and Ryan, and her grandchild. Her family subsequently sent her letters of "Disconnect," which confirmed their refusal to have any contact with her. Within a week, Nan had gone from being a happily married mother and grandmother to being entirely cut off from her friends and family. Sixteen years have passed since the trial, and she has only occasionally seen her three sons and her six grandchildren since. "I was made a scapegoat for the story after Tom Cruise complained. As far as I am concerned, Scientology broke up my family," she says. "They kept my sons and their children from me. We were a nice close-knit Jewish family before this. I have not been able to lead a full life as a mother and grandmother because of this incident."

In August 1990, a month after the investigation was launched to find who had outed Tom, hundreds of Sea Org disciples faced the wrath of their leader after the actor's VIP bungalow at Gold Base was badly damaged in a mudslide caused by heavy rains. It was an act of God, but as Scientologists don't believe in God, David Miscavige blamed the Sea Org for not having proper flood procedures in place. He placed hundreds of Sea Org disciples in a severe ethics condition of "Confusion" as punishment, with gangs of Scientologists working around the clock to repair the damage. "Quite a few people left as a result because they thought he was crazy," recalls Shelly Britt.

At the time, Tom was probably unaware of the severe punishment meted out to fellow Scientologists, just as Nicole would not have been enlightened about Scientology's unbending hostility toward men like her father. As Sea Org disciples worked day and night to restore Tom and Nicole's luxury quarters to its previous pristine condition, the couple flew by private jet to Sydney to meet her father and other family members. Vainly, Nicole tried to dampen the inevitable speculation about wedding bells. "All that talk about us being engaged is just nonsense," she told one Australian magazine. "I'd like to get married one day but I think it would be very foolish to do so at this stage of my life."

A month later they announced their betrothal, Tom buying her a diamond engagement ring costing a reported $260,000. His proposal was in keeping with the way he had wooed the Australian actress, Tom leaving a note on the pillow in her bedroom that said: "My darling Nicole, I chased you and chased you until you finally caught me. Now will you marry me?"

Almost immediately Tom's assistant Andrea Morse and sister Lee Anne DeVette were dispatched to locate a suitable wedding location, eventually finding and renting a $2 million, six-bedroom timber house with spectacular views over the Rockies in the town of Telluride, a former Colorado mining town turned winter playground for the stars. On Christmas Eve 1990, with the house filled with flowers, including a willow arbor laced with white lilies and red roses, Nicole, wearing a 1930s antique brocaded gown she bought in Amsterdam, joined Tom for a simple Scientology wedding service. His auditor, Ray Mithoff, officiated; Nicole's sister, Antonia, was maid of honor; Dustin Hoffman was best man; and guests included David and Shelly Miscavige, Gelda Mithoff, Greg Wilhere, and Nicole's friend, actress Deborra-Lee Furness. The event was choreographed and orchestrated by Miscavige, who arranged for two Scientology chefs and other Sea Org disciples to cater and care for the newlyweds and their guests. While the wedding planning had been cloak-and-dagger, Tom and Nicole were keen to let the world into their little secret, the actress calling a radio station in Sydney two days after her wedding to say that she was now married and "blissfully happy."

A few weeks later, the imperious über-agent Mike Ovitz, head of Creative Artists Agency, and Tom's agent, Paula Wagner, hosted a celebration dinner in honor of Tom and Nicole. Alongside the movers and shakers of Hollywood at the DC3 restaurant in Santa Monica were the upper echelons of Scientology. Here was Mike Ovitz, then the most powerful man in Hollywood, rubbing shoulders with the most powerful man in Scientology, David Miscavige. Sandwiched between this collision of entertainment and religion sat Tom Cruise. It was a symbol of sorts.

CHAPTER 7

The wedding gift from Dustin Hoffman and his wife, Lisa, was unusual but appropriate—his-and-hers tenpin bowling balls. Ever the competitive couple, Tom and Nicole had recently developed a passion for the game, but it was a while before they could continue their sporting duel. As with his first marriage to Mimi Rogers, there was no opportunity to enjoy a honeymoon; four days after her Christmas Eve wedding, Nicole headed to North Carolina to finish filming *Billy Bathgate,* a period gangster movie in which she was starring alongside Tom's best man, Dustin Hoffman.

It was also some time before Nicole was able to enjoy the wedding gift from David and Shelly Miscavige. When Tom confided to the Scientology leader about the couple's fantasy of running through a meadow of wildflowers together, his friend apparently decided to make his dream come true. A team of twenty Sea Org disciples was set to work digging, hoeing, and planting wheat grass and wildflower seed near the Cruises' bungalow. Former Scientologist Maureen Bolstad recalled working until early in the morning in the mud and pouring rain. "It was an emergency project so that Tom could have his fantasy come true. I felt it was strange that we were doing a special favor for him—I was supposed to be a religious worker."

Naturally the work was regularly inspected by David and Shelly Miscavige, who would ride over to the site on his motorbike. They were apparently unhappy with the finished appearance and had the area plowed over and reseeded. These days the Scientology leadership is remarkably coy about the incident, Mike Rinder, head of Scientology International's Office of Special Affairs flatly denying that the wildflower planting ever occurred. Other witnesses, some who have signed legal affidavits attesting to the truth of their accounts, dispute this. As Karen Pressley, a friend of both David and Shelly Miscavige, recalls, "The story of the meadow for Tom and Nicole is absolutely true. I was there."

Perhaps thinking of the great movie pairing of Spencer Tracy and Katharine Hepburn, Tom gave his new wife a wedding present money could not buy—the role of leading lady in his new movie, a rollicking romantic adventure eventually titled *Far and Away*. Even though director Ron Howard had never seen Nicole perform, he didn't have much choice in the matter. For nine years the director of such movies as *Cocoon* and *Splash* had been nursing the project, which was based on the life of his great-grandfather, who'd left Ireland to join in the Great Land Rush of 1893. More in hope than expectation, Howard had sent Tom the script months beforehand, so he was surprised when Tom agreed to star in the story of a brawling Irish laborer who heads west to seek his fortune and finds love in the shape of a spirited landowner's daughter.

Tom's involvement effectively green-lighted the project, and at twenty-eight, he was not shy about imposing his authority. Just as Howard agreed to Tom's choice of leading lady—as well as a reported $10 million fee—so did he give his blessing when Tom insisted that Clearsound, the sound system developed by Scientology, be used in the movie. The young star took Howard to Gold Base to give him a demonstration and to work on the production in peace and quiet. Producer Brian Grazer and scriptwriter Bob Dolman arrived later, flown to the compound in a private helicopter. It was an experience that left Dolman somewhat spooked. His Scientology hosts for the day were "so security-conscious, so military—there was a car waiting for the helicopter, people wearing brown khakis." Once their script conference was finished, they were entertained by David Miscavige.

Before they left for filming in May 1991, Tom and Nicole stayed at the base to rehearse the parts of the young lovers, Joseph Donnelly and Shannon Christie. It was perhaps as well that they were immersed in filming—the movie was shot on location in Ireland and Montana—for that same month their faith was rocked by the most devastating media broadside in its history. A cover story in *Time* magazine—the same journal that had described the actor as "Tom Terrific" in an earlier profile—accused Scientology of being a "Thriving Cult of Greed and Power" that ruined lives and was little more than a "ruthless global scam."

In a withering eight-page article, journalist Richard Behar described the church as a "depraved enterprise" involving illegal activities, legal harassment, mental and physical abuse, and tax evasion. Scientology was a "hugely profitable global racket that survived by intimidating members and critics alike in a Mafia-like manner." In his extensive investigation involving 150 interviews, Behar quoted Cynthia Kisser of the Cult Awareness Network as saying: "Scientology is quite likely the most ruthless, the most classically terroristic, the most litigious and the most lucrative cult the country has ever seen." If the article was not damning enough, a few weeks earlier, members of the Church of Scientology had gone on trial in Toronto, charged with stealing documents from government offices and law firms, and breach of trust. It was the first time a church had been put in the dock in Canada's history. The church was found not guilty of the theft charges, but guilty of breach of trust, and was fined $250,000.

The fallout was immediate and widespread. For example, Scientologist Peter Alexander, a former vice president of Universal Studios, had earlier been instructed by the church to ask a movie friend, Tom Pollock, then president of Universal's Motion Picture Division, to remove a derogatory reference to Scientology from the movie *The Hard Way*. Pollock reluctantly complied. When he read *Time*, Pollock immediately called Alexander and told him never to ask him for another favor on behalf of Scientology.

Realizing the damage to recruitment and existing membership, Miscavige launched an aggressive $3 million counterattack, claiming that the Church of Scientology was the victim of a bizarre and complicated plot involving the cult's bête noire, the drug industry. A subsequent libel action against *Time* was comprehensively defeated. Nonetheless, when Miscavige visited Tom and Nicole on the film set in Ireland in July to celebrate Tom's twenty-ninth birthday, he was prepared, if asked, to deliver a coherent rebuttal of Behar's thesis and soothe any concerns expressed by the Hollywood couple.

Tom and his faith were clearly in the crosshairs. Around the same time, Scientology victim Nan Herst Bowers wrote separately to Tom, in care of his publicist, on the *Far and Away* set, asking him to intervene in her unfolding family tragedy. In a polite, two-page missive, she explained how she had, as far as she was concerned, been falsely accused of revealing that Tom was a member of the Church of Scientology to the media. Her subsequent trial and excommunication meant that she could no longer see her family, who were still members of the church. She wrote, "I felt that maybe if he was made aware of the injustice and grief caused by the Church in their well-intentioned attempt to protect him, he might want to contact them and discuss the situation and the effect it has had on my family. I can't believe Tom would condone breaking up a family on his behalf." She received no acknowledgment, even though she had sent the letter by registered mail. When formally asked about it by journalist John Richardson two years later, Tom denied all knowledge of the letter or of Nan Herst Bowers's plight.

While one family was being broken up, Tom and Nicole were a couple very much in love, referring to *Far and Away* as their "honeymoon" movie. On the set, director Ron Howard was moved to comment: "There was a lot of kissing going on—all day long." Tom was especially attentive toward his new bride, his affection for Nicole proud and public. "He was always taking care of her," extra Tony Leone noted. "He would put a towel around her, making sure that she was feeling good." At organized events they held hands tightly, pressed their bodies close together, and Tom always seemed to be whispering sweet nothings in her ear. As Nicole suffered from panic attacks, their public canoodling was as much to soothe her jangled nerves as from any romantic impulse.

For once this was not an act for outward show, Tom constantly expressing his adoration for his young bride in the roses he sent her virtually every day and the brief yet tender love notes, some written on yellow Post-its, which he left for her wherever they were in the world. (One householder in Toronto who rented her house to the Cruises was bemused to find several love notes in her sofa cushions when she moved back in. At first she thought her husband was being uncharacteristically affectionate. Then she realized they were penned by Tom.) In the early years of their marriage Nicole was enchanted by the way he wooed her. "He's amazingly romantic," she said. "He puts so much work into us."

That work was expressed in lavish gifts of jewelry, the top-of-the-line Mercedes, and even an adorable Labrador puppy. The last gift showed that he had much to learn about his wife—she is no animal lover. When Nicole told her husband that she didn't like clothes shopping, he took over, buying her designer outfits himself or occasionally employing wardrobe mistress Kate Harrington at a thousand dollars a day to find Nicole appropriate attire. As one admiring and rather envious female friend recalled, "I have never met a man who was so loving, caring, and compassionate about another woman. He simply adored Nicole."

Both were keen to start a family. Nicole talked about having children as a certainty rather than a possibility, the actress whimsically remarking that they would have to be raised in Australia "to keep their feet on the ground." On the set, though, Nicole, who celebrated her twenty-fourth birthday during filming, revised her thinking when she saw director Ron Howard and his wife, Cheryl, in action with their four children. She saw them as role models of how to bring up healthy, well-adjusted children in the Hollywood hothouse. That she wanted a child with Tom, married or not, was never a question in her mind. As she confessed some years later, "I was desperate to have a baby with him. I didn't care if we were married. That's what I wish I'd done."

Tom had never made any secret of his ambition to start a family, a desire that was urgent and at times almost visceral. It was as if by becoming a father himself he could expunge the heartache of his childhood, especially his problematic relationship with his own father. Of course, when he did become a dad, he was going to be, like everything else he tackled, the best dad in history. For a man who liked having his family around him—his mother, Mary Lee, visited the newlyweds in Ireland—fatherhood would be a kind of solace and completion. "I would love to have kids," Tom said during his romance with Nicole. "I would turn down an Oscar to see my boy at a baseball game or my girl at a song recital."

For a time it seemed that the extended honeymoon while filming in Ireland had worked according to plan. That summer Tom was quoted as saying, "It's a miracle. She's pregnant. I'm going to be a dad. I can't wait to hold my firstborn in my arms." While these fevered newspaper reports were briskly dismissed by the couple's publicist, it seems that the tabloids had for once gotten something right.

In October, once *Far and Away* had wrapped, Nicole flew to New York on her own to reshoot scenes for *Billy Bathgate*. During the filming, Nicole suffered stomach pains and was taken to a local hospital for treatment. Immediately afterward, she flew to St. John's Hospital in Santa Monica, near her Hollywood home. At the hospital, where she was admitted under a false name, she underwent, according to a widely quoted hospital source, "minor abdominal surgery to remove scar tissue that was causing her pain."

While the real nature of her illness remained a closely guarded secret, the truth was that Nicole was indeed expecting their first child. The couple's joy was brief, as tragically she suffered a potentially life-threatening ectopic pregnancy. This meant that the fertilized egg had settled in the Fallopian tube instead of in the uterus, a condition that resulted in painful bleeding in the abdomen. While ectopic pregnancies can now be dealt with by special drugs, in those days the fertilized egg had to be removed by keyhole surgery to prevent further bleeding. More severe conditions result in the entire Fallopian tube being removed, seriously affecting a woman's chances of becoming pregnant again. While around half of the women who suffer ectopic pregnancies subsequently have successful pregnancies, there is still, according to gynecologist Dr. David Farquharson of Edinburgh Royal Infirmary, a one-in-ten chance of having a second ectopic pregnancy.

The medical prognosis for Nicole was further complicated by her family history. Her mother, Janelle, had believed that she was unable to have children and, after six years of marriage, had become increasingly discouraged about her ability to conceive. While Nicole's birth came as a wonderful surprise, her own gynecological issues may have been passed on to her actress daughter. If that was the case, it truly was a miracle that Nicole had become pregnant at all. It seemed, however, unlikely that she could conceive without miscarrying again. Doctors warned that it would be dangerous to even try, as another pregnancy could be potentially fatal. It was a devastating verdict for the couple, who seemed so eager to start a family. Exhausted and emotionally drained, Nicole flew to Australia alone to spend time recovering with her own family. "It was," she admitted years later, "really very traumatic."

The options facing Tom and Nicole were bleak; if they tried for a baby, they were aware that, even if she was successful in becoming pregnant, Nicole was risking her own health. Ironically, it was a situation that would have far-reaching repercussions not only for their image as a happy, loving couple, but also for the perception of Tom as an all-action screen hero. But that was the least of their worries as they privately struggled to come to terms with Nicole's medical condition.

With unintentional cruelty, a January 1992 *Parade* magazine article reported that Nicole was expecting a baby the following month. While the story was flatly denied by the couple's representative, there was a grain of truth in the yarn, as they were now actively discussing adopting a baby as one of their future options. As Nicole's biographer James Dickerson noted, "The story had gotten twisted in the telling and retelling. Horrified by the story, Nicole and Tom put their secret adoption plans on hold."

For the moment they plunged into work, fielding thousands of questions as they mounted a concerted campaign to promote *Far and Away*. Perhaps bruised by the hurtful and endless speculation surrounding the marriage of Hollywood's most glamorous couple, Tom brought another woman into his life—publicist Pat Kingsley, a media operator with a formidable reputation for the ruthless way she controlled her client's publicity. Control was the language Tom clearly understood, his new publicist ensuring that in the media circus she was the undisputed ringmaster. Before journalists could interview Tom or Nicole, they had to sign contracts about where, when, and how material from the interview was to be published. Those who refused were escorted from the big top. "Increasingly there are indications that he is petulant and demanding, something of a control freak who shows flashes of prodigious ego," noted writer Rod Lurie of Hollywood's golden boy. "Many journalists are coming to believe that they've been bought with an engaging smile."

However much Kingsley cracked the whip, when the circus for *Far and Away* did come to town in April 1992, the critics and paying public were not keen on the performance of Hollywood's latest married double act. There was to be no repeat of the Tracy–Hepburn pairing. Indeed, when the movie was shown at the Cannes Film Festival, some critics loudly groaned their disapproval, even though Tom and Nicole were guests of honor. The public stayed away, too, the film, which cost more than $30 million, grossing only $60 million in America. Hurt by the critical panning—"doddering" and "hackneyed" were two descriptions of the film—Ron Howard retreated into his family, spending the summer reading books and watching movies. Nicole, admitting that she should not have worked with Tom so soon after *Days of Thunder,* auditioned, unsuccessfully, for the female leads in *Ghost, Silence of the Lambs, Sleepless in Seattle,* and *Thelma and Louise.* Out of work for several months, Nicole was philosophical. "Rejection used to be very difficult to take but, as an actor, you learn to deal with that. My mum calls me tenacious."

In a curious case of art imitating life, Nicole finally landed a supporting role in a mystery thriller called *Malice* about a professor's wife who is keen to have children. When her character is rushed to the hospital with severe abdominal pains, a drunk surgeon removes her ovaries, leaving her infertile. It was a scenario that was painfully close to her recent ordeal. A cathartic experience or an acting challenge—either way, it put her back on the Hollywood map, the movie doing brisk business at the box office. Not that the money really mattered—Tom had told her early on in their relationship that he would churn out the blockbusters, leaving her to concentrate on riskier art films.

He was true to his word. In spite of the debacle of *Far and Away,* "Tom Terrific" proved that he was simply Teflon coated. Early in 1992 he walked straight into the movie version of the Broadway show *A Few Good Men,* about abuses of power at the now notorious Guantánamo Bay military base in Cuba. Not only did he command top dollar, earning a reported $12.5 million fee, but once again he called the shots on the sound system used in the courtroom drama. As producer Lindsay Doran said diplomatically, "All I know is we sound-recorded two different ways. I was told one of the ways was a brand-new process and the way of the future."

While Tom had concerns about his voice, there were few doubts about his acting ability, the young man going head to head with the legendary Jack Nicholson, playing a flawed but brilliant military lawyer goading and probing the larger-than-life base commander. As director Rob Reiner noted, this was a high-powered ensemble cast, including stars Kevin Bacon and Demi Moore, which made it Tom's "biggest acting challenge to date. . . . There were no scenes where he could turn on the charm," Reiner noted. "There was no romance."

In this battle of Hollywood's big beasts, the young tyro

proved himself king of the jungle. To underscore his status, in September 1993 he and his agent, Paula Wagner, founded their own production company, Cruise/Wagner Productions, which gave Tom even greater control over future projects— and a bigger slice of the financial pie. They moved into the old Howard Hughes offices on the Paramount lot, with a staff of ten sifting the weekly pile of scripts in search of the pearl that would be suitable for Tom. Paramount president Sherry Lansing was hopeful that their collaboration with the young star would be as fruitful as that between Warner Bros. and Clint Eastwood.

The partnership paid off within months, when Tom starred alongside veteran Gene Hackman in a movie adaptation of John Grisham's legal drama *The Firm,* which Paramount had optioned even before it was written. As a sign of his power in the industry, only Tom's name appeared above the title when the movie was released. Irritated and hurt, his Oscar-winning costar Gene Hackman angrily requested that his name be removed from all publicity materials. It did little to dampen the film's success, the studio giving Cruise a $100,000 Mercedes 500 SL in gratitude when the movie raced past the $100 million mark in a matter of days.

During filming, Tom and Nicole were actively taking steps to start a family, a process that had seemingly been put on hold earlier in the year. Having quietly bought a condo on Marco Island in Florida, they were eligible to adopt in the state that happened to be the East Coast headquarters of Scientology, the town of Clearwater controversially infiltrated by the organization. In December 1992, while Tom was filming *The Firm,* the couple filed formal adoption papers in Palm Beach, Florida. Unlike many hopeful couples, they had to wait only a matter of weeks before being told they were parents. In January 1993 they went to a Miami hospital and picked up a healthy, dark-haired baby girl born a few days earlier, on December 22. The thrilled parents called her Isabella Jane Kidman Cruise. There was no family link; they just liked the name Isabella. As Nicole later recalled, "My mother has an adopted sister, so it's been part of our family, and I knew it would probably play out somewhere in mine. I didn't think it would happen so soon, but it did."

Given the couple's decision to adopt in Florida rather than in their home state of California, there was considerable speculation both inside and outside Scientology that the episode had been engineered by their faith. People close to David Miscavige at the time believe that he was instrumental in orchestrating the quick adoption. Nicole declined to address the speculation, saying, "Some things are personal. We adopted Isabella because she was meant for us."

That failed to stem the swirl of sexual speculation surrounding the couple. There were tabloid stories suggesting that the world's sexiest man was sterile, doubts about his sexual orientation, and rumors that Nicole was unable to bear children. The gossip became superheated a few weeks later when Tom's ex-wife, Mimi Rogers, discussed his desire to be a monk in the March issue of *Playboy*. While she later recanted, publicly stating that Tom was not gay—"I slept with the man for four years; I should know"—the damage was done. Her off-the-cuff remarks became a major fable in the growing body of folklore surrounding the actor's sexuality. For a time the couple tried to let the ill-informed gossip wash over them, as they maintained a discreet silence about the real reasons behind their decision to adopt so early in their marriage. Instead, Nicole discussed her desire of giving birth one day and adopting more children.

For the most part, the couple just blissed out over their new baby, enjoying the daily miracle of bringing new life into their home. Even though the couple had two nannies on call twenty-four hours a day, Tom was very much a hands-on dad, wanting to be the kind of father that he had always longed for, the man whom Isabella could rely on completely. As he grew into fatherhood, he began to realize what he had missed from his own childhood, measuring his father's behavior against his own. It is noticeable that there was now an angrier, less sympathetic edge to his public comments about his own father, observations that perhaps reflected his own experience.

Characteristically Tom, like millions of fathers before him, became an instant and infallible expert on child care. In the Cruise household, it was father who knew best. When he was out, he called home constantly to make sure that baby Isabella was properly fed, bathed, and cared for. He wanted to make sure that everything was just perfect, vetting Isabella's diet, feeding times, and sleeping patterns. In time her daily menu was inputted into a computer and included a long list of ingredients that were banned from her diet. "Being a father is what I always dreamed of, only a hundred times better," he said. "I've never been happier." When he wasn't working, he read to her every night, and when he was at meetings or on set, he was known to take her along with him. "He was born to be a dad," noted a friend who knew the couple at the time. "He absolutely wanted her, he's a wonderful father, very loving, just adored Isabella."

Baby Isabella was entering a household with a routine that was controlled and consistent. Every morning Tom and Nicole were woken at eight o'clock by their staff, who returned ten minutes later to make sure that they were fully awake. Models of healthy living, Tom and Nicole worked out in the mornings following a breakfast of oatmeal while reading *The New York Times*. She liked a regular massage after a workout or a beauty treatment, her stylist and colorist regular visitors to the compound. He read few books apart from the Scientology texts that filled the bookshelves, while spending his days poring over film scripts or reading flying manuals to study for his private pilot's license. In his downtime he played volleyball, went for a round of golf, or simply watched sports on TV, especially the fortunes of the New York Mets, the baseball team he'd supported as a kid.

Just a few years after busing tables, he now had a $9.75 million, five-bedroom house in fashionable Pacific Palisades, employing a plethora of nannies, chefs, gardeners, housekeepers, and security staff. It was said that many were Scientologists who were carefully vetted by Scientology officials, the procedure often taking months in order to find a suitable candidate with the right background and attitude to work for Scientology's poster boy. Candidates would be interviewed on videotape by a Scientology executive before being approved. A Scientology executive later dismissed the claim as "preposterous." There was also a degree of liaison regarding staff matters between Tom's office and that of fellow Scientologist John Travolta. Loyalty and hard work were rewarded—at Christmas and birthdays, staff members at the Cruise home were asked to list their ten favorite "must have" presents, ranging in value from, say, a car to a board game. The couple would pick an item off the list, based on how well they considered a member of their staff had worked during the year.

However loyal his staff, life with "Tom Terrific" was demanding and stressful. He had exacting standards, testing staff on their knowledge of tasks he had previously asked them to perform, insistent that everything be done precisely the way he wanted. If a staff member ever used his initiative to change an order, however slightly, Tom would go "ballistic." It was his way or the highway—no questions asked. "You always had to be on your toes with him, anticipating answers for any questions he had," a former insider said. While Nicole was more disengaged and aloof, she was the kind of employer who would pick up on one fault but never acknowledge how smoothly her home was run. Even though she was a recent convert, Nicole was not above using Scientology techniques to admonish staff.

On one occasion she was infuriated about a flattering but accurate story in the British tabloids about her shopping habits. She was determined to find out who had leaked the information and ordered all the staff to write what Scientologists call a "knowledge report," outlining any involvement in the incident. Both Tom and Nicole read and reviewed the statements by the staff before signing off on them. Staff could be forgiven for thinking that it was like being back at school. The culprit was Nicole's personal shopper, who did not face the same strictures as household staff.

All staff members, whether or not they were Scientologists, had to sign an eight-page confidentiality agreement in which they waived their First Amendment rights to free speech. A word out of place, however innocent, to a friend or

family member about life on Planet Tom could lead to huge
fines and legal fees. If a staff member ever dared reveal all
on TV or in print, they faced huge financial penalties—$5
million for each broadcast and $1 million for every newspaper or magazine featuring an interview.

While the internal discipline and endless demands by their
employers were irksome, most difficult was the constant transition from friend to employee. The Cruises, particularly
Tom, wanted both service and companionship. When people
were visiting the house, Tom and Nicole would treat their
staff as friends, but as soon as the visitors left they expected
them to return to their duties. Holidays were most difficult,
employees trying to do their jobs without looking as if they
were working. Even when they had finished for the day, Tom
liked his staff to hang around simply in order to have, as he
put it, "a warm body in the house." This was a man who hated
to be alone for a moment, a man with a desire for companionship that was almost tangible. In that regard, his private
persona bears remarkable similarities to former President
Bill Clinton—also brought up by an abusive, alcoholic stepfather—who will spend all night carousing and chatting. It
seems neither man ever wants to be alone.

One question that was always on Tom's lips was, "Where
is Nic?" He liked to know where she was and who she was
with every second of the day. It was a constant refrain. "Was
he a control freak? Certainly," recalls one insider. "He was
always checking up on Nic especially." In time she bridled
under the constant attention—and inquisition.

Yet Tom, as boisterous and noisy as their Labrador puppy,
was no match for Nicole's subtle feline skills. Whatever Tom
may have wanted, Nicole always got her way in the end.
Around Christmas or for her June birthday, for example, she
would often consult with art dealer Barbara Guggenheim, the
wife of Tom's lawyer Bert Fields, who provided much of the
artwork in their home. Nicole was always keen to know about
any interesting auctions of paintings or objets d'art and then
ensured that her staff kept Tom apprised of what she wanted.
She got it, too. Tom was a generous husband, always happy

to please the woman he loved. "She was very manipulative," recalls an insider. "He always bowed to what Nic wanted."

If Nicole was traveling, often flying to Australia to see her parents, Tom's mother or sisters came to stay; or his cousin, actor William Mapother, who had worked as a production assistant on Tom's movies, would hang out. While his mother's generous nature and irrepressible spirit added gaiety and laughter to the normally subdued household, the arrival of her oldest daughter, Lee Anne DeVette, changed the domestic dynamic. A few months before the couple adopted Isabella, Tom had hired his elder sister, a fellow Scientologist, to deal with the deluge of press clippings and serve as liaison with charities linked to Scientology. It was not long before Lee Anne, who was seen by others as rather tough and mean-spirited, clashed with Nicole. While Lee Anne, whose two-year marriage had ended in 1981, liked everyone to know that she was Tom's sister—and threw her weight around accordingly—Nicole treated her with ill-disguised disdain, viewing her as a servant rather than a sister-in-law. It was not long before neither could bear the sight of the other. As one insider said, with emphasis, "Lee Anne *hated* Nicole. And she had every reason because Nic treated her like a second-class citizen. But she wouldn't stand up to Nic—no one ever did!"

The final piece in the domestic jigsaw puzzle was an infrequent visitor, but a constant presence—Scientology leader David Miscavige, who was represented in the household by the man Tom called "the Dovenator," his chief of staff, Michael Doven. Tall, well-built, and with the square-jawed good looks of a movie star, Doven was something of a Renaissance man. A world-class skier, fitness fiend, and talented photographer, he could have chosen any career he wanted. Yet he chose to stay by Tom's side, the Colorado-born Scientologist dedicated to ensuring that his faith's most valuable recruit stayed locked down inside the church. His fanatical loyalty to the cause—sacrificing his own career for his faith—was crucial to ensure that Tom or Nicole never strayed off purpose.

No one appreciated Doven's vital role more than the Scientology leader. While Miscavige spoke to Tom a couple of times a week on the telephone, he was in daily contact with Doven, assessing the actor's mood, making plans, calibrating his message, and fine-tuning his control over Tom and Nicole. Doven, who married Tom's assistant Andrea Morse, was first noticed on the set of *A Few Good Men,* where Tom insisted that all members of the crew refer to him as "the communicator." Doven effectively kept Tom's "lines" clear, controlling all the information that reached Tom, filtering everything down to essentials. In a purposeful life, Doven was the man who kept Tom focused on his work—and on his faith.

Not that Tom needed much convincing. "Let's go to CC," he often said to Nicole, his shorthand for Celebrity Centre, the Gothic mansion on Franklin Avenue in Hollywood that was a hangout for Scientology stars. Even within the Hollywood elite, Tom and Nicole were special. They had their own private entrance into an underground garage, their own rooms for auditing, and, of course, dedicated waiter service. Scientology, it seemed, was truly an Orwellian faith in which all men were equal, but some were more equal than others. At Gold, in addition to their VIP bungalow and personal chef and butler, Tom kept two motorcycles, a Mercedes convertible, and a motor home garaged in the compound, while Nicole had her own private garden.

When Tom and Nicole wanted to play tennis, there was a private court built by Sea Org laborers. Just as David had gotten Tom interested in shooting, so Tom encouraged the Scientology leader to see the value of exercise. Not only did Miscavige stop smoking, but he had a gym built for himself and Tom at Gold, which could be used only by senior executives and only when the actor was not around. After the Scientology leader instructed that his father organize the purchase of gym equipment, Ron Miscavige confessed himself "flabbergasted" at the cost to the church, especially when his son's tinkering with the plans for the gym and the bodybuilding apparatus added to the expense, estimated at $150,000. The ecclesiastical largesse did not stop there. Not only did Miscavige send Tom regular gifts of fine wine, but on at least one occasion he dispatched his assistant Shelly Britt with a picnic hamper to Tom's Gulfstream jet for his enjoyment. While Tom bought his friend a Motorola mobile phone and expensive speakers for his apartment, he found that nothing was ever too much trouble for the Scientology leader. When Tom bought his first private jet, his Scientology friend ensured that in-house engineers installed their own Clearsound system.

Tom's exceptional and privileged treatment was matched by the friendship he enjoyed with Miscavige. They were guys' guys, hanging out with each other, smoking Cuban cigars, watching movies, racing their motorbikes at high speeds, challenging each other at basketball or softball or skeet shooting. Everything was a macho competition to see who could be fastest, quickest, bravest . . . the best. Miscavige, who hated to lose anything anyway, always tried to ensure that his teams had the best players. When Tom and Nicole went skiing in Colorado, David would be there, too, trying to outdo his buddy on icy black runs. "They were like glue," recalls Jesse Prince, "two little people who really enjoyed each other. They laughed the same and acted the same. They were like glove puppets, he was a big star and he was head of a religion. They loved each other but it was not gay. It was way more complicated than that."

In this backslapping world inside a macho religion that claimed to cure homosexuality and where the women dressed like men and were addressed as "sir," Nicole tried her best to fit in. As tomboyish as she was, she began to see David—or more accurately Scientology—as the third wheel in her marriage. "She became very frustrated about it," claims Jesse Prince, who says that, in his capacity as deputy inspector general, he was her case supervisor and read her confidential files where she voiced her concerns. "She was tired of David Miscavige being around all the time. She felt that her husband was spending too much time with him. Why do we have to have this constant monitoring?"

Even David Miscavige began to wonder whether he was neglecting his faith for his friend, a concern shared by his father, Ron. Certainly throughout 1993, Miscavige was highly focused on Scientology, primarily on the long-running battle with the IRS to win charitable status. He chaired daily meetings in the base's windowless high-tech "situation room"— based on the underground military nerve center in the White House—where lawyers, Scientology executives, and private investigators met to discuss tactics. At one point the cult was said to be spending $1.5 million a month on lawyers and investigators who were hired to probe the private lives of IRS senior staff to give them bargaining leverage in their quest for charitable status.

Although Scientologists like to perpetuate the myth that the Scientology leader walked in unannounced to see the director of the IRS, the reality was that it took years of intense negotiations before tax officials granted them tax exemption. As New York tax lawyer Robert Fink, who reviewed the agreement, observed, "The IRS normally settles on tax issues alone. What the IRS wanted was to buy peace from Scientology. You never see the IRS wanting to buy peace."

This led to fevered discussion, possibly ill informed, that the unusual tax exemption was granted less because of any legitimate charitable status than because Scientology had dug up enough dirt on senior IRS officials to effectively blackmail them into submission. This gossip mattered little to the ten thousand cheering Scientologists who were told by Miscavige in October 1993 that "the war" was over. It was truly a triumph of the will, David Miscavige's finest hour, the moment the image of Scientology began the transition from a shadowy criminal cult to a law-abiding church. One of the first people he told about his audacious victory was his friend Tom Cruise.

Yet just a few weeks before, the actor had publicly bridled when John H. Richardson, in an article published in the September issue of *Premiere* magazine, questioned his friendship with Miscavige and his involvement with Scientology. The actor was affronted that his religion was up for discussion, dismissing interest in his "good friend" David Miscavige as "off the wall." He denied that Scientologists visited him on film sets, found the idea that he had "handlers" repulsive, and admitted to visiting Gold only once for nonrecreational purposes.

This angry rebuttal came as a surprise to Scientologists at Gold, not least L. Ron Hubbard's son-in-law Guy White, who vividly recalls struggling to carry a refrigerator on his own to Tom's VIP bungalow prior to one of his many visits. As Tom himself said in his tart response to Richardson, who spent two years investigating the "sinister" organization and its "vindictive" gospel, "I know more about Scientology and the Church and its staff than any reporter I've ever met."

Certainly Tom had every reason to claim expertise about the secret inner workings of his faith. By then he had progressed to what Scientologists call "the Wall of Fire," or Operating Thetan III, where the secrets of the universe according to Hubbard were revealed. At that time Scientology's creationist myth was a closely guarded secret, disciples told that the knowledge could prove fatal if they learned about it before they were ready. In the theatrical buildup, candidates were thoroughly audited and warned that they would have to pay huge damages if they ever divulged the secrets. Then they were given a clear plastic folder containing OT III materials as well as a key that they had to use within a matter of seconds to open the confidential cache. For some, it was an experience that was not so much *Mission: Impossible* as *Mission: Implausible*, as they sat in a special room and read, in a facsimile of Hubbard's own handwriting, the hidden truth about the origin of man.

The story, which has since been widely parodied, notably on the TV cartoon *South Park,* revealed that 75 million years ago an alien ruler named Xenu solved the overpopulation in this part of the galaxy by sending 13.5 trillion beings to Earth, then called Teegeeack, and vaporizing them with nuclear bombs after first dumping them in volcanoes. These millions of lost souls, known as thetans, were implanted with numerous false ideas about God, Christ, and organized religion. They later attached themselves to human beings and, Hubbard argued, were the cause not just of an individual's problems but of all the divisive issues in the modern world.

As Tom read this material, he learned that the next stage of his progress up "the bridge to total freedom" was to clear his body of these thetans. While the Hubbardian myth is now widely derided, the story is a test of belief, a leap of faith that vaults over rational doubts. For Tom to make further progress, he had to swallow every last drop of Hubbard's theological Kool-Aid. "When you join OT III you are in a members' only club where you are going all the way with Timothy McVeigh [the Oklahoma bomber]," observes Jesse Prince.

Like many other Scientologists who reach this level, Tom found the knowledge he had just received disturbing and alarming, as he struggled to reconcile the creationist myth with the more practical teachings contained in the lower levels of Scientology. This is not an unusual response. Those who have read the Wall of Fire story are very closely monitored for signs that they are backsliding, becoming disenchanted with their faith. Former Scientologists recall that, during this difficult time, Tom seemed uncharacteristically dazed and out of sorts, with dark rings around his eyes. "He went from a firecracker to a wet noodle," said one insider. It was recalled that around this time relations became "ugly" between David Miscavige and the Hollywood actor, Tom complaining that he had studied all these years and the whole faith was about space aliens. He was treated with kid gloves, carefully wooed back into the fold. A team of senior Scientologists worked diligently to "recover" him, calling the actor into the president's office at Celebrity Centre in Hollywood for auditing and counseling.

Once Tom had been "handled" to cope with the implications of this bizarre myth, the next stage of the lengthy—and expensive—process of enlightenment was to rid his body of thetans. Three or four times a day he had to go into a quiet, sealed room and locate and remove the thetans clinging to his body. As the thetans are invisible and often in a catatonic state, he could only find them telepathically, using his "E meter" to help detect them. Using his telepathic powers, he then asked each thetan a series of questions. The first question was always "What are you?" The thetan might answer, telepathically, in an infinite number of ways, claiming to be anything from a car to a dust mite or even Napoleon. Whatever the reply, Tom had to continue asking the same question until the thetan finally responded, "I am me." Once the thetan had recognized itself, Tom would have successfully rid himself of an unresolved spirit, which would theoretically float away and inhabit another being.

During the twenty-minute session of telepathic conversation he could remove up to ten body thetans. As odd as the process seemed, it had the effect of sending practitioners like Tom into a mild but euphoric trancelike state, the actor feeling good about that day's "wins." As former studio executive Peter Alexander, who attained the level of Operating Thetan VII, recalls, "The theory is that the more you exorcise your body thetans, the more you become yourself. It is a very self-absorbed process. It's all about me, which is why actors love it. It appeals to the narcissist in you. You begin to feel more certain of yourself, that you, and you alone, have the answers to the secrets of the universe. During this time I was walking around spellbound from an endorphin rush. I now realize that I put myself in a light hypnotic trance."

Ultimately, though, the process is seen by many former Scientologists as self-defeating and delusional. Many high-level Scientologists decide to leave the faith when they realize that it is not working for them—and costing them dear. Alexander, for example, reckons he spent around $1 million during his twenty-year membership. With his customary bluntness, Jesse Prince sums up the views of many former high-level devotees: "After a time you either lose your mind or lose your faith. You can spend hours talking to your thumb, elbow, or the crack of your ass, but it is not going to make you a spiritual demigod. Once you realize that, you are gone."

Whatever doubts Tom had, they did not seem to last too long; the actor has been described by his Scientology mentors as a "dedicated and intense" student. There was, however, a question mark about how sincere he was, a sneaking suspicion that he was reading a line from a film script rather than being himself. Longtime Scientologist Bruce Hines, who audited numerous celebrities, including John Travolta,

recalls: "My sense was that he was just acting rather than being genuine." He was not the first, nor the last, to come away
from an encounter with Tom wondering if his whole life was
just an elaborate act.

Hines, a thoughtful former physics student from Denver
who was drawn to Scientology because of the scientific
claims underpinning Hubbard's book *Dianetics,* became an
unwitting participant in the relationship among Tom, Nicole,
and David Miscavige. During the heady first months of her
romance with Tom, the Australian sailed through the entry-
level courses of Scientology, reaching the level of Operating
Thetan II. Not only had she learned how to self-audit, she
was seen as a candidate to go through the Wall of Fire, to be
admitted into the inner sanctum. Yet she hesitated, citing film
commitments. Even though she was shooting the bittersweet
drama *My Life* in spring 1993, David Miscavige wanted to
probe her explanation a little further.

Hines was asked to audit her, looking for any reasons why
she was not making further progress. It seemed to Hines that
there had been some conversation between David Miscavige
and Tom Cruise about Nicole, and the session had been
arranged to find a problem and use that to pull her back into
line. The fact that she was close to her psychologist father—
she began returning home to Sydney with increasing
frequency—would always, by Hubbard's definition, be a
cause for concern. In preparation for the session, Hines reviewed her confidential files, which gave no clue about any
issues or difficulties she had with her new faith. Previous auditors had the impression that she was a young woman who
got on with life, suffering few upsets or setbacks.

During the twenty-minute question-and-answer session
with Hines, Nicole made it clear that she was perfectly happy
and nothing was bothering her. Nor did she give the impression that she was hiding anything, either verbally or while using the E meter. When he proffered his report, saying that
there was nothing wrong with her, Hines was accused of
making a mistake and punished for failing to find a problem.

It was clear that the point of the session had not been to help Nicole, but to find any difficulty to use as an excuse to "handle" her and pull her back into the fold. As Hines now recalls, "They must've been concerned because from this point she started to drop out of Scientology. Obviously they blamed it on me. All they could say was that I didn't ask the questions right. And I still to this day don't think I made a mistake." While Scientology teaches that we are all responsible for our own actions, that clearly does not apply to celebrities.

One woman Tom couldn't "handle" was best-selling novelist Anne Rice. While Nicole may have been having private doubts about Scientology, Rice publicly voiced her concerns about Tom when he was cast in the role of the sinister, sexually deviant Lestat in the movie based on her book *Interview with the Vampire*. Rice much preferred Dutch actor Rutger Hauer for the role, and was equally displeased with Tom's costar, Brad Pitt. "It's like casting Huck Finn and Tom Sawyer in the movie," she raged. "Cruise is no more my Vampire Lestat than Edward G. Robinson is Rhett Butler."

Nor did it help that her comments coincided with calls in September 1993 for an investigation into the celebrity couple's adoption, erstwhile Republican candidate for Senate Anthony R. Martin criticizing "Florida's corrupt interstate adoption baby sellers." While Martin was easy to dismiss as a frivolous publicity hound, Rice proved harder to shake off. Her public campaign, which incited thousands of her fans, resulted in death threats days before Tom began filming. These threats were taken seriously enough for the producers to erect a covered walkway from Tom's trailer to the set, which also stopped paparazzi from taking shots of Tom in full vampire makeup, adding to the air of mystery surrounding the production.

When Tom accepted the award for Actor of the Decade at the Chicago International Film Festival in October 1993 shortly before filming started, he put a brave face on the personal mauling, saying that he "hoped to prove a lot of people wrong." In an attempt to defuse the situation, Tom claimed

he had read Rice's 352-page tome when he was a teenager—
no mean feat for a young man who'd described himself as a
"functional illiterate" when he left high school.

In public Tom was placatory, but in private he was "deeply
hurt" by Rice's ferocious assault on his artistic integrity. Legendary producer David Geffen, who'd convinced Cruise to
take the role in the first place, soothed him by saying that
Rice was a woman gone mad. Nonetheless, it must have been
a bewildering experience for a man who was now constantly
surrounded by those who deferred to his will, sang his
praises, and soothed his ego. What probably rankled most
was the fact that there was no appreciation for the artistic and
commercial risk he was taking by embracing the role of a
creature of fluid sexuality.

For the first time here was the world's sexiest man, whose
audience had become used to seeing him in the role of clear-
eyed hero, playing a villain, a character who seeks love beyond
gender. It was all the more commendable, given the previous
judgments of his friend David Miscavige, who had advised
against his taking on the role of Edward Scissorhands because
of that character's ambivalent sexuality. The role of Lestat was
much darker and riper. Whatever misgivings Miscavige may
have had, Tom put his faith in the judgment of his wife and
David Geffen, the man who had acknowledged his talent a decade earlier by choosing him for the lead in *Risky Business*.

Researching the role with his customary zeal and vigor,
Tom set out to prove Rice and her fans wrong. Not only did
he read all of Rice's books, he went on a drastic diet, learned
to play the piano, and flew to Paris with Nicole to soak up
the decadent atmosphere. They roamed the streets, visiting
museums and galleries—mostly at night, just like real-life
vampires. "We just went wild," he recalled. "Drank fine wine
and danced till dawn." Ironically, while Tom interpreted Lestat as essentially a lonely figure looking for love, the film's
director, Neil Jordan, compared the life of a vampire to that
of a major Hollywood star—kept away from the daylight
and living in a "strange kind of seclusion." It seemed that no
matter how hard Tom tried, he ended up playing himself.

Like the creature of the night he became for a time, he and Nicole enjoyed a restless life, roaming the planet in pursuit of their art, their times together punctuated by innumerable partings. During the filming of *Interview with the Vampire,* Tom was on location or in preproduction from October 1993 onward, spending time in Ireland, Paris, Louisiana, and San Francisco. Only occasionally was he accompanied by Nicole and Bella. As a result, while Hollywood was their home, they used their private Gulfstream jet the way others hail taxicabs. Their differing attitudes to this privileged lifestyle provide some telling insights into the space growing between them.

When he settled back into his kid leather seat, Tom would often look around the beautifully furnished cabin in wonder, literally pinching himself at his good fortune. "I can't believe I have all this," he would say. He never forgot that not so long ago he was stealing flowers to give his girlfriend, but now he was able to provide a life of luxury for the woman he loved. Not that she was overly impressed. Even though Nicole was struggling to establish herself as an actress in her own right, on occasion she behaved like a full-fledged Hollywood diva. If the jet wasn't stocked with beluga caviar and all the trimmings, she appeared deeply irritated, exhibiting a jaded petulance that seems to be the prerogative of the super-rich—or immensely talented.

Perhaps her attitude was born of frustration that her acting career was in a slump. At this stage Nicole was mostly known for her supporting role as Mrs. Cruise, rather than enjoying the spotlight in her own right. A star in Australia, she was seen by Hollywood movers and shakers to be hanging on Tom's coattails, relying on him for introductions, scripts, and projects. She was being paid, as her biographer David Thomson points out, "bimbo money" to appear in movies where she invariably had to disrobe. While she enjoyed a mutual love affair with the camera, with or without her clothes, it was ultimately discouraging.

Even though she was only twenty-six, she questioned her ability sufficiently to enroll at the Actors Studio in New York to help get the creative juices flowing. In interviews she made it clear that she wanted to get her teeth into meatier character roles. So it is easy to imagine her utter distress when her friend from Sydney, director Jane Campion, turned her down for the part of the tragically vulnerable Isabel Archer in her proposed film adaptation of the Henry James novel *Portrait of a Lady*. Campion's decision was the more disappointing as she had initially given Nicole the green light.

As far as the Australian director was concerned, Hollywood—or rather the roles she had accepted since arriving there—had somehow corrupted or blunted Nicole's talent. Doubtless one of those movies was *Batman Forever,* where she played sexy psychologist Dr. Chase Meridian—interestingly, the very profession her faith vowed to wipe from the face of the planet—playing opposite Val Kilmer. "She'd made quite a few films I didn't think suited her, and I don't think she felt suited her, either," Campion later explained. Eventually, after many tears, much heartache, and the indignity of auditioning, Nicole won Campion over and earned her coveted role.

That was in the future. As Tom marched firmly toward the summit of success, it seemed to Nicole that she was spending her days slipping and sliding in the foothills. Her own difficulties in finding a sure footing in the Hollywood hills, even with the help of an expert guide, serve as another reminder of how far and how quickly Tom had come. It was perhaps a sign of her intense desire, even desperation, to succeed that propelled her to dispense with the usual channels and phone director Gus Van Sant and plead for the lead role in his movie *To Die For.* That the producers' first choice, Meg Ryan, had turned it down only seemed to spur Nicole on. She told Van Sant that she felt "destined" to play the cold, calculating, ruthlessly ambitious TV weather girl who has her husband killed by her student lover because she feels he is impeding her career.

For once the outlook was sunny, Nicole winning the role in what was to be her breakout movie. During her research for the part in late 1993, she proved herself as single-minded and driven as her husband, who was on hand to help her with character research. On one occasion the couple checked into a hotel in Santa Barbara on the California coast, not leaving for three long days as they immersed themselves in schlock television. Her new project meant that the Cruise family was on the move once again, renting a house in Toronto, Canada, for the summer of 1994.

While Nicole filmed—she banned her husband from the set when she was involved in steamy sex scenes with costars Matt Dillon and Joaquin Phoenix—he earned his pilot's license, on at least one occasion taking Nicole for a joyride in a two-seater biplane where she climbed out onto the wing, performed an arabesque, and then parachuted to safety. The actor later credited Hubbard's teaching techniques for enabling him to read sufficiently well to understand the technical jargon in the flying manuals. He claimed that when he first became interested in learning to be a pilot, during the filming of *Top Gun* before he joined Scientology, he had to drop out because he couldn't understand the technical terms.

Fortuitously, the high-profile Scientology couple left Toronto before their church was embroiled in yet another controversy. In February 1995, hearings started in a libel case that resulted in the Church of Scientology being ordered to pay $1.6 million in damages, the largest amount in the country's history. The high-profile case made the church's boasts that it had left its dark past behind seem rather hollow. After almost a decade of David Miscavige's leadership, Scientology was as litigious and aggressive as ever.

If his faith was not for turning, one lady was: Tom's toughest critic, Anne Rice. Shortly before *Interview with the Vampire* was released in November 1994, producer David Geffen took the risk of sending a video of the movie to the New Orleans home of the author. She was entranced and told Geffen so. He in turn called an astounded Cruise with the news. "She likes you, she loves it, you know. She really loves it." Tom was amazed at Geffen's chutzpah. "You have the luck of the Irish, David Geffen," Cruise said. The about-face was complete when Rice took out advertisements in *The New York Times* and

Vanity Fair praising the film and Tom Cruise for a performance that "perfectly captured" Lestat's strength, humor, and boldness.

While his bisexual character encouraged yet more rumors about his own sexuality, Nicole and Tom were focused on adding to their family. After spending their fifth wedding anniversary that Christmas in their own ski chalet in Telluride, the chic Colorado resort where they married, the couple quietly filed adoption papers. In late February they became parents for a second time, adopting a baby boy they named Connor Antony Kidman Cruise. His mother was an African-American New Yorker who had given birth on February 6, 1995.

While Connor and his sister, Bella, were too young to appreciate it, they were now part of a family of traveling troubadours. Only weeks after Tom and Nicole signed the paperwork for the adoption, baby Connor was flown out of America. It marked a new stage in the couple's marriage, a journey that took them away from their home for longer than any of them anticipated.

CHAPTER 8

At last he was truly where he felt at home, a place where he instinctively belonged. In the driver's seat. In the cockpit. At the helm. Finally master of his own craft, producing, starring in, and fine-tuning his first blockbuster, *Mission: Impossible.* For the greenhorn producer, still only thirty-two, it was truly a risky business, as he steered a choppy course between the breezy demands of director Brian De Palma and the rocky financial realities of making a movie based on a half-forgotten 1970s TV show about maverick secret agents who foil endless dastardly plots of evildoers who want to take over the world.

Not only did he have the mental and physical pressures of playing a convincing leading man, in this case Special Agent Ethan Hunt, he also had to keep a weather eye on the budget and all the other routine details of sailing a multimillion-dollar project to the safe harbor of myriad multiplex screens. All that, as well as surviving an exploding fish tank, performing a backward somersault on a speeding train, and, famously, starfishing out his limbs as he was lowered 110 feet into a tightly guarded vault while carefully avoiding security laser beams. Perhaps his most difficult feat was not so much evading red lasers as finessing his way through the labyrinth of red tape in the former Communist Czech Republic, where filming took place in the winter of 1995.

For a controlling, driven perfectionist, the convoluted bu-
reaucracy tested his patience to the limit. "Prague ripped us
off. They are still getting used to democracy," he said drily.
Even a man-to-man chat with the country's new President,
playwright Vaclav Havel, failed to bring costs down. Still,
one bonus of filming in the Czech capital was being able to
stroll around the cobbled streets with Nicole, baby Connor,
and Bella without attracting attention. It was a change to go
sightseeing in daylight—normally the couple went out at
night to avoid the attentions of fans and paparazzi.

Not that he had much chance to soak up the sights. As
filming progressed in Prague and finally at the Pinewood Studios outside London, there was no doubt who was in command. Even though De Palma was twenty-two years his senior,
the novice producer insisted he have the final say over every
detail of the production: from ordering daily script rewrites
to rerecording the film score so that he could hear more
flutes. Perhaps his focus on sound quality was inspired, or
even recommended, by his spiritual Svengali, David Miscavige, whose sensitive ear was the final arbiter of Scientology's
own musical offerings.

Certainly there were those in Cruise's faith who saw in
his depiction of Ethan Hunt, a secret agent who lived on the
edge, distinct similarities to the character of the Scientology
leader. "*Mission: Impossible* is fascinating because in Ethan
Hunt I could see David Miscavige," observed Karen Pressley. "Both the character and the man were striving for the ultimate thrill. Just as David was living vicariously through
Tom Cruise, I could see that Tom Cruise was slowly becoming David Miscavige. That transposition in itself was worthy
of a movie script." It was an early appreciation of the direction in which Tom was headed.

While Tom's superagent role echoed the character of his
close friend, Nicole was finally breaking free of the "wife of
Tom Cruise" tag. In May 1995, Nicole flew to Cannes where
her movie *To Die For* was showing at the film festival. For the
first time she walked the red carpet on her own, her dress, slit
to the hip, making almost as big a splash as her movie. Not

only was she nominated for twelve awards, including a Golden Globe for best actress, which she eventually won, she was finally acknowledged as an actress to be reckoned with on her own merit.

As she basked in the critical glow—the film itself was only a modest financial success—she embarked on a serious role, which meant leaving Tom holding baby Connor and his sister, Isabella. Even though, in the summer of 1995, the couple were living in a palatial $15,000-a-week mansion in London, Nicole decided that she needed to be alone to focus on her role as heiress Isabel Archer for Jane Campion's movie of *Portrait of a Lady.* It was a sign of her absorption, some would say self-absorption, and intensity that she had to immerse herself in the character without any distractions.

Such was her obsession with the part that she insisted on wearing a corset that squeezed her waist to a mere nineteen inches, so she could feel the pain that Isabel felt. Several times filming was halted when the actress went pale with fatigue or even collapsed in a dead faint. It was no surprise that at the end of filming in November, she spent two weeks in bed with exhaustion and a temperature of 104 degrees. As with her husband on *Born on the Fourth of July,* the ghost of Laurence Olivier could be heard whispering, "Try acting, it's much easier."

As Nicole was putting herself through self-imposed agony for what she called "her baby," Tom was juggling home, career, and children, filming *Mission: Impossible* at Pinewood Studios but finding time to read Isabella a bedtime story as well as indulge his hobby of flying. He even had the opportunity to flirt a little with Diana, Princess of Wales, when she brought her elder son, Prince William, to the studios. While she was dazzled by his smile and charm during the two-hour visit, he was not her type, the princess preferring tall men.

In the midst of this hectic schedule, Tom found time to read a script by the journalist-turned-director Cameron Crowe, whom he had first met more than a decade earlier through Sean Penn, who worked with him on *Fast Times at Ridgemont High.* Crowe's latest project, *Jerry Maguire,* was about a cynical,

world-weary sports agent who quits his high-powered job in a
ruthless company, taking on just one client, football player
Rod Tidwell, and his secretary with him. The clever script
had Tom from the get-go, the actor gripped by the story of
Maguire's journey from selfishness to self-knowledge. He was
so intrigued that he flew to Los Angeles to see Crowe and his
producer, reading the part aloud for the assembled throng before even asking them to show him the money.

Crowe explained that, as Cruise's name was synonymous
with success, it would be interesting to explore a character
who fails on-screen. The film eventually earned Tom an Oscar nomination, an Oscar for Cuba Gooding Jr., who played
Rod Tidwell, and introduced Renée Zellweger to a wider audience. As Tom's screen love interest, she noticed a quality
in the performer that made him a truly effective actor but
difficult to read as a human being—the ability to switch off
his emotions in a heartbeat.

"His acting was so good it was almost bizarre. You'd look
into his eyes and he'd really be there, he'd really be in love
with you. You could see his heart and soul. And then the director would shout 'Cut,' Tom would leave the set, and you'd
have to go into therapy for six months." It is a not uncommon
observation. Those who have interviewed and even audited
him have come away from an encounter feeling that they have
been subjected to a performance rather than a personality.

Tom's on-screen persona intrigued and attracted the public as well as his peers. Not only did he go on to win a Golden
Globe for *Jerry Maguire,* but by 1996 he was the first actor
ever to star in five consecutive films, including *Jerry Maguire*
and *Mission: Impossible,* to gross over $100 million each at
the American box office. Moreover, in his first outing as a
producer in his own right, he had seen *Mission: Impossible*
earn more than $450 million in box-office sales. He was Hol-
lywood's undisputed Top Gun, a man who was able to make
every artistic mission commercially possible.

Yet taking pride of place on the wall of his office in Hollywood were not posters from his latest blockbuster, but a
framed, if rather faded, fax message. It was sent by the leg-

endary but reclusive director Stanley Kubrick, the genius be-hind *2001: A Space Odyssey, A Clockwork Orange, The Shining,* and *Dr. Strangelove.* The note simply said that he would like to work with Tom and Nicole on a future project and that a script would be sent to them in the next few months. That Tom chose to display the letter showed that even he was not immune to high-caliber flattery. The framed fax was a daily reminder that the breadth and drawing power of his talent went beyond his popularity with the public.

"It was just a damn miracle that he wanted me and Nic to do this," he later recalled. When the script by Oscar-winning screenwriter and author Frederic Raphael eventually arrived, "it took us about two seconds to say yes," recalled Nicole. "And that was it." Even though their previous screen collabo-rations had not been especially successful, the chance to work with a film legend outweighed all other considerations. "They thought they were working on a masterpiece, a career-defining movie," an associate later recalled.

It was the beginning of a bizarre collaboration that would test the limits of their acting, their health, their patience, and their marriage. Their first encounter with Kubrick, in the winter of 1995, set the tone for the strange, surreal life they were to inhabit for the next few years. As Nicole was still busy filming *Portrait of a Lady,* they hired a helicopter to fly them the short journey from London to Kubrick's home near St. Albans in Hertfordshire. Even though they arrived in true Hollywood style, they were as nervous as a couple on a first date, Nicole later confessing herself "terrified" as she shook hands with the figure in a one-piece blue boiler suit waiting to greet them on the lawn of his sprawling estate.

They were there to discuss the film *Eyes Wide Shut,* based on the novel by Arthur Schnitzler, about the sexual fantasies of a married couple, the blurring of dreams with reality, and the unforgiving emotions this can unleash. As Kubrick told them, "This film is about sexual obsession and jealousy. It is not about sex." Even so, he made sure that Nicole agreed to a nudity clause in her contract so that he could film pro-posed sex scenes with her. Kubrick's idea was to convey the mysteries of what goes on between a married couple by casting a real-life couple to play the central characters.

His first thought was to approach Kim Basinger, who had proved in *9½ Weeks* that she was not afraid of exploring sex on the screen, and her husband, Alec Baldwin. Screenwriter Frederic Raphael was wary. "I think it was an odd idea. He thought that if he got a married couple to impersonate a married couple then he'd necessarily get something true or real. It's a naïve idea of what acting and what marriage is." In the face of Kubrick's insistence, Raphael took another tack, suggesting he go for the most famous married couple in Hollywood. Hence Kubrick's fax to Tom.

If Nicole and Tom were nervous as they sat together holding hands on the sofa in the living room of his house, Kubrick was "thrilled" to have snared Hollywood's golden couple, later telling Raphael that they looked "sweet" together. Raphael was more cynical. "Somehow, those words coming out of Kubrick sounded curious. Who knows whether they sit holding hands in meetings all the time or not. But still, it seems that they gave him what he wanted. And he took it that this is what they were actually like as a couple, rather than at least having some cynicism about it. Because after all, if you are putting on a show— however genuine—it is a sign that you are putting on a show." If, as Raphael suspected, this marital display of affection was an unspoken audition for Kubrick's benefit, at that time they had no clue that the show would come to dominate their hearts and their minds.

For a couple who furiously and relentlessly researched their characters, their decision to play effectively themselves, or a version of themselves, left them nowhere to go but on a journey into their emotional interior. Even though they hired acting coach Susan Batson and rehearsed separately at their rented London home, they were, as Nicole admitted, entering "dangerous subject matter" that had frightened even Stanley and his wife, Christiane, when the director first suggested tackling the Schnitzler novel during the early days of their marriage. As Nicole recalled, rather presciently, "But Tom and I decided to take the plunge. It meant talking to each

Bare-chested and "cut," Tom spent his first summer after graduating from high school either commuting to New York for auditions or at the beach with his girlfriend from high school, Diane Van Zoeren. Left to right: Diane, Tom, Scott Spina, and Holli Taylor.

Michele McGarry

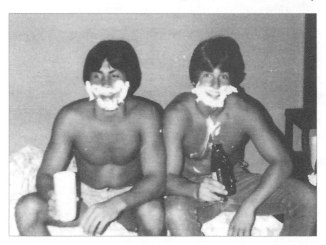

Baby-faced eighteen-year-olds Tom Cruise and friend Bill Claps fooled around with shaving-cream beards when they hung out at a beach house in Lavallette, New Jersey. *Michele McGarry*

In 1849, Tom's first known ancestor, Dillon Mapother, emigrated to America from his home in Southern Ireland, arriving in New York in June onboard the ship *Wisconsin*. The young man, who cited his occupation as engineer, then traveled to Louisville, Kentucky, where he carved out a new life in the New World.

9	Henry Hart	39	m	Engineer	England
10	Dillon Mapother	18	m	Engineer	Ireland
11	Thomas Wallis	53	m	Carpenter	England

Dillon Mapother's name in the ship's passenger list.

Pretty and sporty, Rowan Hopkins was one of Tom's numerous girlfriends during his schooldays in Ottawa, Canada.

Henry Munro School Yearbook

With his fashionably long hair and charming manner, Tom Cruise Mapother, aged twelve, was quite the dashing ladies' man.

Henry Munro School Yearbook

Young Tom Cruise Mapother IV married his first "wife" when he was just eleven on the playground of his school in Ottawa. His bride signed herself Rowan Mapother Hopkins.

As a youngster, Tom was an aggressive rather than a skillful sportsman, chipping a front tooth during a robust game of ice hockey. Years later he needed dental work to give him his trademark winning smile.

www.franciscan-alumni.org

Tom, then aged seventeen, was a keen member of the Glen Ridge High School wrestling team in New Jersey but had to drop out of the end-of-season contests when he damaged his ankle. That accident changed his life. His friend Steve Pansulla suggested he try out for a part in the school musical, *Guys and Dolls*, which launched his rise to stardom.

Glen Ridge High School
Yearbook 1979

Tom in the makeshift makeup room before his performance in *Guys and Dolls*. In the audience one night was the woman who would become his first agent, Tobe Gibson. She told him to change his name from Tom Mapother to Tom Cruise.

©2007 Philip Travisano

The class of '83. Many of the cast of Francis Ford Coppola's movie *The Outsiders* went on to become stars in their own right. Tom, who played a greaser, took the crown off his broken front tooth and had a henna tattoo etched on his arm to make him look more threatening. Left to right: Emilio Estevez, Rob Lowe, C. Thomas Howell, Matt Dillon, Ralph Macchio, Patrick Swayze, and a scowling Tom Cruise.

Everett Collection/Rex Features

In Tom's 1983 breakout movie, *Risky Business*, acting ingenue Rebecca De Mornay played a knowing hooker who captures the heart of middle-class geek Joel Goodsen, played by Tom. Off-screen, the couple started dating and ended up living together for a time in Manhattan.   *Peter C. Borsari*

Laura Baranek, wife of real-life "top gun" instructor Dave "Bio" Baranek, steals a kiss from Tom at the crew party held at the officers' club at the naval air station in San Diego, California, in August 1985. When the movie was released in May 1986, sales of flying jackets and sunglasses went sky-high.

Russ Novak

Tom with his mother, Mary Lee Mapother South, at the 1990 Oscar ceremony. He credits her with passing along her sunny, optimistic view of life. When he was young, he recalls, his theatrical mother would always have a song on her lips, even in difficult times.
Kip Rano/Rex Features

Actress Mimi Rogers and Tom on a date in 1986, the year that Tom was transformed from actor to superstar with the success of *Top Gun*. In May 1987, the couple married, with Tom's new wife encouraging him to investigate Scientology, the controversial faith that now dominates his life.
Frank Trapper/Corbis

L. Ron Hubbard uses what he called an E meter, a crude lie detector, to test a tomato. Normally the E meter is deployed in auditing sessions to assess the authenticity and accuracy of respondents' statements during intense question-and-answer sessions.
Fay Beverley Simcock/ Rex Features

After Hubbard's death in 1986, an aggressive young disciple took over the ailing organization. David Miscavige skillfully encouraged Tom Cruise to dedicate himself to Scientology, the two men becoming lifelong friends.

Fotos International/
Rex Features

Tom Cruise, screenwriter Ron Kovic, and director Oliver Stone celebrate winning Golden Globe awards for the movie *Born on the Fourth of July* in January 1990. At first, Kovic was unsure that Tom could convey the agony felt by disabled war veterans. When filming finished, he gave Tom his Bronze Star in admiration for his performance.

Bettmann/Corbis

Tom Cruise and Nicole Kidman chatting to Diana, Princess of Wales, at the London premiere of their historical action movie, *Far and Away.* They called it their "honeymoon film," since they made the film together immediately after their marriage in December 1991.   *Rex Features*

In January 1993, Tom and Nicole leave a Miami hospital with their newly adopted daughter, Isabella. An earlier adoption attempt in Florida was abandoned following leaks to the press, so they pursued Isabella in complete secrecy. They decided to adopt only after Nicole suffered a miscarriage early in their marriage.

Sipa Press/Rex Features

With her arms raised to the heavens, Nicole Kidman let out a screech of relief as she left her attorney's office in Los Angeles after her divorce settlement with Tom was finalized in August 2001.

X17/allaction.co.uk/EMPICS Entertainment/PA Photos

Tom first met Spanish actress Penélope Cruz when the pair were filming *Vanilla Sky*, shortly before the breakup of his marriage to Nicole Kidman in 2001. Here Tom and Penélope appear together on the red carpet at the London premiere of *The Last Samurai* in January 2004.

Richard Young/Rex Features

Tom met Colombian actress Sofía Vergara at a pre-Oscar party for Jamie Foxx in February 2005. Tom was single at the time, and word has it that he asked the host, Will Smith, to arrange for an invitation to be sent to the South American model. Within a matter of weeks they were seriously dating. Here they are seen leaving Jerry's Famous Deli, a paparazzi hangout, after the Foxx bash.

bigpicturesphoto.com

Publicist Pat Kingsley, pictured in sunglasses, fiercely protected Tom when he joined her client list in 1992. She was responsible for carefully crafting his image as action hero and boy next door. This photo was taken weeks before Tom fired Kingsley in March 2004, replacing her with his inexperienced Scientologist sister, Lee Anne DeVette. With Pat Kingsley and Tom is his mother, Mary Lee Mapother South, who now lives with her only son.

Marc Lecureuil/Corbis

Katie Holmes and actor James Van Der Beek shelter from the rain in Wilmington, North Carolina, where *Dawson's Creek* was filmed. He was her first boyfriend, but her relationship with him ended when fellow actor Joshua Jackson moved in. The two men, previously inseparable, became fierce foes. It was Katie's first bittersweet experience of love, heartbreak, and jealousy.

Scientology has always had a policy of targeting celebrities and enticing them to join the church. Perhaps this explains why Scientology leader David Miscavige (back row) and his wife Shelly (back center) took the trouble to fly to Madrid in late October 2004 to join his friend Tom Cruise and spend an evening watching soccer, not a game he is known to favor, in the company of David and Victoria Beckham and their family. In the background (center right) is Tom's then girlfriend, actress and Scientologist Yolanda Pecoraro.

Aaron Tanner/Rex Features

Ever since he jumped on Oprah Winfrey's couch in May 2005 to declare his love for Katie Holmes, Tom has spawned an entire industry of satire. Parodies of Tom and Katie have been plastered on everything from mugs and mousepads to T-shirts and bumper stickers, often inviting the attention of Tom's lawyers. Web sites mocking Tom's links to Scientology remain phenomenally popular, with one site (www.tomcruiseisnuts.com) still ranked in the top ten of Google searches for "Tom Cruise."

www.promotionaladventures.com/www.cafepress.com/www.tom-cruiseisnuts.com/www.t-shirthumour.com/www.clayboys.com

Over the past few years, Tom has become a "movie messiah," lecturing the world on the virtues of Scientology. Here he appears in Madrid in September 2004 at the inaugural opening of the faith's new center in the nation's capital.

Paul Hanna/Reuters/Corbis

When Tom jumped on Oprah Winfrey's couch, many thought it was a premeditated publicity stunt. Oprah herself was skeptical of his motives. Even though Tom—and John Travolta—have tried to recruit Oprah to Scientology, she has remained immune to their attentions. Tom, Katie, and Oprah attended a Los Angeles party in honor of Mary J. Blige hosted by Jada and Will Smith in February 2007. *Alex Berliner/BEI/Rex Features*

Since her divorce in 2001, it has been noticeable that Nicole Kidman is rarely seen in public with her adopted children, Isabella and Connor. They live with Tom in Beverly Hills and are educated in Scientology values and concepts. She mainly keeps in touch via e-mail and a web cam. Here the children make a rare appearance with their mother at an L.A. Lakers basketball game in December 2004.

TIKIC/KEYSTONE USA/ Rex Features

Katie with her publicist Leslie Sloane Zelnick (center) and "new best friend" Jessica Feshbach Rodriguez, who was her Scientology "minder" during her indoctrination into the faith. As with the rest of Katie's loyal management team, Zelnick was fired and replaced by Tom Cruise's own managerial entourage.

Michael Simon/Rex Features

Paula Wagner first met Tom in 1981 when she was his talent agent at the Creative Artists Agency. She was responsible for getting him an audition for *Risky Business*, his first hit movie. In 1992 they set up Cruise/Wagner Productions together, and *Mission: Impossible* was their first picture. For two years they ran United Artists together, vowing to revive the studio's fortunes. However, they parted company in August 2008 after a 27-year association. *CORBIS SYGMA*

Impetuous in love: Tom had only known Katie Holmes, sixteen years his junior, a matter of weeks before he got down on bended knee, read her a two-page love poem he had written himself, and proposed as the sun set on the Eiffel Tower in Paris. Here the happy couple share a joke at the London premiere of *War of the Worlds* in June 2005, the month Katie said "Yes."

Rex Features

When Tom and Katie hosted a pre-wedding dinner in Rome in November 2006, the real star of the show was six-month-old baby Suri. The couple did not release photographs of their daughter for three months after the birth, leading to speculation that the child had a physical defect, rumors that hurt her mother deeply.

Pignatiello/Rex Features

Tom has always been surrounded by women, being brought up in a house filled with three sisters and his mother. Here are three of the most important women in his life: his sister Lee Anne DeVette, his mother, Mary Lee Mapother South, and his wife, Katie Holmes, at the Giorgio Armani Privé Collection party in Los Angeles in February 2007.   *Sipa Press/Rex Features*

Tom, Katie, and Suri on the set of *Valkyrie* in Berlin, Germany, in September 2007.   *Sipa Press/Rex Features*

Loving embrace: Tom gives a welcoming hug to Suri as Katie looks on. The touching encounter between father and daughter took place as Tom filmed the role of German war hero Claus von Stauffenberg in Berlin. He faced fierce opposition from German politicians and religious leaders, who were dismayed that such a high-profile Scientologist was playing the part of an icon of modern German democracy. Many Germans see Scientology as a totalitarian group, like the Nazis.   *Sipa Press/Rex Features*

other about jealousy and attraction for other people—things you usually skirt around or pretend aren't there. It would be difficult and, at times, very confronting. It was something that was going to either draw us close together or pull us apart."

While the reported $20 million fee was substantial, so, too, was the commitment, the couple agreeing to an open-ended contract. They were so keen to work with Kubrick that, even knowing his reputation for endless retakes, not just during filming but in rehearsal, they signed on for a lengthy shooting schedule of five months. In fact, while the cinematic action takes place in Manhattan over just three days, the filming took four hundred days, landing it in the *Guinness Book of World Records* as the longest constant movie shoot in history. Shooting went on for so long that two cast members, Harvey Keitel and Jennifer Jason Leigh, dropped out in order to pursue other commitments. They were replaced by Sydney Pollack and Marie Richardson. The change had one by-product. During the endless schedule, Pollack and Tom explored their mutual love of aerobatics—Pollack was amazed at how quickly Tom learned complicated maneuvers—while Pollack taught Tom how to cook.

Not that Tom could really enjoy the food, as during filming the actor, then thirty-four, developed a stomach ulcer, a condition often associated with stress. It was not entirely surprising. Tom, who played Dr. Bill Harford, was on set for all but six days of the marathon shoot. During her downtime Nicole organized play dates for Isabella with Princesses Beatrice and Eugenie, the daughters of Sarah, Duchess of York, visited the Lake District to study the poetry of William Wordsworth, learned Italian, and joined the local riding school.

Looking back, Nicole realized that they were living in a "strange, cocooned" world for eighteen months, spending much of their time in an enclosed room. "We didn't see many people," she recalled. "Tom and I had a trailer that we shared, we also had a smaller room, and I would go into that room a lot and read." In the insular world they inhabited, their immediate staff became close companions. Tom spent hours hanging out with his driver Tommy Lee, an avuncular Cockney, as well as with his bodyguard Mickey Brett, a fatherly figure who is popular not just with Tom but also with Angelina Jolie and Julia Roberts.

The shoot was all the more taxing as Tom, an actor whose signature was the release of energy, both physical and emotional, didn't enjoy playing the "contained," disconnected medical man he represented on screen. Containment was not a word normally associated with Tom, an experience he found "unpleasant." A man of dynamic movement and authority, he found his match in the sly subtle manipulations of his director. If Tom was a prince of control, Kubrick was king. He did not just demand control, he desired total obedience, from the script, his cast, his producers, and the studio. Even Nicole, who adored the director, was taken aback by his obsessive behavior. "When you work with Stanley," she said, "you live the way he wants you to live. He wouldn't want me to leave the house. He would get anxious if I was going out. He wanted me to be so dedicated—I mean as every director does, they don't want to think that any other films exist in the world, other than the film you are working on."

For all Tom's star power, it was Kubrick who was ultimately in charge. After all, he was the one who had forced actress Shelley Duvall to perform 127 takes for one scene in *The Shining,* who almost blinded Malcolm McDowell by pinning his eyes open for a scene in *A Clockwork Orange,* and who drove George C. Scott to the brink of insanity during the filming of *Dr. Strangelove.* As Tom said, "He liked filming things in long takes, so we did scenes over and over again, until we got them right. Sure, there were scenes that we did sixty, seventy takes. And there were times when, contrary to popular belief, we'd get something in only a few takes."

When filming started in November 1996 at Pinewood Studios outside London, Kubrick, then sixty-eight, became the third wheel in the lives of Tom and Nicole, a delicately invasive and controlling presence in their work and marriage, which soon became one and the same. Kubrick worked with the couple separately, forbidding them to compare notes or discuss the movie when they were alone, lest they change the existing dynamic where he had ultimate say. During their collaboration they discussed the most intimate details of their lives together, and he, like an avuncular father figure, would intrude into their private lives, on one occasion chastising Nicole for speaking harshly to her husband. In the power play between leading man and director, Tom and Kubrick rarely went head to head, the two men using their aides to relay instructions, tricky messages, and news that might upset and annoy.

As Tom said, "It was just me and Nic and Stanley for years. Sometimes the three of us were literally alone in the room together. He would man the camera himself. The sound guy would mike us for sound and leave. There are things that you do because they're so personal, and there were things that we did that were sexy for the two of us, and there are moments that he got that he wouldn't have got had he not created this intense atmosphere of intimacy. It's confronting for me to have to see it. Nic sometimes said when we were going through it, 'Oh jeez.' It was like running marathon after marathon, emotionally."

This intimacy inevitably changed the dynamics between man and wife, actors and director. While Kubrick encouraged the couple to come up with their own ideas for scenes, he seemed to indulge Nicole far more than Tom, jotting down her ad-libs and accepting her choice of music, Chris Isaak's "Baby Did a Bad Bad Thing," for a sex scene between them. He described Nicole as a "thoroughbred" and Tom as a "roller coaster."

There remained the suspicion that, for all the mutual admiration, there was an element of humiliation involved in Kubrick's treatment of Tom. While Frederic Raphael recognizes but does not endorse the argument, he concedes that for Kubrick "breaking people and feeding them into his machine was maybe a reflex he could not resist." When Kubrick was rewriting the script, he would often fax Tom pages in the middle of the night, ensuring that his leading man was living his life according to the director's body clock. Or when Kubrick filmed a scene in which Tom's character was knocked to the ground by a gang of drunken college louts who accused him of being gay, was this a wink to the audience being aware of the rumors circulating about the actor? Even Raphael is not sure, noting that in the novel the chanting youths accuse the doctor of being Jewish. It was Kubrick who changed the insult.

This ambiguous relationship played out most explicitly when Kubrick filmed the sex scenes involving Nicole and her navy lover. Noticeably, the six-day shoot was the only time in the marathon production that Tom was definitely not needed on set. Not so his scriptwriter. In a knowing aside, Kubrick told Raphael that Nicole had agreed to take off her clothes and he would be filming on a closed set for the next few days. "Might be a good day to happen to drop by the studio, if you wanted to," he told him. Raphael declined, feeling that it would be "cheap" to take advantage of the situation.

Certainly voyeurism had always interested Kubrick, who enjoyed watching porn movies and talked about the possibility of exploring the genre. The sequence that inspired the closed shoot involved Nicole's character, Alice Barford, telling her husband about a recurring sexual fantasy, triggered by her lust for a naval officer she had glimpsed in a hotel lobby the year before. Enraged and presumably excited by this confession, Bill embarks on a series of sexual adventures of his own, culminating in attending a ritualistic masked orgy that ends in the possible murder of a beautiful naked woman.

The man chosen to play the lover of Alice's dreams was Gary Goba, a twenty-nine-year-old Canadian model who had never acted before. When he auditioned, he thought it was for the job of an extra who would be wearing a naval officer's uniform. Instead, in December 1997, he found himself naked on the closed set in front of an equally naked Nicole Kidman. Over the next few days, with barely an introduction, the two strangers performed fifty or so sexual positions, with Kubrick filming from the shadows all the while. The director wanted his naked star to explore every sex act, apart from oral sex, which he dismissed as a cinematic cliché.

"We just tried to do stuff that we had never ever seen before in movies," recalled Goba. "Sometimes she would come up with an idea or I would or Stanley would." In the scene that actually made it into the movie, Nicole is lying on her back wearing a summer dress while Goba caresses her and lifts her dress over her breasts to reveal her body. "Leave [the dress] up there and have those hands continue on down, and, like, grab her tits, kiss them if you want, hands all the way down her body and end up between her legs," said the director. Goba, trying to be sensitive to Nicole, rested his hand on her thigh, knowing that it could make little difference to Stanley, as her other leg was shielding what his hand might actually be doing from the camera anyway. "Whoa! Whoa! Whoa! Gary, you've got to get right in there!" Kubrick instructed.

"I couldn't believe it," says Goba. "I just couldn't believe it. I think he was having fun with it. It was a joke for him, but I think he went a little far for her because as the days went on, she would be like, 'Okay, cut!' Like this is getting too intimate, but he just let it go. It was like he was trying to have things done to piss her off—or the opposite. It was weird. He was laughing. He thought it was so funny."

It was as if he were enjoying the relentless humiliation of another man's wife—and the unspoken emasculation of her husband—by playing out explicit scenes that would inevitably end up on the cutting room floor. In one scenario, Nicole had a wig glued over her private parts and Kubrick ordered Goba to perform oral sex on her. "He really wanted me to go for it," recalls Goba. "I did and he was like, 'You've got to really push in there and really move your head around,' and I'd see him laughing and she would be like, 'Oh God, Stanley!' So I was really grinding away in there, with my mouth on her patch—and there was hair in my mouth, too, and I'd be pulling one out."

As Nicole's biographer James L. Dickerson caustically observed, "The most damning evidence against Kubrick lies in the relentless manner in which he pursued the sex scenes between Nicole and Gary Goba. He asked Nicole to do things that he knew damned well would never make it onto film. It was abusive behavior cloaked in a mantle of professional necessity."

While Nicole is not so censorious, she concedes that she only allowed herself to be used in this way for Kubrick. "He didn't exploit me. I certainly wouldn't have done it for any other director and, yes, it was a little difficult to go home to my husband afterward." It seems that when she did go home, she did not say much about the day job—as per Kubrick's standing instructions. Only after he saw the finished movie a year or so later was Tom aware of some of the intimate scenes played out between his wife and Goba. "Yeah, who the fuck was that guy?" he later said to *USA Today*. (The newspaper removed the expletive.)

If the leading man was in the dark about important aspects of this enigmatic movie, the mass media was in a fever of speculation. One story claimed that Tom would wear a dress in the film, another said that the photographer Helmut Newton, a master at creating sexually explicit images, was hired to snap the couple in a bid to "loosen" them up. Another tabloid tale suggested that the couple had visited sex clubs as part of their research. When Harvey Keitel left the set, it was rumored that he had been fired because a masturbation scene involving Nicole had literally gotten out of hand.

The rumor mill was fueled not just by Kubrick's obsessive secrecy and control, but by the continuing gossip about Tom and Nicole and the nature of their marriage. The most high-profile couple in Hollywood was also the most discussed, prompting endless rumors surrounding Tom's sexuality, their decision to adopt, and Nicole's career ambitions. Gossip about Tom first surfaced in 1986 after his blockbuster *Top Gun* became cult viewing in the gay community. Even Tom's costar Val Kilmer later admitted that the film had "a couple of shower scenes too many." Beefcake pictures from Tom's early years, which apparently appeared in a New Jersey gay magazine, together with his abrupt split from Mimi Rogers in 1990 and her subsequent tongue-in-cheek comments about his desire to be a monk, had given the rumors greater traction.

When Tom played the sexually ambiguous character of Lestat in the 1994 film *Interview with the Vampire,* journalists had the perfect excuse to put the spotlight on Tom's private life. During publicity for the film, he dismissed the gay talk as "hard-line cynicism," telling writer Kevin Sessums in October 1994, "It's not true, but people are going to say what they want to say. . . . I don't care if people are Martians. I really don't care. Straight. Gay. Bisexual. Catholic. Jewish." The rumor mill kept churning even after Nicole rallied to his defense, telling *Vanity Fair,* "I'll bet all the money I've ever made, plus his, that he doesn't have a mistress, that he doesn't have a gay lover, that he doesn't have a gay life."

In 1995, when *McCall's* magazine published an article suggesting that Tom and Nicole's marriage was a sham and that Nicole only had a Hollywood career in exchange for hiding Tom's gay lifestyle, the couple decided to act, Tom instructing his lawyer Bertram Fields to file suit. While many actors ignore the gossip, seeing it as part and parcel of life in Hollywood, Tom was much more sensitive, especially as both he and Nicole knew the medical reasons behind their decision to adopt two children. While *McCall's* printed a retraction and apology, his lawyer was to spend many more years damping down flames of gossip that flared up all over the world. When the German magazine *Bunte* claimed in 1996 that Tom was gay and sterile with a "zero sperm count," Tom instructed Fields to slap the journal with an $80 million libel suit. "The actor's career depends on his fans' willingness to believe that he does or could possibly possess the qualities of the character he plays," said Fields. In other words, no woman would go weak at the knees at the sight of Tom if they thought he was gay or impotent. If the rumors persisted, his image as a clean-cut American sex symbol could be compromised. The magazine duly caved.

The acid test came during the filming of *Eyes Wide Shut.* In October 1997, just a few weeks after the couple had attended the funeral of Diana, Princess of Wales, the *Sunday Express* newspaper published a story claiming that Tom and Nicole's marriage was a business-driven partnership of "convenience" designed to hide their homosexuality. The article also implied that the reason Tom and Nicole had adopted their children was because Tom was sterile and impotent. In keeping with previous policy, Tom decided to sue for libel, telling friends, somewhat oddly, that the story exposed his children, then ages two and four, to ridicule. For once the newspaper called his bluff and announced that it was prepared to defend the action. That meant that if Tom should decide to go ahead, he would have to appear in the witness box at the High Court in London and face hostile questioning about his marriage, his sex life, and his previous sexual partners.

He hired the best lawyer in Britain, the flamboyant George Carman, famous for defending, among others, Elton John, politician Jeremy Thorpe, comedian Ken Dodd, and cricketer Imran Khan. When the couple was ushered into his chambers, Carman was immediately struck by how nervous these Hollywood A-listers were at the prospect of going to court.

For all his bluster, Tom was particularly anxious about the prospect of facing a rigorous cross-examination. Few would blame him. In the sober quiet of his book-lined office, the silver-haired barrister walked Tom and Nicole through the financial and personal costs of appearing in court. In Britain, while the courts tend to favor celebrity plaintiffs, libel cases are notoriously unpredictable and ruinously expensive. Winners often end up losers, their reputations in tatters. Litigants who lie in court for the sake of protecting their good name can end up in jail, like novelist Jeffrey Archer and former Cabinet minister Jonathan Aitken.

During their conversation Carman ran through the allegations about the couple, asking them individually if they were prepared to repudiate the newspaper's claims under oath. Carman's son Dominic, who wrote his father's life story, recalls: "My father formally asked Tom Cruise if he was gay. He categorically denied it. However, he warned him that he would have a rough time in court and asked him point-blank if there were any relationships that he may have forgotten about that the other side might bring up." Again Tom denied that he had any skeletons in his closet that could embarrass him. Carman was impressed. "George felt Tom would make an excellent witness as he was highly cooperative and had a certain charm without seeming arrogant," remembers Dominic. "George was more than satisfied with his honesty."

Certainly Tom's replies would have come as no surprise to the women in his life—past and present. Not only had Nicole and Mimi publicly testified to his virile heterosexuality, but his earlier lovers were equally perplexed by the constant whispers about his sexual preferences. High-school girlfriends Nancy Armel, whom he'd wanted to marry, and Diane Van Zoeren both found Tom a regular red-blooded teenager. As Diane, who dated him from high school until he made the movie *Taps,* recalled, "I don't get it. I find these stories just hard to believe. We romanced in my dad's Oldsmobile doing what you are not supposed to."

If anything, Tom was uncomfortable around gay men. Those who saw him in the company of some of Nicole's gay friends, who included designer John Galliano, noticed that he was awkward and ill at ease, much preferring the company of jocks who talked about football rather than fashion. His discomfort was understandable, given Scientology's view of the gay community. In *Dianetics,* Ron Hubbard famously described homosexuals as "sexual perverts" who should be taken from society "as rapidly as possible and uniformly institutionalized." Indeed many men—and some women—joined Scientology in the hope that their homosexuality would be "cured." After spending $500,000, painter Michael Pattinson, who reached OT VIII, the highest level attainable, sued Scientology for his money back because after years of auditing he was still gay. He eventually dropped the suit when his funds ran out.

While Tom could step into the witness box with a clear conscience, the upcoming trial troubled him greatly, the actor frequently asking George Carman to visit him on the set of *Eyes Wide Shut* and at his rented Hertfordshire home.

From time to time he and Nicole, or Tom on his own, drove to Carman's chambers in central London. Even though Carman found Tom's need for such extensive hand-holding "bizarre," he did not begrudge them his time, charging them about three thousand dollars an hour for consultations that could last several hours. It was not only the impending court case that bothered Tom; he was "obsessed" about his public image, continually pointing out articles that irritated him and discussing the possibility of seeking redress. Over the next few years he consulted George Carman on at least a dozen occasions.

In the end it was not Tom's demeanor in the dock that won the day, but Nicole's admission that she had suffered at least one ectopic pregnancy during the early years of their marriage. It was the smoking gun, proof not only that Tom was fertile but that the couple were involved in a regular, loving marriage. Once Express Newspapers was informed of these medical facts, they threw in the towel. While their decision came as a relief to Tom and Nicole, it rather robbed George Carman of his moment of glory. Instead, the newspaper agreed to pay $200,000 in damages and publish a comprehensive apology and retraction.

In October 1998, just a year after the original libel suit, Carman and Tom Cruise appeared at the High Court to confirm that the money would be given to charity. In an eloquent address, Carman told the court that Tom and Nicole "married solely because they loved each other and their marriage is a close and happy one; they both love and are very devoted to their two young adopted children. They have brought proceedings to put an end once and for all to these highly offensive rumors which have been so hurtful to their married life together and to their role as parents."

The only thing missing as Carman made his victory address was Mrs. Cruise. While Tom, Carman, and Bert Fields, calling from Los Angeles, had pressured Nicole to attend the triumphant occasion so they could stand side by side on the court steps, she had consistently refused. Even though Carman judged Nicole "cold and distant" during their meetings, he still found her decision one of the "oddest" in his professional career. Tom explained her absence by saying that she had a cold. Carman didn't believe a word and pressed him further. The plain answer was that she did not want to be part of the circus. As with most libels, the winner was really the loser. In order to prove that her husband was virile and heterosexual, she had to have the secrets of her womb placed on public display. She had gone along with the case, probably reluctantly, to support her husband in his legal pissing contest with an unimportant British Sunday tabloid. There was a price to be paid, as was shown on the steps of the High Court, where Tom was alone in waving to the crowds and accepting the applause of well-wishers.

Although George Carman feared that it would look "terrible," the media failed to comment on Nicole's absence. Only those associated with the couple appreciated the significance, seeing it as a further sign of the growing distance between them. In the year between the publication of the *Sunday Express* article and the court victory, cracks were beginning to appear in the marriage. Nicole bridled more and more at Tom's controlling behavior, finding fault in everything he did for her. His constant love notes became irritating, the endless gifts of flowers a bore.

Romantic gestures like spontaneously taking her to their favorite London restaurant, the Ivy, or for a weekend away to the Cipriani Hotel in Venice with dinner at Harry's Bar no longer made her heart sing. "She was an unhappy wife," noted an associate. "She was constantly wrestling with the fact that she did not love him anymore." For his part, the more he tried to woo her with gifts, the more she pulled away. "There came a point where nothing Tom did pleased her," recalls an associate. "Tom adored Nic. I have never known a man who was so loving and giving. But that love was not reciprocated by Nic."

Nicole's disgruntlement with her husband was increasingly played out through their friends. For example, Tom's buddy Emilio Estevez, best man for his first marriage, was no longer as welcome as he once was, and on the odd occasions

Tom saw his old school friend Michael LaForte and his wife, Fran, Nicole seemed ill at ease and distracted, as though the rough-talking New Jerseyan was not quite socially acceptable. However, in the company of her girlfriends, like actors Naomi Watts and Rebecca Riggs, as well as gay men from the world of fashion, she was a different person, smiling, relaxed, and full of fun, happy to sing and dance the night away at places like the Buffalo Club in Santa Monica. Curiously, if she went out on her own, she would often take the couple's driver Dave Garris, who had worked for them since *Days of Thunder,* along for company. If they went to the movies, she would even allow Garris, who has been described as a Tom Cruise wannabe, to choose the film they were going to see.

As she pulled away from Tom, by necessity Nicole became much less involved with the children's upbringing than her husband. When she was away filming or, increasingly, flying to Sydney to spend time with her parents and sister, it could be days before she would phone to see how Isabella and Connor were coping. Those who saw the family close up concluded that Tom was much more comfortable and enthusiastic as a parent. The actor was in constant—and controlling—touch with the youngsters and their nannies no matter how busy he was.

In keeping with Hubbard's theory that children were small adults, Tom never babied his children, striking a balance between mentoring and nurturing. Unsurprisingly, Tom was an energetic, noisy dad, always chasing, joshing, playing with the children, his hearty laugh echoing through the normally quiet house. Thankfully, after a stage in which Connor gave Bella terrible bites, the youngsters bonded, Tom appreciating the differences in their characters: Connor bright but mischievous, Bella assertive but playing by the rules. As soon as Connor was walking and talking, Tom took him off on boys' adventures, whisking him away in his private plane for the weekend with only his communicator, Michael Doven, for company. Like most fathers, he wanted to re-create the happy aspects of his own youth for his son, building a ramp at the family home in Telluride so that Connor could be taught daredevil jumps on a tiny motorbike.

When Nicole won a leading role in the comedy *Practical Magic,* it came as no surprise that she left the children with Tom in London while she flew to Los Angeles in January 1998 to rehearse her part. A couple of weeks after beginning work, she was rushed to the hospital for surgery to remove what was officially described as a benign ovarian cyst. Given that her mother had a history of breast cancer and that Nicole had her own gynecological difficulties, it was a worrying time, Tom flying out to the West Coast to be at his wife's side. She recovered sufficiently to continue work on the movie, which was shot in Washington state, allowing Tom to return to London to conclude filming of the interminable *Eyes Wide Shut.* An illicitly recorded telephone conversation between the increasingly distant couple, published in March 1998, gave the world an insight into their fractious marriage.

Celebrity photographer Eric Ford, who recorded the conversation, was subsequently fined and jailed, but in the meantime everyone could listen in to the Cruises uncut and in private. Away from the glamour and smiles of the red carpet, they were revealed as a tired and spoiled married couple getting tetchy with each other. During the chat, made on a car phone, Tom is clearly more conciliatory, Nicole unwilling to be soothed. Noticeably, the love notes and flowers are now weapons in a war of emotional attrition rather than tokens of affection.

After Tom tells Nicole that she makes him "feel like shit," Nicole responds by saying, "We've been hanging on by a fucking thread, okay? A thread. You know it and I know it." Even though Tom says that he wants their relationship to work, Nicole continues to carp, asking why he hasn't sent her a rose or a love note. The conversation continues in this vein, sometimes lightening up, sometimes getting more serious. The couple changes gears, like most married couples, between discussing practicalities—notably plans for Connor's third birthday—and issuing serious complaints.

Nicole tells her husband baldly, "Tom, there's no love here, right? You're under emotional abuse, I'm abusing you, you're abusing me. Tom, this isn't worth it! You have two un-happy people, okay, who spend too much time apart and in the past have hurt each other too much. . . . And I tell you something, we haven't spent any time together, Tom! You just don't make an effort. I come home and all you ever say is, 'I'm exhausted.'"

After a brief interjection from her husband, Nicole con-tinues her litany of complaints: "I'm sick of it, I'm sick of it! And if it's not, 'I've got to get the kids from school,' it's 'I'm working, I don't have time for you.' And Tom, I've heard this for so long now and you're not working now and you're still saying it."

In an attempt to placate his wife, Tom is cajoling and con-soling. "I miss you. I love you. I think about you all day long. You're a knucklehead, a knucklehead for thinking that I don't care, I'm not loving. I'm embarrassed that I was tired last night. I apologize, okay?" Like many married couples who have a fight, by the end of the conversation the couple is managing to laugh, and signing off by saying "I love you" to each other. Unlike most married couples, however, Tom and Nicole had to justify their spat to the gossip-hungry world, their spokeswoman Pat Kingsley issuing a statement saying that the conversation was taken out of context and the cou-ple's words edited to make their discussion sound like a row. When she was asked, Nicole sensibly made light of the squab-ble. "We were fighting about how many people to invite to our son's birthday party," she said. "And about which one of us was more tired and who was working harder. Quite boring, actually."

Others who witnessed Tom and Nicole's daily life were more frank. "To me," says an associate, "their marriage wasn't a 'happy marriage,' but it was one that had found a certain groove, and they went with it. Tom chased after Nicole, who was always unobtainable, and that cycle continued. I think he was in love with her up until the end, but that she had grown out of love with him and was unhappy in the marriage. She seemed so much more mature than he was. He's a jock; a guy's guy. He isn't sophisticated. She is. I believe she loved him when she met him, but she outgrew him. He seemed happier in the marriage than she was and she was always finding fault with everything."

It was not just her husband she found fault with. Nicole often seemed bored or disenchanted with her life as a Hollywood star, expecting a luxurious lifestyle as her birthright. During publicity for *Practical Magic* in the fall of 1998, Warner Bros. arranged for a private G5 jet to ferry her around. It was, as far as she was concerned, a given, not a privilege. "She had no sense of wonderment about the world," recalls an associate. "So many wonderful things happened to her, but she had an enduring sense of boredom like some 1920s flapper. She never delighted in anything."

Whatever the state of their marriage, that summer was artistic business as usual—Tom working on the money-spinning blockbusters, Nicole choosing low-paying art projects. When Tom finally finished work on *Eyes Wide Shut* in June 1998, the couple decided to stay on in London, renting another luxurious house in central London. Tom worked on preproduction for a sequel to *Mission: Impossible,* which was scheduled to be filmed in Australia, while Nicole tried her hand at the theater, earning a modest five hundred dollars a week to star in *The Blue Room* at the fashionable Donmar Warehouse Theatre. She would play five characters, ranging from a Cockney harlot and a politician's mistress to an unfaithful wife. The role involved simulating sex five times and appearing naked, albeit briefly, in front of the audience. Nor was Nicole the only one to take her clothes off; her costar, Iain Glen, had to perform a naked cartwheel across the stage each night.

In September 1998, just weeks before the court case against Express Newspapers, *The Blue Room* opened to rapturous reviews, Nicole's performance memorably described as "theatrical Viagra" by theater critic Charles Spencer. "She's drop dead gorgeous and bewitchingly adorable. The vision of her wafting round the stage with a fag in one hand and her knickers in the other as a delicious French au pair will haunt my fantasies for months."

Nicole had managed something that had eluded her in the movies: Now she was not only considered a beauty, but taken seriously as an actress and a sex symbol. It was intoxicating. Director Sam Mendes, who went on to direct *American Beauty,* noted the change in her. "I feel for Nicole it was a very special time. It was the moment she became a special entity from Tom Cruise. And I'm sure she was aware that was happening."

In public, both Nicole and her stage partner Iain Glen were keen to emphasize that their respective partners—Glen was married at that time to actress Susannah Harker—were "secure" about watching them have sex onstage. Tom was so "secure," in fact, that he came to see the play more than twenty times. Perhaps he was wholly admiring of his wife's work and absolutely comfortable watching her act out having sex with Iain Glen over and over again. Certainly Glen, who first met Tom when he watched them perform the play at a preview, implied that they were all mates together. "He was such an extraordinary bundle of brilliant, positive energy. You couldn't have a more enthusiastic and generous person as a friend."

Behind the scenes, it wasn't quite so convivial. The handsome Scotsman, who was considered for the role of James Bond, was a talented stage and film veteran who refused to be impressed by Tom's achievements. Glen, who was the same age as the Hollywood star but six inches taller, looked down on Tom, belittling his ability while flirting with his wife. The general consensus of those in Tom's circle was that the Hollywood actor was pleasant to the Scottish thespian— but only through gritted teeth. "Tom and he did not get on, whereas there was real chemistry between Iain and Nicole. She always laughed at his jokes." Those who watched the trio in action could not help but admire Tom's sangfroid in the face of considerable provocation. As one associate said bluntly, "Iain Glen was a dick who had no respect for Tom and who would openly flirt with Nicole. Tom refused to show any agitation, as he was a real gentleman."

For a man used to admiration and easy authority, the incestuous, clubby landscape of theatrical London left him feeling isolated. This cliquey world, with its in-jokes, witty banter, and storytelling, was alien to the film actor who was no longer the instant center of attention. Even his famous smile failed to impress. More than that, he was used to the rhythm of the film set, where early mornings rather than late nights were the norm. This lifestyle, however, was meat and drink to Nicole, who reveled in the adrenaline-fueled rush after nightly performances, hanging out until the early hours at the members-only Soho Club, chatting, laughing, and carousing.

For the first time in their marriage, rumors and whispers raced around London about Nicole, claiming that she and Iain were involved in a passionate offstage romance. The gossip was hardly helped by Glen's breezy attitude in interviews. "We had to get very intimate with each other very quickly as actors," he told *In Theater* magazine. "It's easy to kid yourself that you're getting on really well, but with Nicole—through Sam's help—we immediately established a very easy relationship. I think that was very important. People who come to the play see us do five different characters each; in a way, it's curiously about the relationship between Nic and I as much as anything."

Once the play finished its London run at the end of October, Nicole and Iain flew to New York, where the show was scheduled to open on Broadway in mid-December. In order to give extra zest to her role as a prostitute, Nicole hired her acting coach, Susan Batson, to help her explore the part further. Batson took her to a seedy part of downtown Manhattan where Nicole spent time talking to real streetwalkers. The problem was that the sight of Nicole mingling with hookers began to draw attention—and customers. "Here was a hot white woman on the street," Batson remembers. "Cars were coming left and right. We finally had to really get out of there because it got a little dangerous."

While the extra homework may have helped her performance, the play was not quite as well received as in London. Even so, Nicole and Iain were the talk of Broadway, invited to the famed annual ball at the Metropolitan Museum of Art. Unlike his counterpart, Iain Glen was not used to walking the red carpet or, for that matter, wearing a suit. So Nicole arranged for the fashion house Prada to lend him a suit and pair of shoes for the big occasion. When he demurred about sending them back, Nicole generously bought them for him. Her largesse extended to inviting Iain, his wife, Susannah Harker, and their child to Telluride for Thanksgiving, as well as flying them to Sydney to join her family for the millennium celebrations. Although Tom played the gracious host, Glen's constant put-downs and disrespect infuriated him. If it had been his choice, they would never have been invited in the first place.

As with Kubrick, Tom was all about putting on a show. Tom would regularly visit Nicole backstage, though it was noted that there was little conversation or other interaction between them when they were alone. As soon as photographers were around, it was camera, lights, action, the couple kissing, canoodling, and pawing each other to the point where observers were thinking, "Just get a room." Once the photographers were gone, the emotional lights went off and the couple reverted to their normal world of silence and distance.

During the Broadway run of *The Blue Room*, another man came into her life who would have a dramatic impact. At the end of one performance, Nicole walked into her dressing room to find a dozen long-stemmed red roses. At first she thought Tom had sent them, but when she read the note she realized they were from Australian director Baz Luhrmann. "She sings, she dances, she dies. Please meet me," read the note. Intrigued, Nicole found herself talking to Luhrmann about the role of Satine, the beautiful and tragic courtesan who would be the star of his proposed screen musical, *Moulin Rouge*. The part would be a stretch for Nicole, who was not a trained singer or dancer. Buoyed by her success in *The Blue Room* and lured by the prospect of filming in her hometown of Sydney, Nicole decided to take on the challenge.

It proved to be contagious. As Tom was preparing to reprise his role as special agent Ethan Hunt in *Mission: Impossible II,* he, too, found himself seduced by a challenging script. This one was by Paul Thomas Anderson, young director of the cult film *Boogie Nights,* who had visited Tom during the long hours of waiting on the set of *Eyes Wide Shut* to say he had written a role for him in his upcoming movie, *Magnolia.* Tom, who devours scripts the way others read newspapers, was immediately taken with the character of Frank T. J. Mackey, a macho, misogynist self-help guru who teaches men how to snare women at his "Seduce and Destroy" seminars. Like the film, his character was over the top, ripe, and rather gamey. Anderson based Tom's character on the teachings of California author Ross Jeffries, whose speed seduction techniques were the basis for a series of self-help books.

While many were surprised that Tom was prepared to join an ensemble cast, which included Julianne Moore, Jason Robards, and Philip Seymour Hoffman, Tom relished the part, inviting his pals to the set to watch when he conducted a seminar in which his character yelled at his enraptured male audience to "respect the cock and destroy the cunt." As he later told director Cameron Crowe: "When I read the script I thought, 'When do you get a chance to go to seminars like that?' I'm an actor. I'd never played a character like that. I like humor. I thought it was dark and funny."

It was believed that Anderson had written a scene in which Mackey visits his estranged father on his deathbed with Tom in mind. In fact, Anderson didn't know that Tom had last seen his father in similar circumstances in real life. The actor did, though, draw on his own experience, Tom later admitting that he was "skating on the edge." He was sensitive enough to ensure that his mother, Mary Lee, and stepfather, Jack South, saw the film privately before the premiere, lest it bring back painful memories for her. She loved his performance, as did audiences and his peers, Tom duly rewarded with a Golden Globe award and an Oscar nomination.

Shortly after filming ended in early 1999, Tom received an invitation he could not refuse. It was from Scientology executives, politely requesting that he undertake the rigors of what is known as the Potential Trouble Source/Suppressive Person course. The course is designed to anchor an individual's faith while pinpointing those in his life who create problems and difficulties—Suppressive Persons, who stop a Scientologist from achieving "wins" on his journey up the bridge. The Potential Trouble Source in the sights of the Scientology hierarchy was Nicole Kidman.

Alarm bells had been ringing ever since they had read a December 1998 interview in *Newsweek,* where she described her faith: "There's a little Buddhism, a little Scientology," she said. "I was raised Catholic and a big part of me is still a Catholic girl." That was not good enough. Not only was she married to one of Scientology's poster boys, but her father was a psychologist, which automatically made her a Potential Trouble Source. Even though, as a celebrity, Nicole was treated with kid gloves by Scientology leaders, the storm clouds were gathering.

Shortly after Kidman's *Newsweek* interview, senior Scientology leaders, including David Miscavige, Ray Mithoff, and others, discussed their strategy to keep Tom firmly in the fold. The fear was that a lukewarm Nicole could fatally compromise Tom's commitment to his faith. Somehow Tom had to be inoculated against the virus of doubt. The surefire cure for skepticism was the Potential Trouble Source/Suppressive Person course, which reinforced wavering Scientologists' loyalty while making them more suspicious of those around them who were not members of the faith.

Often, on completion of the course, Scientologists would of their own free will write letters "disconnecting" from loved ones who were not members of Scientology. For example, after he completed the rigors of the PTS/SP course, Peter Alexander's seventeen-year-old son calmly sat down and wrote him a letter saying that he never wanted to see him again. The fact that such letters were voluntary meant that when questioned, Scientology officials could argue that these individuals were acting in their own best interests and without any coercion.

When she read the *Newsweek* article, Karen Pressley, who had watched Nicole's waning enthusiasm for Scientology, realized that it was the beginning of the end for her marriage. "By the late 1990s, Nicole was dragging her feet. Tom was much more involved and advancing much faster than she was. I realized that she wasn't going to make it and it really upset me." At the time Karen wanted to leave Scientology. She knew that if she left and her husband, Peter, wanted to stay inside the organization, he would have no choice but to divorce her, which is what happened. Karen now feared that Nicole would go down the same path and lose her children into the bargain.

In early 1999, Tom dutifully attended rigorous auditing sessions with Marty Rathbun, Scientology's inspector general. On one occasion, as part of a drill, he had to ask strangers this question: "What is the most obvious thing about me?" He carried out the drill so enthusiastically that, rather than confine his questioning to fellow Scientologists, he went out onto the street and collared complete strangers. One startled passerby told him: "Well, you look like Tom Cruise—but only at a stretch."

His decision to embark on such a tough course coincided with a period of "real loss and pain" in his life. On March 2, 1999, a few days after *The Blue Room* ended, Nicole and Tom watched *Eyes Wide Shut* for the first time at a private screening room in Manhattan. Except for two executives from Warner Bros., they were alone. They watched the movie twice, Tom calling Stanley Kubrick in London to tell him how much they loved it. Four days later, Kubrick was dead of a massive heart attack.

"I broke down when I heard," Tom said about the news. "I was in absolute shock and disbelief. We had shared two years of our lives together." Tom was a pallbearer at the funeral, which was held in a church in St. Albans, Hertfordshire. At the request of his friend Terry Semel, chairman of Warner Bros., the stunned actor channeled his grief by taking charge of all things relating to the movie.

An acknowledged control freak, Kubrick could not have chosen a better executor, Tom overseeing every detail of the film's distribution, marketing, and publicity. He was furious when scriptwriter Frederic Raphael penned a short book about working with Kubrick without asking permission. For their part, Raphael's publishers, Penguin, were astonished at Tom's reaction to what he considered an act of treachery. As Raphael recalls, "Penguin said they'd never seen anything like it—him trying to stop them publishing the book. But then he is one of these people crazed with wanting total control."

Tom's reputation for control faced a further challenge when the noted film critic Roger Ebert refused to sign a two-page "loyalty oath" before interviewing the actor about the long-awaited film. The contract insisted on editorial control, stressing that no interview could portray Tom in a "negative or derogatory manner" and that "the artist" had the right to delete any parts of the interview he didn't like. When Ebert refused to sign, for once it was Tom who caved, the film critic sitting down for a "frank and forthcoming" chat with the Hollywood star about the movie.

Much as Tom tried to tame the media tiger, he could never truly control the unruly beast. Shortly after Kubrick's funeral, two American tabloids claimed that two sex therapists had been hired by the director to give Tom and Nicole lessons in loving. The couple was less than amused, Warner Bros. issuing a statement denying the story while their lawyers filed suit. Nowhere was Tom's hair-trigger sensitivity more exposed than when mention was made of his involvement with Scientology. During the filming of *Eyes Wide Shut,* the magazine *Us Weekly* stated that Tom felt that actor John Travolta's involvement with the production of *Battlefield Earth,* based on an L. Ron Hubbard novel, was a "mistake." Within a week the magazine was forced to print a prominent retraction declaring that Tom was an "active and committed member of the Church of Scientology," who had neither said nor even "hinted" at anything negative to do with *Battlefield Earth.* That did not stop the film from being described as the worst movie ever made.

"I don't like suing people," Tom told *Harper's Bazaar.* "I take no pleasure in it. But there comes a point where it's beyond silly; it's destructive. I will sue. I will sue every single time that I can until it stops. And when they stop, I will stop."

After all the controversy, when *Eyes Wide Shut* actually opened in July 1999, it was a huge anticlimax. Even though it was the first of Kubrick's films to open at number one at the American box office, the critics were uncertain, some finding the movie dull and unconvincing, others describing the 159-minute film as Kubrick's last masterpiece, a fitting end to a brilliant career. Naturally, much of the attention focused on the sex scenes, with Nicole viewed as passionate and sexy in her encounters with Gary Goba, but distant and unengaged when coupling with her husband. In time, the movie would be seen as much as a coda to their unraveling marriage as an epitaph to Kubrick's career.

Tongues were kept wagging that same month when Nicole gave an interview to writer Tom Junod, who had flown to Sydney, where she was rehearsing *Moulin Rouge* while Tom, also in Australia, worked on *Mission: Impossible II.* Clearly she enjoyed Junod's company, taking him around to local bars, showing him the Sydney Harbor bridge, which her grandfather had helped build, and ending up in his hotel bed with Junod, fully clothed, next to her. Just then the phone rang; it was Tom seeking the whereabouts of his wife, as he and the children were waiting for her in a Chinese restaurant. When Junod told him where she was, Tom responded by saying, "In your dreams, buddy," only for Nicole to interject with, "I'm afraid so, darling. I'm afraid I'm right in his bed at this very moment."

While Junod insisted he had only been enjoying a "flirtation," it was perhaps a sign of his security that Tom, who had seen his wife make love onstage with a man he didn't particularly like and have sex with a complete stranger for six days straight, seemed to take the unusual news in his stride. In fact, he singled out Nicole for special praise when he accepted his Best Supporting Actor award for *Magnolia* at the Golden Globe awards ceremony in Hollywood. "Her generosity, her support, her sacrifices, her talent—she inspires me," he told the audience.

Nicole's sister, Antonia, was by his side when he walked the red carpet, as Nicole was busy filming *Moulin Rouge*. During the lengthy shoot, rumors inevitably circulated that Nicole was having an affair with her new leading man, another Scotsman, Ewan McGregor. The fact that she got on equally famously with his wife, Eve, and that Tom was on set as much as his schedule allowed, to see his wife and children, was lost in the shuffle. Indeed, Connor and Bella became used to seeing their mother, dressed in high heels, fishnet stockings, and a tight corset, making them supper in their trailer in between rehearsing her song and dance routines. Notably, even though Tom insisted on filming *Mission: Impossible II* in Australia so that he could be close to his wife, no one recalled her ever visiting him on set. Nicole remained his elusive object of desire, playing a role on film, and perhaps in life, where, as director Baz Luhrmann said of her character, "She was a woman at her absolute sexual prime."

There was a price to pay. The long and intense rehearsals took their toll, Nicole twice cracking a rib during a dance sequence and then, in April 2000, badly tearing some knee cartilage. She flew to Los Angeles, where noted surgeon Neal ElAttrache, the handsome brother-in-law of Sylvester Stallone, operated. Nicole saw him frequently afterward for consultations about her injury and the two became friendly.

At that time the whole family seemed accident-prone. After filming for *Mission: Impossible II* wrapped, Tom took the children on an ill-fated fishing trip on a forty-foot boat. During the voyage, they hit a reef, the motor conked out, and a Jet Ski hit the boat's side. When flames from the onboard barbecue flared too high, Tom threw it overboard—becoming, as one wag noted, the first actor in Australian history to throw a barbie on the shrimp. In some ways it was refreshing to see that the all-action hero who races sports cars and motorbikes, scuba dives, skydives, flies acrobatic planes, and dreams of climbing Everest is flawed like mere mortals. He exudes such a mountainous air of competence, security, and invincibility that when he was returning from a wilderness rafting trip, the party had a choice of three helicopters to pick them up. One rafter, who was terrified of choppers, traveled with Tom. "God isn't going to kill him," he reasoned.

Director John Woo exploited that image of the superhero, the guy who always dodges the bullet, in full for *Mission: Impossible II*. Even Woo, who made his name from choreographed violence, was nervous as he watched Tom film the famous opening stunt where he held on to a rock face thousands of feet above the Utah desert with one hand. Woo's mood was not helped by the fact that Tom's mother was standing next to him watching anxiously as a hovering helicopter filmed her son clinging to a rock. "I was more panicked than her," recalled Woo. "I grabbed her hand, turned to her, and said, 'Mom, he's going to be fine,' and actually I was the one worried." It took the cameraman seven takes to get the right shot. When Woo wanted Tom to be a "rock star," he didn't mean him to take it so literally.

Tom told director Cameron Crowe afterward that during the dazzling sequence he was simply admiring the view. That moment symbolized a man at the top of his game, king of his movie world. At thirty-six he was still limber enough to perform his own breathtaking stunts, an actor whose determined nonchalance in the face of danger was his trademark, and a successful producer in firm control of a big-budget movie that took in $70 million on its opening weekend in America alone.

Tom was never content to rest on his laurels as an actor and a producer, always searching for fresh talent, scripts, and challenges. At this time he was intrigued by the work of the young Spanish director Alejandro Amenábar. After a meeting in New York, he signed his latest script, a ghost story called *The Others*.

While Nicole and Tom seemed to be growing apart as a couple, professionally they were more entwined. Nicole signed up for six future projects, including a Paul Verhoeven movie where she was slated to play a suffragette, linked to the Cruise/Wagner production stable. First out of the blocks, though, was *The Others.* As executive producer, Tom cast his wife as the lead in his latest project, even though Nicole, still on crutches after *Moulin Rouge,* protested about playing a religiously neurotic mother of two children who are so sensitive to light that they have to be kept indoors with all the curtains and blinds drawn. Within that enclosed dark world, the icy, high-strung mother is joined by a group of strange servants and the ghost of her dead soldier husband.

It is a creepy, disturbing film, and Nicole, still enjoying the afterglow of *Moulin Rouge,* rebelled. Her husband insisted that she set her doubts aside. It was a shrewd decision, Nicole giving one of her best, and possibly most revealing, screen performances as an obsessive and overwrought mother. As her biographer James Dickerson perceptively noted, "How odd it was that Tom would choose this story for Nicole, for, in its own way, it seemed to mirror their marriage, down to the smallest detail." It was a sentiment Tom agreed with.

When he watched her performance as a cold, neurotic, frigid mother who is suffocating yet unkind to her children, he remarked to his circle that she was perfect for the part. It was not said with affection.

CHAPTER 9

Suddenly it was over: Out of the blue Tom was gone. She faced the new year—and the rest of her life—without the man she thought loved her beyond measure. Yet the husband who had once smothered her in red roses, love notes, and adoration did not even tell her face-to-face, man to woman, that their ten-year marriage was over. Nicole learned that she had been written out of the script of Tom's life from a go-between, his lawyer. The parting in the first weeks of 2001 was blunt, brutal, and businesslike. No mess, no fuss. Now she knew what Mimi Rogers must have felt like. As one of his first lovers, Diane Van Zoeren, had put it, "When he was done with you, he was done with you." Tom in love—or in love with the idea of being in love—and Tom out of love were stark opposites. While Nicole was away from their home at Pacific Palisades, a moving van took away all his personal belongings, the actor hiring five cottages at a Beverly Hills hotel for himself and his entourage.

As Nicole sat in her study, twisting a white handkerchief sodden with tears and rubbing her knee, injured during the filming of *Moulin Rouge,* the telephone on her desk was a mute, reproachful reminder of what she had lost. She might have resented her life in a cocoon of caviar and control, might have pulled away from her husband, but this sudden rupture tore at her heart and her spirit. Their personal friends, their professional colleagues, and their business acquaintances all saw which way the wind was blowing and went with the gardeners, the housekeepers, the communicators, and the personal assistants. With Tom. It was the way of the world—certainly the way of Hollywood.

She was left with only her loyal driver, Dave Garris, outside polishing her $72,000 black GMC Denali, for company. As she pondered her future, she spent hours on the phone to Sydney, talking to her parents and sister, who were furious at Tom's abrupt treatment of her.

Inevitably, her thoughts turned to going home to Australia. In her darkest moments, her faith—her Roman Catholic faith—sustained her. She talked through her options with her mother and father. She had heard of nunneries in Australia that would admit women who had been married, and wanted to explore the idea further. At the very least she wanted to spend time in a Catholic retreat, regrounding herself, finding out who she was and where she was headed. After that, who knows? Maybe she would enroll at the University of Sydney to take the English degree she had talked about for so long.

With the dawning of 2001, it certainly seemed that her days in Hollywood were numbered. If the exodus of staff and friends was not enough of a clue, the belligerence of Tom's lawyers expunged any doubts. They told her she would never make another movie and recommended she buy a one-way ticket back to Sydney. She knew they were projecting the anger of their client; hell had no fury like a scorned Tom Cruise. Meanwhile, the mass media screeched with stories, presumably orchestrated by Tom's circle, that blamed her cold, selfish temperament for the split and speculated that she had had dalliances with other men.

Things got worse when the shock jock Howard Stern announced that Tom had hired the notorious private investigator Tony Pellicano, known as the "celebrities' thug," to investigate Nicole's behavior. Still, Tom's reps insisted that this was "an amicable parting." Nursing a broken heart, an injured knee, and a shattered career, Nicole then discovered she was expecting her husband's baby. As she looked back over the last few months, she thought, "How has it come to this?"

Perhaps it all began in the summer of 2000, as Tom sat through a private screening of the Spanish movie *Abre los ojos,* about the relationship between Sofia, a beautiful dancer, and a rich publishing tycoon. As with Nicole ten years before, he was enticed by the screen presence of the leading lady, twenty-seven-year-old Penélope Cruz. As he watched the title credits, he was on his cell phone trying to buy the rights to re-make the film in English. Later that summer, when he met the film's director and screenwriter Alejandro Amenábar in New York, Tom said that he wanted Cruz to reprise her role for the English version, to be called *Vanilla Sky.*

While Cruz was not well known outside Spain, many men had been similarly entranced by her darting eyes, slim figure, and vivacious, teasing personality. "As a person, and on film, she invites you in, and she's incredibly romantic and yet real," Tom would later observe. The daughter of a Madrid hair-dresser and a businessman, Penélope had been romantically linked to several Hollywood stars, including Matt Damon. When Cruise's chosen director, his friend Cameron Crowe, went to Greece, where she was filming *Captain Corelli's Man-dolin,* it was rumored that she was having an affair with her married leading man, Nicolas Cage.

Tom had worked with Amenábar before, on *The Others,* with Nicole as the lead. When filming for *The Others* began in Madrid in August 2000, Tom, as executive producer, was with his wife and children. Indeed, the movie was the first of a six-film deal between Nicole and Cruise/Wagner Productions—which suggested that, in spite of her distance and dissatisfaction, she and Tom planned to stay together at least professionally. Meanwhile, as Nicole was playing a wife left by her soldier husband in *The Others,* Tom de-parted the set in November for New York to take the lead in *Vanilla Sky.* As director Cameron Crowe later pointed out, the chemistry between Tom and Penélope was crucial if they were going to sustain the intense love story that lies at the heart of the film. "Penélope had to appear to fall truly in love. And Tom's character falls in love with her. You watch them going through that hideous great, awful, intoxicating moment. Without it we couldn't have a movie. The first time we screened the movie—just in-house—it was the kind of situation where at the end you get a reaction of 'Wow! They really were in love.' " It didn't take long for fiction to become fact.

While Tom was filming in New York, Nicole completed work on *The Others* and returned to the U.S. from Spain just before Christmas. In spite of their hectic filming schedules, the couple was together to celebrate Paula Wagner's fifty-fourth birthday in New York on December 20. Guests reported that as Tom moved from table to table, laughing with friends and signing menus, a silent and sullen Nicole sat on her own, making little effort to speak to other revelers.

From this date forth, Tom's story and the actual events differ markedly. In his court filing, Tom claimed that the couple separated in December 2000, presumably while Nicole was in Spain finishing filming. His camp made it clear that they went their separate ways on December 21, the day after Paula Wagner's birthday party and the day before their daughter Bella's seventh birthday. (It was thought, wrongly, that his choice of separation dates was influenced by California law, where a marriage lasting ten years or more is classified as a "lengthy" union. While a "lengthy" marriage ruling can affect the size of alimony payments, it does not affect the division of assets. California is one of nine "community property" states where from day one of the marriage all assets are split equally. With houses around the world, private jets, and a reputed $450 million fortune to be split fifty-fifty, alimony was never going to be an issue for Tom and Nicole.)

On the day that Tom says they separated, they flew home to Hollywood. A couple of days later, on Christmas Eve, they hosted an intimate party at their Pacific Palisades home to celebrate their tenth wedding anniversary. By the accounts of those present, both Tom and Nicole, given their private heartache, put on Oscar-worthy performances, dancing to their favorite songs and gazing lovingly into each other's eyes. They were even said to have renewed their wedding vows during the evening.

While this may be open to question, what is incontestable is that the Cruise entourage then decamped to Las Vegas for the Christmas holidays. Tom even arranged for the Big Shot ride at the Stratosphere Hotel to stay open late so that Nicole and the others could enjoy the thrilling experience. Just to confuse matters further, at the time Tom said that they had separated, Nicole later claimed that they'd had sex and she'd conceived a child. Finally, if Tom had paid a lawyer to tell her their marriage was over in December, why was he in her company at all during Christmas? For a couple on the eve of a bitter divorce fight, this was an odd way of drawing up the battle lines.

As soon as the family returned from Las Vegas, Tom was back on the set of *Vanilla Sky,* now filming in Hollywood. It did not take long for the media to get wind of the couple's troubles, especially as Tom had now moved into a hotel. Their behavior at the Golden Globes ceremony in Hollywood on January 21 gave the gossip further credence. Both Tom and Nicole presented awards at the ceremony, but they arrived in separate cars, Nicole escorted by her father, Antony, and sat at separate tables.

With the *National Enquirer* about to break the story, publicist Pat Kingsley issued a statement on February 5 confirming that the marriage was over. She said that the split was due to "the difficulties inherent in divergent careers which constantly keep them apart," emphasizing that there was absolutely no third party involved and that Scientology had not influenced Tom's decision. For once, even the credulous entertainment media was skeptical, pointing out how both Tom and Nicole had often boasted that they had never spent more than two weeks apart throughout their ten-year marriage. The split generated a frenzy of reports linking Nicole to her *Moulin Rouge* costar Ewan McGregor, actor George Clooney, her former boyfriend Marcus Graham, *Blue Room* beau Iain Glen, and others. As for Tom's on-screen love interest, Penélope Cruz denied having an affair.

Even though there were two children involved this time, Tom refused to consider any kind of marriage guidance or counseling—not even the Scientology counseling he and Mimi Rogers had gone through at the end of their brief marriage. Two days after the media announcement, Tom filed for divorce in the L.A. Superior Court, citing "irreconcilable differences" and stating, "I do not believe professional counseling or the assistance of any mental health professional, lapse of time, or any other factor will change this breakdown." Publicly, he remained tight-lipped about the breakdown. "Nicole knows why" was all he would say, his petulant tone more suggestive of a high-school breakup than the dignified end of a ten-year marriage.

On the set of *Vanilla Sky* he seemed relaxed and jaunty, even attending a party hosted by his friend Steven Spielberg. Behind the scenes, however, was a man who appeared to be out to control and intimidate his estranged wife and anyone else who felt tempted to step out of line. Security on the set was drastically beefed up, Tom constantly surrounded by five bodyguards. Crew members who worked in close proximity to the star had to go through a metal detector to check that they were not carrying cameras, mobile phones, or recording devices. It got to be too much for one film executive, who was angered at the sight of a female extra being made to empty her handbag. He shouted, "Tell Tom these are professional actors and are to be treated with respect. This is not the Federal Bureau of Investigation." Tom's publicist, Pat Kingsley, brushed aside these concerns. "Yes, he is insisting on tight security," she said, "but only to protect the safety of himself and others."

Meanwhile, Nicole was suffering, barely able to leave their home. She had started working on a new film, *Panic Room,* in mid-January, but dropped out within the month, ostensibly because of her knee injury. "Even though there were strains," said Nicole's friend, Australian director John Duigan, "the final breach was sudden and jarring." A few days after the split was formally confirmed in early February, her mother, Janelle, and sister, Antonia, and her two children flew to Los Angeles to comfort and support the distraught actress. She felt under siege, both by the media, who were throwing out a confetti of possible names for her lover, and by Tom's lawyers and the news that he had hired the notorious investigator Tony Pellicano to look into her private affairs.

Not only did Tom and Nicole have an agreement not to use detectives, but she knew her husband had always despised the man and his dubious methods. It seemed that Tom's mood was so vengeful that only the venom of Pellicano could express it. Pellicano, a friend and associate of Tom's lawyer Bert Fields, was known as the "ultimate problem solver," a thug who intimidated victims with an aluminum baseball bat he carried in his car trunk. "I can't do everything by the book," Pellicano once boasted. "I bend the law to death in gaining information." It was not until 2002 that it became clear how far he would go to bend the law.

An FBI raid on his offices uncovered two live grenades, plastic explosives, wiretapping equipment, and literally thousands of pages of transcripts of illegal recordings of telephone conversations. He subsequently boasted to Corinne Clifford, a client in a domestic case, that he had bugged Nicole's phone while working for Tom's lawyer Dennis Wasser during the divorce case. "I'm the number one private eye in the world," he said. "I made Dennis Wasser's career." Since then, both Tom and Nicole as well as Bert Fields have been interviewed by FBI agents investigating Pellicano, who is currently in prison facing 110 counts, including wiretapping, racketeering, conspiracy, witness tampering, identity theft, and destruction of evidence.

While that scandal lay in the future, Nicole was sufficiently aware of Pellicano's bullying reputation to ask her lawyer Bill Beslow, a New Yorker who had handled divorces for Mia Farrow, Tatum O'Neal, and Sarah, the Duchess of York, for advice. He recommended that she bring in her own man to handle countermeasures. So it was that Richard DiSabatino, a Hollywood private eye who first got into the business thanks to Nicole's friend Robert De Niro, found himself sitting in her cool, elegant study while her lawyer idly fingered a jazz tune on the grand piano in the sitting room. Dressed simply in jeans and an oversized sweater, Nicole looked the picture of misery, her face porcelain white, her eyes red-rimmed with crying. "She looked terrible," he recalls. "This was not an act, and it was clear that the breakup had hit her hard." As she was talking, she would break down in tears, the actress constantly rubbing her injured knee. Her mood was bleak and pessimistic. "I feel so vulnerable," she told him plaintively. "People want to stop me from continuing what little career I have."

After listening to her tale of woe, he explained that he would be responsible for protecting her, making sure her phones could not be tapped, and ensuring that she only dealt with people she knew and trusted. She was, however, insistent that they not investigate her husband, even though DiSabatino had contacts at the Carlyle Hotel in New York, where Penélope Cruz stayed during the filming of *Vanilla Sky* before Tom filed for divorce.

As he left her home at Pacific Palisades, DiSabatino realized that he was backing the wrong horse, that Hollywood would automatically side with her powerful husband. Nevertheless, his job was now to protect his vulnerable client. On a subsequent visit he swept her phones and installed an encryption device so that she couldn't be wiretapped. "We tried to keep one step ahead," he recalls. Realizing that Pellicano was a resourceful opponent, however, Nicole would say things during phone conversations with friends and family like "Tom, are you listening?" or "Am I saying what you want me to say, Tom?"

For all her bravado, this was a woman on the edge. She was bruised, angry, but above all bewildered, obsessed with the reasons behind Tom's rapid exit from her life. Not only had she been informed by an associate that the marriage was over, but when she called him in January to ask him why, all he would say was, "You know why." He repeated his mantra even when she yelled at him: "You fucking bastard, don't you realize I'm pregnant?" She pleaded with DiSabatino to find out why her husband had left her, adamant that he was the father of her child. DiSabatino was blunt, telling her that if Tom wasn't going to tell his own wife, he had no chance even if he tied him down and tortured him. "Even then you only have a fifty-fifty chance of success of getting information out of Tom," he said.

What concerned him most was the steady drip, drip of insinuation and gossip in the media about his client. When negative stories about Nicole started appearing in the *National Enquirer,* Pellicano's tabloid of choice, he realized that the gloves were well and truly off. One story suggested that Tom left because he could no longer take Nicole's "eternal moaning," while others speculated about the possible identity of the baby's father—expanding the roll call from the actors she knew to her knee surgeon, Neal ElAttrache, and her driver Dave Garris. Certainly, Garris acted like much more than her driver, behaving with the confident air of the man about the house. She seemed to enjoy the company of a man who treated her like a woman rather than a star.

With Pellicano digging for dirt, DiSabatino needed to know if there were any skeletons in his client's sexual cupboard. He sat her down and asked Nicole point-blank if she had been fooling around with another man. "She looked me in the eyes and said absolutely not," he recalls. She admitted that the only person who came close to any type of inappropriate relationship during their marriage was the actor Iain Glen and that "Tom had known all about it."

Meanwhile a parade of men—and often their partners—publicly denied any romantic attachment to the Australian star. A persistent rumor concerned her *Moulin Rouge* costar, Ewan McGregor. "I can't believe people are saying there was something going on between us," Nicole said. "Ewan is a lovely guy and he's a friend. We spent a long time on *Moulin Rouge.* During all that time Ewan's wife, Eve, was there and she's a mate of mine. It's absolutely crazy."

Another candidate was Nicole's close friend Australian actor Russell Crowe, because Tom had reportedly been angry to discover a series of e-mails between them. When Iain Glen offered her a shoulder to cry on, the gossips went into overdrive, causing his then wife, Susannah, to publicly exclaim, "Nicole's an old friend of mine, too. Nothing can be read into Iain speaking to her. It's something I approve of. He's a friend of hers and so it's all positively okay."

Of more interest to Hollywood insiders was her friendship with orthopedic surgeon Neal ElAttrache. ElAttrache was married to actress Tricia Flavin, whose sister Jennifer was Sylvester Stallone's wife, and had a thriving practice treating athletes and celebrities at the Kerlan-Jobe Clinic. After tearing her cartilage during the filming of *Moulin Rouge,* Nicole began treatment at the clinic in May 2000, returning often for physical therapy. There were rumors all over Hollywood that ElAttrache had become overly friendly with the injured actress. When the gossip reached the ears of Sylvester Stallone, he was concerned that a vengeful Tom Cruise might target the aging actor and destroy what was left of his career.

As a result, Jackie Stallone, Sylvester's formidable eighty-year-old mother, called an Italian family "sit-down" to get to the heart of the matter. According to one insider, it was only after two of these sit-downs that Neal ElAttrache was able to calm the fears of the Stallone clan. Stallone later confirmed that his brother-in-law had struck up a friendship with Nicole during treatment and had stayed in touch with her afterward. He told journalist Mitchell Fink, "I sat down with him and I said, 'Look, this story is breaking all over the place, you gotta come clean with me. Did anything happen we should know about?' And he said no. Everything was fine and clean."

There was a twist in this tale. In March 2001, Stallone contacted journalist and former NYPD detective John Connolly, who had just published an article in *Premiere* magazine about allegations of sexual harassment against Arnold Schwarzenegger, now governor of California. Stallone, who loathes the former bodybuilder, was eager to hear more unpublished scuttlebutt about Schwarzenegger and offered inside information on his brother-in-law's friendship with Nicole Kidman in exchange. "It didn't come off," says Connolly. "It was all getting too crazy and I didn't want to get stuck in the middle."

The debate about the father of Nicole's child soon became academic. On March 16 she was rushed to the Iris Cantor–UCLA Women's Health Center, suffering from heavy bleeding and sharp abdominal pains similar to those she had experienced with her ectopic pregnancy a decade earlier. Doctors told her that she was about three months pregnant but had miscarried; in fact, without Nicole realizing it, the fetus had died several weeks earlier. While her loyal driver, Dave Garris, waited in the wings, Nicole phoned Tom to break the news. He sent flowers but did not visit her in the hospital.

Given the strain and her medical history, the miscarriage came as no surprise. "We have a woman who is pregnant, with knee problems and who has been told her career is over in Hollywood," observed DiSabatino. "Lo and behold, she has a miscarriage. I can only believe it was because she was so upset. She wanted a child. She loves children." Shrewdly, he advised her to save some of the fetal tissue in case DNA tests were ever needed to prove the baby's paternity. A story was leaked to the *National Enquirer* about her decision to store the DNA.

It was a brilliant move, putting Tom's camp in a no-win position. In order for Tom to refute Nicole's version of events, he would have to take her to court to prove that the "World's Sexiest Man" was not the father of his wife's child. Even Pellicano, who had a soft spot for Nicole even though he was working against her, acknowledged that Tom had been outmaneuvered.

While Nicole was in the hospital, the religion at the heart of the rift between the couple laid its claim to her estranged husband. On March 18, news organizations falsely reported that the Hollywood actor had severed his fifteen-year association with Scientology, quoting a spokesman as saying that he had left for "personal reasons," but had given them a generous goodwill donation. Within twenty-four hours, Tom's lawyer Bert Fields was on the warpath, denying that Tom had left the Church of Scientology or had any intention of doing so. This rapid response was in keeping with previous stories that dared to suggest a weakening of his ties with the faith that completely cocooned him.

Indeed, as Nicole pulled away from Scientology, Tom was becoming more and more wedded to his belief in L. Ron Hubbard's doctrine. As actress Naomi Watts, one of Nicole's closest friends, said, "Tom has always been far more into Scientology than Nicole. He is somewhat of a fanatic; Nicole never wanted to go down that road." Nicole's waning enthusiasm for Scientology, combined with her ongoing Roman Catholic faith, sowed the seeds for conflict with her husband. By turning her back on Scientology, she was in effect turning her back on her husband. She had become a Potential Trouble Source, tainted by association by her return to Catholicism as well as being the daughter of a psychiatrist.

While Hollywood was rather shocked at Tom's abrupt and clinical dismissal of his wife, his behavior came as no surprise to former Scientologists. Peter Alexander, onetime vice president of Universal Studios, was working on his computer in the same room as his wife, Jolie, when a message came up on his screen saying that she wanted a divorce because he was no longer as committed to Scientology as she was. Then she promptly packed up their three children and drove out of his life. Again, when Karen Pressley decided to leave Scientology and reconnect with her Christian faith, she knew that her marriage was doomed. Similarly, actor Parker Stevenson acknowledged the role of Scientology in his 1997 split from Kirstie Alley. "It doesn't help. I'm Episcopalian, she's a Scientologist, it's different," he told *People* magazine. That same year, actor Tom Berenger split from his Scientologist wife, Lisa, saying that his wife's religious beliefs had been a factor in the breakup.

As Nicole reconnected with Catholicism, she feared that Scientology would attempt to discredit her. If she needed any reminder of the danger, a story in the *National Enquirer* said that Nicole had made a number of taped confessions during her Scientology auditing sessions in which "she bared her soul" and suggested that these personal details might be used against her, especially if there was a battle for custody of their children. Her desire to return to Australia and her hostility to Tom's aim of educating their children inside Scientology made Nicole so anxious that her lawyer, Bill Beslow, asked advice from a former high-ranking Scientologist. He recalls: "Nicole's lawyer called me and said it was a very difficult situation, but all Nicole wants is the kids. He said, Is there anything you can tell me that would help this situation? At this point Nicole hated Scientology but was concerned for the kids. Her mission was to sneak them away from Scientology as much as possible. She did not want to ruin her relationship with them. I told the lawyer if she wants to stay with the children she will have to be quiet and not speak out about Scientology."

If run-of-the-mill celebrity Scientologists were forced to choose between their faith and their relationships, it was even more important for a poster boy like Tom Cruise to have a partner who was as committed to his beliefs as he was. At first glance, Penélope Cruz, who was raised in a poor but devoutly Catholic family in Madrid, did not fit the bill. Indeed, when she met and interviewed Mother Teresa of Calcutta during the 1990s, she was so inspired by her work with the homeless that she started her own charity, the Sabera Foundation, to help tuberculosis sufferers in India.

At the same time, Cruz was open to other faiths and religion. During her six-year romance with Mexican singer Nacho Cano, she was introduced to Buddhism, on one occasion meeting the Dalai Lama during a trip to Nepal. Shortly before meeting Tom in 2000, she described her attitude to faith: "I was raised as a Catholic, but I believe in God in my own way and I pray in my own way and I respect all kinds of philosophies. The one philosophy or religion that I find I am most close to is the Buddhist one."

Scientology likes to market itself, falsely, as an "applied religion," able to coexist with other faiths, which would have appealed to the free-spirited Ms. Cruz. In the early days of their romance, Tom quietly took her to his local hangout, the

Hollywood Celebrity Centre, giving her the full tour, complete with glossy brochures and books by L. Ron Hubbard. It was not long before she was spending days at the CC, reportedly up to seven hours at a time, immersing herself in basic Scientology courses.

Soon the red roses and love notes that he had once showered on Nicole started arriving for Penélope, who much preferred his thoughtful, seemingly spontaneous gestures to lavish presents of jewelry. "Penelope is someone to whom gifts don't mean a lot," Tom said later. "She doesn't really want jewelry or big gifts. She likes written notes and a letter or a phone call at a particular time while she's away."

As in the early days of his romance with Nicole, Tom kept his new love in the background until his divorce was finalized. So when Tom arrived at the Oscar ceremony in March 2001, he did not sit with Penélope. Both were presenting prizes, Tom for Best Director and Penélope for Best Achievement in Costume Design, while Nicole was notably absent. Even though Tom and Penélope tried to disguise their burgeoning relationship, there was no hiding the hostility between Nicole and the Spanish actress when they were photographed for a "Legends of Hollywood" story in *Vanity Fair*. For the cover, photographer Annie Leibovitz shot a group portrait that included Nicole, Sophia Loren, Meryl Streep, Catherine Deneuve, Cate Blanchett, Chloë Sevigny, and, incongruously, Penélope Cruz, who had scarcely a Hollywood movie to her name. That she was now represented by Tom's publicist, Pat Kingsley, and under his management umbrella, CAA, might just have worked in her favor. Significantly, Leibovitz placed the rivals, Nicole looking icy and haughty and Penélope looking scared, in opposite corners of the photo.

If including the relatively unknown Penélope in the photo shoot was a not-so-subtle attempt by Tom's camp to intimidate and humiliate Nicole, their plan was effective. By April, Nicole, still weak from her miscarriage and complaining about her injured knee and a stalker who was hounding her, was sufficiently softened up by Tom's media and legal campaign that she was ready to throw in the towel. According to DiSabatino, "Nicole was talking about settling. Tom gave her a figure that was half of what she eventually got. She called me over to the house and said she was going to settle. I begged with her not to settle for that price—if she hung in there she would get so much more. But she said her knees were bothering her and she wanted to move on with her life." In the end, wiser counsels prevailed and she decided to wait.

Even so, in early May she was telling Oprah Winfrey that her life was "a nightmare . . . You pretend that you're fine and there's days when you're great and there's days when you're not great." She still didn't understand why Tom had left her. When the cameras stopped turning after an interview on the *Today* show, Katie Couric quietly asked her about the split. "I don't know why, I don't know why," Nicole told her. She continued to be overwrought when she attended the opening of *Moulin Rouge* at the Cannes Film Festival a few days later. Nicole, who suffers from panic attacks, was mobbed by over-enthusiastic crowds, later confessing that it was the most frightening moment of her life. Vulnerable and distraught, she felt unable to face the media at the traditional press conference. Seeing his lead actress fading before his eyes, director Baz Luhrmann told her, "Get back up on that horse and be Nicole Kidman." She took his advice, dancing the night away with Ewan McGregor and DJ Fatboy Slim.

As Nicole flew to London to prepare for her role as author Virginia Woolf in *The Hours*, Tom was squaring up for another battle—this time with his old foes in the media. As writer Richard Goldstein noted, "Tom Cruise sues the way Robert Downey Jr. violates his parole. Downey can't pass up a snort and Cruise can't resist a tort." As he had spent many hours—and thousands of dollars—on the phone with his lawyer Bert Fields, asking for advice on the divorce, he had no hesitation in calling Fields when French gossip magazine *Acustar* reported in May 2001 that Tom had had a relationship with gay porn star and erotic wrestler Kyle Bradford, real name Chad Slater.

Slater was slapped with a $100 million lawsuit, Fields stating, "There is not a germ of truth to this vicious, self-promoting story. While Tom Cruise thoroughly respects others' right to follow their own sexual preference, he is not homosexual and had no relationship of any kind with Kyle Bradford [Chad Slater] and does not even know him." Even though Slater denied making the comments and *Acustar* printed a retraction, the gay rumors just kept circulating.

It was turning into a minor cottage industry, not because there was any merit in the stories but because, for those who inhabit Hollywood's underbelly, there was money in exploiting Tom's itchy legal finger, particularly his sensitivity to gay slurs. So it was that in June 2001, gay porn star Big Red— "They don't call me Big Red just because of my freckled face and carrot top"—found himself sitting in the office of Tony Pellicano with fellow private eye and sometimes gay porn producer Paul Barresi. Barresi, who billed himself as Pellicano's enforcer, had earned notoriety in 1990 by claiming to have had an affair with actor and prominent Scientologist John Travolta. Big Red, aka Nathan Hamilton, told the two detectives an elaborate story about his paid dalliances with some of Hollywood's biggest stars, including Tom Cruise. Barresi had already tried to sell Hamilton's account to the *National Enquirer,* but the tabloid had found the porn star's preposterous story too convoluted and contradictory.

Pellicano was less skeptical. "I think the kid is very credible," he told Barresi after Hamilton left. The unspoken implication was that they could make money out of the hapless Hamilton—and Tom Cruise—by reporting their findings to his lawyer, Bert Fields. They reasoned that Fields would set the legal wheels in motion, sending threatening letters to Hamilton and paying Pellicano, his PI of choice, and Barresi for their trouble. It was a win/win play—at least for them; the only losers were Hamilton and Cruise. As Barresi conceded, "The story is perfect because it is never going to see light of day but it's going to be enough to incite Cruise by going for his Achilles' heel. Everyone knows that Cruise goes nuts when he is called a homo. Walking both sides of the street is a great way of making money. Celebrities are naïve and have deep pockets."

In the end, Hamilton went into hiding, claiming that after he received threatening letters from Fields, his phones were tapped and he was being followed by unmarked cars. Not that the detective duo had much sympathy. At a subsequent meeting, Hamilton claimed he'd had an affair with Pellicano's favorite singer, the blind Italian tenor Andrea Bocelli. "What a sick bastard," observed the sultan of sleaze after virtually kicking Hamilton out of his office. For his pains, Barresi eventually received five thousand dollars from Bert Fields, and was so proud of his association with Tom's lawyer that he carries a photocopy of the check to show to friends and acquaintances.

As fiercely as Tom wielded his legal sword, the media proved a many-headed Hydra. That same month, June 2001, Michael Davis, publisher of *Bold* magazine, offered $500,000 to anyone who had photographic evidence that Tom Cruise was gay. Once again Fields reached for his favorite number, filing a $100 million lawsuit against *Bold* in the Los Angeles Superior Court. The magazine published a retraction.

Even though Tom has successfully—and rightly—won every legal battle about his sexuality, at the time of writing he seems to have lost the war. There are more than 2 million Internet sites today relating to "Tom Cruise gay"—slightly more than for a similar heartthrob, Brad Pitt, who has never taken legal action and has publicly stated he will not marry Angelina Jolie until gay marriage is acceptable in America. Indeed, Rob Thomas of Matchbox Twenty has even spoken publicly about the rumor that he and Tom were caught in bed together by his wife. "If I was gay, Tom Cruise wouldn't be on the top of my list," he said. "It would be Brad Pitt."

The irony did not escape Tom's inner circle that, in the midst of quashing gay slurs, he was quietly dating one of the world's sexiest women, Penélope Cruz. In July he took a break from filming his latest movie, *Minority Report,* directed by his friend Steven Spielberg, to fly her on board his private plane—now named *Sweet Bella* rather than *Sweet Nic*—to a private island near Fiji in the South Pacific. Originally the island's owner, Canadian entrepreneur David Gilmour, who started the Fiji bottled water company, had offered the private use of the Wakaya Club resort to Tom and Nicole—a further signal that when the invitation was proffered the couple had not been contemplating divorce. As it was, Nicole and her children, as well as her friend actor Russell Crowe used the resort for the first week, Bella and Connor staying on to join their father and Penélope Cruz for a further two weeks. Penélope's arrival certainly surprised Nicole, the actress later complaining to a friend, "He flat-out swore to me up and down that there was nothing going on. He obviously had her waiting in the wings."

The children knew before the rest of the world that Tom and Penélope were a serious item, and in late July their spokesman, Pat Kingsley, confirmed for the first time that the couple had indeed been dating. In early August, Penélope was diplomatically absent from the Hollywood premiere of *The Others,* where the leading lady and executive producer walked the red carpet separately. The very next day, on August 7, 2001, their divorce was legally finalized, the couple agreeing to joint custody of the children and promising not to talk to the media about each other.

A few weeks later their finances were settled, Nicole winning twice the original offer. While he retained their compound in Colorado, Nicole kept the houses in Pacific Palisades and Sydney, Australia. When she emerged from her lawyer's office after signing the divorce papers, Nicole was pictured letting out a piercing scream of relief.

It was a relief, too, for Penélope, who could now appear in public with her lover. First, though, she wanted him to meet the other man in her life, flying her father, Eduardo, to Los Angeles to see her and Tom. For all her spiritual exploration, Penélope was very family oriented, and her father's approval was important to her. If he had doubts about her twice-married boyfriend, Eduardo kept them to himself, at least for the time being. It would only be later that he looked more carefully—and skeptically—at the man and his controversial religion.

As for Penélope, she was delighted, as Nicole had been a decade earlier, that she no longer had to be kept in the shadows. As her personal assistant Kira Sanchez said, "Penélope has told her friends she's mighty relieved it's all out in the open. She told Tom she didn't like skulking around."

CHAPTER 10

It was Michael LaForte's thirty-ninth birthday, and normally he took the day off to play golf or go fishing. For once he decided to head into the office. He ordered his usual large coffee—milk and one sugar—from Bill Schamber's stand on the train platform in Middleton, New Jersey, before the hour-long ride into Manhattan. As Bill poured the coffee, they chatted about the wonderful weather. It was such a glorious morning that Bill had already decided to shut his stand early and go fishing. Michael was tempted, but kept to his plan—to leave work early and have a birthday party with his two young children and pregnant wife, Fran, at their home in Holmdel, New Jersey.

He never made that birthday party. At 8:46 on the morning of September 11, 2001, Michael was in his office on the 105th floor of the North Tower of the World Trade Center when American Airlines Flight 11 ripped into the building, some fifteen floors down from where he was sitting. At 8:51, Michael phoned home, leaving a farewell message on the answering machine. He told his wife, who was dropping the children at school, that there was no way out. "Franny, I love you. I love you and the kids. A plane hit the building. I don't know what's going on. I will talk to you. Love you, bye."

Although his voice was tense, Michael wasn't the type to panic. Not only had he spent four years as a captain in the Marine Corps, he had been inside the World Trade Center during the 1993 bombing. Of the thousands who faced their fate that day, few would have battled harder to survive than Michael LaForte. He was an easygoing but totally driven, competitive man who had worked his way up to the position of vice president at his brokerage firm, Cantor Fitzgerald.

It was an aggressive spirit that Tom Cruise knew well. He and Michael had been friends since the Glen Ridge days, staying in touch long after his other high-school buddies had gone their own ways. As young men they had gone barhopping and carousing together, and when Tom became famous, he took his friend to the Super Bowl, film premieres, and other Hollywood events. Every so often, Michael and his wife, Fran, had joined Tom and his then-wife, Nicole, for dinner, even though Nicole preferred more glamorous friends.

As Michael's older brother, Sam LaForte, joined Fran in looking for Michael, he thought about the times when his kid brother and Tom had come running to him after getting themselves in some scrape. This was different. Like thousands of others, Sam and Fran walked around New York, looking in hospitals and handing out flyers, searching for anything to end the uncertainty. A heavily pregnant Fran even appeared on NBC TV appealing for information: "You just want to die. I don't know where he is. And I know if he made it out of that building he would have called me up immediately because that's what he did the last time. So I know he's hurt somewhere."

Days later, Sam LaForte got a call saying that they had found Michael. "They said he was okay, in the sense that they had found his body intact. It was a kind of awful closure."

On September 21, Cruise joined a host of other celebrities in front of 89 million viewers on the "Tribute to Heroes" telethon to raise money for victims of 9/11. Before the program, he nestled on a sofa with his lover, Penélope Cruz. When his slot came, Cruise delivered a tribute to Father Mike, the New York Fire Department priest who died during the rescue mission, but made no mention of his good friend Michael LaForte.

For people who knew Tom, this was a surprise. During

the same telethon, Sting dedicated his song "Fragile" to his friend Herman Sandler, who had been killed in the attacks. Tom's failure to make a similar public tribute to Michael LaForte baffled and angered many in Glen Ridge. His high-school buddy Vinnie Travisano knew how close Tom and Michael had been. "I soured on him a lot after that. We watched, waiting for the moment when he would talk about the loss of his good friend Michael. He never said a word. That blew us all away, all of us from Glen Ridge who knew him. It would have brought it home for a lot of people. For Tom not to say anything was so hurtful." Although he sent flowers to Fran LaForte and his mother, Mary Lee South, and attended the funeral, Tom has never publicly acknowledged the loss of his friend.

That said, Scientologists view death in a cold, matter-of-fact way. They call it "dropping the body," believing that an individual's spirit will inhabit another body at some point in the future. As far as they are concerned, Ron Hubbard, who died in 1986, will return any day now, hence the construction of lavish homes around the globe for the dead leader.

While the showman in Michael—his catchphrase was "Life is a cabaret"—would have loved the fame of a televised tribute, the trauma of 9/11 had apparently woken something deeper inside Tom. As Sam LaForte reflects, "I look at life 200 percent differently now; a lot of people do. It doesn't surprise me that Tom Cruise was changed." The feelings of helplessness, confusion, and disbelief that people around the world experienced after 9/11 did not sit well with the self-assured conviction by which Tom had always led his life. "After 9/11, I was so angry. I was devastated. I thought, 'What can I do to help?'" he said later.

Tom Cruise was not so much a man in mourning as a man incensed, those in his inner circle witnessing a genuine transformation. From the smoke clouds over the Manhattan skyline was born Scientology's most influential advocate. He later described the moment when he saw the catastrophe: "Once the towers had gone down and we were faced with the aftermath of their collapse, I could not get out of my mind that huge cloud billowing across Manhattan."

When his close friend and Scientology leader David Miscavige called 9/11 a "wake-up call," Tom was certainly listening. As one Scientology insider observed, "I have no doubt Tom Cruise had conversations with Miscavige about what more he could do to spread Scientology, because obviously time was running out." Certainly the events surrounding 9/11 seemed to confirm L. Ron Hubbard's apocalyptic worldview. Scientology followers were urged to work harder, run faster, to save a planet overrun by "merchants of chaos." They sent scores of so-called Volunteer Ministers in distinctive yellow shirts to Ground Zero, to offer "contact assists"—a kind of spiritual massage—to rescue workers, to recruit new members, and to interfere with the work of mental health professionals. Such was their persistence that the National Mental Health Association warned the unsuspecting public that Scientologists were operating at the site.

Hubbard's words provided clarity for Cruise, showing him the chaos and evil in the world's events from a broader perspective. The vision of time that Scientology provided was inviting. It removed the uncertainty and the desolation that presented itself, by revealing the bigger battle that had been running over several millennia, of which these flashes of devastation were just a part. For Tom, the days of hiding in the shadows were over; he now saw himself as part of his faith's larger purpose. More had to be done by everyone, but on Tom's shoulders rested even greater responsibility. With his fame came a duty to bring Scientology to the masses.

On November 16, 2001, the day that Fran LaForte gave birth to the son who would never meet his father, Tom sealed the final financial settlement in his divorce with Nicole. He was now working from a fresh slate, withdrawing into the intimacy and security of his own family and the family of Scientology. His sisters and their children moved into his new Hollywood home; his mother was a regular visitor, and, in time, like Penélope, would start taking courses at the Celebrity Centre. There was talk that he and Penélope were on the brink of marriage.

The evidence of 9/11 was matched by the siren calls inside his extended family. Without any dissenting voice from Nicole, the message from Tom's sister Lee Anne, a dedicated Scientologist, was to rededicate himself to the church. Scientology had the tools to help him through his marital breakup, the gay rumors, and the destruction of 9/11. While Tom had always been committed to his faith, he had never been vocal, at times almost embarrassed by his association with the organization. In fact, in 1993 his publicist, Pat Kingsley, had attacked questions about his religion as "un-American." At that time, he was indeed questioning his commitment, Scientology leaders working assiduously behind the scenes to "recover" their high-profile Hollywood star. Now the man who had spent so long deflecting questions about Scientology was transformed into a celebrity crusader.

The first indications of his changed perspective came in December 2001, when Tom was promoting *Vanilla Sky,* interestingly a story about a wealthy publishing tycoon who continues his life on Earth after death with the help of the mysterious Life Extension Corporation. When the subject of 9/11 was broached during an interview with *Vanity Fair,* the writer noted with surprise how Cruise's whole appearance seemed to change. His voice fell almost to a whisper and his eyes were "boiling with late-night rap-session intensity," as he said: "Things mean something different than they did before September 11. It's a responsibility not only for our country but for the entire planet." In another conversation, Tom observed, "I think the World Trade Center has kind of ripped the social veneer off this country."

During the worldwide publicity for *Vanilla Sky,* which began in the New Year, for the first time Tom used his star status to aggressively sell Scientology. Noticeably, Penélope joined him as they lobbied American ambassadors in France, Germany, and Spain—all countries hostile to Scientology—to help advance the cause of "religious freedom." When the couple arrived in Berlin, they met with the U.S. ambassador, Dan Coats, lobbying him to urge the German government, which had placed the sect under police scrutiny, to legitimize Scientology. After their meeting, Cruise spent nearly an hour signing autographs and talking to starstruck embassy staff.

This was not the first time Scientology had used celebrities to try to gain a toehold in what they considered an important market. In January 1997, thirty-four Hollywood personalities, including Dustin Hoffman, Goldie Hawn, Larry King, and Oliver Stone, put their names to an open letter to German chancellor Helmut Kohl, likening the plight of Scientologists in Germany to the persecution of the Jews under Hitler. The full-page ad, published in the *International Herald Tribune*, prompted the U.S. State Department to denounce the letter as an "outrageous charge" that bore "no resemblance to the facts of what is going on there." It later became clear that almost all those who signed, while not necessarily Scientologists, were linked to Tom Cruise or John Travolta. In response, the German ambassador made it clear that Scientology posed a threat to Germany's basic democratic principles. "The organization's pseudo-scientific courses can seriously jeopardize an individual's mental and physical health and it exploits its members." Undaunted, in September 1997, celebrity Scientologists Chick Corea, Isaac Hayes, and John Travolta appeared before a congressional commission in Washington to complain about the treatment of Scientologists in Germany.

When the *Vanilla Sky* tour moved on to Spain, where Scientologists were accused of such crimes as kidnapping, tax fraud, and damaging public health (but were subsequently acquitted), Penélope's presence in her hometown of Madrid was a significant bonus. The fact that a famous Spanish Catholic was prepared to stand shoulder to shoulder with her actor boyfriend gave the faith an air of legitimacy. Which, of course, was the strategy.

If anything, opposition to his faith merely inflamed Tom's missionary zeal. He took time off from promoting *Vanilla Sky* to tell a whooping, near-delirious audience of Scientologists in Hollywood that he had just achieved "the most important thing he had ever done" in his life: He had reached the exalted status of Operating Thetan V. It had been an arduous—and expensive—journey, taking him nearly a decade to progress along Hubbard's bridge from OT III to OT V. Tom now had credentials beyond his celebrity—he had been cleared to audit people through the lower levels of Hubbard's New Era Dianetics.

But the attractions of Hubbard's teachings went far beyond that. Hubbard had the expansive imagination of a science fiction writer and the purpose-driven preaching of a cult leader. He conceived of life in different universes and times, claiming to have visited heaven twice and promising to return to Earth after his death. It was Hubbard's galactic vision that provided the basis for John Travolta's much-lambasted 2000 film *Battlefield Earth*. In this vision, Earth is an empty wasteland, where "vicious Psychlo aliens" rule over what remains of the human population they had destroyed a millennium earlier. It is a story in which the last survivors join together in a desperate attempt to drive the Psychlos from the world before man is lost forever.

For Scientologists, this kind of apocalyptic view is not fiction. The church has spent millions of dollars inscribing hundreds of stainless-steel tablets and disks with Hubbard's musings, encasing them in heat-resistant titanium so that they will survive a nuclear blast, and storing them in vaults in at least three remote sites in California and New Mexico. One site in Santa Fe, New Mexico, is marked with huge hieroglyphics, akin to crop circles. It is believed that these signs will indicate to aliens from outer space that there was once intelligent life on Earth, and show where that intelligence is stored—just in case we're no longer around when they arrive. It is revealing that this science-fiction worldview, although widely derided and parodied, could speak to someone like Tom Cruise.

It did. Tom digested every word, clinging to each passage with conviction. Hubbard's writings were scriptural and immutable. Every word, utterance, and thought was the infallible bedrock of the church's scripture—inviolate tablets of stone—or rather sheets of titanium. As a child, Tom Cruise had been a daydreamer who loved star-gazing and watching films like *E.T.* As a man, he viewed the world through a Manichaean lens: Everything was black or white, right or wrong, good or evil. You were in or you were out. My way or the highway. Hubbard's works confirmed Tom's own thoughts and feelings. The man that he called his great teacher and mentor had provided him with a belief system that chimed perfectly with his own personality.

His attraction to technology and the possibilities of the future had found expression a few months earlier, when Cruise organized a secret conference of scientists and technocrats at a hotel in Santa Monica. He was working on the preproduction for the Spielberg film *Minority Report,* and asked them to discuss what the future might look like. The film was to be set in the 2050s, and Cruise wanted it to look as accurate as possible. Scientology's pseudo-technical stance and futuristic worldview appealed to his inner geek. This was a man who enjoyed reading technical manuals, finding the scientific language enticing. Perhaps it made this middle-of-the-road pupil from Glen Ridge feel smart.

In the spring of 2002, Tom seemed to be on the verge of realizing a lifelong dream: becoming the first actor in space.

He had engineered a private visit to NASA in Florida to meet the astronauts on the shuttle program. While this was not normal NASA policy, it was a quid pro quo for Tom's work recording the voice-over for a film about the international space station and for revamping the organization's clunky Web site on what his religion boasted were Hubbard's educational principles. Accompanied only by his Scientology communicator, Michael Doven, Tom spent two days with the astronauts, watching them train, going into the water tanks to replicate movement in space, and even trying on a space suit. After a day's induction, he and Doven were invited to join a group of astronauts at the home of NASA's General Jefferson Howell. As they ate Tex-Mex food and drank cold beers from the local Shiner brewery, Tom could barely sit still with excitement, talking nonstop about his love of flying and asking endless questions about space travel. After he'd talked about mountain climbing, stock-car racing, skydiving, and his other passions, Tom's boy racer approach to life earned a few words of warning from his host. "As an old guy who nearly got killed a couple of times in a jet, I suggested that he should be thinking about the limits of what he is doing," said the host, General Howell, as Tom told him about some of his own aerial near misses.

Tom was in his element, rapping with men he truly admired. Guys, as Tom Wolfe famously described, with "the right stuff," modern-day adventurers and buccaneers. It was all the more piquant as Tom was sporting a beard in preparation for his next film, *The Last Samurai,* a story about warriors who have a code of honor, duty, and courage similar to the values of the men and women sitting around the dinner table that night. While Tom proved that he had the right stuff to take a shot at astronaut training, his dreams of going into space were shattered when, in February 2003, the *Columbia* space shuttle disintegrated during its reentry over Texas, grounding the program for more than two years. Tom took the trouble to call Charlie Precourt, chief of the astronaut corps, to pass on his condolences.

For the time being, Tom had to leave outer space to the purview of his spiritual leader, L. Ron Hubbard. Meanwhile, he was making rapid progress toward becoming his own god, traveling up the bridge to Operating Thetan VI, a sign of how diligently he was ridding his body of the spirits of dead souls during his self-auditing sessions. When he spoke to an ecstatic audience of Scientologists at a graduation ceremony in Clearwater, Florida, in July 2002, he was received with the adoration reserved for the returning messiah, the transformation from celebrity member to tub-thumping preacher complete. As well as thanking his family, mentioning proudly that one sister had just gone "Clear" and another had passed OT III, he singled out "Dave" Miscavige—the shortening of his name a calculated indication of their closeness—and of course his mentor, L. Ron Hubbard, for special praise.

He made a solemn promise to the worshipful throng that from here on in he would dedicate his life to spreading the word of Scientology. While he was doing no more than Hubbard expected of a Scientologist who had attained this lofty status, even the movement's founder would have been impressed by Tom's missionary zeal and commitment. As celebrity writer Jess Cagle observed during a conversation in June 2002: "Cruise is more than a defender of Scientology; he is a resolute advocate."

He was not only an advocate, but a teacher, donor, a preacher, and a recruiting sergeant, using his celebrity and his image as a clean-cut action hero to gain access to the levers of power while making Scientology seem like a middle-of-the-road institution for regular folk—"just like the Rotary Club or the Baptist Church." This was a key part of Hubbard's strategy, using celebrity members to gain recognition and credibility—and recruit more "raw meat."

Tom set about his task with gusto. When he was filming *The Last Samurai* in New Zealand, he gave James Packer, son of Australia's richest man, Kerry Packer, a role as a samurai extra in the movie. Dominated by his larger-than-life father, James Packer cut a sorry figure, overweight and out of shape. Not only had his One.Tel communications business collapsed, but his wife of just two years had walked out on him. His "ruin" was obvious to anyone—and it did not take long before he was reading Scientology literature, attending courses at the Scientology center in Dundas, and flying to the Celebrity Centre in Hollywood. When he attended Tom's fortieth birthday party in July 2002, it seemed that it was the thirty-five-year-old businessman who was going through the midlife crisis and not the older actor. Packer later said that he admired Cruise "enormously. The way he behaves, his humility, his values, his decency."

Packer was a perfect recruit. Not only was he wildly wealthy and emotionally confused, he was a well-known figure in a country that has been hostile to the faith, a 1965 government report accusing Scientology of being "evil." He was but one of a smorgasbord of celebrities Tom endeavored to bring into his faith, targeting those who were not just rich and famous but who had standing in their countries or communities. For example, actor Will Smith and his wife, Jada Pinkett Smith, were courted because of their stature in the African-American community, and Jada apparently home-schools her children using Hubbard's study techniques. And it didn't hurt that Tom's love interest Penélope Cruz came from Spain, a market that Scientology was looking to exploit and develop.

As well as recruiting, he was donating generously to Scientology causes, giving more than $1.2 million in September 2002 to a Scientology-based health center in New York to help 9/11 rescue workers. "When I saw what happened on 9/11, I had to do something. I just knew the level of toxins that would be ripping through the environment. I'd done the reading," he told *Marie Claire* magazine. His center, called the New York Rescue Workers Detoxification Project, claimed to have no direct association with the Church of Scientology, but it offered treatment exclusively derived from the works of Hubbard. It was set up by the Foundation for Advancements in Science and Education (FASE), a Scientology front organization that had been overseeing the research for Hubbard's general detoxification program since 1981.

Dr. David E. Root, who served on the project's advisory board, was full of praise for Tom's involvement. "We will never forget what Tom Cruise is doing for the uniformed officers who serve New York. His commitment to this project and the remarkable results that are being achieved through detoxification are rare bright spots in the aftermath of this horrible tragedy."

Nearly three hundred firefighters and rescue workers attended the free clinic in Lower Manhattan, undergoing a detoxification program based on Hubbard's teachings. It involved sweating in saunas set at high temperatures, drinking polyunsaturated oils commonly used to fry food, and taking questionably high doses of niacin, a form of vitamin B3, which if overused can lead to liver toxicity, heart palpitations, reddening of the skin, and metabolic acidosis—a potentially deadly buildup of acid in the blood. During the program, some rescue workers even stopped taking such prescribed medications as antidepressants, asthma inhalers, and blood pressure pills.

The detox method was Scientology's "Purification Rundown" in all but name—the church's controversial method of "cleansing" its followers. This routine of long saunas and exercise inspired a no doubt apocryphal tale about singer Michael Jackson, who was introduced to the faith by his former wife Lisa Marie Presley in 1994. Jackson had been a Scientology target for much longer than Tom Cruise, Scientology leader David Miscavige learning his famous "moonwalk," which he demonstrated publicly on board the Scientology cruise ship the *Freewinds* in the excitement of securing such a high-profile recruit. Unfortunately, the apocryphal story goes, when Jackson, who has undergone numerous surgical procedures, took the Purification Rundown, his face started to melt in the sauna. He looked, according to one former Scientologist, "like the witch in the wizard of Oz." Shortly afterward, Jackson reportedly left the organization.

Other criticisms of Hubbard's detoxification program were much more coherent, sober, and alarming. After doctors employed by the New York Fire Department checked out the Rescue Workers Detoxificiation Project, they concluded it was not a legitimate detoxification course. Deputy Commissioner Frank Gribbon told the New York *Daily News*: "We don't endorse it." Not only did the city's largest union yank its support, but medical officers employed by the fire department counseled firefighters to keep taking their prescribed medications. "There's no evidence [the clinic's program] works," said Deputy Chief Medical Officer David Prezant.

The conclusions of other experts who had spent time investigating Hubbard's methods were even more damning. In what *The New York Times* called a "blistering report," toxicology expert Dr. Ronald E. Gots, who analyzed a similar event in Louisiana in 1988, called the regimen "quackery" and noted that "no recognized body of toxicologists, no department of occupational medicine nor any governmental agencies endorse or recommend such treatment."

A Canadian doctor, David Hogg, M.D., described many of Hubbard's claims about the Purification Rundown as "fallacious or even mendacious." In a five-page analysis written in 1981, he concluded: "Hubbard is a very ignorant man. He consistently demonstrates a complete and at times dangerous lack of knowledge concerning biochemistry, physics, and medicine. His theories are based on fallacies and lies; there is no scientific data to support any of them. Furthermore his program not only fails to deliver what it promises but may actually be detrimental to the health of those taking it. As such it cannot be recommended that anyone take this program." Another expert, Bruce Roe, professor of chemistry and biochemistry at the University of Oklahoma, similarly dismissed Hubbard's detoxification program as "pure, unadulterated cow pies. It is filled with some scientific truth but mainly it is illogical and the conclusions drawn by Mr. Hubbard are without any basis in scientific fact."

As for Cruise, in his head it was simple: He knew more than the doctors. He was now a medical expert, simply because he had read Hubbard. "I'm the kind of person who will think about something, and if I know it's right I'm not going to ask anybody. I don't go, 'Boy, what do you think about this?' I've made every decision for myself," he later told writer Neil Strauss. In fact, his claims went further than his religion, which describes the Purification Rundown as "a religious practice . . . solely for spiritual benefit."

Scientology had convinced him that he already knew all the answers. He knew the truth because Hubbard *was* the truth; he was Source, as Scientologists see it. Any other point of view was pure ignorance. "A lot of doctors don't have much experience in that area," he said with the confidence of a bar-stool expert. "There are all kinds of toxins in the environment that can act on a person emotionally. When you talk about lead poisoning, for example, that can make a person act as if they're totally insane, depressed. I thought, there are people still living now. These men and women who are risking their lives in the rescue effort. And I knew I could do something that could help."

Celebrity recruiting sergeant, generous donor, and medical expert. Now he tried his hand at lobbying the movers and shakers in Washington as an authority on human rights and education. Scientology had come a long way from the days when it considered the government an enemy and David Miscavige once quizzically asked a fellow Scientology executive why he even bothered to vote. Scientologists now employed high-powered professional lobbyists to argue their cause, augmented by the glitz and glamour of their Hollywood celebrities.

On June 13, 2003, one of the most powerful men in America, Deputy Secretary of State Richard Armitage, met privately with Tom Cruise, together with his friend Tom Davis, head of the Hollywood Celebrity Centre, and Kurt Weiland, an Austrian Scientologist who was director of external affairs for the organization's Office of Special Affairs. For thirty minutes Armitage listened as they expressed their concerns about the treatment of Scientologists in some foreign countries, particularly Germany.

At first, even Tom's star wattage could not obtain a meeting with Armitage, the actor instead palmed off to John Hanford, the State Department's ambassador-at-large for religious freedom. But Tom persevered, writing to Armitage personally to say that he was most interested in speaking with him: "I am familiar with your history and your duties as Deputy Secretary and I am certain that I can, in a brief amount of time, communicate to you what is on my mind."

Tom emphasized that he was well informed about the supposed human-rights abuses of Scientologists in Germany: "I have taken it upon myself to become somewhat educated in these matters and to stay abreast of what continues to occur," he wrote portentously. "I do keep a close watch on the situation in these countries and within the last month, I learned of attempts to sabotage the performances of two American artists solely because they are members of the Church of Scientology."

Cruise was keen to remind Armitage of his various lobbying trips to American embassies in Europe, noting that he had made a number of visits to the U.S embassies in Germany, France, and Spain, and "spoke to each ambassador about the problems of religious intolerance in those countries." He mentioned that he also hoped to arrange a discussion with Vice President Dick Cheney.

The day after his meeting with Armitage, Tom sat down with Cheney's chief of staff, Scooter Libby. In testimony given two years later, when Libby was on trial for perjury and obstruction of justice, Craig Schmall, the CIA intelligence officer who had given daily briefings to the chief of staff, recalls Libby being "excited" and bragging about having a face-to-face meeting with Tom Cruise and Penélope Cruz. Once again, the subject of the meeting was Tom's concern about Germany's treatment of Scientologists.

This episode, which coincided with the government's increasing concerns over the Iraq debacle, illustrates the access and authority that celebrities can wield at the highest levels of government. Tom Cruise was not given an audience with any of these busy, powerful men because of what he knew, but because of who he was. In the old days, political influence was based on class, money, and status. In our celebrity-obsessed culture, starstruck politicians are putty in the hands of the new breed of hustlers from Hollywood.

That same month of June 2003, Tom quickly swapped hats, changing from an authority on human rights to an expert on education, visiting Washington in an attempt to win government funding for L. Ron Hubbard's Study Tech through the Bush administration's "No Child Left Behind" program. This time he cited his personal experience, crediting Hubbard's teaching methods with curing his own learning difficulties. "We have some serious problems with education. I know a lot about it," he said categorically, referring to his own battle with dyslexia. "There are eight million kids that are being medicated with educational medication."

His expertise seemed to know no bounds. "Do you know about Ritalin, Adderall, psychotropic drugs?" Cruise went on. "When you break down the chemical compound, it's the same as cocaine. Bet you didn't know that." As the drug company Novartis, which has been manufacturing the drug Ritalin for more than fifty years, soberly noted, "Ritalin is not addictive when taken as indicated while cocaine is highly addictive. Ritalin and cocaine are two very different substances. While they affect similar parts of the brain, Ritalin and cocaine work differently in those areas of the brain."

Whereas millions of American teachers and educators will never get the chance to speak in person to the man in charge of education, Tom Cruise had lunch with then education secretary Rod Paige and his chief of staff, John Danielson. They were impressed by his coherent and passionate presentation, listening intently as he told them that before Scientology, he had trouble learning to fly jet planes because he couldn't read the manuals. It was only when a friend introduced him to Hubbard's Study Tech that he was able to overcome his difficulties and pass the tests for his pilot's license. It is a testament to the effectiveness of Cruise's lobbying that he and Danielson, who now works in the private sector, became close friends, the two men often meeting for lunch and Danielson eventually visiting a Study Technology center in Missouri.

For once Tom seemed to be speaking from personal experience. But just how true is his story? Over the years he has given two differing accounts of his battle to overcome dyslexia. His first version, before his conversion to Scientology, credits his iron will and his mother's help for enabling him to learn to read. Indeed, in 1985 he was happy to receive an award at the White House from Nancy Reagan for his efforts to raise global awareness of the learning disorder.

After he joined the Church of Scientology in 1986, the story changed. In the flurry of interviews he gave during 2003 to promote Scientology learning techniques, he claimed that before he discovered Hubbard, he was "a functional illiterate." By his own account, young Thomas Mapother had been unable to read or write effectively. The implication was that thirteen years of traditional education had let him down. In a story in *People* magazine titled "My Struggle to Read," he sympathized with his teachers, arguing that they had failed him only because they didn't have the correct educational tools. "I had so many different teachers and I really feel for them. I see how they struggled with me. They were rooting for me and cared about me and wanted to see me do well, but they didn't have the tools to really help me." The tools they lacked, of course, were the tools of Scientology.

The lights went on, he claimed, only in his mid-twenties, after he encountered Scientology techniques and learned to use dictionaries. Looking up words in a dictionary is one of the "technologies" that Scientology offers its members. "No one teaches you about dictionaries," he told writer Dotson Rader. "I didn't know the meanings of lots of words."

As he continued to give interviews about his troubled education, he went even further, claiming that he had never really been dyslexic but incorrectly labeled as such by educational psychologists—the archenemies of Scientology. When he interviewed Cruise in November 2003, talk-show host Larry King asked if he was or ever had been dyslexic. Three times Tom flatly denied it. He looked King in the eye and said that he had never had a problem with reading or writing. Instead, he repeated the story that he had told numerous other interviewers—that he was "labeled" with a learning disability, and it was only when he became a Scientologist in 1986 that the secrets of L. Ron Hubbard's Study Technology released him from this false labeling.

The miracle cure of Study Tech was the reason, he explained, that he had given considerable time and money to the Hollywood Education and Literacy Project (HELP), a supposedly secular organization that offered free tutoring to children and adults—using Hubbard's study technology. It was the same reason that in the summer of 2003 he joined

Jenna Elfman, Isaac Hayes, Anne Archer, and Congressman Lacey Clay to cut the ribbon for the opening of the new headquarters of Applied Scholastics International in St. Louis—a campus entirely dedicated to Hubbard's teaching techniques.

"Do I wish I'd had something like this when I was a kid?" Tom said. "Absolutely. It would have saved me many hours and days and weeks of pain and embarrassment." As he modestly told *Marie Claire* magazine, "I can learn anything now. If I had known then . . . oh man, I'd have been through college at age eleven. I'd have been that bullet train that whipped past our school."

For someone who uses his educational history as a calling card to lobby for government funding, Tom Cruise is cagey when anyone tries to examine his claims. In the past, when journalists have made cursory attempts to review his school days, his response has been the familiar retreat into legal threats and professional bullying. When reporter Stephanie Mansfield spoke to a former school friend, who had only good things to say about Tom, his publicist, Pat Kingsley, angrily told her that she would never work with any of her roster of celebrity clients again. She was true to her word. Although he has lobbied vigorously for freedom of expression for his fellow Scientologists, Tom Cruise has proved relentless at using the law or professional arm-twisting to muzzle others' freedom of speech.

So just what does he have to hide? Teachers, former pupils, and others give a very different picture of Tom's education, a picture that does not jibe with the Scientology propaganda. Pennyann Styles, who was a teacher at Robert Hopkins Public School in Ottawa for thirty years, remembers Cruise very clearly. She recalls that from the age of eight he was placed in a special-education class with about ten other children. In order to receive this special education, he had to be assessed by an educational psychologist, who diagnosed him as having a learning difficulty.

Styles doubts Cruise's claim that Study Tech alone rid him of his problems. "We can't cure dyslexia, but we can assist children with coping strategies so that they can be successful.

He has said that Scientology cured him, but I don't think there is a special-needs teacher going who would believe that. Dyslexia is something that is with you throughout your life. He wants to make Scientology out to be the savior of all things. What a shame!"

Cruise's contention that he was never taught to use a dictionary also provokes a raised eyebrow from his former teacher. "Most certainly dictionaries were used," recalls Styles. "In Tom's day, especially as he attended a brand-new school which had been given plenty of money, dictionaries were plentiful. I even remember his classroom teacher teaching specific dictionary skills, often."

George Steinburg taught drama at Robert Hopkins and had an extremely good relationship with Cruise. It was Steinburg who asked his assistant, Marilyn Richardson, to help Cruise learn lines for drama by reading them out to him. She, too, is surprised to hear Cruise's claims of being a "functional illiterate." She recalls: "Tom Mapother could read, but it took him a long time. He had a very good memory, it didn't take him long to pick up his lines." Marilyn also remembers Tom's mother doing the same—working hard to help him learn his parts. Clearly his dyslexia was not that "mislabeling" by a psychologist that he would now have the world believe.

Although he was diagnosed with a learning difficulty early in his academic career, by the time he was a teenager he seems to have been coping well enough not to need any special help. The care and support that he received from his mother and the special-education teachers at Robert Hopkins had helped him go a long way to overcoming his problems— a full twelve years before L. Ron Hubbard became a part of his life.

When he reached the seventh grade, Tom moved from Robert Hopkins to Henry Munro Middle School in Ottawa. His homeroom teacher, Byron Boucher, taught him in a variety of subjects, including English and math. Now retired, Boucher remembers all the children in that year, and, as far as he is concerned, Tom Mapother had no special learning difficulties. He was certainly never classified as needing special services. If he had struggled with reading and writing, Byron, who later became a special-needs teacher, says that the school principal would have been informed and necessary remedial action taken. "He was just an average kid with no learning disability. The description 'functional illiterate' does not fit with my recollection. I can't believe that story. An illiterate is someone who cannot read or write, and that is not the case with this student. It is not true, simply not true."

According to Boucher, Cruise was at neither the top nor the bottom of the class, but right in the middle. He was not a special-needs student, simply an average student. Boucher's is a common assessment. From middle school to high school, fellow pupils like Glen Gobel and others use exactly the same phrase, "middle of the road," to describe Cruise's modest academic ability.

Certainly his girlfriends like Nancy Armel and Diane Van Zoeren, who sat with him at his kitchen table and did homework, never noticed any problem with reading or writing. When he read scripts with Kathy and Lorraine Gauli, there was no indication that he was having difficulties. This was, after all, a young man who could stand in front of his drama coach and his friends and declaim from the script in front of him.

Perhaps more accurately, the actor's reading trajectory conforms to scientific research that has discovered that while dyslexia cannot be cured, it can be dealt with if caught at a sufficiently early age and a program of remedial education put into effect. This is precisely what he received at his elementary school, Robert Hopkins. By the time he reached Henry Munro Middle School, he was no longer considered to have special needs. As dyslexia is caused by "miswiring" in the brain, it can effectively "rewire" itself while the young brain is growing. This process is more difficult when the brain is fully mature—certainly in one's twenties, which is when Tom said that Study Tech helped him.

Rather than floundering for years among teachers who "didn't have the tools to really help me," Cruise seems to have been fortunate to encounter a series of dedicated teachers—as well as a caring mother—who intervened early and effectively, so that he was able to cope on his own from middle school on.

Of course, the plain fact that conventional teaching works does nothing to help the cause of Scientology or further their applications for tax breaks and government funding for their educational programs. Therefore, history had to be rewritten: Tom owed everything to Scientology.

The new gospel according to Cruise has not gone without criticism. The International Dyslexia Association has publicly attacked the actor's assertions. As executive director J. Thomas Viall commented, "When an individual of the prominence of Tom Cruise makes statements that are difficult to replicate in terms of what science tells us, the issue becomes what other individuals who are dyslexic do in response to such a quote unquote success story. There is not a lot of science to support the claim that the teachings of L. Ron Hubbard are appropriate to overcoming dyslexia."

Once again, Cruise brushed aside such criticism, utterly convinced of his superior knowledge. As he was to say time and again, he had done the reading. But that reading was invariably works by L. Ron Hubbard; to explore further would have been heresy. In the hermetically sealed universe beginning and ending with LRH, no other worldview or even point of view is tolerated. It is the North Korea of religion.

Clearly Tom was comfortable in this country of commitment. In January 2004, not only did he become a gold-level "Patron Meritorious" for donating $1 million to his faith, he reached the exalted level of Operating Thetan VII, where Hubbard promised that man would become his own god. It meant that several times a day Tom clutched his E meter and scoured his body in search of dead spirits. The questioning routine was similar to earlier levels, except that the spirits were harder to discover and eliminate.

The process puts practitioners into a self-induced hypnotic trance that can disconnect them from reality. As former Scientologist Peter Alexander, who reached OT VII, observes, "You believe that all your problems are due to these thetans. So when you come back into reality, you're like, 'Wow, this is a nice day, my dog's been killed but that doesn't matter, I realize that I am a being who has lived endlessly contacting all these long-lost body thetans. So nothing is really a problem.' That is the behavior that you can see in Tom Cruise."

Cruise was seething with Scientology, totally immersed in his faith. He was physically surrounded by Scientologists, intellectually and emotionally cocooned, seeing the rest of the world through Hubbard's ideological prism. Not only did he know all the answers, but in his universe there was no room for nonbelievers, dissenting voices, or even the mildest criticism. Writer Neil Strauss from *Rolling Stone* magazine, which always gave him flattering coverage, was taken aback by the ferocity of Tom's response when he asked him about his faith. "Some people, well, if they don't like Scientology, well, then, fuck you." Then, his face reddening, he rose from the table and jabbed a finger at the imaginary enemy: "Fuck you."

As Tom approached the dark heart of Hubbard's universe, there was absolutely no place for those Scientologists deemed Suppressive Persons or Potential Trouble Sources. Just as many ordinary Scientologists had sacrificed their personal relationships, shunning wives, husbands, children, brothers, and sisters for their faith, so Tom had little hesitation in disconnecting from his longtime publicist, Pat Kingsley, and his girlfriend Penélope Cruz when it became clear that Penélope could not bring herself to join his organization.

Significantly, the ax fell on Pat Kingsley on March 13, 2004, the anniversary of L. Ron Hubbard's birth, the Hollywood actor replacing her with his sister and ardent Scientologist Lee Anne DeVette. Like so many of his partings, professional and emotional, it was cold and clinical. "If I don't feel that [my people] are doing what I need from them . . . hey, I fire them!" he later commented. For fourteen years Kingsley had been his shield and iron fist, ruthlessly protecting him from overexposure and unnecessary intrusion. What *Slate* magazine had called his "Teflon-coated persona" was almost entirely due to Kingsley.

It is commonly believed in Hollywood that the first cracks in their relationship came in the fall of 2003 when Tom, fresh from his lobbying work in Washington, was gearing up to publicize his latest movie, *The Last Samurai*. Feeling that his proselytizing was harming his image and detracting from the films he was supposed to be selling, she came to an informal agreement with CAA, his management agency, and one of Tom's close friends that they would sit him down and let him know that they thought he had gone too far. When they did eventually sit down, it was only Kingsley who spoke out. As one Hollywood insider observed, "From that moment she was doomed."

Kingsley paid the price for saying what many in Hollywood had privately thought for some time. As a senior entertainment industry executive observed, "When he started to use his platform to spew personal opinion, he immediately allowed himself to be questioned. You can't have it both ways. Suddenly everyone has the right to lash back.

"Pat Kingsley did a fantastic job; she sheltered him, his public persona was carefully crafted, but now that the veneer is down and he strongly believes in something the rest of us think is odd, he comes off as self-righteous."

At the same time that he was dissolving a professional partnership, he was saying good-bye to the woman widely thought to be his future bride. Much as he had tried to woo the Spanish actress to join his faith, his three-year love affair with Penélope Cruz came up against an unexpected roadblock— her father, Eduardo. In the early days of their romance in 2001, Eduardo had given the couple his blessing. But it was a mixed blessing, the Madrid retailer telling local journalists that he had to be "110 percent sure" that the twice-married actor would stick around. "Tom is a nice guy, but I have to make sure he loves my daughter enough for life."

While Penélope studiously read Scientology texts, attended auditing courses, and, according to at least one report, even took the Purification Rundown, she was never entirely committed. "I have great respect for all religions, but I do not intend to join any of them at the moment," she said tactfully. She did, however, join Tom's diplomatic mission to spread the Scientology gospel in Europe and was by his side during his lobbying campaign in Washington during the summer of 2003.

It seems that Eduardo Cruz became increasingly alarmed by his treasured daughter's involvement with a group that concerned the Spanish government. Eduardo's alarm over his daughter's well-being was entirely in character. For example, when a Spanish TV host announced that Penélope was pregnant out of wedlock with Tom's baby, he was quick to defend her reputation and that of her family. Now he spent time trawling the Internet for information about Scientology but did not know where to turn for advice. He was concerned that his famous daughter could be drawn into what he considered a cult—and, like so many others, be lost to him and his family forever. Eventually he e-mailed an organization devoted to helping cult members and their families. It was only after a long exchange of correspondence that officials realized that they were dealing with Penélope Cruz's father. Even today, they are reluctant to identify themselves publicly, lest it discourage other families or those who are trying to escape from Scientology from making contact.

Family versus faith. It is an implacable dilemma that many committed Scientologists have confronted with much heartache and sorrow. For Penélope, family had always come first. A ring given to her by her grandmother is one of her most prized possessions, and the actress returns often to Madrid to see her family. "We are very strict about that, about not letting anything interfere with having time for the family," Penélope has said. "We are always here for each other, all of us. We know we can count on the rest so we always find the time."

Whatever family sentiment—or disapproval—was expressed about Penélope's attachment to Tom Cruise and Scientology, it became immaterial in December 2003. While Penélope was filming the Italian movie *Non ti muovere,* her father suffered a heart attack, his daughter rushing to his bedside in Madrid. The six weeks she spent in Spain as her father recuperated seem to have grounded her again in her family and her Catholic faith. In the new year she was noticeably absent when Tom attended the Golden Globes, where he was nominated for his performance in *The Last Samurai,* and later in January 2004 when he appeared on *Inside the Actors Studio,* a TV show intended to showcase the interviewee's achievements in front of an adoring audience. It seemed that the most important man in her life was in Madrid.

The couple announced their breakup in March 2004. It was an "amicable" parting, said her publicist, Robert Garlock, keen to take Scientology out of the emotional equation. "She has taken church courses and she's found them beneficial." His careful phrasing was matched by Penélope's own guarded comments about the organization, saying that she had read a lot of books and "some of the things I have studied have helped me with my life."

Perhaps her reticence was related to the fact that she was called into two meetings with the Office of Special Affairs, the department of Scientology responsible for intelligence operations. It has access to the confidential files of individual parishioners and is able and willing to use previous confessions to attack the characters of those who have left the group. "Presumably she was warned not to say anything," observes a former OSA chief.

Her father was much more open. "She's happier than I am," revealed Penélope's father, Eduardo, a telling phrase that suggested something of her fraught experience. When asked if he was saddened by the breakdown of his daughter's relationship, he was blunt. "No, I've no reason to be." While the split may have delighted Eduardo Cruz, his daughter—unlike Nicole Kidman—and Tom remained friends.

It was not long after the split that the Hollywood rumor mill was linking Tom to actress Jennifer Garner, who divorced her actor husband Scott Foley around the time Tom and Penélope announced their own parting. One story suggested that he had become smitten with the chemistry graduate after seeing her in his favorite TV show, *Alias*. Legend has it that he left messages on her voice mail asking "if she knew what freedom was," sentiments so trite that Garner apparently read them to her girlfriends. One wildfire story that made the rounds inside the higher echelons of Scientology was that Tom learned of Jennifer's fascination with tigers and had sent one around to her house in a cage. Naturally, Garner's representatives dismiss the notion—after all, real live tigers are hard to come by even with a Neiman Marcus charge card—but it demonstrates how all eyes inside Scientology were continually locked on pleasing Cruise.

While his association with Scientology may have harmed his love life, his faith seems to have helped him understand his movie characters. During the filming of *Collateral* during 2004, he explored the personality of Vincent, a coldhearted hired killer, by studying Hubbard's examination of antisocial behavior and personalities. "In Scientology there is a large body of knowledge about antisocials. So I worked to create Vincent's moral code from that." He omitted to mention that in Hubbard's view, these antisocial "merchants of chaos" included politicians, police, journalists, and, bizarrely, undertakers.

Scientology as character background was one thing, but by the fall of 2004, he was literally building a base for his faith on the set of his latest movie, *War of the Worlds*. Tom, his sister Lee Anne DeVette, agent Kevin Huvane, and director Steven Spielberg had to appeal personally to the president of Universal Studios, Ron Meyer, to allow a Scientology tent to be erected at the studio. Permission was given, provided the tent was not used for recruitment purposes.

As a result, throughout filming, Scientology Volunteer Ministers were on duty in the large tent in order to give "assists" to actors and members of the film crew. The delicious irony of a new religion that believes in reincarnation inveigling itself onto the movie set for a film based on a book written by H. G. Wells, an outspoken atheist who categorically rebuffed the idea that either he or his body was immortal, was apparently lost on Tom Cruise—and everyone else, for that matter. When asked about the religious tent, Spielberg rather shamefacedly argued that no one was compelled to visit it. Typically, Tom was much more aggressive when pressed by the German magazine *Der Spiegel.* "The volunteer Scientology ministers were there to help the sick and injured. People on the set appreciated that." Ignoring the traditional role played by doctors and nurses, he moved effortlessly into his new role as omnipotent preacher and healer.

"I don't care what someone believes. I don't care what nationality they are. But if someone wants to get off drugs, I can help them. If someone wants to learn how to read, I can help them. If someone doesn't want to be a criminal anymore, I can give them tools that can better their life. You have no idea how many people want to know what Scientology is."

Tom's zeal was in keeping with his persona as an indestructible godlike figure, able to solve all the world's problems on and off the screen. This was a man who, when he was not saving the planet on the silver screen, was rescuing damsels in distress in real life. Stories were legion: In 1996 he stopped to help a hit-and-run victim in Santa Monica and paid her hospital bills. "If he's not Superman," said a grateful Heloisa Vinhas, "he can be my Batman." That same year he pulled to safety two children who were being crushed in an excited crowd at the London premiere of *Mission: Impossible,* sent a tender from his yacht to assist five people who had abandoned a sinking boat off the island of Capri in the Mediterranean, and consoled a sobbing housewife who had just been mugged of expensive jewelry outside her home near Tom's rented house in central London. During the filming of *The Last Samurai* in 2003, he stopped to change the flat tire of a couple stranded in the remote New Zealand countryside.

A year later, in November 2004, he explained why he was a Good Samaritan in a long congratulatory interview before he was awarded Scientology's first-ever Freedom Medal of Valor at a gala event at Saint Hill Manor in England. He told his audience, "You can't drive past an accident, because as a Scientologist you are the only one who can help." While his assertion confirmed fellow Scientologists in their assumptions that they were a superior species—and that Tom was supreme among these advanced beings—his tone of arrogant, self-righteous certainty was beginning to play badly in the outside world.

That evening, though, everyone was there to worship Tom, his achievements lauded in a lengthy video preceding his award being presented by his great friend David Miscavige. The bond between the star and his spiritual leader was on show for everyone to see. As they met on the stage, they looked each other straight in the eyes, unblinking, then traded effusive words and crisp salutes. Miscavige said that Tom was "the most dedicated Scientologist I know," before presenting him with his unique award. The adulation did not stop there. Miscavige went on to describe his friend in terms befitting a prophet: "Across ninety nations, five thousand people hear his word of Scientology—every hour. Every minute of every hour someone reaches for LRH technology . . . simply because they know Tom Cruise is a Scientologist." That Tom had also donated more than $2.5 million warranted a second award, the Platinum Meritorious.

Even though he doesn't believe in heaven, Tom looked as if he had died and gone there as he soaked up the adulation of this huge congregation. Then it was his turn to laud David Miscavige. "I have never met a more competent, a more intelligent, a more tolerant, a more compassionate being outside of what I have experienced from LRH. And I've met the leaders of leaders. I've met them all." He then turned his verbal firepower on SPs—Suppressive Persons—before announcing that as Scientologists, "We are the authorities on the mind."

When the cheers had faded, however, there were mutterings of discontent among Scientology's most committed followers. Sea Org members know what sacrifice means. They have all signed billion-year contracts, promising to put the advancement of the organization before *anything* else: money, family, fame, prestige. They are the elite. Yet here was a man who already had it all, being showered in glory and awarded honors because of his celebrity rather than his sacrifice. It was as if their unseen, unstinting efforts behind the scenes counted for nothing against the glamour of Tom Cruise.

A month later, Scientology's poster boy was asked, together with Oprah Winfrey, to host a concert in Norway to honor the Nobel Peace Prize winner, Kenyan environmentalist Professor Wangari Maathai. Before the event, Tom spoke not as an actor but as a man of religion. "One of the things that we believe in [as Scientologists] is peace, freedom. I'm just proud to be here, and very proud to be a Scientologist here and to be part of this."

If Cruise expected the kind of reception in Oslo that he had received at the Scientology gala, he was mistaken. Noisy protests were staged against the choice of such a controversial figure for the occasion. The newspapers quoted one priest from Stockholm as saying, "They're a manipulative sect that takes over people's lives and finances." Another Scientology foe, Andreas Heldal-Lund, also spoke out: "It's very wrong to let Cruise lead the gala. I've met tons of people who have had their lives devastated by Scientology, and this is such an important event."

These critics meant as little to Tom as any others. They were so far beneath him, he barely heard them. He was on top of the world, at the top of his game. Celebrity advocate, expansive donor, skillful lobbyist, human-rights activist, medical expert, education guru, healer, inspirational preacher: There was nothing this man could not do. He was a full-fledged master of the universe.

CHAPTER 11

The temperature in Montreal had plummeted, but her work there was nearly done. Stunning actress Sofía Vergara was shooting the final scenes of a bloody family revenge movie, *Four Brothers*. While on the set with former boyfriend Mark Wahlberg, the Colombian-born model received an intriguing invitation to join actor Will Smith and his wife, Jada Pinkett Smith, at the pre-Oscar party they were hosting in Los Angeles. Their friend Jamie Foxx had been nominated for his performance as the blind jazz pianist Ray Charles—this was an A-list congratulatory bash. The sun and glamour of Hollywood would be a welcome change from the subzero February chill in Canada.

On a balmy Tuesday evening in February 2005, Sofía walked up the steps of the Los Angeles Museum of Modern Art, where the party was already under way. She was wearing a black-and-white print silk dress and chunky turquoise jewelry that offset her olive skin and dark hair, but even more striking than her looks was the absence of a man on her arm. Although she had been voted one of the one hundred sexiest women in the world by *FHM* magazine, Sofía was arriving on her own. No man meant little interest from the press. There were hundreds of beautiful people in L.A. Sofía might have been famous in Latin America as a TV host, a model, and an actress, but she had yet to make it to the next level. Tonight the paparazzi had other prey in their sights.

Tom Cruise arrived as part of a perplexing trio, making his entrance alongside his former girlfriend, Penélope Cruz, and her new boyfriend, actor Matthew McConaughey. Cruise was smiling and waving patiently as Penelope showed Matthew off to the cameras. Hollywood heartthrob Tom Cruise without a date: Now, that was a story. It was not, however, a story that would last for long. There was a plan in place. Inside the party, Tom had eyes only for one person: Sofía Vergara. As soon as he spotted the Colombian beauty, he left Penélope and Matthew and introduced himself. He was charming and friendly, frequently flashing his famous megawatt smile.

Maybe he knew that a guy's smile was the way to the heart of this onetime dental student. As her aunt Lilita Jamarillo observed, "For Sofía the most important thing in a man is that he has good teeth." Whether or not he knew about her dentistry past, he did seem to know a lot about her career. The flattery rolled off his tongue.

Caught up in the moment, she accepted his invitation to go for coffee at Jerry's Famous Deli in Hollywood. It was a classic late-night celebrity hangout—a professional Tom Cruise look-alike is a regular—and the paparazzi would always swing by there as a last call after the Ivy or Mastro's. When celebrities turn up at Jerry's, they know they are likely to get "papped." Sure enough, they were photographed, Tom waving as his "mystery" girl, a pashmina shawl over her slender shoulders, walked by his side. In one evening, Sofía had gone from party outsider to talk of the town.

Pictures of the new couple hit the gossip columns the following day, pushing talk about Penélope Cruz and Matthew McConaughey down the page. Maybe this was what Tom Cruise had in mind. The next day, Sofía faced a blizzard of phone calls, text messages, and e-mails from the remorselessly romantic Mr. Cruise, who sent her flowers, notes, and chocolates. She was flattered and excited—as were her friends, giggling over his texts and admiring the bouquets he sent her.

Naturally, Vergara's publicist, Karen Tenser, was delighted, eager to see her client's name in the headlines with a

star of this magnitude. Sofía was cooler. She took Tom's wooing in her stride, airily dismissing him as "the shortest guy she
had ever dated." After all, the shapely Ms. Vergara—at five
feet, seven inches the same height as her new beau—had already dated some very eligible bachelors. Her first boyfriend
had been Latino superstar Luis Miguel, the South American
equivalent of a young Frank Sinatra. Nonetheless, Tom's
charm offensive was working.

Sofía agreed to delay her return to Montreal, accepting
Tom's offer to hang out at his Hollywood home. She brought
her son, Manolo, born when she was eighteen, along, too.
Manolo played with Cruise's children, Connor and Isabella,
and was thrilled when Tom took him out on the back of his
trail bike. If this relationship was going to work, both Tom
and Sofía knew that their children would lie at the heart of it.
Sofía once told an interviewer that her favorite date was a
night in with her twelve-year-old son. As a close friend
noted, "She is a mother first, not a careerist."

Besides being single parents, the couple had much else
in common, beginning with early fame. When Sofía was
seventeen, a photographer "discovered" her as she lay on a
Colombian beach. That first modeling session earned her
other deals, notably the starring role in a Pepsi commercial
shown all over Latin America. Like Tom, she had a passion
for adventure, growing up on a cattle farm in Barranquilla,
Colombia, where she spent her childhood riding horses and
swimming in rivers. This headstrong girl, who her family
nicknamed "La Toti," was an ideal choice to host a travel
show called *Fuera de Serie* (Out of the Ordinary) in which
she was sent to extreme locations around the globe. For a
guy who listed skydiving, jet planes, and trail biking among
his hobbies, Tom recognized that this was a woman who
spoke his language.

Their spiritual pasts were similar, too. Both Tom and
Sofía had been brought up in the Catholic faith. As she embarked on her acting career, she had relied on the guidance
of the nuns at her school, following their advice to turn down
big-money offers from *Playboy* magazine to display her

32DD assets. Tom, however, no longer found guidance from his Catholic past. He now had a very different moral compass.

It was not long before Cruise casually suggested that Sofía join him on a trip to what he calls "CC," the Celebrity Centre in Hollywood. When she arrived, David Miscavige, the diminutive head of the church, was there to greet her and show her around. He was charming and attentive. She was given some Scientology literature to leaf through. It was a pleasant introduction to the world of Scientology.

But it was on this trip that Sofía realized something else: Tom was never alone. Everywhere he went, he was surrounded by Scientologists. They were at his home, they were in his car, they were at the restaurant. They were never short of smiles, but she found them "powerful and authoritarian."

At the end of February, when she returned to Montreal to complete filming, Cruise bombarded her with calls. He was obsessed with the new woman in his life. After she flew back to Hollywood in early March 2005, the couple spent every moment together. If they were not at his home, they were at the Celebrity Centre. Sofía even took her mother, Margarita, along for a look around the palatial Scientology mansion. Unlike her daughter, this devout Catholic was not given an armful of literature as she left. All conversion efforts were focused on Sofía—they had been ever since she first met Cruise.

Although they had known each other only for a matter of weeks, the relationship had become so intense that marriage looked like the logical next stage. One friend told me: "She met his children, there is no doubt he was auditioning her for the part of his wife. If she had been interested, she would today be the next Mrs. Cruise. Was it going to go further? No doubt about it. He wanted to marry her—that was the idea." The "audition" was going according to plan. Cruise had found a feisty, athletic, adventurous woman. The winning factor was that she had a child. Vergara had a proven track record; she could provide him with exactly what he was after. They could be together forever—Scientology's poster boy and first lady.

As the days passed, however, Sofía started to connect the

dots, and didn't much like the pattern that was emerging. As affectionate and attentive as Tom was, she found his world cloying and suffocating, and was never quite sure if his actions were motivated by passion or were part of a well-practiced performance. She felt she was being followed or watched and that her phone calls were being monitored. It was as if he and Scientology were trying to take over her life. Certainly her longtime manager, Luis Balaguer, and his team thought their days were numbered, fearing that they would be replaced by management chosen by Cruise.

It was made clear that if their relationship were to continue, she would have to renounce her Catholic faith and convert to Scientology. For Tom, this was supremely important. It would be unacceptable for Hollywood's and Scientology's leading man to be married to anyone other than a member of his faith. "She was fundamentally terrified by Scientology," recalls a friend. "She sincerely believed that she would be struck down by God and burn in hell if she joined. That is what she said." The lighthearted frivolity that had characterized her early discussions with friends was replaced by their genuine concern for her well-being. "Her friends got scared for her," admits one of her close circle.

They need not have worried. Although educated by nuns, Sofía had graduated from the school of hard knocks. Not only was she a single mother, but her brother had been killed in a botched kidnap attempt and she had survived thyroid cancer three years before. As she later admitted, "It was terrifying. But I knew I'd beat it." Sassy, street smart, and obstinate, she proved immune to the blandishments of Cruise and Scientology. Her friend said, "Sofía comes from Colombia, where the women have balls. There is no sense you can control her. If you know her, it makes perfect sense. . . . She had plenty of opportunity to hitch her wagon to Hollywood and to Tom. She is not swayed by that—she is her own person."

Sofía told her friends that she had been deliberately targeted not only as a possible bride for Tom, but as a high-profile Scientology recruit who would be an alluring figurehead for a future recruitment drive in Latin America. The unexpected invitation to Will Smith's party, the "impromptu" decision to go to Jerry's Famous Deli, the "casual" visits to Celebrity Centre—they all began to make sense. They were to impress and ultimately win her over.

Instead of impressing her, all this drove her away. Tom's constant "love bombing"—the endless texts, calls, and e-mails—was too much. She saw it as a performance to serve the higher purpose of his faith. On Easter weekend—March 27, 2005—she and Tom had arranged to go to Clearwater, the Scientology center in Florida. Instead, she stood him up, packing a bag and "disappearing" for a few days. For five days he left messages and texts, but she resolutely refused to return his calls. Even now, the location is kept secret in case she needs to use the same bolt-hole again. As one friend put it, "The guy's a freak and she ran for the hills."

Sofía is kinder. While she admits that she likes Tom as a friend and found their affair "fun," having seen him in action she has a very clear vision of who he is and how he operates. "You have to have respect for his beliefs and trying to get his religion out there in any way possible," notes a close member of Sofía's circle. The bottom line was that she was not prepared to sacrifice herself or her faith to further her career—or to become the next Mrs. Cruise.

Sofía was savvy enough to see the consequences of the game being played. It seems that Tom, for all his protestations of love and affection, saw it as a game, too, albeit a game with high stakes. Even before the blooms on Sofía's flowers from him had faded, Tom was already sending bouquets to a new girl—a wholesome, wide-eyed actress from America's heartland.

For days, John Carrabino's phone had been ringing off the hook. Every call to his Beverly Hills office seemed to be about the young actress he was managing—Katie Holmes—and her love life. Since March 5, 2005, when she had publicly called off her engagement to longtime boyfriend Chris

Klein, star of the teen comedy *American Pie,* all the talk had been about a new man in her life. She had been spotted kissing heartthrob actor Josh Hartnett in a coffee shop in New York. The rumor mills whirred into action. Managing this kind of attention is never easy; Carrabino was deflecting inquiries from all over the country. So it must have been something of relief, as well as a surprise, when in early April he received a call from the office of Tom Cruise rather than from another gossip columnist. The request, which came out of the blue, was for a meeting between Hollywood's leading man and the aspiring star.

If her manager was surprised by Tom Cruise's invitation, Katie Holmes was ecstatic. She had dreamt of meeting the Hollywood action man since she was a little girl growing up in Toledo, Ohio, her childhood crush a long-standing family joke. She told her three older sisters that she would marry him someday and live in a beautiful mansion where she would start the day by sliding from her bedroom into her own swimming pool. Even in 1996, when she snagged the part of Joey Potter, a teenage girl growing up in a suburban town, for the hit teen soap *Dawson's Creek,* her crush continued. Indeed, it was her unworldly innocence—and her playful green eyes—that won her the role in the first place.

"She had these incredible eyes, it was all about the eyes," recalled writer Kevin Williamson. Educated by nuns and raised by a protective, God-fearing family, Katie, just seventeen, was a real greenhorn when she first arrived on the TV set in Wilmington, North Carolina. Her artlessness was exploited by her costars, James Van Der Beek and Josh Jackson, who teased her about her teenage crush and sexual naïveté.

Close to her family and friends from Toledo, she daily phoned her mother, Kathy, who was recovering from ovarian cancer. Kathy visited the set often, while Katie's longtime pal Meghann Birie, who impressed the cast with her loyalty and levelheaded nature, stayed with her friend for six months to keep her company. Her father, Martin, a partner in a law firm, was on hand to look over the contract when she bought her first condo, just as he was there when she signed up for the series. "She trusted him absolutely, and rightly so," said a crew member.

The family became anxious when they realized their youngest daughter was caught in a tug-of-love contest between Josh and James. The love triangle was like a real-life episode of *Dawson's Creek*. At first she dated the mild-mannered, likable James, but then fell for the bad-boy charms of Josh, who once claimed that his Irish roots gave him a divine right to get drunk. The two young men, so close that they shared a room during the first season, became sworn enemies, on numerous occasions nearly coming to blows. They couldn't even be in the makeup trailer together.

Katie's relationship with Josh, a notorious womanizer, worried her parents. As her sex education from school boiled down to the nuns telling the girls to practice abstinence, a *Dawson's Creek* crew member decided to give her more practical advice. "I talked to her about condoms and the need for contraception," the crew member recalled. "I can tell you she was certainly careful after that."

This tug-of-love made her grow up. By the third season she was no longer the sweet little innocent thing from Toledo, but a determined young woman—more savvy and cynical about the industry, yet still determined to make her mark in Hollywood. After her first film, *Go,* an action comedy, in 1999, she had small parts in several films, notably appearing opposite Michael Douglas in the 2000 movie *Wonder Boys,* about a college girl who is infatuated with her professor. It was a real thrill for Katie, the starstruck young woman even enjoying an on-screen kiss with the Hollywood legend. "Katie was so excited but very nervous," recalls a *Dawson's Creek* friend. "She was blessed by the fact that they could see she was young and inexperienced and took her under their wing."

As her career was moving onward and upward, so was her love life. Friends introduced her to actor Chris Klein, riding high with the hugely successful teen comedy *American Pie.* With appearances on TV's *Saturday Night Live* as well as several movies, including *Phone Booth* with Colin Farrell, under her belt, Katie was ready to talk about her life and career for an hour-long TV special with host Jules Asner.

In fall 2002 her family spent days with Asner's film crew, allowing them total access to their rambling, clapboard home in Toledo. In a fascinating documentary, first screened in October 2002, the young actress came across as a wry, confident, strong-willed, occasionally stubborn girl with a wide streak of sparky, self-deprecating humor. It was clear, too, that her adoring family had supported, nurtured, and advised her every step of the way. She was a bright, much-loved, well-understood jewel in a solidly conventional Catholic family.

When they all attended midnight Mass at their church, Christ the King, on Christmas Eve 2003, just after Katie's twenty-fifth birthday, they had special reason to give thanks. That night Katie's longtime boyfriend, Chris Klein, had asked her to marry him—after first nervously asking her father for his official blessing. As proof of his serious intent, Klein had spent a reported $500,000 on a wedding ring—the kind of money that could have bought a substantial five-bedroom house in Toledo. The excited couple planned to marry in Los Angeles during the fall of the following year.

In the meantime, she had work to do. Katie spent months in London, where she had been given the chance to star in a Hollywood blockbuster, playing the love interest, Rachel Dawes, opposite Christian Bale in *Batman Begins*. She also attended film premieres—including the one for Tom Cruise's action thriller *Collateral*—and was a guest at numerous fashionable parties, rubbing shoulders with the likes of model Elle Macpherson, actress Sienna Miller, and actor Jude Law. She had clearly left behind her tomboy Joey Potter image, emerging as a beautiful and talented star.

When she returned to Hollywood in September 2004, the strain in her relationship with her fiancé became apparent. Although she was a rising name, Chris was struggling to find work, having turned down the chance to appear in the final *American Pie* film. A public argument in a restaurant in October confirmed media rumors of a rift.

While the wedding was postponed until after Christmas, the couple spent the festive season together skiing in Aspen, Colorado, a place that Chris said "held a lot of good memories." But their holiday "honeymoon" did not last long. Katie was working on a starring role in the comedy *Thank You for Smoking*. She was unimpressed when Klein was caught driving drunk outside San Diego in February and given 150 hours of community service and an eighteen-hundred-dollar fine. It was the final straw for Katie, the couple officially calling off their engagement in March. By then they were not speaking. Chris was enigmatic about the reason for their parting. "We grew up. The fantasy was over and reality set in."

The reality was that her star was rising. That is what probably appealed to Tom. When his office called Katie's manager, they said the meeting would be about work and should take place as soon as possible. They said Tom had been interviewing actresses for weeks in search of a leading lady to play Ethan Hunt's fiancée in *Mission: Impossible III*. It was Katie's big chance, but she seemed to be one of many, and it did not take long for rumors to start circulating that there was more to this auditioning process than met the eye. It was the choice of candidates that gave rise to this story.

It was said that the list included Jessica Alba, who had split from her fiancé the previous year, as well as Kate Bosworth—she, too, had split from her boyfriend, actor Orlando Bloom, back in February. Next was Scarlett Johansson; she was single but had expressed a keen interest in older men. The word among gossip columnists was that Cruise might be looking for more than just a leading lady for a film: There was a gap in his own life that needed filling.

Katie Holmes was on the same list as the rest of them. While she may have been excited, Cruise had cast his celebrity net wide. She did fit the bill, but so did many others. What really mattered was whether she passed the test. As soon as Carrabino called Katie about the meeting, she flew to L.A. from New York, where she had been living. That was around April 11, 2005—less than three weeks after Tom's frantic pursuit of Sofía Vergara. Katie would not be seen again by friends or family for over two weeks. She seemed to have disappeared. The time she spent with Cruise that fortnight was all-transforming. It was the period that separated her from the rest of the women who had tried out for the role.

As with the first meeting between Tom and Nicole Kidman, the connection was immediate and powerful. "It was instant," she told talk-show host Jay Leno. He took her on her first motorcycle ride, to the beach at Santa Monica. "It was amazing and fast," she recalled later. "I was in love from the moment that I shook his hand for the first time." As Katie was not cast for *Mission: Impossible III,* it was clear that she had made a different kind of connection. Soon after their meeting, a limousine filled with chocolates and flowers arrived at Katie's place. In a generous gesture, he apparently had her own car cleaned and repainted. Courtship was something Cruise had mastered—it was only weeks since he had been doing the same thing for Sofía. Just for good measure, he also presented Katie with a copy of a Scientology handbook.

Their first proper date was a sushi dinner held in one of his parked private jets at Santa Monica airport. It was a taste of things to come—not just because of the luxury, but because they were not alone. Cruise's close circle of Scientology friends joined them throughout the dinner. It is impossible to know exactly who attended—but it is likely the guests included church leader David Miscavige and the tall, watchful figure of Katie's designated new best friend—Jessica Feshbach Rodriguez. Katie would be seeing more of these people than she could possibly have imagined.

It seems that she passed her social audition. Tom was eager to introduce the young actress to his children, Isabella and Connor, who had been playing with Vergara's son, Manolo, a few weeks before. Katie flew back to New York with a sparkle in her eye. A few days later, in a Starbucks on Waverly Place, not far from her SoHo apartment, she was overheard gushing to a friend about her new love. "He introduced me to his kids!" she whispered. "And he's taking me to Rome on a private jet this weekend."

Tom picked Katie up in New York on April 23 and flew

her to Italy to stay in the $3,500-per-night suite in the Hotel Hassler in Rome. He had arranged for the double bed to be scattered with red rose petals, and took her to the same restaurant where he and Penélope Cruz had dined just over a year before. They were spotted by the paparazzi, and this became their first appearance as a couple who were head-over-heels in love. It was a picture that would become very familiar in the following months. Back in the U.S., Sofía Vergara saw the images of Tom and his latest love on television. Only then did she fully recognize her own narrow escape. A friend said, "Sofía privately pitied the poor girl. Katie is a much weaker, more innocent person than Sofía."

If Sofía felt sorry for the girl who had taken her place, Katie's family and friends in Toledo could be excused for being in shock. It had been only six weeks since she had split with her fiancé, Chris Klein. Now she was dating a twice-married man sixteen years her senior. As they watched the footage of Katie walking the red carpet with Tom at the David di Donatello Awards on April 29, they must have noticed other changes in their normally vivacious daughter. While she smiled, kissed her new love, and posed for photos, Katie was uncharacteristically silent—and stooping. It set the pattern for future public appearances; Tom occasionally giving an impromptu interview to tell the world how "amazing" and "beautiful" Katie was, and how much in love they were. All the while Katie would smile but say absolutely nothing.

Spontaneity was alien to Tom Cruise. He knew about control and command, about calculating and calibrating the odds. There was no risk in his business. As one friend, choosing his words carefully, told me: "He is meticulous and particular. Just like Martha Stewart." In May 2005, a few weeks into his romance with Katie Holmes, he joined Oprah Winfrey in Chicago for her TV show, ostensibly to publicize his latest movie, *War of the Worlds*.

Tom was an old hand at the publicity circus. Under the glare of the studio lights, he was in charge, affable and jovial but with a reputation for giving away only those personal details he wished to divulge. As Oprah later observed, "Tom's usually very closed and has his own ideas about what he's going to tell you and not tell you." Oprah was an old hand at this, too, fully accepting her role as cheerleader for his new movie while trying to tease out some tidbits about his latest romance. Months after his marriage to Nicole, for example, the newlyweds had taken a seat on Oprah's sofa and told her how happy they were, while managing to plug their new movie, *Far and Away.*

Both Oprah and Tom knew the rules of the game. After all, they had been sparring with each other for years, professionally and socially. Indeed, at various times both Tom and her neighbor John Travolta had tried to recruit her to their faith. Today, though, it seemed as though Tom had thrown away the rule book, leaving Oprah wondering what his game really was.

As soon as he walked into her studio, he put on a performance worthy of that elusive Oscar. In front of an audience of howling, near hysterical women, he dropped to one knee as though the Romeo from New Jersey were about to propose to the astonished talk-show host. He punched the air. He laughed hysterically. He leapt backward onto the couch, which is no mean feat even when not on live TV. He held his head in his hands as though completely overcome. Oprah shrieked at him, both in amazement and encouragement as he spoke, at times incoherently, about his new love. As Tom burbled about romance, red roses, and scuba diving, Oprah yelled, "You're gone!" some nineteen times.

"I'm in love! I'm in love," Cruise proclaimed loudly, throwing his hands in the air. "I can't be cool. I can't be laid back. It's something that has happened, and I feel I want to celebrate it. I want to celebrate her. She's a very special woman . . . she's amazing." Once he hit his stride, there was just no stopping him, Tom praising Katie's "generosity, her élan, her vital life force." During the extraordinary performance, he revealed that the now-infamous motorbike ride was on a machine given to him by Steven Spielberg. The director appeared on a video link, pleading in vain with the actor to plug the film rather than himself and his new love. "Talk a little bit about *War of the Worlds* because we're opening really soon!"

It was only when Oprah asked how long he had known the woman who had rocked his world that Tom adopted his default interview position, saying they should talk about his new movie. Oprah had uncovered an uncomfortable fact: Tom had known Katie for only a little over a month. Still, he seemed ready to marry her, indicating that he didn't want to disappoint the girl who had once told *Seventeen* magazine that her dream was to be Mrs. Tom Cruise.

Oprah, who had met the couple at her Legends Ball in Santa Barbara two days before the interview, later confessed that Tom's behavior left her mystified—and not a little suspicious. During the interview, she was trying to decide whether this was real affection or a premeditated act. She said, "It was wilder than it was appearing to me. I was just trying to maintain the truth for myself because I couldn't figure out what was going on. I was not buying—not buying. That's why I kept saying, 'You're gone, you're really gone.'" One clue of his intentions was that he had warned Katie about his "spontaneous" nature: "I told her, 'Look, you never know what I'm going to do, Katie.' That's the point." Perhaps Oprah might have been even more confused if she had also had him on the show a few weeks earlier. Then he could well have been jumping on the sofa about Sofía.

Certainly the public shared Oprah's misgivings, viewing the romance and his on-screen antics as little more than a gimmick. A poll in *People* magazine showed that nearly two-thirds of the public thought the romance was a publicity stunt. This view was echoed not only by the supermarket tabloids, but even by the venerable *New York Times,* with an article titled "I Love You with All My Hype."

Tom's behavior on *Oprah* set the whole world talking. It was compared to the moment when Michael Jackson dangled his baby son over the edge of a hotel balcony. The phrase "jump the couch" even entered the language; it was named the Slang of the Year by the editors of the *Historical Dictionary of American Slang*, who defined it as "Tom Cruise–inspired slang meaning to exhibit frenetic or bizarre behavior."

Tom's motives came under scrutiny, too. Why was a forty-two-year-old man with two marriages behind him and two impressionable children watching him on TV acting in this way? Even if he seemed to be the picture of happiness, it was not normal behavior, certainly not for a man who had given new meaning to the phrase "Cruise control." He had acted out an erratic, uncontrollable, overpowering ecstasy, almost as if he were experiencing a heightened mental state. As Janet Carroll, his screen mother from *Risky Business,* drily observed, "People say to me, 'Did you know that when you worked with him, your son was going to be a nut?' "

Watching Tom jump up and down like a man possessed, former Scientologist Peter Alexander recalled his own behavior. Like Tom, he had reached the level of Operating Thetan VII, where man is ostensibly on the cusp of becoming a superman. "The jumping on the couch was directly attributable to the fact that he is not in touch with reality," Alexander said. "No normal, sane man would react that way to a love relationship because he would have a sense of himself and a sense of where he was in reality. When you are on OT VII you lose that sense because part of you is still in that hypnotic trancelike state."

Just forty-eight hours later, Tom's faith was front and center in a publicity merry-go-round, the actor effortlessly switching from soap opera to soap box. The man who had already claimed to be an authority on education, human rights, religious freedom, detoxification, and drug rehabilitation added another arrow to his quiver. Cruise unveiled himself on national TV as an expert on postpartum depression. The target of the attack was actress Brooke Shields—the woman who had starred in his first movie, *Endless Love*.

In an autobiography published a few weeks earlier, Shields had recounted taking antidepressants to help her cope with postnatal depression. Cruise used the platform of an *Access Hollywood* interview to berate the actress for using antidepressants. "I care about Brooke Shields because she is an incredibly talented woman—[but] where has her career gone?"

It seemed that *War of the Worlds* was going to miss out on more publicity. "These drugs are dangerous. I have actually helped people come off them," Cruise said. "When you talk about postpartum depression you can take people today, women, and what you do is you use vitamins." This was an article of Tom's faith, that mental illness should be treated with vitamins and not clinically developed drugs.

Shields, appearing in a musical in London, later responded to Cruise's criticism in a wry op-ed piece in *The New York Times*. Articulating the feelings of many outraged women and doctors, she wrote: "I feel compelled to speak not just for myself but also for the hundreds of thousands of women who have suffered from postpartum depression. I'm going to take a wild guess and say that Mr. Cruise has never suffered from postpartum depression. . . . Tom Cruise's comments are irresponsible and dangerous. . . . Tom should stick to saving the world from aliens and let women who are experiencing postpartum depression decide what treatment options are best for them."

Watching the furor was a previously stalwart ally who was less than pleased with Tom's recent performances. Just as Tom Cruise had a well-deserved reputation for focus and drive, *War of the Worlds* director Steven Spielberg is known not only for his creativity but for his intense dedication to his films. Spielberg did not seem pleased by the way his old friend's couch-jumping antics and attack on Brooke Shields were derailing the expensive publicity machine for the movie. From this time on, Spielberg's friends noticed that he spoke of Tom in the past tense.

Spielberg had first met Tom on the set of *Risky Business* in 1983. Both men prided themselves on their focus and commitment, singing each other's praises in public. When it looked as if *Minority Report* was going to be canned because each man was asking for too much money, it was Spielberg who picked up the phone and convinced the younger actor to reduce his fee. Nor did he have a problem with Tom's faith.

While he had not looked very deeply into Scientology until the group pitched a tent on the set of *War of the Worlds,* he had always found Scientologists to be personable and polite, making good eye contact and showing interest in the other person. He liked to tell a story about how a former Scientology boyfriend of his now-wife, Kate Capshaw, had given her a test using the E meter to see if she was having an affair with the Hollywood director. While she had passed the Scientology test, she left him shortly afterward for Spielberg.

Even when Tom and Steven Spielberg were joined by David Miscavige during the filming of *War of the Worlds,* Scientology was not on the menu during lunch, when they discussed the merits of flight simulators. When Tom did mention his faith, it was in the context of helping one of Spielberg's children who was having reading difficulties. The actor suggested that Spielberg take the youngster to a Scientology center in Hollywood. Spielberg did so, but when he was informed that his son would have to be taken off his medication in accordance with Scientology principles, he declined their offer of help. In the mythology surrounding Cruise and Scientology, this story was transposed into a yarn in which Spielberg mentioned the name of the psychiatrist treating one of his children, and within a matter of days the psychiatrist supposedly found himself being picketed by Scientologists.

While the exaggerated gossip burnished the Scientology myth, the cooling friendship between the director and actor was a typical Hollywood tale—it was all about the bottom line. Spielberg simply feared that Tom's behavior was affecting the potential audience for their film. As one of his longtime associates said, "What ended the friendship is that Steven saw him behaving not on the team. He knocked the movie PR off track by jumping on the sofa. Steven is focused on what he is working on totally and then he moves on. He is ruthless and dedicated to his craft. If someone lets him down, he doesn't work with them again."

If Spielberg disapproved of Tom's behavior, it is not hard to imagine the emotions of Katie's parents as they watched a man whom they had never met proclaiming his undying love for their daughter to Oprah Winfrey. This was car-crash TV, and they were the hapless passengers. At least her previous fiancé, Chris Klein, had asked Mr. Holmes for his consent before proposing.

Just a few years before, Katie's family and friends had welcomed camera crews to Toledo as they chatted happily about Katie and her success on *Dawson's Creek*. Now there was a re- sounding silence. Noticeably her friend since kindergarten, Meghann Birie, who was seen as a levelheaded influence on Katie, was totally out of the picture. Tom's sister Lee Anne De- Vette sent letters to their local church, Katie's former school, and even the local newspaper asking them to respect the fam- ily's privacy and not discuss Toledo's famous daughter. While Toledo was proud of Katie Holmes, it seemed TomKat was a toxic subject. Local Catholic priest Father Mike Brown was typical, shying away from any comment about Katie's involve- ment with Scientology. "Scientology affects just one family here, and I want to respect their privacy," he said.

As with Tom, then Nicole, so did Scientology quickly co- coon Katie Holmes inside circles of control. Lee Anne De- Vette's demands for silence from the residents of Katie's hometown were just the beginning. Very quickly Katie was integrated into life on Planet Tom, even the most casual ob- server noticing her transformation from vivacious young ac- tress to a modern-day Stepford wife. A Web site called FreeKatie.net, dedicated to "the movement to liberate Katie, a young, gifted actress held captive by forces we may never understand," did a roaring business in T-shirts, trucker hats, stickers, and coffee mugs bearing the message FREE KATIE.

First to go was the name. Tom preferred Kate, so Kate it was. Her appearance was next. The girl whose sparkling green eyes had intrigued the director of *Dawson's Creek* now looked as if the lights had been switched off. "My family can't lie to save themselves," she once said. "We always get in trouble. Our eyes give everything away." As she did the publicity rounds for *Batman Begins,* interviewers remarked on her hol- low and lifeless eyes. Writer Robert Haskell noted that her eyes "focused on nothing in particular." Other interviewers nicknamed her Katie "Dead Eye" Holmes.

It was not just her eyes but the rest of her face that came under close scrutiny. An eruption of sores and marks was blamed on Scientology's Purification Rundown, a process designed to purge the body of toxins through vitamins, exercise, and prolonged periods in a sauna. In fact, the marks were cold sores—a condition that afflicts the Holmes family and in Katie's case was brought on by stress.

Katie's natural animation seemed replaced by a sort of deadpan elation as she recited the liturgy of love. "I'm thrilled. I'm so happy," she told entertainment journalist Ruben Nepales. "I'm happy, so I'll just keep on smiling," she said to Christopher Goodwin of *Tatler* magazine. At the end of one interview, a security guard entered the room carrying a Chanel diamond necklace, a gift from Tom. "He's my man, he's my man!" Katie exclaimed when she opened the package. Tom had used a similar technique during his marriage to Nicole Kidman, calling her or sending gifts or messages in the middle of an interview. It was a reminder that Tom was ever present even when he was not physically there.

Tom was also represented by Katie's official new best friend, Jessica Feshbach Rodriguez. She was her Scientology handler, a member of the elite Sea Org who had been transferred from her higher spiritual mission to accompany Katie on her promotional tour for *Batman Begins* during the summer of 2005. Not only was Jessica brought up and educated in Scientology, she was from a wealthy family of bond traders who had donated millions of dollars to their faith, her aunt managing a Scientology center in Florida. Her presence was a sign of the importance Scientology placed on rapidly converting Katie to their cause.

When Katie spoke, Feshbach monitored her words. Or uttered them for her. During an interview with writer Robert Haskell, when Katie found herself stuck for words to describe how she felt about Tom, Jessica was on hand to help. "You adore him," she prompted. Katie soon found her way back on track: "I feel so lucky and so—like I've been given such a gift." When a journalist asked Katie about the widespread skepticism concerning her new romance, Jessica replied for her. "The truth is, we don't read that stuff because it's just rude." Others on the tour recall Feshbach as being condescending to staff, suspicious of the publicity process, and often disruptive in interviews.

Jessica was a central figure in the new team quickly placed around Katie. Within weeks the actress's stalwart professional advisers and personal friends were cast into outer darkness. At the beginning of June, her agent at CAA, Brandt Joel, was fired and replaced by Tom's men at the same agency, Rick Nicita and Kevin Huvane. Her longtime manager, John Carrabino, who also represented Renée Zellweger, was next. When Renée accepted a Screen Actors Guild award for her role in *Cold Mountain,* she singled out Carrabino for special praise. "Everybody needs a John Carrabino. I'm lucky to hear your words of wisdom." Wisdom that Katie no longer required. Last to go was her publicist of nine years, Leslie Sloane-Zelnick, replaced by Tom's sister and ardent Scientologist Lee Anne DeVette.

Katie's friends back in Toledo fared just as badly. Along with Meghann Birie, other friends lamented losing touch with the young actress. One old pal, speaking anonymously, described the TomKat relationship as "weird," comparing it to the ill-fated match between Liza Minnelli and David Gest. Their comments were remarkably similar to those of Sofía Vergara's friends, excitement giving way to unease. "It was exciting at first that Katie was dating Tom, but then when she started drifting away and I realized it was because we weren't into Scientology, it got a little weird."

It was not until the premiere of *Batman Begins* in June that Katie's parents got to meet Tom. His famous smile was on overdrive, charming his future in-laws and, according to at least one report, he showed the couple around the Celebrity Centre. Here was a man who didn't smoke, drink, or do drugs, and his mother even cooked a fried chicken dinner for them.

What was there not to like? Still, the suspicion remained that while they were gaining a son, they were losing a daughter.

Days after that first meeting, Katie effectively wrote off her old life when on June 13, she put pen to paper and signed up with Scientology. Few religions expect their followers to sign legally binding documents to ensure their commitment, but Scientology is no ordinary religion. The contract had become fundamental to the church following the death of Scientologist Lisa McPherson in 1995. McPherson, who suffered psychiatric problems after a car accident in Florida, died of a pulmonary embolism while in church care in Clearwater, Florida. She was apparently dehydrated and had cockroach bites on her emaciated body. As a result, the church was indicted on two felony counts, criminal neglect and practicing medicine without a license, effectively putting Scientology practices and beliefs on trial. The argument was that she had not been taken to the hospital for treatment earlier out of fear that she would be put into psychiatric care, which Scientologists fundamentally oppose. Instead, she was given what Scientologists call the Introspection Rundown, where a "psychotic" Scientologist is isolated and audited frequently. The criminal charges were eventually dropped and the death formally ruled an accident.

Lisa's death led not only to a protracted civil court case that resulted in the judge ordering an out-of-court settlement, but to the introduction of a contract colloquially known as "Lisa's clause," which said that new members or their families could not sue the church for death or injury associated with an Introspection Rundown. Katie Holmes signed a clause that ended with: "I accept and assume all known and unknown risks of injury, loss, or damage resulting from my decision to participate in the Introspection Rundown and specifically absolve all persons and entities from all liabilities of any kind, without limitation, associated with my participation or their participation in my Introspection Rundown."

The contract fundamentally changed Katie's human rights and those of her future children, requiring that if she or any of her children were ever to suffer from mental or terminal illness, they must turn only to Scientology's treatments. She must never use psychiatric care or psychiatric drugs. If she suffered postnatal depression like Brooke Shields—or the one in ten other women who experience the condition after childbirth—she would be in the hands of Scientologists. She had bound herself to the Scientology mantra: "The spirit alone may save or heal the body."

Concerned former Scientologists recognized the seriousness of Katie's contract. A onetime Sea Org member took the initiative and sent Martin Holmes a copy of the Scientology contract, the first legal document that Katie had signed in her life without her lawyer father looking it over beforehand. The contract was a watertight promise to allow Scientologists full control over her life. She had given permission to Scientology to isolate her from seeing her family again, or any other "sources of potential spiritual upset," during the Introspection Rundown. Not only had she lost her religion, there was the real possibility of losing contact with her family—like hundreds of Scientologists before her. Katie was experiencing exactly what Sofía Vergara had feared would happen to her. Everything that had alarmed Sofía, Katie seemed to accept.

Four days after signing the Scientology contract, Katie had another decision to make. In keeping with the very public nature of the romance, Tom proposed to her in Paris, at the top of the Eiffel Tower. After going down on one knee and reading her a self-penned two-page poem, he held out a five-carat yellow solitaire diamond engagement ring. The timing suggested that her conversion to Scientology had been a necessary proviso for Katie to get the ring, the fairy-tale wedding, and the childhood dream. It was a world away from the proposal by Chris Klein, who had asked Katie's father's permission and proposed in the family home.

Without having slept, Cruise called a press conference in Paris. This news could not wait. He announced he would be marrying Katie Holmes. "Today is a magnificent day for me; I'm engaged to a magnificent woman." Halfway across the world, Katie's friend Meghann Birie was leaving a movie theater in Toledo after watching *Batman Begins* when her phone began to bleep. It was a voice mail from Katie, excitedly telling her about her engagement. Even though she hadn't seen Meghann since her whirlwind romance with Tom Cruise, it was thoughtful of Katie to tell her oldest friend before the news hit the wires. Sad, too. A voice from the past, saying farewell to her old life.

CHAPTER 12

It was just a typical day in the office for TV host Matt Lauer—a real-life rescue miracle, a car with a mind of its own, and the invasion of Earth by Aliens from Outer Space. Oh, and a cookie-tasting contest. On June 22, 2005, Matt left his Westchester home as usual at four-thirty in the morning, arriving in Manhattan to catch the sunrise. On his way to the NBC studios in Rockefeller Center, he leafed through his notes for that day's edition of the *Today* show. First up was a heartwarming tale about the rescue of Boy Scout Brennan Hawkins, who had been missing for four days from his camp in the Utah backwoods. Actress Lindsay Lohan would be talking about her latest movie, *Herbie Fully Loaded,* while actor Tim Robbins was slated to chat about his role in the science fiction drama *War of the Worlds*.

After the show wrapped, Matt was scheduled to prerecord an interview with Tom Cruise about the Spielberg movie. He was relaxed about the upcoming chat with Cruise; he had interviewed him several times in the past and found Tom, unlike some Hollywood stars, to be affable and professional. More than that, Matt was interested in the subject. He and his production team had seen and enjoyed the movie, and he was keen to explore the themes that visionary author H. G. Wells had raised in the novel on which the film was based. Matt was well prepared; after all, he had done the reading.

Before the interview, Lauer met Tom in his dressing

room, where the two men asked about each other's children. Tom was in top form, chatting animatedly with NBC's entertainment reporter Jill Rappaport, as Lauer talked through the parameters of the interview with Tom's sister and publicist, Lee Anne DeVette. Although Tom's new fiancée was present in the studio, DeVette made it clear that Katie didn't want to be brought on set like some prize exhibit; she would watch Tom from the wings. Other than that, Tom was happy to talk about anything; just fire away.

Once they were perched on high stools and miked up, Matt introduced his T-shirted guest and asked wryly if anything interesting had been happening in his life. Of course, for the last few weeks Tom had been making daily headlines. His couch jumping, his rapid-fire engagement, and his unprovoked attack on Brooke Shields had turned him from a bland, self-contained star into a figure of controversy—and fun—though Tom didn't get the joke when a TV camera crew in London shot him with a water pistol before the premiere there of his new movie a few days earlier. After the initial banter, Lauer began to explore how Tom was coping with the heightened publicity. "I'm just living my life, Matt," Tom repeated like a mantra.

Finally the gloves came off. As Lauer questioned him about his belief in Scientology, the actor physically changed, transforming from an easygoing star to an exasperated preacher, closing his eyes and shaking his head in irritation at Lauer's seeming ignorance about his faith, psychiatry, and drugs. "Scientology is something you don't understand," he scolded the TV host, like a schoolteacher talking to a slow-witted pupil. At that moment Lauer sensed a shift in Tom, the actor visibly discarding his professional mask as he morphed from polished talk-show guest to belligerent lecturer. "It was like he couldn't help himself," Lauer told friends afterward. "Like he had been waiting for years and this was his chance."

In the end, Lauer was more interested in talking about Tom's new movie than the leading man was. Tom launched into what appeared to be a premeditated harangue on the evils of psychiatry, mixing pity for Brooke Shields and her medical choices with vitriol against the medical profession. While his sentiments were not new—the year before he had called for psychiatry to be outlawed—this time there was a messianic zeal in his diatribe and a patronizing tone toward his interlocutor: "I have never agreed with psychiatry. Ever. Before I was a Scientologist, I never agreed with psychiatry, and then when I started studying the history of psychiatry I began to realize why I didn't agree with it."

Just a few minutes earlier he had shrugged off criticism of his behavior by repeating that he was living his life as he wished. Clearly he did not want to extend that opportunity to the rest of the world, who were supposed to live by his values and choices. When Lauer challenged him and asked what was wrong with Brooke Shields's choices if they worked for her, Tom evaded the question, widening the discussion to a familiar Scientology rant against so-called psychiatric abuses, singling out the involuntary drugging of children: "Do you know what Adderall is? Do you know Ritalin? Do you know now that Ritalin is a street drug? Do you *understand* that?"

In the face of his guest's hostile tone, the experienced TV host stayed focused and persistent, politely pointing out that Brooke Shields had made her own decisions; nothing had been done to her against her will. Shaking his head in exasperation, Tom went on, "Matt, Matt, Matt, Matt . . . no, you see. Here's the problem. You don't know the history of psychiatry. I do." Nor, according to Tom, did Brooke Shields. It was an audacious statement, but Lauer stayed with the topic, knowing, as he said later, that he was "capturing TV lightning in a bottle." The actor argued that drugs merely masked the problem and that the solution was vitamins, exercise, and "various things," effectively Hubbard's Purification Rundown.

Then came the killer question, Lauer asking: "If antidepressants work for Brooke Shields, why isn't that okay?" Tom replied: "I disagree with it. And I think that there's a higher and better quality of life." He seemed angry, implying that Matt Lauer did not want him to discuss these important issues. Here was Tom applying classic Scientology techniques, deflecting intelligent inquiry by attacking the accuser. He had worked precisely the same trick the previous week with Australian interviewer Peter Overton, who, like other journalists, had been forced to spend hours hearing about Tom's religion before being admitted into the presence.

When he had asked a perfectly straightforward question about whether Tom and Nicole Kidman still had a parenting relationship and talked professionally, Tom snapped, "You're stepping over a line now." Then he told him to "put his manners back in." Once Overton apologized, Tom continued with the interview as though nothing had happened. It seemed that Tom's anger, like much in his life, was a performance, an act that relied heavily on Hubbard's strategy of "always attack the attacker."

Similarly, with Matt Lauer, Tom used a bogus slight as a tool to deflect coherent conversation and argument. When the discussion moved on to giving the drug Ritalin to hyperactive children, Tom accused the TV host of being "glib"— a loaded word in Scientology connoting a person who skims over a subject without doing proper research. "You don't even know what Ritalin is," Tom jeered. "You have to evaluate and read the research papers on how they came up with these theories, Matt. That's what I've done. And you should do that also . . . you should be a little bit more responsible, Matt." The tone was hectoring and condescending, with Tom implying that an influential broadcaster like Matt should have a better command of important issues. It was almost unheard-of for a seasoned veteran of the publicity circuit to launch a personal attack on an interviewer who had effectively invited him into his studio and given him the opportunity to sell his film and his faith.

By the end of the interview, Lauer knew that he had captured something interesting, but he wasn't sure what to make of it. Tom, on the other hand, had no doubts; he was delighted with his performance. So, too, was his Scientologist sister. As he later told *GQ* magazine, "I thought I was pretty restrained. I thought it was a terrific interview. I wasn't pissed; I just was intense on wanting to communicate." In fact, he was keen to carry on the chat, Tom asking the host if he had been in touch with Brooke Shields. Then, after giving Matt Lauer his trademark one-armed hug, he was gone, leaving Matt and his executive producer to scramble to edit the tape for airing two days later.

Although it was rumored that significant sections of the interview were left on the cutting room floor, in reality very little, apart from the occasional repetition, was omitted. When the interview aired it created a firestorm of debate and publicity, which was precisely what Tom and fellow Scientology leaders wanted. If the American public was taken aback by Tom's outburst, former Scientologists were even more alarmed: They could see Tom Cruise morphing into Scientology leader David Miscavige before their eyes. Every jabbing gesture, each patronizing inflection, every angry remark mirrored a trademark Miscavige tirade. Tom was speaking with His Master's Voice. "When I watched him he sounded exactly like David Miscavige," observed Karen Pressley, who had worked closely with the Scientology leader. "It's almost as if Miscavige has merged his personality into Tom. It's scary."

All over America, other former colleagues of the Scientology leader independently came to the same conclusion. As a onetime Scientologist who worked with Miscavige for seven years said, "I swear I was watching David Miscavige talk. He's bombastic, certain about what he believes, and never admits he's wrong." Former Scientologist Bruce Hines, who audited Nicole Kidman, had the same response: "When he was talking about psychiatry, he was talking like David Miscavige. When Tom Cruise gets overzealous, you are seeing a reflection of David Miscavige. They are very close, they mirror each other."

For those outside Scientology, the *Today* show outburst was shocking, prompting more than a thousand responses—three hundred more than a typical interview with the President. Many berated Tom for the way he spoke to Matt, as well as for his invective against Brooke Shields. She personally responded in *The New York Times*: "To suggest that I was wrong to take drugs to deal with my depression, and that instead I should have taken vitamins and exercised shows an utter lack of understanding about postpartum depression and childbirth in general." David Rice, president of the National Coalition of Human Rights Activists, agreed, urging Tom to "stand on a milk crate and apologize to Ms. Shields face-to-face for the gross insult he has committed against her and hundreds of thousands of other women who suffer from postpartum depression. He should also learn to shut up on matters he is utterly ignorant about."

Tom's views were not just inflammatory but potentially life-threatening. Medical experts and psychiatrists were concerned that vulnerable individuals might listen to Tom and stop taking their medication, with dire consequences. Crime novelist Patricia Cornwell, who studied psychiatry during her research for a psychological thriller, described his comments as "ridiculous" and "incredibly irresponsible," while *The Journal for Clinical Investigation,* published by an honor society of physician-scientists, warned that his celebrity could prevent those in need going for treatment. That was just the start. The Congressional Mental Health Caucus, a bipartisan coalition of over ninety members of Congress, criticized his remarks, saying that he reinforced negative perceptions.

The American Psychiatric Association, the National Alliance for the Mentally Ill, and the National Mental Health Association issued a joint statement condemning the actor: "Mental illnesses are real medical conditions that affect millions of Americans. . . . It is irresponsible for Mr. Cruise to use his movie publicity tour to promote his own ideological views and deter people with mental illness from getting the care they need." They pointed out that around ten children every day die from suicide as a result of untreated mental illness. Republican congressman Tim Murphy said if attitude adjustment, as advocated by Tom, had any sway, then mental illness could have been cured during the Salem witch trials: "By promoting such a theory, Cruise is providing false hope that deters people from getting the help they need."

Shortly after Tom's appearance on the *Today* show, a concerned mother anonymously posted this message on the NBC Web site:

> I would like to tell how Tom Cruise has impacted our family's life. I have a daughter who is bi-polar and must take medication. It is a disorder that, so far, no one can help other than with medication. When Tom was everywhere doing his rants about medication, she listened intently (bi-polar folks can be led very easily so please don't pre-judge) and decided that Tom probably was right. She was feeling just great so she decided to stop her meds and then she began a downward spiral. We were told last night, since she has now decided to self-medicate with alcohol, that she may have 2 weeks to live. Thank you, Tom, so much. You are a complete fool and I'd like you to come and do your magic on her and help our family through our grief.

There were similar posts on the Web site for the *Dr. Phil* show after he hosted an on-air discussion of the issues raised by Tom.

While there was no way to verify the accuracy of the posting, and Scientologists could dismiss an unsigned comment as mischief making, there is nothing anonymous about Jeannine Udall. As she watched Tom's rant on the *Today* show from her home in California, she could barely contain her anger. A tall woman from a solid Mormon family, Jeannine joined Scientology at the age of twenty-five, when she was working as a secretary at Universal Studios. A fellow staff member had been pestering her for months, but what finally sold her was the fact that John Travolta and Tom Cruise were members. If it was good enough for Tom Cruise, she reasoned, it was good enough for her. That reasoning nearly cost her her life.

At first all was well. She joined a Scientology-front organization and earned good money in sales, progressing to Operating Thetan V. Jeannine spent seventeen years as a loyal and hardworking foot soldier for the Scientology cause, then a combination of unfortunate events sent her into a downward mental spiral. In 2001 this once happy-go-lucky girl drove to Santa Barbara, wrote notes to her friends and family, and prepared to throw herself in front of an oncoming train. She was suffering from severe mental illness and had become morbidly depressed.

Yet because of her Scientology beliefs, Jeannine refused to see a psychiatrist. Even when her family forced her to go for help, her conditioning fought against it. Eventually, after treatment at the WindHorse Clinic, in Boulder, Colorado, she checked into the Wellspring retreat in the Midwest. After many hours of counseling, she was finally able to address her guilt and sense of worthlessness after escaping Scientology. Her message to Tom Cruise? "God forbid he or his children ever gets sick as a Scientologist. Psychiatry saved my life. It is not the evil he says it is."

Jeannine was lucky: She is still alive today. For others the association with Scientology has proved fatal. After Tom's appearance on *Today*, an ad appeared in *LA Weekly* that blamed the actor and his church for the death of Scientology auditor Elli Perkins, a fifty-four-year-old wife and mother who was stabbed seventy-seven times by her schizophrenic son. He had stopped taking the medication prescribed for his condition because of the precepts of Scientology. Significantly, the stabbing took place on the annual celebration of L. Ron Hubbard Day, March 13. The ad read: "Thanks, Tom Cruise and the Church of Scientology, for your expert advice on mental health. Elli Perkins was killed on March 13, 2003, by the schizophrenic son she was told to treat with vitamins instead of psychiatric care."

When Tom was lecturing Matt Lauer in June, his fiancée was watching from the wings, silent and unseen. By late October, Katie Holmes was front row center—she, Tom, and Sea Org disciple Jessica Feshbach Rodriguez guests of honor at the annual Patron Ball at Scientology's British headquarters, Saint Hill Manor. At first glance the black-tie evening seemed like a conventional social occasion. It was only when a video came on showing the violent destruction of the psychiatric profession as part of a campaign of "global demolition" that the zealous nature of the gathering became clear. Whatever her misgivings, Katie stood with Tom and applauded wildly as David Miscavige roused his audience with colorful rhetoric about the enemies of Scientology while rattling off rapid-fire statistics about the organization's successes.

One disillusioned member of Scientology, who attended the event, compared the evening to a fascist rally. "It can be extremely unpleasant to be a live witness to evil," she said. "It's not something you're reading or watching on TV. You're there. And the indoctrinated are there with you. You see the evil and you want to do something. But you know that if you do, you'll be taken away, turned over to 'the authorities,' and that will be the end of you."

It was a baptism of fire for Katie Holmes, who was surrounded by Scientology, completely immersed in it. As one former member noted ironically, "Maybe Tom will show a video of the event to Katie's parents. I'm sure they will love it." Throughout, Katie looked at Tom with "unblinking adoration," not only when he received a standing ovation for his donations to the cause, but when he was praised by Mike Rinder, commanding officer of the Office of Special Affairs, for his stance against psychiatry. According to Rinder, such was the impact of Tom Terrific that, just one day after one interview and two days after another, the Food and Drug Administration issued so-called "black box warnings" on two psychiatric drugs. When Tom spoke, the world listened.

As the Scientologists listened to Tom, they watched Katie intently. There was perhaps a knowing curiosity in the way that Sea Org disciples looked at her. Or rather at what she was carrying. Days before the Saint Hill event, Katie had severed one of the remaining links with her old life by firing Leslie Sloane-Zelnick, her publicist since the early days of

Dawson's Creek. On October 5, Sloane-Zelnick had been re-placed by Lee Anne DeVette, who wasted no time in an-nouncing to the world that Katie was pregnant with Tom's child. This had not been part of Katie's career game plan.

During her days on *Dawson's Creek*, Katie, then twenty-one, had visited a tarot card reader in New York's East Vil-lage. She was horrified when the cards predicted that she would be a mother in 2006. "I don't want to be a mother at twenty-seven," she wailed. Her Catholic parents, who had disapproved of Katie's plans to live with her previous fiancé, Chris Klein, were reportedly unhappy that she was pregnant out of wedlock. Despite a letter from Katie's new publicist urging parishioners at her church in Toledo to refrain from public comment, a family friend, Kathleen Jensen, spoke out. "I can't imagine what her parents are going through right now," Ms. Jensen said. "She really needs to get that baby bap-tized in a Catholic church."

Under normal circumstances, Scientologists would also have taken a dim view of pregnancy outside wedlock. As public Scientologists, Tom and Katie would have been forced to appear before an ethics officer and been deemed to have committed an "overt," a harmful act that is a sin. If a Sea Org disciple had committed the same "overt," she would have been sent to the Rehabilitation Project Force, the Scientology version of a labor camp.

Tom and Katie, of course, did not live by the same rules as other Scientologists. If Tom was ecstatic at the news of Katie's pregnancy, inside the world of Scientology there was excitement bordering on hysteria. Some sect members sin-cerely believed that Katie Holmes was carrying the baby who would be the vessel for L. Ron Hubbard's spirit when he re-turned from his trip around the galaxy. True believers were convinced that Tom's spawn would be the reincarnation of L. Ron Hubbard. Some Sea Org fanatics even wondered if the actress had been impregnated with Hubbard's frozen sperm. In her more reflective moments, Katie might have felt as if she were in the middle of a real-life version of the horror movie *Rosemary's Baby,* in which an unsuspecting young woman is impregnated with the Devil's child.

Ironically, as absurd as this theory sounds, within the sect it was entirely plausible. The Scientology founder predicted he would return to Earth in some form some twenty years after he had "dropped his body." Nor was this the first time that Scientologists had been gripped by this frenzy. When Hubbard's daughter Suzette gave birth to a red-haired son—the same coloring as the sect's founder—the infant was followed around the base at Hemet by curious believers. It became so unnerving that Suzette's then husband, Guy White, decided it was time to leave the movement. This belief in Hubbard's return goes to the very top of the organization.

During the mid-1990s, Bonnie View, the home built at Hemet especially for Hubbard, was renovated in anticipation of his imminent return. Both David Miscavige and Mike Rinder verbally cracked the whip over the gangs of Sea Org disciples who worked to build and furnish the house, berating them and urging them to work harder because time was running out before the great man returned. At one memorable briefing, Miscavige furiously told Sea Org disciples "If you think you are building a house for nobody to live in, you are all dreaming." Once the building was completed, Miscavige installed a housekeeper to prepare the mansion for Hubbard's return. For a true believer like Tom Cruise, already hailed as a messiah by fellow Scientologists, it was entirely plausible that his unborn child was somehow destined to take L. Ron Hubbard's place.

Certainly the way Tom prepared for the child gave the impression that he was in tune with the mood of breathless anticipation in which Scientologists awaited their spiritual equivalent of the Virgin birth. Even the womb was no hiding place, the actor spending $200,000 on a sonogram machine to monitor the baby's development. In the first weeks he took endless pictures of the growing embryo. "I'm a filmmaker— I need to see the rushes!" he explained. When he told one incredulous interviewer that the machine was strapped to Katie "twenty-four hours a day," it was hard to know if he was joking or not. Katie later downplayed the issue, saying that they only had a sonogram at home for when their doctor was there. When physicians warned that unnecessary use of the sonogram machine could put mother and baby at risk, Tom retorted that he had not exceeded FDA guidelines.

If the sonogram machine was not enough, he also reportedly bought a fetus learning system that was strapped to Katie's stomach. The device was apparently designed to impart information to the baby in the womb. On one occasion Katie was asked to leave a movie theater in Florida because the device, which emits a low buzzing noise, was annoying other patrons. It was also reported, and subsequently denied, that Tom had fitted Katie's cell phone with a tracking device so that he would know where she was day and night.

The rest of the universe was more difficult to control. By now Tom was something of a laughingstock. Not only had the phrase "jumping the couch" entered dictionaries, but bloggers were saying that Katie had gone from "A list to alien, hip to hypnotized." It was perhaps a sign of the panic inside Camp Cruise that only hours after returning from England, where he had basked in the adulation of Scientologists, he effectively fired his sister Lee Anne DeVette as his chief publicist.

On November 7—just a month after taking charge of Katie's publicity—she was demoted to looking after his philanthropic activities, which were mainly Scientology related. Paul Bloch and Arnold Robinson, of the established Hollywood PR firm Rogers & Cowan, took her place. That Robinson joined Tom on a normally routine trip to Shanghai and Xitang, where he spent two weeks in November shooting *Mission: Impossible III*, demonstrated how little they trusted Tom to stay on track and on message. Once Tom Reliable, he was now seen by many Hollywood insiders as a loose cannon.

Even with Bloch and Robinson piloting the Cruise ship, there was no stopping the tsunami of gossip and ridicule engulfing the Hollywood star. Famously humorless—and litigious—in the face of speculation about his religion and his sexuality, he had little to laugh at later in November 2005 when the cartoon series *South Park* screened an episode, provocatively titled "Trapped in the Closet," that poked fun at Scientology and the endlessly mutating rumors about his sexual orientation. It was bad enough that the half-hour show, penned by series creators Matt Stone and Trey Parker, already had a running joke in which Tom refused to leave a clothes closet, the implication being that he was refusing to acknowledge his homosexuality. But perhaps more damaging was the tongue-in-cheek explanation of Scientology's creationist myth, dealing with how the evil warlord Xenu sent millions of people to Earth to be blown up, their spirits floating in eternal torment. Not only was the exposition of this myth highly accurate—Stone and Parker had used a Scientology expert to write a background paper—there was a caption underneath that read: THIS IS WHAT SCIENTOLOGISTS ACTUALLY BELIEVE. It was comedy genius, both funny and informative, eventually earning the show an Emmy nomination. Indeed, Steven Spielberg later told friends that he had learned more about Scientology from *South Park* than he ever had from Tom Cruise.

South Park airs on the Comedy Central network, owned by media conglomerate Viacom—which in turn counted Tom Cruise as one of its most important clients. When the episode aired, it caused a wave of controversy both inside and outside the company. Tom was reportedly so angry that he insisted the show not be broadcast again in America or aired elsewhere in the world. In Britain, Channel Four, which held the *South Park* franchise, pulled the episode for fear of attracting a lawsuit from the actor. Although Tom later denied being aware of the program—a tad disingenuous, given his obsession with his public image—the damage was done, as media and public rallied to the beleaguered writers. Stone and Parker received flowers from the makers of *The Simpsons* for their bravery, while the team behind *King of the Hill* sent them a message that they were doing "God's work."

It was a story that refused to go away—much to publicist Paul Bloch's frustration. In March, singer and Scientologist Isaac Hayes, who had voiced the character of Chef on *South Park,* announced that he was resigning from the show, ostensibly because the controversial episode was scheduled to be aired again later that month. In his resignation letter, which used the unmistakable language of Scientology, he accused Matt Stone and Trey Parker of "religious intolerance and bigotry." In response, Stone noted that "in 10 years and more than 150 episodes Isaac never had a problem with the show making fun of Christians, Muslims, Mormons and Jews." Moreover, when he had talked about the episode in an earlier interview, he had sounded relaxed about it, admonishing Stone and Parker to "take a couple of Scientology courses, and understand what we do."

It seems that Hayes's Scientology masters were behind his resignation, especially when it was revealed that Hayes had suffered a mild stroke in mid-January and, according to friends, was still recovering when he decided to "resign" in March. In fact, it was eventually reported that the announcement had actually come from the singer's Scientologist manager Christina "Kumi" Kimball. Observers concluded that Scientology had made an ailing man, whose wife was expecting a baby, quit his job to protect the organization's reputation. As *The Washington Post* commented, "Hayes's action makes Scientologists look like what many, many people assume they are: intolerant, humorless, and under the thrall of a demonic, soul-eating cult that brooks no dissent."

Still, the dispute rumbled on, Tom Cruise reportedly issuing the ultimate warning—if the show was repeated, he would not do any publicity for his upcoming blockbuster *Mission: Impossible III*. In the face of this threat, the Viacom organization, the company behind both *M:I & III* and *South Park,* backed down. When the episode was finally pulled, Matt Stone and Trey Parker issued a statement saying, "So, Scientology, you may have won THIS battle, but the million-year war for Earth has just begun! You have obstructed us for now, but your feeble bid to save humanity will fail!"

Cruise's victory over *South Park* came at considerable cost. Hollywood insiders were realizing that Tom Cruise's championship of Scientology was becoming a nuisance that could affect the bottom line. Previously favorable magazines became more critical. In March, *Rolling Stone,* edited by Tom's friend Jann Wenner, carried a thirteen-thousand-word article minutely detailing the nefarious activities of Scientology, while *Vanity Fair* printed a cover banner asking: "Has Tom Lost His Marbles?" Retribution was not long in coming. For once *Rolling Stone* was not given access to the *Mission: Impossible* set to interview Wenner's friend.

Yet the normal excitement surrounding a Cruise action movie was focused less on the film's star than on his fiancée, the actor answering endless questions about Katie's health as the days ticked down to the birth of his first biological child. Even though Katie's mother attended a baby shower in late March at the Celebrity Centre in Hollywood, the tabloids portrayed the actress as a "prisoner of the cult" who was rarely allowed out without Tom or her Scientology minders. Sightings of Katie going out on her own, to a local farmers' market or for coffee, became regular staples of the gossip columns.

Certainly, when she moved in with her fiancé, she inherited an instant family, joining his mother, Mary Lee Mapother South, and younger sister, Cass Darmody, and her two children, Liam and Aden, in the sprawling Beverly Hills compound. As Katie was embarking on her new life, Mary Lee and Cass were rebuilding their worlds. In an extraordinary about-face, Tom's mother had abruptly given up everything in 2005 to be with the son she doted on. Not only had she renounced her Catholic faith—she was a Eucharist minister—but also her husband of twenty years, Jack South, and her circle of friends in Marco Island, Florida. As a friend from her local Catholic church observed, "She left her faith and went to Scientology. I'm so sad I can't believe it." When Tom's younger sister, Cass, went through a divorce in 2004, she and her two children came to live with him. Like her brother, Cass was dyslexic but insisted on homeschooling her two children in Scientology's Applied Scholastics.

In this home environment, the precepts and principles of their faith reigned supreme, Katie accepting and adopting the rituals of Scientology as she approached her due date. If moving in with the future in-laws was daunting, Katie didn't let on, saying enthusiastically, "There's always something going on in the house and I love it." Perhaps it reminded her of the noisy home life she'd enjoyed in Toledo, where, Katie told TV interviewer Jules Asner, she always felt a little bereft when her older siblings went to school and the house fell silent.

It was the manner in which she would be giving birth that caused the most comment. Hubbard's followers have adopted a ritual known as a "silent birth," the assumption being that any loud noises or words uttered as the baby is born, or even in the first week after birth, can have a detrimental effect on the infant. Hubbard is not alone, many believe that the "initial insult of birth," when the infant goes from a warm, cozy world to bright lights and noise, can cause psychological trauma. The science fiction writer thought that such noise could produce damaging "engrams," which would increase the need for auditing in the baby's later life. From start to finish of the reproductive process, Hubbard counseled quiet. "Be silent during and after the sex act," he exhorted his followers in his book *Child Dianetics*. Shortly before Katie went into labor, a number of six-foot boards were put up in Tom's Beverly Hills home, reminding everyone who would be around Katie during the delivery to maintain absolute silence and stay calm.

On March 24, 2006, Tom's nephew Liam even helped carry a stack of large cue cards into the couple's home: "Be silent and make all physical movements slow and understandable," read one. As Tom explained, "We've been doing seminars with the family just to educate them, so that everyone in the family understands. The kids, and even friends and different people." He did point out to interviewer Diane Sawyer that the mother was allowed to make noise but not say words. When he announced that he was going to eat the baby's placenta, it was consistent with the bizarre nature of Katie's pregnancy.

Staff inside Tom's compound needed no reminders of the need for quiet—and discretion. From the moment they were allowed through the high-security gates, they entered a world of controlled calm, with the emphasis on control. Staff were monitored by a German governess, everybody watching everyone else. They were encouraged to remain silent, and if they did speak, it was in hushed tones. The daily cleaning crew, which started at dawn and left by eight A.M. so as not to disturb Tom and Katie, was under strict instructions to operate in silence. The home itself had the feel of a tasteful but anonymous upmarket hotel suite or upscale private hospital. As one insider said, "The place was as quiet as you can get. It was unreal."

At the entrance stood a giant portrait of Tom and Katie, but their closeness in the picture was not reflected in the home. They lived in separate wings, with separate bathrooms, bedrooms, and sitting rooms, Isabella and Connor in their father's quarters. Ostensibly, they slept apart because of Tom's snoring. How Hubbard would interpret the effect of that sound on the baby's development was uncertain. On April 18, 2006—twenty years and three months after the death of L. Ron Hubbard—Katie was driven to St. John's Health Center in Santa Monica, where she gave birth, not to a red-haired boy, but to a baby girl, seven pounds, seven ounces, and twenty inches long. After carefully scrutinizing a couple of baby name books, the couple called their first daughter Suri, which they later discovered means "red rose." Within twelve hours Katie and Suri had left the hospital, Tom flying his precious cargo to his four-hundred-acre ranch in Telluride, Colorado, for their week of Scientology silence.

While her birth was not quite the Second Coming diehard Scientologists had hoped for, the arrival of Tom's first biological child garnered worldwide attention, the hospital and their Hollywood home surrounded by dozens of photographers, reporters, and camera crews. As writer Mark Lawson noted drily, "There have previously been children whose birth attracted a certain amount of attention—Jesus Christ, Elizabeth Windsor, Brooklyn Beckham—but the arrival of Suri Cruise set a new record for interest in an infant."

It did not take the attendant media long to point out the irony that along the same corridor in the same hospital on the same day, Brooke Shields, so recently berated by Tom for taking drugs for postpartum depression, was giving birth to her second daughter, named Grier. Nor did it escape comment when Nicole Kidman's publicist pointed out that, contrary to media reports, she had not sent congratulations to Katie on the birth of Suri. It was hardly surprising. Her friends described the announcement of Katie's pregnancy as akin to a "kick in the stomach." At the time, Nicole was trying to have children with her future husband, troubled country singer Keith Urban. She was on the margins of Tom's life—and, it seemed, the world of her adopted children. Not only were Connor and Isabella educated in the gospel according to Ron Hubbard, but Nicole saw them only rarely. Katie had effortlessly assumed the role of their stepmother, she and Tom endlessly photographed watching the youngsters play soccer for their school teams.

It appeared that Katie's parents were as much on the sidelines as Nicole Kidman. While their daughter was giving birth according to Scientology ritual, they were three thousand miles away in their vacation home in Florida. It was Tom's Scientologist mother, Mary Lee, who lived with the couple, who was present when a Scientology-sanctioned epidural was administered to Katie to ease her pain during labor. It was another two weeks before Katie's parents, who had been by her side throughout her Hollywood career, saw their granddaughter. In the tabloid soap opera that Tom and Katie's life had become, her lawyer father, Marty Holmes, was characterized as fighting a futile rearguard action to protect his daughter's interests. If he couldn't stop her from becoming a Stepford wife, at least he could ensure that she was a wealthy Stepford wife. By the end of May, Katie's father and Tom had come to a $52 million prenuptial agreement, the deal reportedly ensuring Katie $3 million a year for every year of marriage as well as a $19 million trust fund for his daughter and grandchild whether the marriage went ahead or not. Marty may have lost his daughter, but Katie had gained a small fortune. It was said that the reason Katie was pushing for a prenuptial agreement was to speed up the marriage so that, once they had gone their separate ways, she could fight him for custody of Suri. Otherwise, she would be no match for his financial big guns—or his formidable clout in Hollywood. *Newsweek* magazine quoted a Holmes family friend as saying: "If she walks now, Tom will fight her for custody of Suri and Katie can't outlast him in court. She knows she needs to marry him to get the money to fight him for custody." This constant speculation was hard on Katie, who admitted to seeing all the gossip in the tabloids and on entertainment television. "Some of the crap that's out there—the stuff that's said about my parents and my siblings—it's really frustrating," she told writer Jane Sarkin.

While she put on a brave face in public, it was not long before cracks began to appear in the façade.

CHAPTER 13

While Katie and baby Suri were quietly bonding in the Rocky Mountains under the watchful gaze of Scientology staff members, Tom was making as much noise as he could promoting *Mission: Impossible III*. In April 2006, less than a week after Suri was born, he flew to Rome for the film's premiere, and for the next few weeks toured the planet attempting to re-create the movie's breathless excitement. For the New York premiere in May, he traveled around Manhattan by motorbike, speedboat, sports car, subway, taxi, and helicopter before arriving at the movie theater. When he promoted the film in Japan, he hired a bullet train for himself and 150 of his fans.

Although the movie, directed by J. J. Abrams, the creative force behind the TV series *Lost* and *Alias*, had its fair share of leaping from skyscrapers, exploding bridges, and edge-of-the-seat, life-and-death drama, the star of the show, at least as far as the media was concerned, was sleeping in a crib in the Cruises' mountain retreat in Telluride, Colorado. Nothing was too much trouble for mother and daughter, Tom reportedly dispatching his Gulfstream jet to California for crates of diet cherry soda and special organic food. When Katie appeared at the Hollywood premiere in May, the eyes of the world were on the young mother.

While Tom talked gaily of having ten children and getting Katie back in shape for their wedding, professional Katie watchers concluded that she appeared "tired and miserable." Then she was whisked back to Colorado for what Tom called "b and b." She did the breast-feeding and he did the burping—and changed the diapers. If they fed Suri on Hubbard's barley baby formula—a recipe he claimed he recalled from Roman soldiers two thousand years ago—they kept it secret. Mother and daughter spent the summer out of the limelight, surrounded by his and her family, who entertained themselves with golf, gliding, and barbecues. While Tom took Isabella and Connor on the homemade motocross course, Katie diligently made a quilt that incorporated family photos in the patchwork.

The couple's seclusion and the fact that it took a further three months for Suri to make her public debut—naturally on the cover of *Vanity Fair,* photographs courtesy of celebrity snapper Annie Leibovitz—caused all kinds of wild speculation that her parents were afraid to show her off because she had a birth defect. When the world finally got a glimpse, it was clear that she bore no resemblance to L. Ron Hubbard. With a head of thick black hair and big, wide brown eyes, she was the image of both parents. The shoot itself took five days, rather more than the thirty minutes it took Leibovitz to photograph the Queen of England.

In June, as a telling counterpoint to the media madness engulfing Tom, Katie, and baby Suri, Nicole Kidman married country singer Keith Urban in a traditional white wedding in a Catholic church in the suburbs of Sydney, Australia. "For Nicole this is a spiritual homecoming, to the church and her faith," observed Father Paul Coleman, who married the couple. The conventional ceremony drew a line in the spiritual sand, the actress clearly and completely distancing herself from her former dalliance with Scientology.

While the rest of the world cooed over baby Suri, in Hollywood all eyes were on Tom's latest movie offspring, *Mission: Impossible III.* Even though Tom's bold decision to let TV director J. J. Abrams helm the movie had paid off with generally favorable reviews, the crucial U.S. opening weekend took in only $48 million, compared to $58 million for

M:I and *II*. While the movie, which cost $200 million to make, went on to earn nearly $400 million worldwide and half as much again from DVD sales, the consensus in Hollywood, particularly at his parent company, Paramount, was that Tom's proselytizing on behalf of Scientology had cost up to $100 million in profits. This was a high crime in Hollywood, where you can worship any God you like, so long as it is Mammon.

Tom was now on trial in the court of his peers. Witnesses for the prosecution cited the fact that, according to a Gallup/*USA Today* poll in May 2006, just over a third of the public had a favorable opinion of the star, a sharp drop from nearly 60 percent a year earlier. More than half now viewed him unfavorably, compared with under a third in 2005. Most significantly, the onetime World's Sexiest Man had lost considerable ground among his female fan base, primarily because of his attack on Brooke Shields. By the end of August, when Tom visited Shields's Hollywood home and made his peace with her over tomato and basil omelets, it was way too late.

As leading marketing guru Paul Dergarabedian observed, "It's hard to ever know why a film fails to live up to expectations, but in this case you can't fault the marketing campaign. The reasons lie elsewhere." In his defense, producer Garth Drabinsky, who gave Tom a starring role in his early movie *Losin' It*, lauded his achievement in making the *Mission: Impossible* series so commercially and artistically successful. As he said, "The *MI* trilogy is a staggering accomplishment as an actor and producer. It took a Herculean effort to do this and you cannot make light of it. He works his ass off on the movie set, and as a producer he will continue to produce great work."

The fact that *Forbes* magazine named Tom the world's top celebrity in June 2006 cut little ice with the suits at Paramount. When his contract came up for renewal at the end of July, he was found guilty of committing a mortal sin: Tom simply cost too much. Even though he had earned the studio over a billion dollars during his fourteen-year association with them, during contract negotiations Paramount executives tried to reduce his production company overheads from $10 to $2 million a year. Tom and his production partner, Paula Wagner, balked. At the time, they were looking for another studio to call home, but not one had invited them in. As negotiations continued, it was reported that, when leaving his office one night, Paramount Studio boss Brad Grey was approached by a dozen or so Scientologists who attempted to put pressure on him to give Cruise a good deal. Grey, apparently, stood his ground and refused to bend to coercion.

When the sentence was finally pronounced, it was Tom's Scientology faith rather than his up-front costs that took the rap. Sumner Redstone, the octogenarian chairman of Paramount's parent company Viacom, made the announcement in an interview with *The Wall Street Journal*: "As much as we like him personally, we thought it was wrong to renew his deal," Redstone said. "His recent conduct has not been acceptable to Paramount." In a stinging barb, he added: "It's nothing to do with his acting ability, he's a terrific actor. But we don't think someone who effectuates creative suicide and costs the company revenue should be on the lot."

He later told *Vanity Fair* that Cruise had become a "hate figure" for women over his criticism of Brooke Shields. "He didn't just turn one off, he turned off all women and a lot of men." There was talk that Steven Spielberg, who was effectively employed by Paramount, stood by as Cruise was taken down, Tom's behavior during the *War of the Worlds* tour apparently still rankling. Soon, however, fingers were pointing at Redstone's wife, Paula Fortunato, who was "incensed" by Tom's criticism of Brooke Shields, telling friends, "I never want to see another Tom Cruise movie." A Viacom spokesman conceded that Fortunato "disagreed" with Tom's views, but insisted that she saw all his movies.

Tom's camp hit back quickly, his partner, Paula Wagner, maintaining that she and Tom had been the ones to terminate contract talks in favor of independent financing. According to Wagner, Redstone was "just trying to save face." Tom's lawyer Bert Fields was furious: "That a mogul like Sumner

Redstone could make a statement so vicious, so pompous, so petulant . . . it tells you more about Sumner Redstone and Viacom than about Tom Cruise."

Over the next few weeks, Wagner and Cruise scrambled to finance their own production company. Eventually Tom's good friend Kevin Huvane interested a group of investors, including Mark Shapiro, who runs Six Flags amusement parks; Daniel Snyder, owner of the Washington Redskins; and real estate magnate Dwight Schar. As one agency executive told the *Los Angeles Times*, "It all feels very knee jerk. This feels very Plan C, maybe even Plan D. When you lose your studio deal and you get into business with amusement parks, that's a problem."

Historically, though, splits between studios and stars go all the way back to 1919, when silent movie stars Charlie Chaplin, Mary Pickford, and Douglas Fairbanks set up their own studio, "United Artists," so that they could keep a bigger share of the profits. In October, in a fitting historical coincidence, Cruise and Wagner were approached by MGM and given the chance to take over the ailing United Artists studio. Wagner became the CEO and Tom executive producer, the duo cracking open a $550 bottle of vintage champagne at Mastro's in Beverly Hills to celebrate. Their aim was to "revive" the company to its glory days, with United Artists producing about four films a year.

Film star, father, movie mogul; Tom capped a tumultuous year by becoming a husband for the third time in his life. On November 12, 2006, he and Katie tied the knot legally at a small, private, civil ceremony in Los Angeles. Six days later they married again in a fairy-tale castle in Italy in front of family and Hollywood celebrities while the media, ever the bridesmaid, waited outside. Even though the local Catholic parish priest refused to give his own blessing, the Scientology ceremony at the fifteenth-century Odescalchi Castle in Bracciano near Rome made headlines around the world as a host of celebrities, many of them members of Scientology, swelled the congregation. Guests included singers J-Lo and Marc Anthony, Will and Jada Pinkett Smith, Jim Carrey,

Jenny McCarthy, Jenna Elfman, Victoria Beckham, and even Brooke Shields, who said, "I'm thrilled for them."

Notable absentees included Oprah Winfrey, who had publicly questioned Tom's couch-jumping antics, as well as fellow Scientologists John Travolta and Kirstie Alley, who also did not attend a party in Los Angeles subsequently hosted by Paula Wagner. Naturally, Nicole Kidman was not invited, but she sent a four-thousand-dollar vase as a wedding present—presumably, suggested one wag, because it saved her the expense of throwing it. There were few of Katie's friends from her days in Toledo or *Dawson's Creek,* but plenty of Scientologists, like her Scientology handler Jessica Feshbach Rodriguez, to take their place. David Miscavige was best man and Katie's sister Nancy Blaylock was the matron of honor.

After a "simple yet eloquent" twenty-minute Scientology ceremony, which included bizarre vows about Katie needing pots, combs, and a cat as well as a reminder that young men can't be expected to remember their promises, the couple exchanged rings and rounded off the proceedings with what was by now trademark behavior—a lengthy public kiss. Most guests agreed that, apart from the ceremony, the most moving moment was when the blind Italian opera singer Andrea Bocelli serenaded the assembled throng, although as a practicing Catholic he declined to attend the Scientology ceremony itself. "This was," declared gravel-voiced David Miscavige as he toasted the couple, "a marriage of true minds." Katie's father, Marty Holmes, put aside any misgivings to declare that his new son-in-law was "the right guy" for his precious daughter.

Later, the newlyweds flew to the Maldives for a scuba-diving honeymoon on board the luxurious yacht of Tom's friend and Scientology convert Jamie Packer. They were apparently not alone—David and Shelly Miscavige were seen boarding the private jet at Rome's Ciampino Airport for the eight-hour flight to Male, the islands' capital. Unfortunately, bad weather spoiled the holiday and the couple flew home early. While the church subsequently denied that the Miscaviges went on the honeymoon, it was not long before Tom and his best friend were reunited.

Tom and Katie spent their first New Year's Eve as a married couple with two thousand other Scientologists at the Shrine Auditorium in Los Angeles, applauding enthusiastically as David Miscavige spoke luridly about the "global obliteration" of psychiatry, using "smart bombs" and grenades to exterminate the profession. Once again, comparisons to Nazi rallies sprung to some onlookers' minds.

As he outlined the organization's plans for world domination and what he called "planetary clearing," it was clear how critical Tom and Katie were to the strategy. After reeling off statistics about the miles of newsprint and hours of television devoted to Scientology, Miscavige heralded what the media had dubbed "the wedding of the century" as a chance to introduce the planet to the concepts and values of Scientology. It confirmed the suspicions of those wedding guests who felt the occasion was as much a marketing opportunity for Scientology as a union between two people. Of course, the event was both. David Miscavige, who once confessed to an associate that if he weren't a Scientologist he would be selling laser art at the side of the road, had succeeded brilliantly in selling his faith through the medium of his best friend. From the Scientology tent on the *War of the Worlds* set and the attacks on Brooke Shields, to the silent birth of Suri and the spectacle of Tom and Katie's wedding, Scientology had piggybacked on the actor's celebrity, with Tom prepared to sacrifice his credibility and his popularity for his faith.

Miscavige had a further challenge for his worldwide ambassador. While it wasn't *Mission: Impossible*, it was certainly *Mission: Difficult* to join with John Travolta in spearheading the expansion of Scientology into Britain and the rest of Europe. In contrast to its tax-exempt status in the U.S., Scientology had been investigated in France, Spain, and Belgium, banned for a time in Britain, and, because of the country's own totalitarian history, treated with grave suspicion in Germany. During 2006, Tom had provided behind-the-scenes technical and financial assistance when Scientology bought a building in the City of London for $31 million from a Saudi

Arabian property company. "It's like the tipping point, with this base we'll be recruiting the people who control the planet," observed one excited Scientologist at the grand opening of the London headquarters in October 2006. Apart from local worthies, however, the celebrity turnout at the opening was negligible. Part of Tom's mission was to change that.

David and Victoria Beckham were obvious candidates, the most high-profile celebrities in Britain, with an avid following in Europe and the Far East. The actor first met England's former soccer captain David Beckham in 2003 after watching him play for his team, Real Madrid, during a visit to the Spanish capital. Apart from a love of sports and fast cars, the son of a gas fitter from London's poor East End and the Hollywood star would seem to have little in common, but their friendship flourished. Interestingly, both men had met their wives by watching them on the big screen: Tom had spotted Nicole Kidman when she starred in *Dead Calm*, while David fell for singer Victoria, also known as Posh Spice, when she appeared in a Spice Girls video. "Posh and Becks," whose worldwide popularity made them grade-A Scientology celebrity material, became a permanent fixture in Tom's Rolodex.

More than that, he introduced them to his friend Scientology leader David Miscavige as early as 2004. Just six weeks after Tom and Miscavige opened a new Scientology center in Madrid, Miscavige flew back to Spain to spend time with Posh and Becks and their family. While he knows little about soccer, at the end of October Miscavige gamely sat through a match, watching David's team, Real Madrid, at the Bernabéu stadium in the Spanish capital. He joined David, who was not playing, his mother, Sandra, his wife, Victoria, and their two boys, Romeo and Brooklyn, as well as Tom in a box at the venue. It is a sign of the couple's importance to the organization that Miscavige was prepared to fly halfway around the world to see them.

As with Penélope Cruz and Sofía Vergara before them, Tom gave the Beckhams introductory information on his faith. In October 2005, Victoria was seen reading a book, *Assists for Illnesses and Injuries,* by L. Ron Hubbard. It was thought that she was reading the self-help guide because her son Romeo suffered from epilepsy, the attacks triggered by photographers' flashlights. There was one problem, though: If the Beckhams did join, Romeo would have to stop taking any prescribed drugs for the condition. This could have dire consequences, as Tory Christman, a former Scientologist, discovered. When she first joined, Christman followed the dictates of her new faith by refusing to take prescription medicine for her epilepsy, which led to numerous life-threatening seizures.

That was a consideration for the future. For now, David Beckham was being courted not only by Scientology but also by another American conglomerate, Anschutz Entertainment Group, who wanted to lure him to Hollywood to play major league soccer for the Los Angeles Galaxy. When Anschutz finally got their man in the fall of 2006, David telephoned "his wise friend" Tom Cruise for advice, the actor encouraging him to head out west.

While Tom was guiding David's career, Katie was acting on Victoria's fashion tips. In October 2006 the duo went on a girls-only trip to Paris during Fashion Week, appearing in similar or complementing outfits, often chosen by Victoria, who had published a best-selling book of fashion advice, *That Extra Half an Inch.* They became friends and confidantes, Katie asking her to be her stylist when she did a shoot in December 2006 for the February cover of *Harper's Bazaar.* Even though Katie has her own fashion ideas—she's a fan of Marc Jacobs and Armani—it was noticeable that when she revamped her hairstyle in spring 2007, she appeared in a bob just like her English friend.

It was as if Katie had been given the "Catherine Zeta-Jones" makeover, like the Welsh actress who changed from fresh and funky glamour to a vision of classic style following her marriage to Hollywood royalty, veteran actor Michael Douglas. Similarly, the new Mrs. Tom Cruise was transformed from a longhaired, laid-back ingenue into a sleek, sophisticated fashionista, her shorter, more sophisticated locks matched by elegant designer outfits and towering heels.

The changes in the intelligent, if unreflective, actress had come at a high price. Although she was in love with Tom, the early illusion of romance had long been shattered. She had fallen for an image that had taken shape in her mind when she was a carefree teenager who boasted to her sisters that one day she would marry Tom Cruise. The reality was somewhat different. As commentators made the inevitable comparisions to Princess Diana's whirlwind courtship with Prince Charles, the marriage did indeed seem a bit crowded. Katie and Tom were living the lives of Hollywood royalty, always surrounded by people, never alone. At home there was a team of nannies and governesses to care for baby Suri, Connor, and Isabella, cooks and housekeepers and gardeners to attend to her every whim, and if she went shopping—and she shopped a lot for a "career" woman—she was accompanied by a bodyguard to swat away the swarming paparazzi. Inevitably, Tom was hard at work giving his studio, United Artists, the kiss of creative life, as well as breathing the oxygen of publicity into his controversial faith.

The newly married Katie simply wanted to spend time with her husband—not share him. She could be excused for beginning to feel isolated and alone, living separately from Tom in their new home in Beverly Hills, snatching the occasional hour with him as he focused most of his attention on promoting his film studio and his faith. In other ways, he was ever-present, constantly phoning to check on her well-being and that of his precious daughter, asking about her sleep patterns and eating habits. The controlling behavior that had rankled with Nicole was now clearly apparent to Katie, who was much less of a prima donna than her predecessor. Nor did it help that his mother and sister were living with them, the young mother, according to published reports, sometimes feeling constrained and "stifled" by the endless proximity to his relentlessly cheerful mother and his sister and children. She often went shopping in Beverly Hills just to get out of the house and be her own person for a time.

While in public with her husband she was all smiles, clinging to his side, in private a rather different Katie was on show. She seemed constantly tired and rather forlorn, as if she were carrying a heavy emotional burden on her slim shoulders. "Away from the cameras she was a different person," noted a business associate. "I wouldn't call her happy or acting like a woman in love—quite the opposite. She seemed so sad and depressed, not at all like a woman who was just married and looking forward to a new life. Every time I saw her, she was like this, listless and negative, just a very down person."

In the first few months after the birth of Suri, Katie's physical and emotional fatigue could have been attributed to postpartum depression, a condition that affects one in ten new mothers. Of course, Tom had publicly criticized Brooke Shields for taking medicine to cope with the black moods and despair associated with depression after the birth of her first child. Now that Katie was a Scientologist, it would have been utterly unthinkable for her to have gone down this medical path. Certainly the carefree girl of the *Dawson's Creek* era was long gone; those who saw her up close and personal remarked that she seemed older than her years, sadder, and emotionally and physically worn out. Those who dared to make any connection between Katie's new, subdued persona and the state of the newlyweds' marriage very quickly faced the wrath of Tom—or rather his lawyers, who were vigilant in tackling tabloid stories suggesting that Katie was anything other than blissfully happy.

While baby Suri was an utter delight, it seemed to those who knew Katie that she was having doubts about the path she had embarked upon. With her acting career on the back burner, she appeared miserable, giving the impression that she was somehow now "trapped," uncomfortably aware that she had married one of the most powerful men in Hollywood. However, when she told *Harper's Bazaar* magazine that it would be an "honor" to work alongside Tom in a movie, it was a sign of how much she wanted the marriage to work both professionally and personally.

When she took on her first film role since the birth of Suri, Tom vowed to be by her side during the six-week shoot of *Mad Money* in Shreveport, Louisiana. While his intentions were good, in the end his own work commitments meant that he often flew her back and forth from their Beverly Hills home on a three-hour commute on board their private jet.

Whatever misgivings Katie may have had about the future of her union to Tom, the treatment of Nicole Kidman could only serve as a road map—and a warning. Katie knew that Nicole had been reduced to keeping in touch with her adopted children by Internet camera or e-mail. Tom effectively had custody, bringing up both youngsters in his faith. In the summer of 2007, for example, Isabella and Connor were sent to a Scientology summer camp in Portland, Oregon, rather than spend time with their mother. Nicole's revelatory interview in *Vanity Fair* in September 2007, where she irritated Tom by revealing that she had had a miscarriage early in their marriage, was seen by observers as a warning shot to Tom to give her some parental latitude—otherwise, she would spill the beans on their ten-year marriage. Indeed, it seemed at one level that the interview was a coded conversation between Nicole and her former husband. Not only did she pose with her sister's baby clutched to her chest—perhaps symbolizing the baby she longed for—but she hinted that one day she would fully explain the "complicated" background to the adoption of Isabella in Florida in 1993. At the time, the hand of Scientology was believed to be behind the adoption, although neither Tom nor Nicole ever commented on suggestions that the birth mother was an impoverished Sea Org member or, for that matter, the identity of the birth mother.

Whatever the private turbulence in her heart, Katie was discreet, her downbeat demeanor and aura of wistful sadness the only clues she gave to associates and others in her circle that perhaps motherhood and marriage were not quite how they had appeared in the brochure. In public, she was the perfect Hollywood wife, putting a brave face on her new life. "I have a husband and children I adore," she said, looking relaxed and happy by Tom's side. When David and Victoria Beckham finally arrived in Los Angeles in July 2007, Katie and Tom were waiting to welcome them with an exclusive A-list party at the Museum of Contemporary Art. The six-hundred-person guest list included cohosts Will Smith and Jada Pinkett Smith, Oprah Winfrey, George Clooney, Steven Spielberg, and Jim Carrey. Tom was going all-out to impress his British guests. While in Hollywood there is no such thing as a free lunch—or a free party, for that matter—at the time of writing, the Beckhams have yet to be beguiled by his faith.

It may just be a question of time. Few can resist the Cruise squeeze, the actor concentrating on those who influence specific ethnic or geographical communities. At the welcoming party, where David Miscavige was a brooding presence, were numerous celebrities who had at first balked at Tom's blandishments, only to succumb later. He tried to recruit actress and singer Jennifer Lopez, whose father had been a Scientologist for twenty years, in an attempt to reach a wider Hispanic audience. As with Oprah Winfrey, Will Smith—who knocked Tom off the top spot to become *Newsweek*'s "Most Powerful Actor on the Planet" in 2007—and wife Jada Pinkett Smith became targets because of their popularity in the African-American community. Similarly, the woman who got away, Sofía Vergara, had an avid following in South America.

Smiling and ever affable, pressing the flesh, Tom had a way with fellow celebrities and starry-eyed fans alike. He exuded the confidence and panache of a politician—or a Hollywood big shot—which is precisely what he now was. In early 2007, Tom, now heavier and often photographed wearing a suit and tie rather than his trademark T-shirt and jeans, gave the green light to his first movie as a United Artists producer, *Lions for Lambs*, a political drama directed by and starring screen legend Robert Redford. Billed as Tom's comeback movie following his messy divorce from Paramount, the film was already causing controversy before its November 2007 release in the U.S., the movie's tagline—"If you don't stand for something, you might fall for anything"—infuriating conservatives, who accused it of being not just antiwar but anti-American. Interestingly, the world premiere took place in London—high on Tom's Scientology target list—rather than in the United States.

Before Tom arrived in London's Leicester Square for the premiere of *Lions for Lambs* on October 22, 2007, he insisted that the bags of all photographers be searched for water pistols. He did not want a repeat of the incident two years before, when a TV film crew squirted him with water as he worked the crowd. Although he spent nearly two hours meeting and greeting his fans, the movie received a lackluster reception from the critics. "The drama glows as brightly as a five-watt bulb," wrote James Christopher in *The Times,* the newspaper that sponsored the film festival where the movie was showcased. The review described Tom, in his role as a Republican hawk, as "a desk-thumping, ultra-smooth flirt who beams at [Meryl Streep, playing a cynical journalist] with total insincerity." Even though the film dealt with the controversial subject of the conflict in Iraq and Afghanistan, the Hollywood star smoothly sidestepped questions about the War on Terror. He did, however, reveal that he planned to take his friend David Beckham for a fast car or plane ride to cheer him up after his new soccer team, the L.A. Galaxy, failed to reach the playoffs in Beckham's injury-prone first season.

If Tom's first feature with United Artists signaled his studio's intention to take on edgier issues, his next was an audacious fusion of faith and film, a symbol of his utter immersion in the promotion of Scientology. As Tom and his colleagues were sifting through potential scripts on the lot of United Artists, David Miscavige and his lieutenants were in Scientology's war room at Hemet, planning the invasion of Germany. From time to time they were joined in their desert bunker by Tom, who these days is the organization's second-in-command in all but name, involved in every aspect of planning and policy. Just as the denizens of the Kabbalah Centre do nothing without the approval of their great champion and paymaster, Madonna, so the marketing strategy of Scientology is molded around Tom Cruise.

Germany was a hugely desirable prize, a potential market of 82 million people. What's more, it would be an immense public relations triumph to gain legitimacy in a country where Scientology is officially viewed as a commercial rather than a religious enterprise, a totalitarian organization that takes advantage of vulnerable individuals. In short, as far as Germany is concerned, Scientology poses a risk to democratic society. Over the years, various German states have taken measures to protect their citizens from infiltration by the group, whose activities are monitored closely by the Office for the Protection of the Constitution.

In turn, Scientology has aggressively argued that Germany's attitude is a denial of fundamental religious freedoms, their lobbying in Washington causing a rift between the U.S. and Germany on this human rights issue. In January 2007, Scientology established a major beachhead in its campaign when it opened a glossy 43,000-square-foot building in the heart of Berlin. Two months later, in a brilliant pincer move, Scientology effectively parked its tanks on Germany's ideological lawn when Tom Cruise announced that he would produce and star in a movie about Colonel Claus Schenk Graf von Stauffenberg, the German aristocrat whose failed attempt to assassinate Adolf Hitler in the dying months of World War II earned him a place in the pantheon of German heroes.

Not only would a leading Scientologist be playing a symbol of the new German democracy, but the moviemakers wanted to film in the exact locations in Germany where the plot was hatched and dispatched. This was the Cruise/Miscavige axis at its most Machiavellian, planning to march their ideological storm troopers through the streets of Berlin, camouflaged in the garb of artistic integrity and religious freedom. The film could be seen as the stalking horse.

Tom's presence on German soil provoked debate among all sections of society about the rights and wrongs of Scientology. Which was precisely the master plan. "The subject of

Stauffenberg was chosen deliberately," claims a former Scientologist who was privy to the organization's plans for European expansion. "It was a brilliant way to rub it into their faces. The Scientology high command was laughing their asses off. It created controversy in Germany, set politicians against politicians, which was just what they wanted."

Controversy was not long in coming, as members of the Stauffenberg family, the German church, and politicians robustly attacked the film. The hero's eldest son, Berthold Graf von Stauffenberg, a retired general, declared, "Scientology is a totalitarian ideology. The fact that an avowed Scientologist like Mr. Cruise is supposed to play the victim of a totalitarian regime is purely sick." Tom was compared to infamous Nazi propagandist Joseph Goebbels by the German Protestant Church, whose spokesman, Thomas Gandow, divined the underlying purpose behind the movie: "This film will have the same propaganda advantages for Scientology as the 1936 Olympics had for the Nazis."

When it was discovered that United Artists planned to film in Germany, politicians clamored to man the barricades. Defense Ministry spokesman Harald Kammerbauer said, "United Artists will not be allowed to film at German military sites if Count Stauffenberg is played by Tom Cruise, who has publicly professed to being a member of the Scientology cult. In general, the Bundeswehr [German military] has a special interest in the serious and authentic portrayal of the events of July 20, 1944, and Stauffenberg's person."

Tom's battalions valiantly threw themselves into the fray, *Shrek* star Rupert Everett publicly saying that Scientology was no more ridiculous than other religions. Whether the openly gay actor was aware of Hubbard's policy stating that homosexuals should be "disposed of quietly and without sorrow" is not known. Paula Wagner fired her own broadside, arguing that Tom's personal beliefs "had no bearing on the movie's plot, themes, or content." This was no more than the truth, as screenwriter Chris McQuarrie and director Bryan Singer, the creative duo behind the slickly intelligent crime drama *The Usual Suspects,* had no idea that their von Stauffenberg project was possibly being used as a Trojan horse to promote the cause of Scientology.

The man at the center of this war of words was statesmanlike and disarmingly low key. After paying a three-hour Sunday-morning visit to the new European headquarters of Scientology during a June reconnaissance of the film's Berlin locations, Tom coolly opened a second front, diplomatically and unusually inviting selected journalists for a cocktail party to meet other members of the cast, which included Bill Nighy, Kenneth Branagh, and Terence Stamp, and to watch the filming of a scene on set. He spoke humbly about the Catholic aristocrat who was executed the day after the bomb he was carrying in a briefcase injured but did not kill the Führer. "He was someone who realized that he had to take the steps that ultimately cost him his life. He recognized what was at stake. It's compelling when people stand up for things."

His last sentence was a sentiment that could serve as a metaphor for the world's fascination with the actor. Certainly the scene in which, as Stauffenberg, Tom watched his children play just before embarking on his dreaded mission reminded the watching media why he had been at the top of his trade for more than two decades. "Without the aid of dialogue, his face obscured by an eye patch, Tom still manages to convey grief and turmoil," observed entertainment writer Ruben Nepales. "Watching the scene reminded us why we've always believed that Tom is an underrated actor. The controversies have often succeeded in eclipsing the fact that the guy is one of the finest actors of his generation."

Within a matter of weeks, the strategy paid off. The German defense ministry waved the white flag and agreed to his demands to film at military locations. After their abject surrender, another government ministry paid "reparations," giving the film $6.5 million in subsidies because the movie dealt with issues of national history. So, on July 17, 2007, without a shot being fired, fighter planes emblazoned with swastikas, the banned symbol of the Nazi regime, flew low over the village of Loepten outside Berlin as filming began. Only a few Germans realized that they were being invaded.

Although he may have won this battle, the war was by no means over. As Tom continued filming in Berlin's Babelsberg Studios—once favored by Goebbels for making Nazi propaganda—Scientology suffered assault after assault. First, a fourteen-year-old girl and her stepbrother, children of a high-ranking German Scientologist, made headline news after fleeing their home in Berlin to escape the organization. They sought refuge in Hamburg, which has safe houses for those leaving cults. Then Ursula Caberta, who had spent fifteen years investigating Scientology as the commissioner of the Scientology Taskforce for the Hamburg Interior Authority, released *The Black Book of Scientology,* a scathing critique of the organization that became an instant best-seller. In Belgium, after a ten-year investigation that concluded that the group should be labeled a criminal organization, prosecutor Jean-Claude Van Espen recommended that Scientology should stand trial for fraud and extortion. The organization vowed to fight the charges.

It was the enemy within, however, that was potentially the most damaging. As Tom, in his character as Stauffenberg, loaded his briefcase with explosives, a Scientology renegade was about to detonate his own device. Behind bullet-proof glass in a building in Stuttgart protected by armed guards, a man who claimed to be a former Scientology minister, Christian Markert, spent three days telling secret agents about his experiences inside the organization. Fearing that he would not be safe in America, where many former Scientologists believe—sometimes with good reason—that the local police work hand in glove with Scientology organizations, Markert, a German citizen who had been living in Buffalo, New York, fled to Germany for safe haven. It was an ironic inversion of the dark days when Jews escaped Nazi Germany and took refuge in America.

The story Markert told the German intelligence agents was familiar yet chilling. A difficult relationship with his parents, a checkered career, including arrest warrants for fraud in France and Ireland, and a search for meaning in his life after the death of his mother had led him to Scientology a decade before. To verify his identity, Markert, now thirty-six, had a letter from the Scientology legal department in Buffalo attesting that he was a good and long-standing member of the organization. He said he worked for Scientology in Ireland and California before his stint in Buffalo.

Not only did Markert run the bookstore, but for a time he claimed he was the director of the Office of Special Affairs in charge of intelligence, in particular harassing former Scientologists who had criticized the organization. As proof, he handed over sensitive OSA documents that conformed to similar directives and orders held in the extensive archive in the Scientology commission in Hamburg. He told the German police that he had coordinated the systematic harassment of families and individuals. Those who stayed silent were left alone; those who attacked their former faith were dubbed "Suppressive Persons" and faced "the full wrath of the organization." The method, as per training, was always the same. First, he would gather the so-called confidential "ethics" files that contained confessions about sex, drugs, and rocky roads, looking to find and exploit an individual's "ruin."

According to Markert, one family, a husband, wife, and daughter, was harassed every day for a year, receiving thousands of unsolicited visits, telephone calls, and threatening letters. Markert told the secret agents that as a result of the pressure, the wife, then judged a Suppressive Person, had made two unsuccessful suicide attempts. The third succeeded. "I didn't think anything of it at the time," he said. "As a Scientologist you don't view death as much of a big thing, you just talk about dropping the body." Markert and his staff did not see themselves as engineering her death. After all, the actions were consistent with instructions outlined years before by L. Ron Hubbard when he declared that an enemy of Scientology could be "tricked, sued, or lied to or destroyed." Even the interviewing agents, who knew about Scientology's tactics, were shocked by his allegations of calculated cruelty at the dark heart of an organization that calls itself a religion.

"It was the first story he told me when I met him," recalls Ursula Caberta, the commissioner for the Scientology Taskforce in Hamburg.

Markert was a walking blueprint for Scientology's future policy, a strategy that placed Tom Cruise at the heart of their expansion into Britain and Europe. He claimed that these plans were unveiled at a meeting with David Miscavige in Hemet in April 2007, where Markert was offered the chance to help build the organization in Europe. Scientology was desperately short of linguists, for example using non-German-speaking staff from England in Berlin. During his first—and last—visit to the base, Markert reported feeling as if he were entering a high-security prison. There was a pervading sense of paranoia about the place. Before meeting David Miscavige, Markert had to undergo rigorous security checks, as if he were meeting the President of the United States.

While the group traditionally treats the outside world with grave suspicion, at that time many inside the organization were discussing the way that a classic Scientology strategy had neutralized an imminent threat from the media. John Sweeney, an award-winning journalist working for BBC Television in London, had been sent to America to see if Scientology was a cult or a religion. Certain that Sweeney would be critical, they rolled out a familiar Scientology tactic to discredit him. The plan was simple but effective, to harass Sweeney and his camera team around the clock until he eventually lost his cool and "freaked out"—ideally, with the shadowing Scientology camera team there to capture the action. Showing critics to be angry or out of control fatally undermined any arguments, however coherent, they advanced about Scientology. As a former Scientologist observed, "It's a very straightforward plan. They 'bull bait' you until you blow, pressuring you for so long that they mess up your mind."

The scheme worked better than expected. In March, at Scientology's alarmist Psychiatry of Death exhibition in Hollywood, Sweeney finally lost his temper, shouting and screaming at senior Scientologist Tommy Davis, son of actress Anne Archer, who had been hounding him throughout his trip. As Sweeney later explained, "I have been shouted at, spied on, had my hotel invaded at midnight, been denounced as a 'bigot' by star Scientologists, and been chased around the streets of Los Angeles by sinister strangers. Back in Britain, strangers have called on my neighbors, my mother-in-law's house, and someone spied on my wedding and fled the moment he was challenged."

When the confrontation was screened on the BBC's flagship investigative TV show, *Panorama*, in May, it earned record ratings—and 2 million hits on YouTube worldwide. While Scientology took full propaganda advantage, spending an estimated sixty thousand dollars on promotional DVDs and other materials, the majority of comments were in favor of the beleaguered reporter. "After a week of Scientology, I had lost my voice but not my mind," Sweeney said, now realizing, with the benefit of hindsight, that he was set up.

Even as Scientologists were discussing their coup against the BBC, Eugene Ingrams, a notorious private investigator regularly employed by Scientology, was probing the family background of Southern California radio talk-show host Vince Daniels after he had dared to criticize the work of Narconon, the group's drug rehabilitation program, on his show. By August he had resigned from KCAA radio station, citing differences with the management.

While Scientology founder L. Ron Hubbard placed great credence on black propaganda, Miscavige had succeeded beyond Hubbard's dreams in executing the founder's policy of using celebrities to bang the drum for the faith. Markert claimed that Miscavige indicated that stars like Tom Cruise and John Travolta would be used to spearhead the drive into Britain and Europe. Tom would build on his existing role as a roving ambassador, using his celebrity to gain access to politicians and other movers and shakers in business and showbiz. As Miscavige observed, a politician did not have to be a Scientologist to promote the cause; he just needed a good Scientologist behind him. "He made it clear that celebrities like Tom Cruise are doing everything they can to get into Europe and give Scientology a higher profile," recalled

Markert. "Miscavige sees it as a big market—Scientology has already been successful in Italy. He talked about it in depth." The Scientology leader even boasted that Tom's studio, United Artists, was seen within the organization as essentially a pro-Scientology outfit. He hoped to see the studio increasingly staffed by dedicated Sea Org disciples who had cut their technical teeth at the Gold production studios in Hemet. In *Lions for Lambs,* actor Michael Pena, composer Mark Isham, cameramen, musical technicians, and other production staff were Scientologists.

Within weeks of meeting Miscavige, Markert, sometime Scientology bookseller, intelligence officer, and church minister, wanted out and was helped to escape by a former Sea Org member before flying to Germany. His defection, as he anticipated, brought the wrath of the movement on his head, with Markert accused of being a con man, a convicted criminal, a "plant" by German security forces, someone who was only briefly in the organization and, bizarrely, a psychiatrist. The efforts of Scientology and its front group, Religious Freedom Watch, were partly successful, in that a German broadcasting station concluded that his story was contradictory and not entirely credible. However, the ferocity and extent of the attempts to discredit him could be seen as evidence of his previous value to the group, prompting Ursula Caberta to ask him if he was hiding vital information about the group.

Here the story becomes as murky as any when trying to penetrate the labyrinthine world of Scientology and the mind-set of its followers. When I formally asked a lawyer acting for Scientology why they had devoted so many resources to vilifying someone they claimed had only been a member for a brief period of time, his response was intriguing. In a written reply, he categorically stated: "Christian Markert has never met with or spoken with Mr. Miscavige and has never been to Golden Era Productions' facilities. The first time he set foot in a Scientology church was when he joined staff at the Church of Scientology of Buffalo at the beginning of April 2007, claiming he had a desire to enlighten people about Scientology. He was hired to become that church's bookstore clerk."

Yet a letter, dated March 9, 2007, which originates from the Church of Scientology's own legal office in Buffalo, directly contradicts that assertion. The letter was in support of Markert's application for a visa as a temporary religious worker: "Mr. Markert is fully qualified to receive an R-1 Visa as he has been a Scientologist for about ten years and in the past three years has demonstrated his high skill in the field of Dianetics. His knowledge and skill in Church scriptures is very much needed by the Church in Buffalo to assist as a minister at the church."

A church minister or con man? Ursula Caberta believes that the fuss surrounding Markert stems directly from Tom's friend David Miscavige. Under Scientology policy it is a high crime for a church member to fail to write a "knowledge report" about anyone they suspect of being about to leave or "blow" the organization. It would be inconceivable for Miscavige to be seen to be associated with a renegade so soon before his departure. Technically, he would be failing in his duty and would have to be punished. Hence the vigorous attempts to discredit the hapless Markert.

If he was in fact a practitioner of Scientology's dark arts, Markert saw into the heart of the organization. "Scientology is not about money," he said. "It is not a religion; it is an extreme political organization. All Hubbard wanted was world power. He wanted to run the planet." Tom Cruise's work in spreading the word about his faith gave what Markert now considers to be a "dangerous and criminal cult" a spurious legitimacy. "He makes Scientology seem innocent and safe, especially to the young. After seeing what I have seen, I have no hesitation in saying that Tom Cruise is one of the most dangerous celebrities in the world."

While this is a statement by a disillusioned defector, it is by no means an isolated or maverick opinion. Perhaps a fairer assessment is that Tom Cruise achieves his power and influence by cleverly exploiting the fact that we live in a sound-bite media society and worship at the temple of celebrity. He is a leading member of a modern breed of celebrity advocates who use their star status to gain access to the corridors of power, the TV studio, and the cover story.

Just as Bob Geldof and Bono have effectively used their contacts and celebrity to fight against Third World poverty, so Tom Cruise has campaigned for his controversial religion. The difference is that Bono and Geldof want to change the world, while Tom is part of an organization that wants to conquer the planet. Whereas Geldof and Bono's mission is out in the open, Tom's organization operates by disguise, hiding behind focused campaigns against specific drugs like Ritalin or antidepressants when its true purpose is the "global obliteration" of psychiatrists and other health-care professionals.

Unlike politicians, celebrity advocates like Tom Cruise are able to avoid detailed scrutiny of their policies or positions. Media outlets are simply delighted to have them in front of the camera or on the magazine cover. As long as Tom's presence or picture boosts ratings and sales, journalists are prepared to jump through any hoop, such as attending Scientology courses, in order to gain access. For that matter, as then White House aide Scooter Libby demonstrated, politicians love to feel the warm glow generated by a Hollywood star in their midst. In this sycophantic climate, Tom has become the master of the sound bite, promoting his controversial cause by assertion rather than argument, offering slogans instead of intellectual substance. For instance, how many politicians could have stated unchallenged, as Tom did during a TV interview on *Entertainment Tonight* in 2005, that psychiatry was a "Nazi science" and that methadone, a drug used to fight heroin addiction, was originally called Adolophine after Adolf Hitler? Although neither statement is accurate, Tom's popularity as an actor inevitably give his pronouncements weight and authenticity.

In an era when Tom is much more powerful than the average senator, with a worldwide reach and influence, he and Scientology are given a free pass, one that they have used to great effect. For example, according to the Mental Health Matters Political Action Committee, some twenty-eight Scientology bills have been introduced by members of the Arizona state legislature aimed at limiting access to treatment and medication for children with mental health disorders. On its Web site, the lobbying group asks voters if they want Tom Cruise to make future decisions about mental health care in their state. It is therefore ironic that, unbeknownst to the actor, Dr. Gary Lebendiger, Tom's stepbrother from his father's second marriage, is a child psychiatrist.

Of course, Tom is merely a smiling conduit for the philosophy of the man he calls his mentor, L. Ron Hubbard. By definition, everything LRH wrote about psychiatry—and, for that matter birth, marriage, and life—is deemed sacred and inviolable. His word is Scientology lore. Neither Tom nor any other Scientologist can deviate from his teachings or his policies. This is one of the fatal flaws in Tom's prognosis for the planet. Take Hubbard's obsession with psychiatry. Apart from the personal slight he felt when mental health experts dismissed his book *Dianetics,* the bedrock of Scientology, Hubbard was learning and writing about psychiatry in the 1940s and '50s, when inquiry into what makes the brain tick was still in its relative infancy.

Psychiatry, like computing, is an evolving science. For Hubbard to make universal rules and edicts about the science of mental health is akin to laying out iron laws about computing based on the cumbersome machines of the postwar period, when it took rooms full of equipment to perform fewer functions than today's microscopic silicon chips. Philosophically, Hubbard's worldview was defined by the state of the planet just after World War II. It is intellectually static, unable to accept or absorb any progress in civilization since then. It is no exaggeration to state that Scientology is the intellectual equivalent to the Flat Earth Society, a group locked in a time warp, inexorably bound by the rules defined by its founder. Even today, for example, high-ranking Scientologists communicate by encrypted telex—rather than more modern methods such as e-mail—because Hubbard decreed it.

If, like the Flat Earth Society, Scientology were content to be a parochial, inward-looking club, there would be little enough harm in it. But it is not. The relentless expansion of the organization and its front groups has been made possible by the charm and persuasiveness of its poster boy, whose modernity, familiarity, and friendliness mask the totalitarian zeal of his faith. Perhaps the media, politicians, and public should examine Tom's claims with greater rigor and skepticism. When comedians ridicule Tom Cruise, the joke may be on him—but it is also on ourselves.

More than any star today, Tom is a movie messiah who reflects and refracts the fears and doubts of our times, trading on the unfettered power of modern celebrity, our embrace of religious extremism, and the unnerving scale of globalization. While advances in science, medicine, and technology give the illusion of modernity, the world is seemingly gripped by a harking back to apocalyptic fundamentalism. Current discourse all too often resembles that of the period before the Age of Reason and Enlightenment when messianical theories held sway. In the marketplace of ideas, rational debate and scientific method are frequently shouted down by the most extreme—and unproven—dogmas. And Tom has been one of those shouting the loudest, selling the dubious, unproven wares of his faith.

In an age of material plenty and spiritual famine, Tom Cruise is compelling—and dangerous—because he stands for something, extolling the virtues of a faith that is parodied and feared in equal measure. This faith, like his own personality, exists and thrives by disguise. Truly theirs is a match made in heaven—if they believed in it.

While he is clearly "one of the premier American actors of his generation," taking his rightful place alongside such luminaries as Al Pacino, Robert De Niro, and Julia Roberts when he received this honor from New York's Museum of the Moving Image in November 2007, there is another dimension to Tom's appeal. What you see is not what you get. With his boy-next-door good looks, energy, and winning smile, he should join the likes of Tom Hanks and Jimmy Stewart as one of the ordinary guys with universal audience appeal, an actor who makes us feel safe and secure in an uncertain world. Yet his history suggests that the man behind the smile is altogether more edgy, threatening, and even sinister. Steven Spielberg recognized this quality when he directed him in *Minority Report*. Spielberg instructed Tom not to smile for the role because he understood the iconography of the Cruise grin. On one occasion he burst into a characteristic smile and Spielberg found himself thinking, "I get it. He has that deliciously indescribable magic that cannot be analyzed or replicated. He is in every sense a movie star."

He is a man, too, of contradictions: an uncertain child waiting for an undeserved blow from his father, an adult searching for certainty and control. An alpha male who does his own stunts, lest there be a challenge he could not meet, seeking approval from the ghost of his bullying father. Now a father himself, he clearly loves family life and yet crusades for a faith that routinely sets loved ones against one another. A romantic who falls in love in a heartbeat and yet walks away without a backward glance. A certain, purposeful presence but a man who hates to be alone. During a career spanning a quarter of a century, he has played pilot, doctor, secret agent, warrior, assassin, vampire, and war hero. Perhaps the most complex character he has ever played is Tom Cruise himself.

UPDATE

It was the Tom Cruise blockbuster of the year, watched by an audience of millions around the world. Yet even though the sensational film was the talk of the water cooler for weeks, the nine-minute solo performance, entitled "Tom Cruise on Tom Cruise," did not have its premiere in a movie theater.

From this humble debut on the Internet, the film of Tom, unshaven and dressed in a black turtleneck as he talked about his passion for Scientology, rapidly exploded into a global phenomenon. Viewers gawped and giggled as the movie star, in a performance both rambling and inarticulate, tried to explain his religious credo. The only people not smiling were Tom Cruise and his church. As the actor later told Oprah Winfrey about the video, "I was receiving an award that evening for global literacy. It was a very private moment. I'm actually talking to my congregation."

Actually he was being awarded Scientology's first-ever Freedom of Valor medal at a 2004 gala for thousands of fellow believers at Scientology's English headquarters, Saint Hill Manor. Although I mentioned salient features of his pre-taped interview in the original edition of this book, the video proved that a picture, especially a moving picture of the biggest Hollywood star in the world, was worth 10,000 words.

Its release ignited a firestorm of controversy. This was Tom Cruise as never seen before, unguarded, unvarnished and, to many, unhinged. He spoke as though in a dazed reverie, almost as if he were communing with himself. From time to time, he would laugh maniacally for little or no reason. His speech was peppered with Scientology jargon, confirming his credentials as an ardent follower of his faith.

As the *Mission: Impossible* theme played in background, he explained how Scientologists were the "authorities on getting people off drugs, the authorities on the mind," and the only people who can bring peace and unite cultures. As an ambassador for his faith, he insisted that the world's politicians were waiting for Scientologists to provide solutions to global problems. "Traveling the world and meeting the people that I've met, talking with these leaders . . . they want help, and they are depending on people who know and can be effective and do it and that's us. That is our responsibility to do it." Such was his dedication to "clearing the planet" that he had little time to enjoy his private jets, custom-made motorbikes, race cars, $35-million home in Hollywood, or skiing and snowmobiling at his mountain retreat in Colorado. "I wish the world was a different place. I'd like to go on vacation and go and romp and play . . . but I can't."

Despite his absolute certainty that only he and his fellow believers could solve the problems of the planet, he warned his congregation that the journey would be "rough and tumble . . . wild and woolly." Finally, a portentous voiceover announced that "Tom Cruise has introduced LRH [L. Ron Hubbard] technology to over one billion people of earth. And that's only the first wave he's unleashed. Which is why the story of Tom Cruise, Scientologist, has only just begun."

As comedians around the world ransacked their wardrobes for black turtlenecks and practiced the Cruise guffaw and chopping hand gestures, it became an iconic moment in his career. Just as the famous shots of Tom in *Risky Business* and *Top Gun* cemented his image as a controlled, cocksure, effortlessly attractive boy next door, so the abiding impression left by the Oprah couch-jumping episode and this new video was of a man out of sync with the real world. As Gawker's Nick Denton noted in his media column, "If Tom Cruise jumping on Oprah's couch was an 8 on the scale of scary, this is a 10."

The *New York Post* was more direct, inviting its readers to vote on whether Tom had gone off his rocker. German historian Guido Knopp ratcheted up the hysteria factor even further after he compared Tom's rousing sermon at the end of the Scientology ceremony with the call to war by Nazi propaganda minister Joesph Goebbels.

The impact of the Cruise video, which was first leaked by media commentators on the West Coast, was particularly pronounced because it coincided with the January 2008 publication of this biography. As anticipated, its release proved to be a "wild and woolly" ride. In the week before it hit the stores, the book was assailed by Tom's lawyer, Bert Fields; the Church of Scientology, which released a 15-page rebuttal; and Tom's public relations agents, Rogers and Cowan, who issued a hostile statement and pressured major media outlets not to publicize the book or interview me as well as the star's famous Hollywood friends.

His veteran lawyer fumed that my book was "sick and demonstrably false." For good measure, the legal eagle, who has written contentious books disputing Shakespeare's authorship of his plays and arguing the proposition that King Richard III never killed the two princes locked in the Tower of London, dismissed as "nutty" my assertion that his client was the *de facto* second in command of Scientology.

He was joined by Scientology spokeswoman Karin Pouw, who also described the notion that Tom held informal office inside his faith as "ludicrous." "He is neither second or 100th," she averred. The actor was merely a "parishioner," albeit a parishioner who stirred the church into a paroxysm of media activity on his behalf.

His business partner Paula Wagner issued a statement condemning the book and the "mockery" of the Cruise video, while stars like Adam Sandler, Dustin Hoffman and Ben Stiller rode to his rescue, arguing that Tom had the "right to freedom of speech and freedom of religion." There was fevered talk that Bert Fields was considering reaching for his favorite number, $100 million, as he prepared a lawsuit against myself and the publisher. At the time of writing no such suit has been produced—although Tom's lawyers did send a cease-and-desist letter to a baby clothes outlet in Hollywood in May for talking about the couple's possible purchases for their daughter, Suri. The fact that, because of the litigious nature of both Scientology and Tom Cruise, the book was not being published in Britain, Australia or New Zealand, where freedom of expression is hedged by such strict libel and privacy laws that Britain is known as the world's capital for "libel tourism," merely fueled the Cruise bandwagon.

The clamor in the mainstream media was reminiscent of the hue and cry that followed the publication of my biography of the late Diana, Princess of Wales, in 1992. Then the British media were baying for blood, eager to pay obeisance to the royal family as they attempted to undermine the book, which, unknown to them or anyone else, was written with her full cooperation and involvement.

Although my biography of Tom Cruise was deliberately unauthorized—as I have argued frequently, a book authorized by Scientology would lack credibility—the response from some sections of the established American media was as deferential toward Hollywood royalty as the British media were to the House of Windsor.

There was, for example, deafening silence from the Hollywood entertainment media when it came to author interviews. The reason became clear when the press office at St. Martin's received a hysterical phone call from a senior producer at an entertainment show. She had been contacted by a rep from Rogers and Cowan, Cruise's publicity agents, who had erroneously suspected the show of planning to air an interview with me. Dire consequences were threatened, so the agitated producer pleaded with St. Martin's to call Rogers and Cowan and tell them no such interview was scheduled.

The self-censorship of some in the mainstream media was demonstrated most clearly when Katie Holmes was doing the publicity rounds for her film, *Mad Money*, a crime caper also starring Diane Keaton and Queen Latifah. Anyone who wanted to interview Katie had to stick to certain topics. TV host Diane Sawyer, who sat on the sofa with the young actress for eight long minutes, was castigated by the *New York Post* for giving Katie a "free ride," asking only innocuous questions about her hair, her clothes, baby Suri, and her movie. When quizzed about Suri's first words, Katie replied, "She said Mama, then Dada and then everything else. She's a great mimic." Although the show's producer Jim Murphy insisted that its coverage was not a whitewash, *The Washington Post* let the cat out of the bag when it explained why they had passed on interviewing the latest member of Hollywood royalty: "The *Post* was not able to acquiesce to Holmes' publicist's requests—especially that the celeb not be asked about a certain Los Angeles-based church."

Meanwhile, the original video and comments about the book, both positive and negative, were spreading like wildfire in the anarchic world of the Internet. Even as Scientology spokespeople were saying the video had been good publicity for their faith, their lawyers were sending threatening letters to media sites ordering them to take down the offending film. At Scientology's request, YouTube and other sites removed the copyrighted video, but Gawker refused. The site claimed fair use, arguing that the nine-minute film was only a fraction of the three-hour filmed event, and said "it's newsworthy; and we will not be removing it." (It also made commercial sense. The site's traffic, normally steady at one million hits a month, soared to 3.9 million hits.) Others did heed the church's threats, Bill O'Reilly explaining on Fox News that his station, like many others, had decided to stop showing the movie in the face of hostile letters from Scientology lawyers. It seemed that the church was going out of its way and at some cost to aid Tom Cruise, parishioner.

Yet there was a whiff of rebellion in the air. The bullying Goliath of Scientology was about to face its David, a faceless, leaderless group of tech-savvy youngsters. Initially this merry band of hackers and Web geeks were infuriated by the removal of the Cruise video from YouTube. They decided to investigate Scientology further and didn't like what they saw, angered by what they saw of Scientology practices, but mainly what they viewed as Scientology's history of "speech-suppression tactics."

On January 21—just a week after Tom's Scientology video first appeared—the anarchic group, appropriately called Anonymous, declared war in a mission statement on YouTube. It was a creepy but highly sophisticated piece of agitprop, with a flat, computer-generated voice warning the leaders of Scientology that "with the leakage of your propaganda video into mainstream circulation, the extent of your malign influence over those who trust you as leaders has been made clear to us. Anonymous has therefore decided that your organization should be destroyed."

The declaration, which attracted three million hits, ended with a phrase that was to become their signature: "We are Anonymous. We are legion. We do not forgive. We do not forget. Expect us." They were as good as their computer-generated word. Within hours, they launched a coordinated series of attacks on the main Scientology website, effectively shutting it down. This was followed by "black fax" transmissions to Scientology offices across the country, prank phone calls, and the inevitable bogus pizza deliveries. For three days they maintained their Internet war, until long-time critics of Scientology asked them to call off their attacks, arguing that they were behaving just like the church by denying freedom of speech. They complied but planned a series of worldwide demonstrations for February 10—to commemorate the death of Lisa McPherson while in Scientology's care.

In a remarkably well-organized and coordinated campaign, some 8,300 people worldwide gathered in protest outside Scientology buildings in Los Angeles, New York, San Francisco, Berlin, London, Melbourne, Dallas, Houston, and elsewhere. (Tom and Katie were resident at the Hollywood Celebrity Centre during the protests, as their home was under renovation.) Wearing Guy Fawkes masks—from the movie *V for Vendetta*—to protect their identity, they chanted anti-Scientology slogans against a background of the 1980s pop song, "Never Gonna Give You Up," by singer Rick Astley. As writer Chez Pazienza wryly observed, "It's kind of satisfying to watch someone turn the tables on Scientology, using the same brand of furtive cloak and dagger absurdity to publicly shame an adversary that the church has used for decades."

While the demonstrators, mainly young college students, did not take themselves too seriously, Scientology did. In retaliation, they made their own video of allegations accusing the group of terrorism and hate crimes. They claimed they had received harassing phone calls, death and bomb threats, and envelopes containing white powder that could be anthrax. To long-time anti-Scientology activists, their protests had the familiar ring of humorless exaggeration and hysteria that greets even moderate criticism of the church. No infraction escapes notice. A snarky comment by a *US Weekly* writer about a shiny suit worn by Nicole Kidman—"Bonus: This specially designed suit repels Scientologists"—earned a lawyer's letter from celebrity Scientologist Kirstie Alley demanding that the writer be fired and that the publication "apologize and commit to a thorough examination of why you have chosen to foster animosity and bias against Scientologists."

Meanwhile, many former senior officials and upper-echelon members came out publicly in support of my book. The response of one former high-ranking official who worked at the Hemet base for twenty years was typical: "I saw Scientology's denial of all sorts of things you reported which just burned me up, especially how they don't separate families— biggest lie in the world." Another former member posted the names and details of thirty couples who had been split up because of Scientology.

Most prominent was Jenna Miscavige Hill, the niece of church leader David Miscavige, who wrote an open letter to spokeswoman Karin Pouw in January 2008. The 24-year-old former Scientologist, who was brought up in the faith, launched a withering assault on the church and its most prominent supporter, Tom Cruise: "I am absolutely shocked at how vehemently you insist upon not only denying the truths that have been stated about the church in that biography, but then take it a step further and tell outright lies." She went on to denounce Tom Cruise for "supporting a religion that tears apart families, both in the media and monetarily."

Jenna described how her own family—her father Ron is David Miscavige's elder brother—was scattered by the organization's policies. When her parents left the church in 2000, she decided to stay but was prevented from contacting them. She said that Scientology officials intercepted letters from her parents and friends, kept her from speaking to them on the phone, and only allowed her to visit them once a year for four days—and then only after her parents threatened legal action. "Hell, if Scientology can't keep his family together then why on earth should anyone believe the church helps bring families together," she wrote. For her pains, Jenna, who teamed up with other disillusioned Scientology "aristocrats" to form an organization to help Scientology children, ExScientologyKids.com (Motto: "I was born. I grew up. I escaped."), found herself harassed by church officials. She told the *New York Post* that the church ordered friends to "disconnect" from her.

Her experience failed to deter celebrity Scientologist Jason Beghe from speaking out several weeks later. The one-time Scientology poster boy and star of *G.I Jane* and TV series like *Melrose Place* and *American Dreams* blew the whistle on the fourteen years—and one million dollars—he had spent inside the organization. He accused the church of being a "rip-off" and a "dangerous cult" whose purpose was to create a "brainwashed, robotic version of you."

As Beghe and others spoke out, other former high-ranking Scientologists were simply baffled by the church's insistence that Tom Cruise held no official or unofficial position inside the organization. For example, film producer Marc Headley, who was brought up inside the faith and worked closely with David Miscavige for fifteen years, recalled that the church leader had told him and others at Gold base in Hemet: "If I could make Tom Cruise IG [Inspector General, second in command] I would." Moreover, Headley considered the actor effectively the "dean" of the organization's celebrities, re-calling the time that Tom ordered fellow Scientology stars in-cluding Anne Archer, Giovanni Ribisi, Jenna Elfman, and Jason Lee to attend a meeting at Celebrity Centre, where he lectured them for failing to work hard enough for the cause, accusing them of being "out ethics," essentially not pulling their weight. The message got home.

Second in command or not, he was treated as anything but an ordinary parishioner. A number of former Scientol-ogy executives, several of whom were personal friends of L. Ron Hubbard, recalled the building of Bonnie View, the home designated for the church's founder after he had fin-ished his planetary peregrinations. For the overwhelming majority of Scientologists, this shrine to Hubbard—with a freshly laundered set of clothes laid out every day in case the founder turns up unexpectedly—is strictly off-limits. Not only did Tom regularly tour the mansion, he was wined and dined there by David Miscavige. As always, he was treated like royalty when he visited the remote base; for example, if he was arriving by helicopter, the hillsides had to be freshly planted and brown patches of grass removed and replaced.

Then there was the surprise birthday party for Tom on *Freewinds,* the church's own cruise ship. Every year the church organizes a special celebration to commemorate the birthday of L. Ron Hubbard, flying in musicians, entertainers, cooks and camera crew at an estimated cost of $300,000. After the festivities in the summer of 2004, they were all flown back again for Tom's lavish birthday concert—along with the chefs and staff from his favorite sushi restaurant. When he walked into the ship's ballroom, a solo guitarist on stage played the *Top Gun* theme. For the next hour, singers and dancers enter-tained the star, singing a medley of tunes from his movies while film clips played in the background. At the end, Tom, casually dressed in jeans and a T-shirt, joined singers and dancers on stage to reprise the Bob Seger hit, "Old Time Rock and Roll," which he had danced to as a fresh-faced actor in *Risky Business.* "It's the best birthday ever, ever, ever, ever,

ever, and I mean ever," he told the assembled throng, which included David and Shelley Miscavige. Probably the most expensive, too. Former Scientologists who helped organize the bash estimate it cost the church $300,000—the same as the Hubbard birthday celebration—to entertain the multimillionaire. As Gawker wryly noted when they first aired the video on their website in March 2008: "If Cruise was merely a humble parishioner why in Xenu's name did the sect spend six figures to celebrate his birthday in 2004?"

Why, too, did David Miscavige personally supervise every aspect of the event, from the camera positions to the dance choreography? According to Scientology producer Marc Headley, he also edited and approved the commemorative video, which he presented to Tom. He did the same thing before the now-infamous gala at Saint Hill where Tom told the world that only Scientologists could help at the scene of a car accident. Not only did Miscavige produce the video preceding Tom's award of the Freedom Medal of Valor, according to Headley, he instructed the camera crews filming the audience what and what not to shoot. Strictly off-limits were photos of Tom and his new girlfriend, aspiring actress Yolanda Pecorara. Tom had first met the 19-year-old daughter of a Nicaraguan mother and Italian father at the opening of a new Scientology centre in Madrid in September 2004, a few months after his breakup with Penelope Cruz. With her big brown eyes and striking looks, she bore a remarkable resemblance to the Spanish actress. There was, however, one big difference: Yolanda had been a Scientologist since the age of 13. The 42-year-old actor and his teenage girlfriend, whose only claim to fame was appearing as a bikini babe in the TV drama *Dr. Vegas,* dated for a few months. Tom invited her to join the Beckhams and the Miscaviges at a Real Madrid soccer game in October 2004, and a month later, dressed in a long coral satin gown, she was by his side when he accepted his award. By February 2005, he had moved on to another Cruz look-alike, Sofia Vergara.

That evening the cameramen clearly forgot their orders, as brief shots of the couple were evident when the video surfaced in January 2008. The emergence of a Scientologist teenager as a possible partner encouraged the whispers previously alluded to in the original biography, that church elders had played cupid for the Hollywood star. In March 2008, Marc Headley, who was audited by Tom when he worked at Hemet, claimed in a British tabloid that church officials had actively tried to find him a bride. According to Headley, church officials put out a casting call to actresses for a part in an upcoming Tom Cruise movie. Auditions were held in a room at the Celebrity Centre in Hollywood, where Headley was in charge of taping the interviews to be screened personally by David Miscavige. First they rounded up Scientology actresses like Erika Christensen, Erica Howard and Sofia Milos, but none was deemed acceptable. "They had to look outside the herd, so to speak," Headley told writer Lewis Panther. "They went for Jennifer Garner, Scarlett Johansson and Jessica Alba, in that order. Jennifer and Jessica didn't bite, but Scarlett took the bait and came in for an audition. When she arrived at the audition address and found out it was the Scientology centre in Hollywood, she freaked out and didn't do a tape." Finally they hit on Katie Holmes after they read an interview saying that she would like to marry him. Headley claimed they sent a senior Scientologist to New York, where she was then living, to vet her.

For all the furor surrounding Tom and Scientology—a Gallup poll released in April 2008 revealed that Hubbard's church was the most negatively viewed religion in America, behind the Mormons, Muslims, and atheists—his enthusiasm for his faith remained undimmed. It was revealed that he had donated $5 million to the cause, beaten only by Nancy Cartwright, the voice of Bart Simpson, who gave $10 million to spread the word of L. Ron Hubbard. Nor was his friendship with church leader David Miscavige impaired; the pals were spotted at a motorcycle race track in Monterey, California, in the summer of 2008. By then Scientology membership had become a toxic issue for other celebrities. Tom's friend and sword-fighting partner Will Smith spent much of the year fencing with journalists about his possible involvement with the controversial church. In a confrontation with members of Anonymous in September, he denied that he was a member.

Tom's unwavering support for his spiritual constituency came at a price. The electorate who really called the shots, the movers and shakers in Hollywood, began to voice their doubts about his future. Peter Bart, the editor-in-chief of *Variety,* the Bible of the entertainment industry, captured the hostile mood in January 2008. It did not make reassuring reading for the man who had recently been the biggest box-office draw in the world. Bart wrote, "Since the appearance of the Cruise salute [Tom's Scientology video], I have been peppered with anecdotes from top players in the industry describing instances in which Cruise has used his bully pulpit to advance his cause. His fervor is tilting the entertainment community against him. He is a target of suspicion rather than respect." Arguing that a film star's brand should remain bland, Bart continued, "Cruise's advocacy of Scientology and its satellite causes seems to have become even more strident and contentious. More than ever, his actions reflect the conviction that he, Tom Terrific, has sole and unique access to the ultimate truth about life, science and cinema."

Whatever his views on life, Hollywood was beginning to doubt his cinematic choices. The financial and artistic failure of *Lions for Lambs,* his first movie as the head of United Artists, placed more pressure on his second big feature, *Valkyrie,* about the doomed attempt to assassinate Hitler. It was a troubled shoot, dogged by bad publicity and misadventures on the set, such as a studio fire and injuries sustained by a number of extras. The frequent change of the film's release date merely added to the air of pessimism. Obituary writers were beginning to sharpen their pencils. "Is Tom Cruise's career over?" asked a headline in *The Week.*

For once it seems that the actor was prepared to listen to the warning voices inside the industry. In March 2008 he swallowed his pride and invited Viacom head Sumner Redstone—the man who had publicly sacked him from Paramount—out for lunch. Their very public rapprochement at the Beverly

Hills Hotel seemed to signify that Tom was once more back in the fold—and back with a chance of making *Mission: Impossible 1V.* "We agreed that past is the past and we would put it behind us and renew our relationship," said Mr. Redstone afterwards. "It seems clear," noted Hollywood insider Kim Masters, "that Cruise has begun to appreciate the magnitude of career damage that he has inflicted upon himself, though he may not completely grasp the cause." Operation Career Recovery was now underway.

The rebranding—or as Peter Bart might say, the "reblanding"—of Tom Cruise began in earnest when he invited Oprah Winfrey to join him at his ranch in Telluride, Colorado. After giving Oprah a tour of the sprawling property—the highlight was a miniature "office" for baby Suri—he sat sedately on his overstuffed sofa and attempted to explain away the pitfalls and pratfalls of the recent past. Oprah obligingly helped out whenever he struggled for the right language; it was less of an interview than Hollywood royalty communing with itself.

In the hour-long chat, he regretted his attack on Brooke Shields but not the sofa- jumping incident. He denied that Nicole Kidman was prevented from seeing their two adopted children, Connor and Bella—the teenagers flew to Nashville to meet with Sunday Rose, Kidman's baby daughter, a couple of weeks after her birth in July; suggested that his opposition to psychiatry was focused on drugs for children; and argued that his now-infamous video was taken out of context. (On this issue he was correct; if the public had been allowed to see the three-hour Scientology extravaganza where David Miscavige talked of using "smart bombs" and "booby traps" to "globally obliterate" psychiatry, they might have been even more alarmed.)

"Listen, I feel like definitely things have been misunderstood and there are things I could have done better," he explained in a performance that was uncharacteristically sober and low-key. "From now on when I'm dealing with my humanitarian issues, I'll talk about my humanitarian issues and when I'm promoting a film I'm just going to promote the film. And that's just the way it's going to be." His announce-ment may have been a blow to his church, but it was music to the ears of Hollywood honchos—and to his fans, who were now able to chart his cinematic life on his new website.

Tom's appearance on *Oprah* was seen as a smart move by media professionals. "I think Tom learned his lesson," said Howard Bragman, founder of the L.A. PR firm, Fifteen Minutes. "The lesson was that sometimes your personal beliefs can get in the way of the projects."

He also seemed to have heeded the advice of George Clooney, who suggested he learn to laugh at himself. In the next stage of his comeback, he reminded moviegoers why he had been at the top for twenty-five years—because he is a good actor. In *Tropic Thunder,* a satire of the movie industry by Ben Stiller released in August 2008, he played a fat, ugly, bald, and foul-mouthed executive. His cameo as a kind of "Hollywood Satan" earned high praise from the critics. "Who could have foreseen Tom Cruise nearly stealing the movie in a fat suit, a prosthetic nose, a skinhead wig and an Austin Powers–style mat of chest fur?" wrote Slate's Dana Stevens. Cruise and Stiller had talks about making another comedy, an updated version of *The Hardy Boys.* First, though, he planned to move back into familiar territory, making an international spy thriller called *The Tourist.*

It was clear, however, that Cruise was at a career cross-roads. While still a popular and attractive actor, he was no longer a sure bet to open a movie. Now at forty-six, his time as a heartthrob who could carry a picture armed only with his gleaming smile seemed to be coming to a close. As film critic Richard Crouse observed: "The days of line-ups around the block for the new Tom Cruise are gone even if he tried to revive his career with another *Mission: Impossible* or *Risky Business Two.* The smart money would be on him mor-phing into a character or supporting actor in big films."

His "divorce" from his long-time business partner Paula Wagner, who had been by his side during his golden age, was a portent for the future. In August 2008 she departed as chief executive of United Artists, the studio she and Tom had

taken over with ambitious ideas to make "edgy" films. Originally the plan was to release four films a year, but in two
years they had released only *Lions for Lambs.* Hollywood
insiders, quoting MGM executives, cited Wagner's inability
to green-light projects as the reason for the abrupt parting of
the ways. "It had been simmering for some time. Tom likes
action, Paula was not doing the business," noted one movie
veteran. Notably Tom snapped up the rights to author Dun-
can Preston's thriller, *The Monster of Florence,* a couple of
weeks after Wagner left.

Even as the studio issued statements that Tom was still "a
full partner in charge of UA," events were rapidly moving
out of his control. In September 2008, Wall Street went into
meltdown as financial institutions struggled to cope with a
mountain of bad debt resulting from the sub-prime mort-
gage scandal. One of the casualties was United Artists's financial backer, Merrill Lynch, the 100-year-old firm sold in
haste to the Bank of America to save it from bankruptcy. As
shell-shocked bankers dusted themselves off, the future of
the movie industry was not high on their agenda.

Although a spokesperson for MGM, the parent company
for UA, stated that the credit line was still in place, the *New
York Post* quoted one banker as saying that Tom and his
company might have to wait in line for cash to fund future
films. "Reworking a $500-million-dollar credit line for UA
is going to be way down Bank of America's list of things to
do. It could take six months to a year before they even get
around to looking at it."

In many ways the crisis on Wall Street could serve as a
modest metaphor for Tom's career. They were all masters of
the universe, indomitable, invulnerable and inviolable, and
they all fell crashing to earth. After their near-death experience, they lived to fight another day. More contrite, more
considered and more controlled perhaps. But still standing.

It was a warm, balmy evening in mid-September, bringing
out crowds of tourists and theatergoers on Broadway. On
West 45th Street, a line snaked one hundred yards down the

block as the audience waited patiently to take their seats for the first public performance of Arthur Miller's 1947 play, *All My Sons,* starring John Lithgow, Dianne Wiest and a certain Katie Holmes.

The drama began several hours before the curtain went up. Outside the venerable Gerald Schoenfeld Theater, which has hosted such luminaries as Glenn Close, Richard Burton, Peter Ustinov and Tallulah Bankhead, about thirty demonstrators from the Anonymous Internet group, some wearing Guy Fawkes masks, gathered in protest. They held up banners reading, "Free Katie" and "Run Katie Run," and handed out fliers saying that Scientology is a "dangerous scam that ruins lives." For the most part the theatergoers who lined the sidewalk were bemused or mildly irritated, but the demonstration was a welcome photo opportunity for the banks of waiting TV cameras and paparazzi.

The predominantly white, middle-class audience did not seem particularly interested in Scientology. There were the curious who had come to take a closer look at the girl whose life had morphed into a daily tabloid drama; the thrill-seekers who wanted to watch Katie's high-wire act, without the safety net of a retake; and, of course, theater buffs arriving to see award-winning director Simon McBurney's take on Miller's family drama.

However Katie performed during the play's run, she would inevitably be measured by the success of Tom's second wife, who had Broadway critics swooning after her performance in *The Blue Room.* It jet-propelled Nicole Kidman's movie career, bringing Oscar glory and success independent of her former husband. Certainly the equally ambitious Mrs. Cruise III could do with a boost for her film career.

Rather rashly, she had turned down the chance to reprise her *Batman Begins* role in the latest blockbuster, *The Dark Knight*—Maggie Gyllenhaal took the part—while the crime caper *Mad Money* was deemed bankrupt of humor and made only loose change at the box office. The *New York Post* described her reappearance on the big screen as "the most cringe-making return since *Love Boat—The Next Wave.*"

When Katie first joined her fellow cast members for rehearsals in New York in May, the vultures began to circle. Redoubtable theater critic Michael Riedel predicted that the play was going to be a "resounding flop," as the erstwhile leading lady had failed to sell the expected number of tickets. Describing Holmes as a "nice little actress," he argued that she was only in the public eye because she was Mrs. Tom Cruise and that these days that was no draw.

With every seat in the house filled, the audience at the first preview performance seemed to think otherwise. Before the curtain opened, they were treated to a cameo role from Tom Cruise. Flanked by two bodyguards, he smiled, waved and posed for pictures as ushers vainly tried to stop the audience from snapping the grinning figure. The arrival of his friend, actor Dustin Hoffman, merely added to the buzz. It was an effortless display of star power, a consummate ability to light up a room. As Tom soaked up the adulation, the start of the performance was delayed by ten minutes.

The leading man, John Lithgow, caught the mood when he led the cast on stage and asked the audience not to take pictures. "Can we take just one?" yelled one woman from the gods. "No," answered Lithgow firmly. Standing behind him was the tall, slim figure of Katie Holmes, wearing a curly wig to cover her new pixie hairstyle and a '40s-style print dress. Was this cool, skinny, half-smiling young woman the tyrant who had, depending on the contradictory tabloid, tale of choice, thrown Tom's family out of their Hollywood home, sought a separation from her husband, been pregnant four, or was that five times, and was so sick and wan that she had collapsed outside a Beverly Hills restaurant?

Her life might have been turned into make-believe, but now she had to convince the audience—and the critics—to believe in her. She had a secret weapon. For much of the play she was effectively reprising her role of Joey Potter, the winsome girl next door who won the nation's hearts in the teen TV soap, *Dawson's Creek*. Her stage character, Ann Deever, was another girl next door. But unlike Joey, this character called for a range of emotions as dark secrets were gradually revealed, the drama building to a tragic climax.

For the first couple of scenes, Katie was Joey redux, cute and lively, her eyes and gestures brimming with the anticipation of a bright future. It amused some of the audience that in the play an unseen character, a certain "Mr. Hubbard" kept calling on the telephone, proof perhaps that even on stage Katie could not escape the attentions of the founder of her newly chosen religion.

As the emotional mood intensified, she was less convincing; one theatergoer compared her to "the star actress in a high-school play" who was out of her league among the big boys—and girls—of Broadway. Of course, that was not the way Tom saw it. As the play ended, he was true to type, jumping out of his seat as if he were reprising his role on *Oprah*. After leading the standing ovation, he described her performance as "extraordinary."

Outside the theater, several hundred fans—including Scientologists holding up banners saying "Well done, Katie"—waited for a glimpse of the leading lady. So many well-wishers gathered that mounted police were called to control the throng. Many stood out of idle curiosity, and yet the traffic-stopping scenes were reminiscent of the late Diana, Princess of Wales.

The comparisons did not end there. In the early days of Dianamania, she was defined by her marriage, her fashions and her children, Princes William and Harry. Her most inconsequential remark made headlines around the world.

As the new poster girl for modern celebrity, Katie Holmes seems to have, however unconsciously, learned those lessons, a star who is both beautiful and bland, a blank canvas for us—and especially the tabloids—to paint our fantasies. In interviews her responses are brief, guarded and inconsequential, endlessly repeating the numbing mantra that her life is "magical," while dispensing trivial details of marital bliss and motherhood. Out in public she lets her fashions do the talking for her, sparking a craze, for example, when she started wearing rolled-up "boyfriend" jeans to rehearsal.

It was noticeable that when her acting colleague Dianne

Wiest won her third Emmy for her role in *In Treatment* during the first week of the play's run in September, it was pictures of Tom, Katie and baby Suri that captured media attention. What seems to be undeniable is that the new queen of bland has a growing constituency of other girls next door who admire the fact that she has made it and is living her dream. As she and John Lithgow emerged from the stage door to be greeted by cheers and a halo of flashlights, her blossoming popularity suggested that a star, if not a future Oscar-winning actress, was being born that night.

If so, Tom Cruise was not there to see it. For once he was waiting for her in the shadows, happy to let his bride take a bow.

ACKNOWLEDGMENTS

Tom Cruise is one of the best-known and intriguing celebrities in the world, a Hollywood star as controversial as he is talented. In the writing of this biography I owe a huge debt of gratitude to a large number of people who shared their recollections, insights, and assessments.

Without the guidance and support of the following people, this portrait of Tom Cruise would have been much less substantial and textured. I would in particular like to thank Patricia Greenway, Nancy Many, and Tracy Nesdoly for their insights and commitment, as well as Daisy Garnett, Fiona Gray, Ali and Lydia Morton, Delissa Needham, Tom Rayner, Jack Shenker, and Bronwen T.

Inevitably, given the passion for litigation exhibited by Tom Cruise and Scientology, many witnesses have chosen to give guidance and insight on a background basis. Their contributions have been no less valuable or appreciated. I have, however, been surprised by how many people have been prepared to speak openly about the movie star and his faith.

In the hothouse Hollywood jungle, where most like to stay in the shade, I would like to thank Peter Alexander, Paul Barresi, Janet Charlton, John Connolly, Richard DiSabatino, Mark Ebner, Marlise Kast, Sharlene Martin, Kim Masters, and Skip Press.

With its technical jargon, checkered history, and apocalyptic vision, learning about Tom's faith is a not inconsiderable task, and many are still too scarred from their own experiences to talk openly. My thanks to those guides who "walked" me across the bridge to understanding: Chuck Beatty, Graham Berry, Maureen Bolstad, Nan Herst Bowers, Shelly Britt, Ursula Caberta, Tory Christman, Paulette Cooper, Vince Daniels, J. C. Hallman, Bruce Hines, Professor Stephen Kent of the University of Alberta, Canada, Christian Markert, Frank Oliver, Michael Pattinson, Karen Pressley, Jesse Prince, Phil Spickler, John Sweeney, Dave Sweetland, Michael Tilse, Professor Dave Touretzky of Carnegie Mellon University, Jeannine Udall, and Guy White.

While Tom and his agents have actively discouraged those who wished to examine the claims he has made about his childhood and schooldays, the fact that so many of his former teachers, school friends, and others were happy to reminisce, usually with much affection, about the boy they called Maypo, helped build an authentic portrait. I am most grateful to Asta Arnot, Lionel Aucoin, Bryon Boucher, Kathy Burns, Cathy Carella, Angelo Corbo, Diane Cox, Lorraine Gauli-Rufo, Sean Gauli, Amy, Babydol, and Tobe Gibson, Glen Gobel, Sam LaForte, Alan, Irene, Jennifer, Murray, and Scott Lawrie, Jonathan Lebendiger, Dr. Kevin McGrath, Carol McLaurin, Nancy Maxwell, Cathy Mindel, Nancy Price, Marilyn Richardson, Wendy Santo, Pamela Senif, Krystyna Smith, Pennyann Styles, Phil, Ron, and Vinnie Travisano, Sharon Waters, and Val Wright.

I would also like to thank Dave "Bio" Baranek, Dominic Carman, Janet Carroll, Eileen Collins, Richard Corliss, Richard Crouse, Garth Drabinsky, General Jefferson D. Howell, Dayna Steele Justiz, Michael O'Keefe, and Frederic Raphael. Their insights and memories added valuable perspective to the narrative.

I am grateful for the indefatigable and inspirational support of my publisher, Sally Richardson; editor, Hope Dellon; and publicist, John Murphy.

Andrew Morton
London
January 2009

SELECT BIBLIOGRAPHY

Atack, J. *A Piece of Blue Sky: Scientology, Dianetics and L. Ron Hubbard Exposed.* New York: Lyle Stuart, 1990.

Bergman, R. *Dustin Hoffman.* London: Virgin Books, 1992.

Bonderoff, J. *Tom Selleck: An Unauthorized Biography.* New York: New American Library, 1984.

Breitbart, A., and M. Ebner. *Hollywood Interrupted: Insanity Chic in Babylon—The Case Against Celebrity.* Hoboken, N.J.: Wiley, 2004.

Clarke, J. *Ridley Scott.* London: Virgin Books, 2002.

Clarkson, W. *Tom Cruise: Unauthorized.* Norwalk, Conn.: Hastings House, 1997.

Dickerson, J. L. *Nicole Kidman.* Citadel Press, 2004.

Ellis, L., and B. Sutherland. *Nicole Kidman: The Biography.* London: Aurum Press, 2002.

Fleming, C. *High Concept: Don Simpson and the Hollywood Culture of Excess.* London: Bloomsbury, 1998.

Freedman, M. *Dustin: A Biography of Dustin Hoffman.* London: Virgin Books, 1989.

Goodwin, M., and N. Wise. *On the Edge: The Life and Times of Francis Coppola.* New York: William Morrow, 1989.

Gray, B. *Ron Howard: From Mayberry to the Moon . . . and Beyond.* Nashville: Rutledge Hill Press, 2003.

Hallman, J. C. *The Devil Is a Gentleman: Exploring America's Religious Fringe.* New York: Random House, 2006.

Hubbard, L. R. *Dianetics: The Original Thesis.* Copenhagen: Scientology Publications Organization, 1970.

———. *Science of Survival.* Hubbard College of Scientology, 1967.

———. *Scientology: The Fundamentals of Thought.* Denmark: Publications Department, 1972.

———. *The Second Dynamic.* Oregon: Heron Books, 1981.

———. *What Is Scientology?* Los Angeles: CSC Publications Organization, 1978.

Jenkins, P. *Mystics and Messiahs: Cults and New Religions in American History.* New York: Oxford University Press, 2000.

Johnstone, I. *Tom Cruise: All the World's a Stage.* London: Hodder & Stoughton, 2006.

Johnstone, N. *Sean Penn.* London: Omnibus Press, 2000.

Kelly, M. P. *Martin Scorsese: A Journey.* New York: Thunder's Mouth Press, 1991.

Kelly, R. *Sean Penn: His Life and Times.* London: Faber and Faber, 2004.

King, T. *David Geffen: A Biography of New Hollywood.* London: Hutchinson, 2000.

Lefkowitz, B. *Our Guys: The Glen Ridge Rape and the Secret Life of the Perfect Suburb.* Berkeley and Los Angeles: University of California Press, 1997.

O'Brien, D. *Paul Newman.* London: Faber and Faber, 2005.

Pattinson, M. *Celebritology: The Mystery of Why Some Celebrities Are So Deep into Scientology.* celebritology.net

Phillips, G. D., and R. Hill, eds. *Francis Ford Coppola: Interviews.* Jackson: University Press of Mississippi, 2005.

Quirk, L. J. *Totally Uninhibited: The Life and Wild Times of Cher.* London: Robson Books, 1991.

Riley, L., and D. Schumacher. *The Sheens: Martin, Charlie and Emilio Estevez.* New York: St. Martin's Press, 1989.

Robbins, T., and S. J. Palmer. *Millennium, Messiahs, and Mayhem: Contemporary Apocalyptic Movements.* New York: Routledge, 1997.

Sargant, W. *Battle for the Mind: A Physiology of Conversion and Brain-Washing.* Cambridge: Malor Books, 1997.

Schumacher, M. *Francis Ford Coppola: A Filmmaker's Life.* New York: Crown, 1999.

Schwartz, R. A. *The Films of Ridley Scott.* Westport, Conn.: Greenwood Press, 2001.

Thomson, D. *Nicole Kidman.* London: Bloomsbury, 2006.

Toplin, R. B. *Oliver Stone's USA: Film, History and Controversy.* Lawrence: University Press of Kansas, 2000.

INDEX